—————THE NEW CONCISE—————

CHILDREN'S ENCYCLOPEDIA

Contributors

David Lambert M.A.
Brian Murphy M.A.
Brian Williams B.A.
Keith Lye B.A. F.R.G.S.
Christopher Maynard B.A. M.Sc.
Anita Townsend B.A.
Jenny Vaughan B.A.
Catherine Dell L. es L.

Educational Advisers

Harry le Comte
Headteacher
St Martin of Porres School,
London
Joan Jacobs
Headteacher
The Holy Family Primary School,
Hertfordshire

Editorial

John Grisewood B.A.
Leslie Firth B.A.
Jennifer Justice B.Sc.
Vivian Croot B.A.
Jane Olliver B.A.
Simon Franklin B.Sc.

Michael Dempsey M.A.
Markie Robson-Scott M.A.
Hillary Bunce B.A.
Belinda Hollyer B.A.
Caroline Royds B.A.
Denise Gardner

THE NEW CONCISE
CHILDREN'S
ENCYCLOPEDIA

G-ZUMP

**Edited by
John Paton**

KINGFISHER BOOKS

This edition (completely revised and reset)
published in 1988 by Kingfisher Books Limited
Elsley House, 24–30 Great Titchfield Street,
London W1P 1AD

First published in 1982, revised 1986, 1988

BRITISH LIBRARY CATALOGUING IN PUBLICATION DATA
Kingfisher new concise children's
    encyclopedias.—Rev. ed.
    1. Children's encyclopedias in English –
    Texts
    I. Paton, John, *1914–*
    032

ISBN 0-86272-390-6

Phototypeset by Southern Positives and Negatives
(SPAN), Lingfield, Surrey.

Printed in Italy

About Your Encyclopedia

An encyclopedia is a book of knowledge. By using the **The New Concise Children's Encyclopedia**, you will discover a wealth of fascinating information about people, ideas, events, and the world around you. Hundreds of subjects that you are interested in or curious about are included here.

This book is very easy to use. All the entries are arranged in alphabetical order. You should find most of the information you want by first looking up the main entry word. If the subject you are looking for does not have its own entry, check the Index at the back of the book. Usually you will find some information about your subject in another article. You may also enjoy just browsing through the book, discovering new things to read about and looking at the pictures.

Throughout the encyclopedia you will find words printed in small capitals, like this: ALLIGATORS. These words are *cross-references*. When you see one, you will know that there is a separate entry on the subject in the encyclopedia. That entry may have more information about the subject you are looking up.

This is an old Chinese abacus. The beads in the upper part count five when they are down on the central divider. Those on the lower part count one each when they are up. Can you work out the number shown on the abacus? The first two positions on the left are not being used, so the number is 1,532,786.

Aardvark

The aardvark is an animal that eats termites. When it has broken open a termite nest with its powerful claws, it pokes in its long, sticky tongue and pulls it out covered with the insects. The aardvark lives in central and southern Africa. It has large ears like a donkey and is an expert burrower. If caught away from its home it can dig a hole for itself at astonishing speed. The word 'aardvark' is Dutch for 'earth pig'. These shy animals can be over 2 metres long and nearly 1 metre high.

The aardvark is a strange-looking animal that lives in the dry parts of Africa. It spends the day in holes which it digs in the ground with its long, strong claws.

Abacus

The abacus is a simple counting machine first used by the ancient Greeks and Romans. It consists of rows of beads strung on wires; those on the first wire count as ones, those on the second wire count as tens, on the third wire they count as hundreds, and so on. The abacus is still used in Eastern countries such as China and Japan. The Romans sometimes used small stones as counters. They called these counters *calculi*, and it is from this that we get our word 'calculate'.

Abbreviation

An abbreviation is a shortened form of a word or a group of words. Words and phrases are shortened to save space. Sometimes the first and last letters of a word are used, such as *St* for 'Saint' or *Dr* for 'Doctor'. Sometimes only the beginning of the word is used, as in *Sept.* for 'September'. A full stop may be placed after the abbreviation to show that it is a shortened form.

This Aborigine still follows a primitive way of life. Many others now live and work in towns and cities.

Aborigine

The word 'aborigine' really means the first people who lived in any country. But it is now used to identify the original inhabitants of AUSTRALIA. The Aborigines are slim black people with black wavy hair. They came to Australia thousands of years ago from south-eastern Asia. In Australia they did not build permanent homes but wandered about the desert hunting or gathering their food. Their chief weapons were the boomerang and the throwing spear.

The Aborigines were very badly treated by the white men who came to Australia. Today Aborigines have rights as Australian citizens.

Acid

An acid is a liquid chemical compound that has a sour taste. Some acids, such as sulphuric acid, nitric acid and hydrochloric acid, are very strong and can *corrode*, or eat away, even the strongest metals. Other acids are harmless. These include the citric acid that gives lemons and oranges their sharp taste, and the acetic acid in vinegar. Lactic acid is produced when milk goes sour. All acids turn a special sort of paper called *litmus* from blue to red.

Acupuncture

Acupuncture is an ancient kind of medical treatment in which thin needles are used to puncture various parts of the body. The treatment was developed by the Chinese about 5000 years ago, and it is still used today. Chinese doctors have performed surgery with acupuncture as the only anaesthetic. In recent years, acupuncture has begun to be accepted in the West as a branch of alternative medicine. It is often used in the treatment of such things as headache, asthma and arthritis.

Addition

When we collect things together to find out how many there are, we are using addition. Three sets of dots can be counted or added like this:

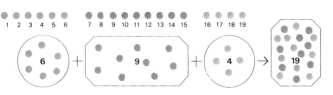

It does not matter in which order we add things together. In other words, $4 + 3$ is the same as $3 + 4$:

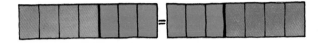

Give 4 the letter a and 3 the letter b: $a + b$ is the same as $b + a$.

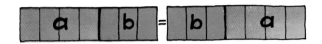

Adjective

An adjective is any word that describes or modifies a noun. 'A grey horse' is more exact than just 'a horse'. We can make it more exact still by writing 'a big, friendly, grey horse'. The words *big*, *friendly* and *grey* are adjectives describing the noun *horse*.

Adjectives usually come before the noun, but they can also come after it: 'The pie is *delicious*'. The word *delicious* describes the pie. It is an adjective.

Africa

Africa is the world's second largest continent. It covers an area of 30,319,000 square km, one-fifth of the world's land. Africa stretches from the Mediterranean Sea in the north to the Cape of Good Hope at its tip in the south. Large parts of Africa are empty wasteland. The SAHARA Desert spreads over much of the northern part of the continent. Near the equator, which runs through the centre of Africa, are thick rainforests. There the trees grow so close together that their leaves blot out the sunlight.

More than a third of Africa is a high, flat plain, or plateau. Grassland called *savanna* covers much of the plateau region. Great herds of grazing animals roam the savanna. They include zebras, giraffes, wildebeest and impala. Other animals, such as lions, cheetahs and hyenas, prey upon the grazing animals. In the past, many animals were killed by

This giraffe is standing among thorn bushes. In the background is Mount Kilimanjaro (5,895 metres), the highest mountain in Africa. Although it is near the equator, the top of the mountain is covered with snow.

hunters, but today special reserves have been set up to protect them.

Mt Kilimanjaro, the highest mountain in Africa, rises 5,895 metres in Tanzania. Africa's largest lake, Lake Victoria, lies between Kenya and Tanzania. The continent's great rivers are the NILE, Zaire, Niger and Zambezi.

Many different types of people live in Africa. In North Africa are ARABS and Berbers, who mostly follow the Muslim religion. So-called 'black Africa' lies south of

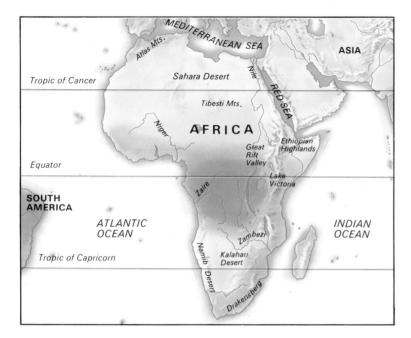

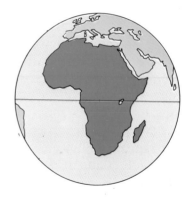

Africa is a huge continent with the equator running across its middle. There are two big desert areas – the Sahara in the north and the Kalahari and Namib in the south. Near the equator, the lowlands are covered with tropical forests.

This beautifully carved ivory mask was worn as an ornament by the king of the West African kingdom of Benin. Great empires grew up in Africa before white people came. Another of these was the civilization of Zimbabwe, built in the 800s.

the Sahara Desert. The black people who live there make up three-quarters of Africa's population. People with European and Asian ancestors make up the rest.

Most Africans are farmers, growing crops such as cocoa, coffee, cotton, sisal and tea. Africa produces nearly three-quarters of the world's palm oil and palm kernels, which are used to make soap and margarine. The continent has valuable mineral resources, too, including gold and diamonds, copper, tin, and bauxite for making aluminium.

The Dark Continent

For centuries Africa was called the 'Dark Continent' because Europeans knew little about it or its people. The Phoenicians and Romans had built trading centres along the north coast and they knew of the great early civilization in Egypt. But the lands to the south remained a mystery.

The first Europeans to learn more about this huge unexplored continent were the Portuguese. They were the first to find a sea route to India by sailing around the southern tip of Africa. They hugged the coast, fearing to sail out of sight of land. Soon the African coastline was charted. But it was still a long time before people became interested in exploring inland. From the 1400s, European sailors began to ship slaves from Africa. About 14 million slaves

were taken to the Americas between 1500 and the 1800s. Usually these slaves were bought from tribes that lived along the African coast, so Europeans did not need to travel into the interior of the great continent.

By the 1800s the countries of Europe were becoming interested in setting up colonies in Africa. Brave explorers like David Livingstone, Mungo Park and Henry Stanley travelled into the interior and soon the continent had been carved up between the European powers. The Europeans brought new ways of life to Africa. Missionaries brought the Christian religion and set up schools.

After a while, Africans began to resent being ruled by foreigners. During the 1950s and 1960s most former colonies became independent African countries. Many are poor and some have had bloody civil wars as different rulers fought for power. But today the countries are working together to help one another and to develop industry and their natural resources. Many of the richer nations of the world are helping them in this task.

Dr Livingstone went to Africa as a missionary and made friends with the Africans. During his travels he explored the Zambezi and Zaire rivers, and discovered the Victoria Falls and Lake Nyasa.

Air

Air is all around us—it surrounds the earth in a layer called the *atmosphere*. All living things must have air in order to live. Air is colourless and has no smell. Yet it is really a mixture of a number of different gases. We can feel air when the wind blows, and we know air has weight. Air carries sounds—without it we would not be able to hear, because sounds cannot travel in a VACUUM.

The chief gas in air is nitrogen, which makes up nearly four-fifths of the air. About one-fifth of the air is made up of OXYGEN. Air also holds some water in very fine particles called *vapour*. We find the degree of HUMIDITY in the air by measuring the amount of vapour.

Air expands when it is heated, and when it expands it becomes lighter. This is why warm air rises.

The air that surrounds the earth gets thinner the higher you go. All high-flying aircraft have to keep the air in their cabins at ground-level pressure so that passengers can breathe normally. In the same way, mountaineers carry their own air supply because the air at the top of high mountains is too thin for normal breathing.

Below: Air presses on everything. To show this, take a glass of water and place a card over the top (left). Turn the glass upside down (centre). When you take your hand away (right) the card stays in place. This shows that the air pressure beneath is greater than the weight of the water.

Above: When air is heated it expands and becomes lighter. In a hot-air balloon, air is heated by a jet of burning gas. The balloon rises when the weight of the gas plus the balloon is lighter than the surrounding air.

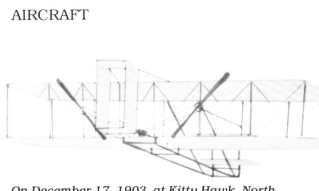

On December 17, 1903, at Kitty Hawk, North Carolina, Orville Wright made the world's first flight in a fully controlled heavier-than-air machine.

Aircraft

People have always dreamed of being able to fly like birds. At first, they attached artificial 'wings' to their arms and tried to flap them. But people failed, because their muscles were not strong enough to keep the wings in the air.

In the 1800s, the British scientist Sir George Cayley suggested that a vehicle could be built that was designed like a bird but with fixed wings. Many people tried to build such a machine, and some built gliders. But these could fly only short distances and were difficult to control.

In 1903, two brothers, Orville and Wilbur WRIGHT, built the *Flyer*, a flimsy-looking machine with a petrol engine at the back. They were successful. The first powered flight in the world took place at Kitty Hawk, North Carolina, on December 17, 1903. The new means of transport did not catch on right away. But by 1908, after the Wright Brothers had demonstrated their planes all over Europe, many others had caught the flying 'bug', and the development of aircraft was rapid. During WORLD WAR I, aircraft were used both for watching enemy movements (called *reconnaissance*) and, later, for fighting.

The war proved that aircraft were not only useful but a necessity. In 1919 John Alcock and Arthur Whitten Brown made the first Atlantic crossing; Charles LINDBERGH made the first solo crossing in 1927. In 1936 the Douglas DC-3, or *Dakota*, went into service

The SR-71A Blackbird *is one of the most advanced aircraft in the world today. It holds records for both speed and altitude. It can fly at about 3,500 km/hr.*

and proved itself the most successful airliner ever built. WORLD WAR II saw the development of fast fighter aircraft and heavy bombers, and by the end of the war jet aircraft had appeared.

The first aircraft to fly faster than the speed of sound (*supersonic* speed) was tested in 1947. Today, military fighter aircraft and some airliners such as the *Concorde* are designed for supersonic speeds. Others, like the jumbo jets, carry more than 500 people and big freight loads.

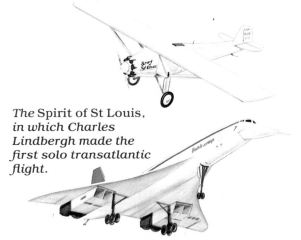

The Spirit of St Louis, *in which Charles Lindbergh made the first solo transatlantic flight.*

The supersonic Concorde airliner. *It flies at twice the speed of sound.*

Getting Off the Ground

To fly, an aircraft must have *lift* to raise it against the pull of the earth's GRAVITY. This lift is produced by the movement of air over the aircraft's wings. The force (*thrust*) needed to push the aircraft forward comes either from propellers or from jet engines. The tail on the aircraft steadies and helps to control its flight. The *rudder* and *elevators* on the tail and the *ailerons* on the wings all help the pilot to control the craft. A modern airliner also has a wide variety of controls to help the pilot keep a check on all the aircraft's systems and to navigate a course.

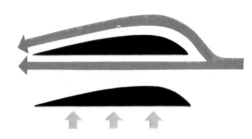

A cross-section through an aircraft's wing shows its aerofoil *shape—curved on top and flat on the bottom. When air passes over and under the wing, a difference in air pressure is created because of the curved shape. This lifts the wing, and the aircraft flies.*

Albania

Albania is a small, rugged country that lies between Yugoslavia and Greece on the eastern shore of the Adriatic Sea (see map on page 123). Most Albanians live in small, remote mountain villages. Albanian farmers grow wheat, barley, tobacco and cotton. Beneath the ground there are deposits of chrome, copper, iron, oil and natural gas. Albania was ruled by Turkey for over 400 years. After World War II it became a communist state.

Alexander the Great. This is part of a mosaic found at Pompeii in Italy.

Alexander the Great

Alexander the Great (356–323 BC) was a ruler of GREECE and one of the greatest generals that ever lived. The son of Philip of Macedon, Alexander conquered the Greek city-states after he became king when Philip

Above left: The F-15 Eagle is one of the world's best fighter planes.
Left: The Boeing 747 jumbo jet is a great airliner. It can carry more than 500 people at a speed of more than 980km/hr.

died in 336 BC. He then marched east to conquer Persia, which was at that time the greatest empire in the world. By 327 Alexander's empire stretched from Greece to India. When his armies reached India they were worn out from marching and fighting. Alexander turned back. When he reached Babylon he became ill with a fever and died. He was only 33. Alexander's body was carried back to Alexandria, the great city he had founded in EGYPT. There it was placed in a magnificent tomb.

Alfred the Great

Alfred the Great (849–899) was a wise and able ruler who saved England from being conquered by the Danes. He formed an army and a navy to defend his Kingdom of Wessex from the invaders, and drove out the Danes in 896. When peace returned, Alfred did much to bring justice and education to his people. Under his direction the ANGLO-SAXON Chronicle was begun. It was a record of the events of each year, and much of our knowledge of King Alfred's time comes from this record.

Alligators and Crocodiles

Alligators and crocodiles belong to the same family. There are few differences between them. They both lay their eggs on land, but they spend a lot of time keeping cool in the water. There are two species of alligator: the American alligator of the south-eastern United States and the Chinese alligator that lives in the Yangtze

Crocodile

Unlike the alligator, when a crocodile closes its jaws, the fourth tooth in its lower jaw sticks out.

Alligator

River. Crocodiles spend much of their time floating just below the surface with only their eyes and nostrils showing. They are waiting for an unwary zebra or antelope to come down to the river.

Alps

The Alps are the greatest mountain range in EUROPE. They are centred in SWITZERLAND, but they stretch from France all the way to Yugoslavia. Mont Blanc, 4807 metres high, is the highest mountain peak in Europe.

Amazon, River

The Amazon is the world's second largest river. It flows for 6400km from Peru through Brazil to the Atlantic Ocean. Almost the whole of the Amazon basin is dense tropical forest. In the 1540s a Spanish explorer saw female Indian warriors on the Amazon's banks, and so the river was named after the Amazons of Greek legends.

America

The word 'America' is often used to mean the United States, but it originally covered a much larger area that today is more properly called the Americas. The Americas include North America, Central America and South America, and the islands of the Caribbean and northern Canada. The Americas were named after the Italian navigator Amerigo Vespucci, who explored part of the South American coast.

American History

The Spanish were the first European nation to settle in North America. In 1565 they established a fort at St Augustine, Florida. English colonies were not started until after 1600. But the English, unlike the Spanish, French and Dutch, had really come to stay. They gained control of most of the Atlantic coast from New England to Georgia, an area that was to become the original 13 states.

In 1607, Jamestown Colony was founded. Then, in 1620, the Pilgrims set sail from Plymouth, England, to found Plym-

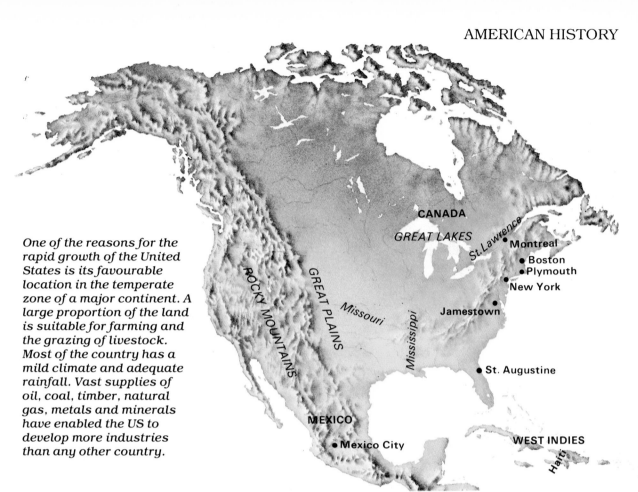

One of the reasons for the rapid growth of the United States is its favourable location in the temperate zone of a major continent. A large proportion of the land is suitable for farming and the grazing of livestock. Most of the country has a mild climate and adequate rainfall. Vast supplies of oil, coal, timber, natural gas, metals and minerals have enabled the US to develop more industries than any other country.

outh Colony in Massachusetts. By 1700, most of the East Coast was dotted with settlements.

During the 1700s, wars were fought by Britain, France and Spain in various parts of America. These were the French and Indian Wars (1754–1763). By 1763, Britain had gained most of the land in western North America.

Without the consent of the colonies, Britain decided to keep a standing army in America. Britain also forbade the colonists to move west of the Appalachian Mountains. In addition, it levied some new taxes that the colonists thought were unfair.

Relations grew worse, and in 1776 the colonists declared their independence from Britain. (See REVOLUTIONARY WAR, AMERICAN.)

The Revolutionary War ended after the Battle of Yorktown in 1781. The United States was an independent nation. George Washington became the first president in 1789.

During the 1800s, the British navy controlled the seas and began to interfere with American shipping. This led to the War of 1812, which neither side could claim to have won.

After the war, the issue of slavery began to divide the nation. The North wanted to abolish slavery; the South needed slave labour on the plantations. The victory of the anti-slavery candidate, Abraham Lincoln,

The signing of the Declaration of Independence in Independence Hall, Philadelphia.

in the presidential election of 1860 helped start the Civil War. (See CIVIL WAR, AMERICAN.) The years after this war were difficult, but soon the United States began a period of prosperity.

When Europe went to war in 1914, Americans thought they could avoid becoming involved. But by 1917 they were drawn into World War I, joining forces with Britain and France against Germany.

After the war, the United States became more and more prosperous. But in 1929 the stock market crashed and the Great Depression began. The government under Franklin Roosevelt started many new projects, building great dams, public buildings, and bridges to provide jobs for Americans.

World War II broke out in 1939 between Adolf Hitler's Germany and Italy on one side and France, Britain and their allies on the other. The US did not want to enter another war, but in 1941 the Japanese, who had become allies of the Germans, bombed Pearl Harbor, Hawaii. From that moment, the United States was at war. (See WORLD WAR II.)

The United States leads the world in technology. This is a space shuttle booster rocket being prepared at the Kennedy Space Center at Cape Canaveral.

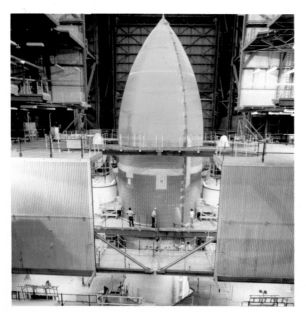

When the war ended with the dropping of atom bombs on two Japanese cities, everyone decided that there must never again be a world war. The United Nations was founded, but there were still limited conflicts in Korea and Vietnam which involved US troops. Today the main threat to world peace is still the mutual distrust between the US and her allies and the Eastern Bloc headed by Russia. Each side has built up vast nuclear armaments, which everyone hopes will never be used; however, a treaty signed in 1987 brings closer the prospect of future world peace.

The United States is now the wealthiest nation on earth, and US technology has advanced tremendously. On July 20, 1969, two Americans became the first men to set foot on the moon. The message they left there said: "We came in peace for all mankind."

Amphibians

Amphibians are animals such as FROGS, toads, salamanders and newts. They can live in water or on land, but most of them start their lives in water. Amphibians are cold-blooded creatures. They do not drink like other animals but absorb water directly through their skins. For this reason they must keep their skins moist. Amphibians were one of the earliest groups of animals on earth. They crawled out of the water and onto the land about 400 million years ago.

All amphibians have backbones. Nearly all of them lay their eggs in water, in a layer of jelly, which protects them. When the young amphibians hatch, they feed on algae (tiny water plants). A young frog at this stage is called a tadpole. It breathes the oxygen dissolved in water through gills. After two or three months the tadpole begins to change into an adult. Its tail gradually disappears, and its gills turn into LUNGS. Hind legs and then front legs appear. The little frog leaves the water and spends the rest of its life as an air-breathing adult. But it must return to the water to mate and lay its eggs.

Angle

An angle is formed when two straight lines meet. The size of all angles is measured in degrees. The angle that forms the corner of

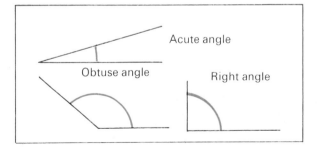

a square is called a *right* angle and has 90 degrees (90°). An *acute* angle is less than 90 degrees; an *obtuse* angle is between 90 and 180 degrees.

Anglo-Saxons

Anglo-Saxon is the name given to the group of Germanic tribes who settled in Britain during the 400s and 500s AD. These tribes were the Angles, Saxons and Jutes. They gradually occupied all of England, driving the original Celtic people of Britain into

The frog usually lives close to water. Its large hind legs are used for jumping and swimming. It eats insects and worms.

The Anglo-Saxons were fond of highly decorated jewellery like the solid gold brooch above.

Wales and Cornwall. By the 700s there were seven main Anglo-Saxon kingdoms – Wessex, Sussex, Kent, Essex, East Anglia, Mercia and Northumbria. The Anglo-Saxon language is one of the two main ingredients of modern English.

Ant

Ants are 'social' insects—they live together in colonies. Some colonies are in heaps of twigs; others are in chambers deep in the ground. Still others are hills of earth or sand. There are three types of ant: males, queens, which lay eggs, and workers or females that do not mate or lay eggs.

The legionary or army ants march across country in a great horde that may have as many as 100,000 ants. If they reach a house

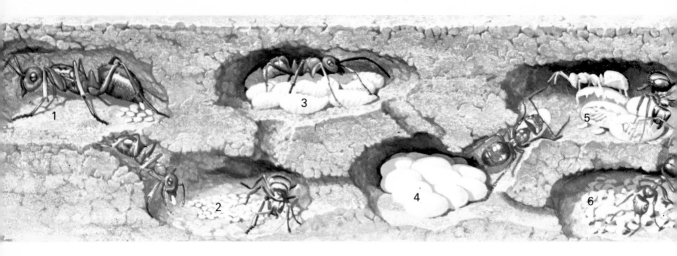

they will strip it of anything that can be eaten, even tied-up animals. Most kinds of male ants and most young queens have wings for a while.

The life cycle of the ant begins when the queen lays her eggs (1). Worker ants carry the eggs to the nursery where they hatch into larvae (2). The larvae are fed by worker ants (3). The larvae then spin cocoons, in which they turn into pupae (4). In the hatching chamber the young ants come out of the cocoons (5). Waste material is taken away and stored in a refuse chamber (6).

Antarctic

The Antarctic is the continent that sur-rounds the South Pole. It is a vast region of cold waste, with very little animal or plant life. Nearly all of the Antarctic is covered by an ice cap, broken only by a few mountain

Antarctica is a vast wilderness of ice and snow. Scientists go there to study the rocks buried deep beneath the ice. They use tractors to get around. The penguins huddle together against the biting wind.

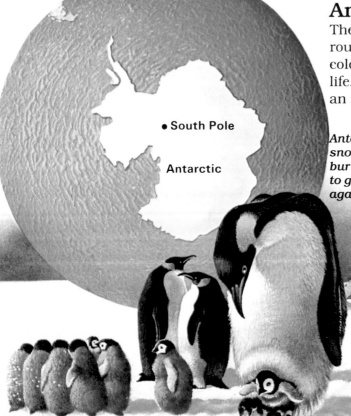

● South Pole

Antarctic

ranges. This ice cap averages 2500 metres in thickness, but is as much as 4700 metres thick in places. Antarctica has nine-tenths of all the world's ice.

Anteater

The anteater of South America is a curious creature with a long, tapering snout. The snout is specially shaped to take ants, termites and grubs from their nests. The anteater catches the insects with its long, whiplike tongue. An anteater may measure over 2 metres from the tip of its tail to its snout. It uses its strong front claws to tear open ant and termite nests.

Antelope

Antelopes are a family of grazing animals with horns and hoofs. They look something like DEER but are actually related to the goat and the ox. Most antelopes live on the African plains. They are fast runners and often live in large herds, fleeing suddenly at any hint of danger. Some of the best known are the impala, the waterbuck, the harte-beest, the gnu, the eland and the little dik-dik, which is about the size of a rabbit.

Right: The greater kudu has handsome corkscrew horns. The hartebeest's horns are short and screwed. Longest of all are the curving horns of the sable antelope. The strange four-horned antelope is unusual.

Ape

Apes are people's closest animal relatives. We share the same kind of skeleton and have the same kind and number of teeth. We also have the same kind of blood and catch many similar diseases. Apes have large brains, but even the gorilla's brain is only half the size of ours. Unlike monkeys, apes have no tails. There are four kinds of ape: the GORILLA and chimpanzee are African; orang-utans live in Borneo and Sumatra; gibbons live in South-East Asia.

Greater kudu

Hartebeest

Sable antelope

Four-horned antelope

The claws on the front feet of the giant anteater are so long that the animal has to walk on the sides of its feet instead of the soles.

19

Arab

Arabs were originally those people who lived in Arabia. But from the 600s AD Arabian Arabs, inspired by their new faith, Islam, swept through western Asia and North Africa, conquering and settling a huge area. They taught the inhabitants the Arabic language and the Islamic religion. Today, Arabs are those people whose mother tongue is Arabic and who share a common history and religion. This includes Arabic-speaking peoples from countries such as Algeria, Syria, Iraq and Libya. Muslims in Iran, India and Pakistan pray in Arabic but do not use it in everyday speech, so they are not considered Arabs.

The Arabs ruled North Africa and Southwest Asia for 900 years, until they were defeated by the Turks in the 1500s. They lived under Turkish rule until World War I. After World War II many Arab countries became extremely rich from the production of huge quantities of valuable OIL. There have been several attempts to unify the Arab nations, though in recent years conflict with the state of Israel has contributed to a split in the Arab ranks. The oil-producing countries hold great political power in the world because of their control of important oil resources.

We can learn a great deal about the past from objects dug up at places where people lived long ago. These places are usually known as 'sites'. They must be very carefully dug so that the exact place where each object is found can be noted down. The picture on the right shows part of a site where a 'dig' is going on. Finds are placed in the labelled boxes; all the earth is taken away to be sieved in case any small find has been missed. The grid of strings helps to map the site at different stages.

Archaeology

Archaeology is the study of history through the things that people have made and built. These may include tools, pottery, houses, temples or graves. Even a rubbish pit can help to reveal how people lived. Archaeologists study all these things, from the greatest monuments to the tiniest pin. Modern archaeology began during the REN-AISSANCE, when people became interested in the culture of ancient GREECE and ROME. At first, archaeological sites were ransacked for the treasures they contained. But by the early 1800s archaeologists had

begun to uncover sites carefully, noting all they found and where they found it. Many exciting and important discoveries were made, including the remains of ancient Troy (1871); the early Greek civilization at Mycenae (1876); and the tomb of the pharaoh Tutankhamun in Egypt (1922).

Today, science helps the archaeologist in his work. Radiocarbon dating and *dendro-chronology* (dating by tree rings) help tell when particular objects were made. Infrared and X-RAY photography can show up designs under the rotted surface of a bronze bowl. Archaeology has even gone under the sea. With modern diving equipment, archaeologists can explore sunken wrecks and other long-lost remains of the past.

Archimedes

Archimedes (282–212 BC) was a famous Greek scientist who lived in Sicily. Among many other things he discovered Archimedes' Principle, which tells us that if we weigh an object in the air and then weigh it again submerged in a liquid, it will lose weight equal to the weight of the liquid it displaces. Archimedes is supposed to have discovered this when he stepped into a bath full to the brim, and water spilled onto the floor.

Architecture

Architecture is the art of designing buildings. If we look at old buildings still standing we can learn a great deal about the people who built them.

Architecture as we know it began about 7000 years ago in ancient EGYPT. The Egyptians built huge pyramids as tombs for their kings, and many of these pyramids still stand.

Greek architecture began to take shape about 600 BC and developed into the

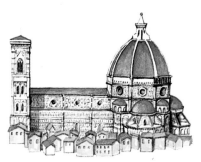
Renaissance: Florence Cathedral, Italy.

Byzantine: Sancta Sophia, Turkey.

Greek Doric: Temple of Neptune, Greece.

Why should a hollow vessel float in water? Why should a block of wood float but a piece of lead sink? The answer lies in the density of the objects and of water. *Archimedes' Principle* says that when any object is placed in a liquid, it experiences an upthrust equal to the weight of liquid displaced. As an object sinks into the liquid, it displaces more and more liquid, and there may come a point when the upthrust is equal to the weight of the object. The object floats. Wood floats on water because it is less dense.

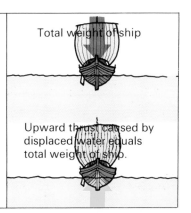
Total weight of ship

Upward thrust caused by displaced water equals total weight of ship.

Roman: Arch of Constantine, Rome, Italy.

Ionic

Doric

Corinthian

There were three main styles of Greek capital (the top part of a column). The Doric style was simple; the Ionic style was carved and scrolled; the Corinthian style, which was popular from the 5th century BC onward, was decorated with scrolls and acanthus leaves.

beautiful styles we can see today on the Acropolis in Athens.

When the Romans conquered GREECE they copied Greek architecture. But when they discovered how to make an arch, they were able to build larger, stronger buildings. They also began to make domes for the first time.

About AD 800 the Romanesque period of architecture began. Romanesque architecture at first imitated the style of ancient Rome but soon took on a style of its own—a style that was strong and heavy. This style was followed by the Gothic. Many fine old cathedrals are in the Gothic style. They have graceful pointed arches over doors, windows, and often in the roof as well. The roof of a Gothic cathedral is usually made of a series of crisscross arches which support

Gothic: Bruges Cathedral, France.

the weight of the ceiling. Roofs like this are called *vaulted* roofs.

In about 1400 a new style of architecture began in Italy. This was called the RENAISSANCE (the word means rebirth), and it spread all over Europe. Renaissance architects paid almost as much attention to public buildings and people's houses as they did to building churches and other places of worship.

Later, many famous architects changed the building styles to fit the times in which they lived. Christopher Wren (1632–1723) designed buildings such as St Paul's Cathedral in London and parts of Hampton Court.

Today people still build with brick and stone, but they also use newer materials that have changed the way in which buildings are constructed. Concrete and steel, glass and plastics now shape the world in which we live. Architects are designing offices, factories and sports arenas so as to make the best use of these materials.

Arctic

The Arctic is the region around the North Pole. At the very North Pole there is no land, only a huge area of frozen sea. The land in the Arctic region is frozen solid for most of the year. In the short summer the surface

North Pole

Greenland

Arctic Circle

soil thaws and some plants can grow, even brightly coloured flowers. There are now more people in the Arctic than there used to be. This is because valuable minerals and oil have been found there.

It is cold near the North Pole because the sun never rises high in the sky. In winter there are days when it does not rise at all. In summer there are days when it can be seen all day and night.

Argentina

Argentina is the second largest country in SOUTH AMERICA. Most of the country's 30,000,000 people are ranchers and farmers, for much of Argentina's wealth comes from livestock and crops. Argentina is one of the world's top producers of beef and veal, fruit, wheat, millet and sorghum, and wool. The chief farming region is on the *pampas*, a Spanish word meaning 'plains'. The pampas lie to the north-west and south of Argentina's capital, Buenos Aires. Here, farmers raise millions of cattle and sheep, which graze on the rich pasture. Northern Argentina is an area of tropical forests and is little developed. In the far south, near the tip of South America, is Patagonia, a desert wasteland. The western part of the country is dry, and the land rises to the Andes Mountains, including Aconcagua, at 6960 metres the highest peak in South America. Argentina was ruled by Spain from 1535 to 1810. Today most Argentinians are descended from Europeans, though there are still about 20,000 native Indians.

Argentina is a land of contrasts. Tierra del Fuego in the south is a cold, wet land where penguins live. The pampas, a vast, treeless, grassy plain, spreads out across the centre of the country. In the west are the towering Andes Mountains that separate Argentina from Chile.

Aristotle

Aristotle (384–322 BC) was a Greek philosopher and a student of another famous Greek philosopher, Plato. At the age of 17 Aristotle went to Athens to become Plato's pupil. He worked there for 20 years and then became tutor to ALEXANDER THE GREAT. Aristotle invented the method of thinking called *logic*. His writings cover many areas, including nature and politics.

Arithmetic

Arithmetic is the branch of MATHEMATICS that deals with counting and calculating, using numbers. The four operations in arithmetic are addition, subtraction, multiplication and division.

We use arithmetic every day to count money, to tell the time, and to buy or sell anything.

Armada

Armada is a Spanish word for a great fleet of armed ships. The most famous armada was the Spanish fleet that tried to invade England in 1588. The 132 Spanish ships were large, clumsy and heavily armed. The English ships were faster and easier to manoeuvre, and were manned by more skilful seamen. The English sent fire ships towards the Spanish fleet, which retreated out to sea. Later, several Spanish ships were sunk and many damaged in battle. The Armada was forced to flee around the northern tip of Britain, and many of its ships were wrecked in a storm. Only 67 of the original 132 ships reached Spain.

The Spanish plan was to sail through the English Channel to Belgium. There they would join forces with the Spanish troops fighting the Dutch and Belgians. The combined force of 30,000 men would then sail to the Thames and march on London. Bad weather and superior English seamanship ensured the failure of this plan. The Spanish ships were driven round the north of Scotland, and many went to their doom in bad weather.

The fate of the Spanish Armada

SCOTLAND

North Sea

IRELAND

Howard pursues fleeing Armada
23 July 1588

ENGLAND

Armada attacked by fireships
22 July 1588

197 English ships mostly small & 16-17,000 men

Portland

Plymouth

Armada sighted
20 July 1588

Armada sighted
19 July 1588

Atlantic Ocean

Armada sighted
14 July 1588

The Spanish invasion plan was based on picking up troops in Belgium. These never materialized.

Armada scattered by squalls

FRANCE

4 June 1588

La Coruna   Santander

SPAIN

PORTUGAL

Madrid

Mediterranean Sea

Lisbon

14 May 1588
Armada leaves with 132 ships

Armadillo

Armadillos are unusual animals that live in Central and South America and in Texas. Their backs are covered with an armour of bony plates. Some kinds of armadillo can roll themselves into a ball when attacked, giving them complete protection. They have strong claws which they use for digging burrows and tearing open termite nests to find food. There are ten different kinds of armadillo; the biggest of these is about 1.2 metres long.

Right: The armadillo's body is protected by a series of bony plates.

Armour

Armour is covering used to protect the body in battle. It goes back at least 5000 years and was originally made of tough leather.

KEY TO PARTS
OF ARMOUR
1. Visor
2. Breastplate
3. Gauntlet
4. Couter
5. Cuisse
6. Greave
7. Sabaton

Plate armour
about 1500

Norman

Saracen

Crusader

13th-century helmet

Then men made metal breastplates, helmets and shields. But the rest of the body was still protected by leather or *chain mail*, many small iron rings linked together to form a flexible metal coat. In the Middle Ages, knights rode into battle encased from head to toe in plate armour which weighed up to 30 kg. When firearms were invented, armour was no longer worn, except for the helmet. The weight of metal needed to stop a bullet was too great.

Today, tough, lightweight metals and plastics are used in armoured jackets worn by soldiers and police officers.

Art

Since the very earliest times people have painted and made sculptured objects. We can still admire cave paintings that were drawn over 20,000 years ago. Beautiful wall paintings and sculptures from ancient EGYPT, GREECE, and ROME still survive.

The Christian religion had a great influence on art. During the Middle Ages painters depicted religious scenes in a rather stiff way. But when the RENAISSANCE came in the 1300s, art began to flower and artists became famous for their work. Painters such as LEONARDO DA VINCI and MICHELANGELO began to make their subjects more lifelike. Great Dutch painters such as REMBRANDT painted everyday scenes. In the 1700s and 1800s many artists went back to making their work look something like early Greek and Roman art.

Later, painting became more real-looking, but by the 1870s a new style called Impressionism was starting. Artists such as Monet (1840–1926) and Renoir (1841–1919) painted with little dabs of colour, making soft, misty outlines. Painting in the 1900s became even freer. Styles included Abstract Art and Cubism, with famous painters such as Cézanne (1839–1906) and PICASSO.

Below left: The history of art is as old as the history of people. This African cave painting dates from the Stone Age. Below: A self-portrait painted by the Dutch artist Rembrandt. Bottom: A Madonna and Child by the Italian Renaissance artist Raphael.

Above: A figure by the great modern sculptor Henry Moore. Above, right: An ancient Chinese bronze elephant.

The oldest pieces of sculpture we know were made in the STONE AGE, about 30,000 years ago. The ancient Egyptians made very fine sculptures between 2000 and 4000 years ago. Many of them were huge statues of kings and queens. Some of the world's most beautiful carving was done by the sculptors of ancient Greece and Rome, in what is known as the Classical period. During the RENAISSANCE, especially in Italy, the art of sculpture advanced by leaps and bounds. MICHELANGELO carved superb statues such as his *David*, which can be seen in Florence.

Modern sculptors often carve sculptures into abstract shapes rather than showing the likeness of a figure.

Far right: A beautiful porcelain vase made at Sèvres in France about 1785. Sèvres porcelain is famous for its rich colours. Right: A tiny Easter egg of gold, enamel and precious stones made by the Russian goldsmith Fabergé (1846–1920).

A busy street in Hong Kong. The total area of the small British colony in China is only 1060 square km. In this area there are more than 5 million people, nearly 5000 per square kilometre.

The Japanese 'bullet' train speeds past Mount Fuji at over 250 km per hour. Fuji (3776 metres) is the highest mountain in Japan, and is a sacred place to the Japanese. Its top is the crater of an inactive volcano.

Asia

Asia is the largest of all the continents. It also has more people (2,693,000,000) than any other continent. Places such as the Ganges-Brahmaputra delta, the river valleys of CHINA, and the island of Java are among the most thickly populated areas in the world.

Northern Asia is a cold, desolate tundra region. In contrast, the islands of INDONESIA are in the steamy tropics. The world's highest mountain range, the HIMALAYAS, is in Asia, and so is the lowest point on land, the shores of the Dead Sea. Asia's people belong to the three main races: Caucasoids live in the south-west and northern INDIA; Mongoloids, including the Chinese and Japanese, live in the east. A few Negroids are found in the south-east. All the world's great religions began in Asia – JUDAISM, CHRISTIANITY, ISLAM, Buddhism, HINDUISM, Confucianism and Shinto.

Most Asians are farmers, and many are very poor. The chief food crops are wheat and rice. Other crops are exported, including tea, cotton, jute, rubber, citrus fruits and tobacco. Many nations such as China are developing their industries, but JAPAN is the major industrialized nation.

Asia was the birthplace of civilization and was the home of many great civilizations, including those of Mesopotamia, Babylon, China and the Indus Valley in what is now Pakistan. Europeans began to visit Asia in the 1400s, and trade quickly grew up between the two continents. Later, for several centuries, China and Japan closed their doors to trade with Europe. By the late 1800s most of the rest of Asia was ruled by European powers. But after World War II, during which Japan occupied parts of East Asia, most European colonies became independent. In 1949 the Chinese Communists took control of mainland China. In 1975 Communists took over VIETNAM, Laos and Cambodia after a long war for control, fought mainly in Vietnam.

In Japan and other crowded Asian countries, farmers have learned to cultivate carefully the soil that can be farmed, so that their crop yields are among the highest in the world. They have built terraces on hillsides for growing rice and other crops. Terracing the slopes helps stop erosion of the soil.

Astronaut

See SPACE EXPLORATION

Astronomy

Astronomy is the scientific study of the heavenly bodies and is the oldest science in existence. Early observations of the heavens enabled men to divide the year into months, weeks and days, based on the movements of the SUN, EARTH and MOON. The development of the calendar helped the early astronomers to forecast the appearance of COMETS and the dates of ECLIPSES. For many centuries people believed that the earth was the centre of the UNIVERSE until, in the 1540s, Nicolaus Copernicus revived the idea that the sun was the centre of the SOLAR SYSTEM.

In 1608 Hans Lippershey, a Dutchman, invented the TELESCOPE, an important new tool for astronomers. Today, big telescopes are aided by radio telescopes, which collect radio waves sent out by objects in space, such as pulsars and QUASARS.

Astronomers are now using satellites and telescopes in space to study the universe. Space probes such as *Viking 1* and *2* and *Voyager 1* and *2* have sent back to earth new information about our neighbours in space.

Atmosphere

The blanket of air and moisture that surrounds our planet is called the atmosphere. It is divided into four bands. The lowest level is the *troposphere*. Most of the air is concentrated here, from sea level to about 18km high. Then comes the *stratosphere* to 80km, where jet aircraft often fly. The third layer is the *ionosphere* to 500km, above which is the *exosphere*. This is the fringe of the atmosphere and the start of outer space. Even in outer space there are still a few molecules of air.

Atom

Everything is made of atoms. Things you can see, such as a table; things you cannot see, such as air, are all made of atoms. You are made of atoms, too. If the atoms in something are packed closely together, that something is a solid. If the atoms in something are not so tightly packed—if they move around more—that something is a

Below: A homemade reflecting telescope made almost entirely of wood. A simple telescope like this will show Saturn's rings and the Great Red Spot on Jupiter. Right: The Pleiades are a cluster of stars that can be seen with the naked eye. They are white giant stars thousands of times brighter than our sun. This photograph was taken through a telescope.

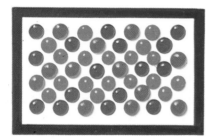

In a solid, atoms pack tightly.

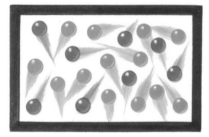

In a liquid, atoms move around.

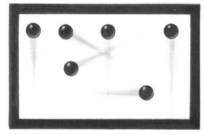

In a gas, atoms move around a lot.

of the light gas HYDROGEN. In the centre is a tiny body called a *proton*. Around it spins an *electron*. Other atoms are much more complicated than the hydrogen atom. The carbon atom, for example, has at its centre six protons and six other things called *neutrons*. Around these spin six very tiny electrons.

Atomic Energy

An atomic bomb produces an enormous amount of heat in a fraction of a second. Atomic energy is produced in an *atomic reactor* in a similar way, but the energy is controlled. Heat is produced much more slowly and safely.

To make useful power from the atom, scientists use a special kind of metal called URANIUM. The atoms in uranium are always breaking up and making heat. To control the amount of heat, the uranium is made into long rods. The rods are put into a *reactor core* and are separated by other control rods which are often made of CARBON. With the right number of uranium rods and carbon rods, the reactor goes on making a lot of safe heat.

Water or sometimes carbon dioxide gas flows around inside the reactor. The water boils and the steam is made to drive turbines. The turbines drive generators which make ELECTRICITY. This electricity is made available to us, just like electricity from power stations which run on oil or coal. The diagram below shows how the energy gets from the uranium rods to your home.

liquid, like water. And if the atoms move around a lot, we have a gas, like air.

It is very difficult to imagine how small atoms are. We cannot see them – they are far too small. Look at the full stop at the end of this sentence. It has in it about 250 billion atoms! But even atoms are made up of smaller parts. The simplest atom is that

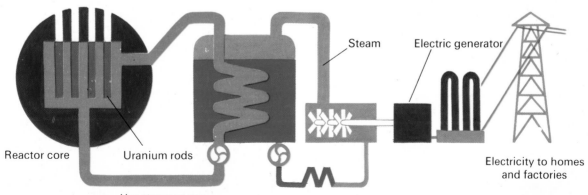

Reactor core   Uranium rods   Steam   Electric generator

Hot water or gas

Electricity to homes and factories

Australia

Australia is one of the world's seven CONTI-
NENTS. It is a huge island, almost as big as
the United States without Alaska, but the
population is only about 15 million compared to the US's 240 million. The heart of
Australia is a vast desert, with very few
people. Ringing the coasts on the east of the
country is a long chain of low-lying mountains. But Australia is a flat land with few
high mountains. Off the north-east coast is
the world's longest underwater CORAL reef,
the Great Barrier Reef. It is over 2000km
long.

Australia was almost unknown until
1770, when the explorer Captain James
COOK landed in Botany Bay, on the south-
east coast, and claimed the land for Britain.
The only people living there were the
ABORIGINES, who had arrived on the continent about 30,000 years before.

Australia is one of the world's richest
lands, with great wealth in minerals and
farmland. The country exports large quantities of wool, meat and wheat.

Australia has only a few kinds of animals
of its own. Among them are the famous
marsupials—animals that carry their
young in pouches. These are the KANGA-
ROOS, wallabies, wombats and KOALAS. The
duckbilled platypus is a strange mammal
that lays eggs.

Australia has a federal form of government with the national parliament in Canberra. It is a member of the Commonwealth
of Nations.

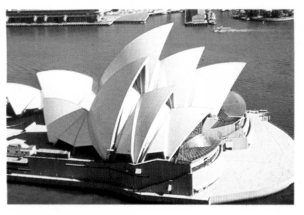

*The Sydney Opera House was built to look like
the sailboats in the harbour. Sydney is the
largest city in Australia.*

*More than half the people of Australia live in
the four largest cities—Sydney, Melbourne,
Brisbane and Adelaide. Vast areas of the
interior of the country have very few people.
On an average there are only about three
Australians to every square kilometre.*

*Left: Ayers Rock rises high above the flat
desert in the Northern Territory. It is the
largest rock in the world.*

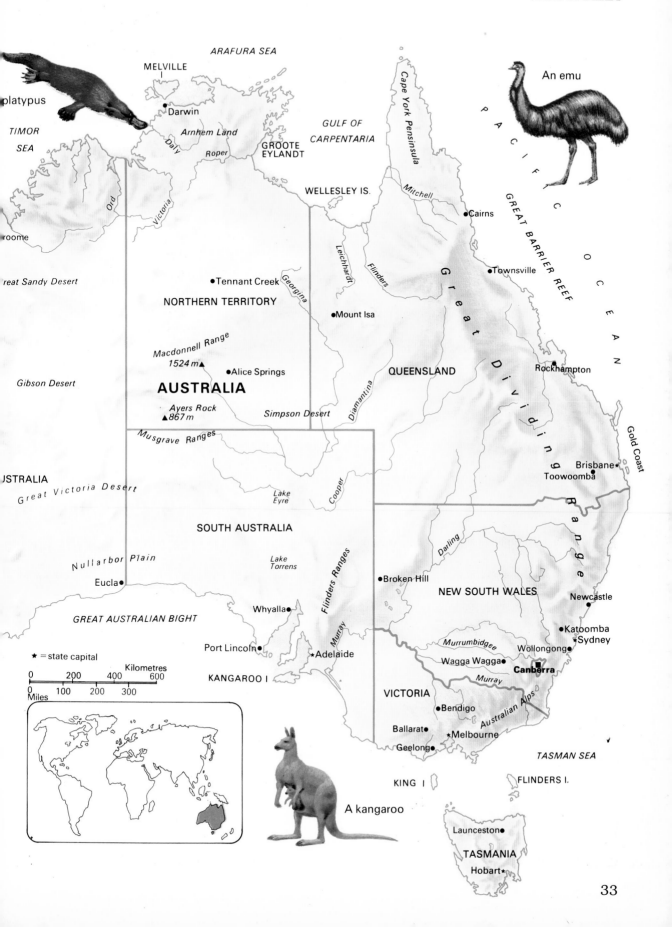

platypus

An emu

ARAFURA SEA

MELVILLE

Darwin

TIMOR SEA

Arnhem Land

Daly

Roper

GROOTE EYLANDT

GULF OF CARPENTARIA

Cape York Pensinsula

P A C I F I C

roome

Od

Victoria

Great Sandy Desert

WELLESLEY IS.

Mitchell

GREAT BARRIER REEF

Cairns

Tennant Creek

NORTHERN TERRITORY

Georgina

Leichhardt

Flinders

Mount Isa

Townsville

O C E A N

Macdonnell Range
1524 m ▲

Alice Springs

Gibson Desert

AUSTRALIA

Ayers Rock
▲867 m

Simpson Desert

Diamantina

QUEENSLAND

Great Dividing

Rockhampton

Gold Coast

Musgrave Ranges

Cooper

Brisbane ★
Toowoomba

USTRALIA

Great Victoria Desert

Lake Eyre

Range

SOUTH AUSTRALIA

Darling

Nullarbor Plain

Lake Torrens

Flinders Ranges

Broken Hill

NEW SOUTH WALES

Newcastle

Eucla

GREAT AUSTRALIAN BIGHT

Whyalla

Murray

Katoomba
★ Sydney
Wollongong

Port Lincoln

Adelaide

Murrumbidgee

Wagga Wagga

■ **Canberra**

★ = state capital

Kilometres
0   200   400   600
0   100   200   300
Miles

KANGAROO I

Murray

VICTORIA

Australian Alps

Bendigo

Ballarat
Geelong

★ Melbourne

TASMAN SEA

A kangaroo

KING I

FLINDERS I.

Launceston

TASMANIA

Hobart ★

33

Austria

Today this small country is not much bigger than Ireland. But once it was one of the largest and most powerful nations in Europe. (See map on page 123.)

For more than 600 years, from 1278 to 1918, Austria was ruled by a dynasty of kings and queens called the Hapsburgs. Their lands covered most of central Europe. They included Hungary, Czechoslovakia, large parts of Italy, Yugoslavia, Poland, Germany, Spain and the Netherlands.

The Austrian Empire collapsed after World War I. But there are many relics of the rich court life of the Hapsburg emperors. Vienna, the capital city where over $1\frac{1}{2}$ million Austrians live, is filled with castles, beautiful buildings and churches, statues and royal parks.

Above: An outdoor cafe in a busy Vienna shopping district provides a meeting place for friends.

Aztec

The empire of the Aztecs was a great Indian civilization in Mexico and Central America when Spanish soldiers discovered it. A Spanish commander named Hernando CORTÉS landed with 600 men on their shores in 1519. Within two years he had destroyed the Aztec empire.

Emperor Montezuma was the last ruler of the Aztecs. He was captured by Spanish soldiers soon after a small army of them arrived in his capital city. By holding him hostage, they were able to control his subjects even though they were greatly outnumbered.

The Aztecs were famous for their grim religious practices, such as sacrificing human beings to the gods.

Above: An Aztec warrior. Not until he had captured three prisoners could a warrior wear his hair in a tuft. Left: The Aztecs wrote their histories in books made of leather. The pictures represent words.

Bach played the violin and the viola. He studied music passionately, often creeping out of bed to copy music from his brother's collection.

At the age of 38 Bach moved to Leipzig, where he lived for the rest of his life. Here he wrote some of his greatest pieces of music—mostly choral works and music for the organ.

When Bach died, his music was almost at once forgotten. No one put up a monument to him. Almost a hundred years passed before people began to realize what a genius Johann Sebastian Bach had been.

Bacteria

There are thousands of different kinds of bacteria. These tiny living things are too small to be seen with the naked eye. They are one of the simplest forms of life and are more like plants than animals, though they show characteristics of both.

Bacteria take many shapes. Some are round, others are wormlike or spiralled. Still others are rod-shaped. These microscopic organisms are found everywhere—in our bodies, in the soil, in food, on just about everything we touch.

Many bacteria are helpful. There are bacteria in the soil that help to break down, or decay, animal and vegetable matter. Those in our digestive systems help break down food into nutrients for the body. Harmful bacteria include germs that cause disease

Bach, Johann Sebastian

Johann Sebastian Bach (1685–1750) was one of the greatest composers of all time. He was born in Eisenach, Germany, and all his family were musical. From an early age

Johann Sebastian Bach was one of the greatest composers of all time. Below right: Part of the score of one of Bach's Brandenburg Concertos.

and those that make food spoil. Bacteria multiply very quickly. From one bacterium there can be millions in only a few hours. Louis PASTEUR was the first to study the effects of bacteria and to discover that it was bacteria that made food spoil.

Badger

Badgers are big weasel-like animals. They are common in North America, Europe and Asia.

Badgers are MAMMALS. They have thickset bodies, long blunt claws used for digging, sharp teeth and powerful jaws. A fully-grown adult badger measures about 75cm from nose to tail and stands almost 30cm high.

People rarely see badgers during the day. They are night creatures. After sunset they emerge from their underground dens to begin feeding. They browse on plant roots and hunt worms, mice, rats and voles, insects, frogs and other small animals.

Badgers build elaborate underground burrows which are called *sets*. A set has several entrances, a system of long tunnels and a number of rooms. Here, a badger couple makes its home and raises from two to four young at a time. Badgers are quite peaceful animals. However, they can fight fiercely if they are attacked.

The badger is seldom seen during the day. It is a powerful animal, but it eats mainly worms and plant food.

Baking

Baking means cooking food in dry heat, usually in an oven. This method of preparing food is thousands of years old, as old as the making of bread itself.

Early humans ate food more or less as they found it. With the discovery of fire they could roast meat. But it was not until people realized that the seeds of some wild grasses could be ground to make flour that bread-making began. Baking ovens have been found in the remains of the earliest civilizations. Baking has changed little since earliest times, though the fuels we use today are different.

At first bread and cakes were unleavened; they contained nothing to make them rise. Eventually yeast was discovered. Today baking powder is often used in cake baking. It is a combination of bicarbonate of soda (baking soda) and a weak acid. The acid makes it produce the gas carbon dioxide when it is in contact with a wet cake mixture or batter. The tiny bubbles of gas spread all through the cake, making it puff up as it cooks.

Ballet

Ballet is a precise and beautiful form of dancing that is performed in the theatre. A kind of ballet first appeared in Italy in the 1400s, but ballet as it is danced today began in France. During the reign of King Louis XIV, in the 1600s, it was officially recognized as a form of art. The French Royal Academy of Dance was founded in 1661 to promote ballet.

Traditional, or *classical*, ballet follows strict rules and conventions. There are standard positions for the arms, legs, and hands, and special movements that make the dance flow smoothly.

Classical ballet uses orchestras, elaborate scenery, and splendid costumes. Many ballets tell a story. But the dancers do not speak any words. They mime (act out) the story, using their bodies. The person who arranges the dance movements is called the *choreographer*.

Some ballets are very famous. They have been danced for many years. *Giselle*, a story of a young village girl who dies in love-stricken grief, was first performed in 1841. Two other long-time favourites are *Swan Lake* and *The Sleeping Beauty*. These two ballets are as famous for their music as for their dancing.

Modern ballets often look very different from classical ones. They include freer, more modern dance steps. Sometimes, instead of telling a story, they dwell on certain moods or themes.

Swan Lake, *by the Russian composer Tchaikovsky has long been a favourite ballet.*

Ballet dancers perform a number of exercises, some of them at the barre *(top right). Assemblés (right) are jumping steps. The dancer springs from one foot, brings both feet together, and lands.*

Below: Louis XIV's dance master, Pierre Beauchamp, devised the five basic ballet positions over 300 years ago. Each foot position has an arm position to go with it.

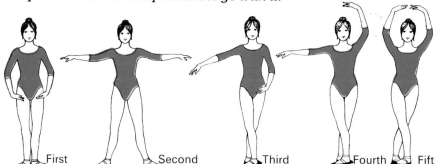

First   Second   Third   Fourth   Fifth

The first hot-air balloon to carry people was built by the Montgolfier brothers in 1783.

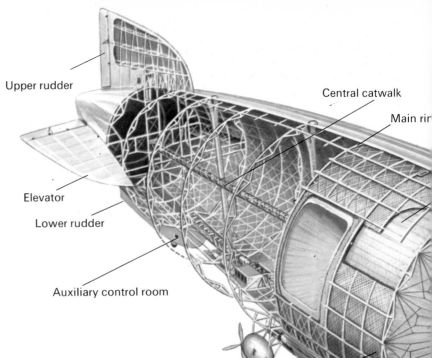

Upper rudder

Central catwalk

Main rir

Elevator

Lower rudder

Auxiliary control room

Engine nacelle (two each side) houses 1100 HP diesel engine

Wire mesh between gas bags and outer envelope

Four-bladed wooden propeller

Balloons and Airships

Balloons and airships use lighter-than-air gases to fly. Balloons can only drift in the wind, but airships can be flown and steered.

The first manned balloon was a hot-air craft launched in 1783. It was built by two French brothers, the Montgolfiers. Their balloon was an open-ended bag. A fire burned under the opening to keep it filled with hot air. The biggest problem the Montgolfiers had was to keep the balloon from bursting into flames. It had to be drenched with water throughout the flight.

In the same year, the first gas-filled balloon took to the air. The gas used was HYDROGEN, and it was a simpler craft to fly. To go down, one simply opened a valve and let some gas out.

In the 1800s, manned balloons were used by the military for observations. Today most balloons are used to study the weather.

Airships

Most airships are much bigger than balloons. The simplest kind looks like a huge, cigar-shaped bag, under which is slung a cabin and the engines. More advanced kinds of airship have a rigid skeleton

covered with fabric. Inside the skeleton are a number of large gas bags that give the airship its lift.

The first successful airship flew in 1852. It was powered by a steam engine and could manage a speed of 8km/hr. During World War I, airships were used to bomb cities. In 1919, the British-built R34 made the first Atlantic crossing. In 1929 the famous *Graf Zeppelin* of Germany flew around the world. But a series of disasters brought the building of airships to an end. They were simply not safe enough for regular passenger use. Today airships are filled with helium, a gas that doesn't burn as hydrogen did. They are therefore much safer.

38

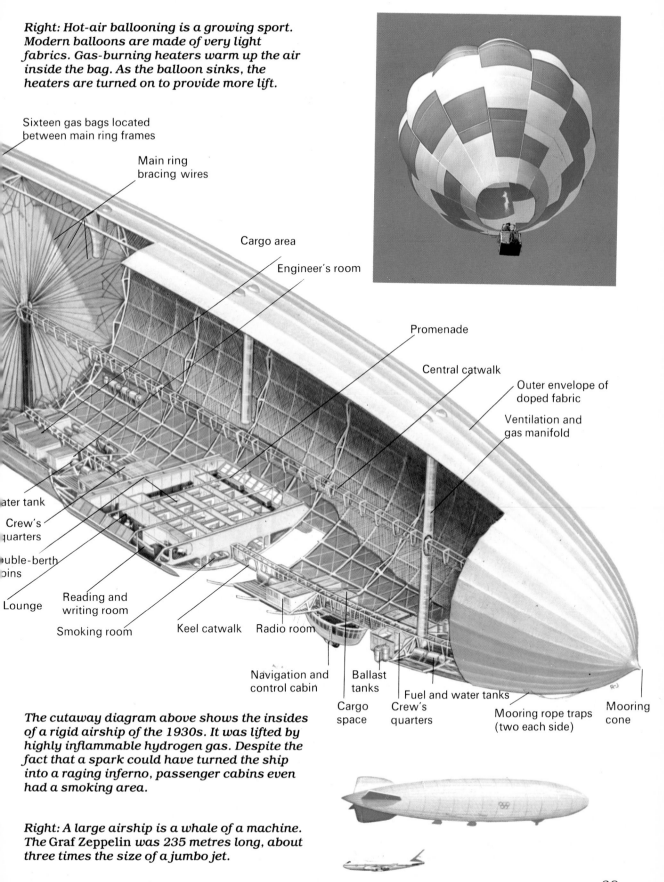

Right: Hot-air ballooning is a growing sport. Modern balloons are made of very light fabrics. Gas-burning heaters warm up the air inside the bag. As the balloon sinks, the heaters are turned on to provide more lift.

Sixteen gas bags located between main ring frames

Main ring bracing wires

Cargo area

Engineer's room

Promenade

Central catwalk

Outer envelope of doped fabric

Ventilation and gas manifold

ater tank

Crew's quarters

ouble-berth bins

Lounge

Reading and writing room

Smoking room

Keel catwalk   Radio room

Navigation and control cabin

Ballast tanks

Cargo space

Crew's quarters

Fuel and water tanks

Mooring rope traps (two each side)

Mooring cone

The cutaway diagram above shows the insides of a rigid airship of the 1930s. It was lifted by highly inflammable hydrogen gas. Despite the fact that a spark could have turned the ship into a raging inferno, passenger cabins even had a smoking area.

Right: A large airship is a whale of a machine. The Graf Zeppelin *was 235 metres long, about three times the size of a jumbo jet.*

Ballot

Voting by ballot is popular in many countries because each voter can make his choice in secret. When the voter has marked his or her ballot paper, it is dropped into a box. After the voting has been completed, the box is opened and the ballot papers are counted.

Voting by secret ballot is quite a recent way of holding elections. Ballots of this type were not used in Britain until 1872. Before then, voting took place at open meetings, often by a show of hands.

Bamboo

Bamboo is a GRASS, but it often grows so tall that it looks more like a tree. Over 200 different kinds of bamboo grow in tropical regions all over the world. Bamboo grows in such thick clumps that a forest of bamboo is almost impossible to walk through.

Bamboo stems are woody. They are very long and thin, hollow on the inside, and smooth to touch. The stems of the giant bamboos may grow as high as 36 metres above the forest floor, and measure anything up to a metre around in the steaming monsoon jungles of southern Asia.

Bamboo has hundreds of uses. Young shoots are tender enough to be eaten. Even slightly larger plants are soft enough to weave into mats and baskets, and to make fences and thatched roofs. Larger bamboo trunks may be used to make furniture, water pipes, or planks for building. In the Far East, bamboo is also used in preparing certain kinds of medicine. These are made from a fluid found in the stem joints.

Bark

The outer layer of WOOD on the trunk and branches of a TREE is the bark. Bark is dead wood. It is tough and waterproof and protects the living wood underneath. In this way it serves the same purpose as the outer layers of skin on our bodies.

As trees grow, they form layers, or rings, of new wood and become thicker. When this new wood is formed inside a tree it pushes against the dead bark and makes it crack and peel off.

Barometer

Put simply, high air pressure is a sign of good weather. Low pressure is a sign of changing and bad weather. The barometer is used to measure such changes.

There are two kinds of barometer, the aneroid and the mercury. The aneroid is more widely used. Inside it is a flat metal box. The air inside the box is at very low

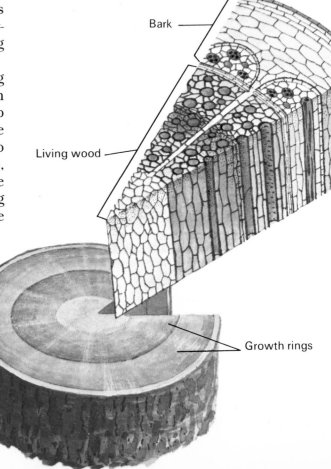

Bark

Living wood

Growth rings

The bark of a tree is waterproof. It protects the living wood against the weather and sudden changes of temperature. A growing tree forms a ring of new wood each year, so by counting these rings on a tree stump you can find the age of the tree.

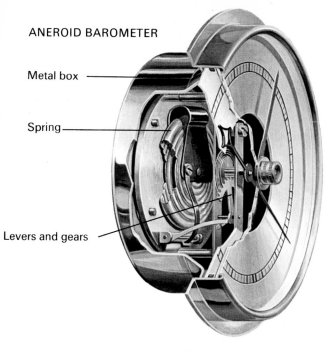

ANEROID BAROMETER

Metal box

Spring

Levers and gears

Basketball

Basketball is an American game which has won popularity all over the world. It was invented in 1891 and quickly became popular as an indoor winter sport. Basketball is played in many countries and has been an Olympic sport since 1936.

Professional basketball is played by two teams of five players each. Each team tries to score points by shooting a ball into a net, or basket. The basket is 10 feet (3 metres) from the floor and 18 inches (45.7 cm) in diameter at the top.

The ball can be advanced by bouncing it along the floor (dribbling) or by passing it to a teammate. A player cannot take more than one step while holding the ball. The opposing players try to block him or her without making physical contact. A field goal counts two points. Free throws count one point.

pressure. The metal walls of the box are so thin they will bend very easily.

As air pressure drops, a spring pushes the sides of the box apart. As it rises, the sides of the box are squeezed together. These movements are picked up by levers and gears that move a pointer around.

Baseball

Baseball is the national sport of America. No one knows quite how it began. It may have come from the similar British game of rounders. In 1845 Alexander Cartwright set up the Knickerbocker Baseball Club of New York. The rules as he laid them out established a game of nine innings, with teams of nine players each. The baseball diamond would have four bases 90 feet (27.4 metres) apart.

Today baseball is played with a bat not more than $2\frac{3}{4}$ inches (7 cm) in diameter and 42 inches (106 cm) in length. The ball is 9 inches (23 cm) in circumference. The pitcher's mound is 60 feet 6 inches (18.4 metres) from home plate.

Professional baseball today is big business. Each year millions of fans watch the teams of the two major leagues (American League and National League) battle for a chance to play for the championship in the World Series, held in October.

Basketball—the Harlem Globetrotters play the Washington Generals.

Bat

Bats fly like birds, yet they are MAMMALS.
They are the only mammals that can truly
be said to fly. Their wings do not have
feathers. They are made of a thin sheet of
skin stretched between the long 'finger'
bones. In most bats the wings are also
joined to the legs and tail.

There are more than 2000 different kinds
of bat. Most live in the tropics and warm
parts of the world.

The biggest of all bats are the fruit-eaters,
or flying foxes. One, the kalong, has a
wingspan of 1.5 metres. The insect-eaters
are usually smaller. Their wingspan is
rarely as much as 30 cm. They live in most
parts of the world. Where winters are cold,
they HIBERNATE.

The vampire bat of South America has a
very unusual way of feeding. It bites animals with its teeth and drinks their blood.
However, vampires do not suck blood, they
merely lap it up as it flows.

Most bats are nocturnal—they sleep during the day and fly at night. Scientists have
shown in experiments that bats do not need
good eyesight for flying. They find their way
in the dark by using a 'sonar' system. They
make high-pitched shrieks that no human
ear can hear and use the echoes bouncing
off objects to tell where they are.

Battery

A battery is a device that stores electricity.
Car batteries are rechargeable. The battery
contains lead and lead oxide plates bathed
in dilute sulphuric acid. The acid changes
the material in the plates and makes them
produce electricity. The plates are arranged
in pairs. Separator plates keep them apart.

To produce current, the acid attacks the
plates, changing them into lead sulphate.
Electrons are produced in the process, flowing from the lead plate to the lead oxide
plate and creating an electric current.

Dry batteries, used in transistor radios
and torches, cannot be recharged.

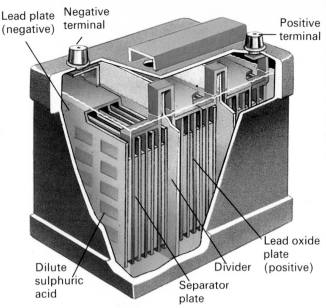

A cutaway view of the inside of a car battery. Plates made of lead sit in a weak solution of sulphuric acid.

Bear

Bears are found in most parts of the world
except for Australia and Africa. They are
some of the biggest meat-eaters on earth.

The largest of all bears are the brown
bears of Alaska. These can reach a weight of
over 750 kg. Other giants include the polar
bear of the Arctic, and the grizzly of western
North America.

A brown bear cub playfully wrestles with its mother. Mock fighting strengthens the cub's muscles. It also helps to develop the skills the young bear will need later for hunting.

The only bear that lives in South America is the small spectacled bear. Its name comes from the ringlike markings around its eyes.

The smallest bear in the world is the sun bear of the jungles of South-East Asia. It weighs no more than 65kg. Sloth bears, found in India and Sri Lanka, have enormously long tongues for lapping up insects, which are an important part of their diet. They have long claws for digging termites from their nests.

Bears are slow, lumbering beasts. They have short, powerful limbs and heavy, broad heads with powerful jaws. They also have long, dangerous claws for tearing.

Right: A beaver fells a tree with its large front teeth. It is a skilled dam and lodge builder (below).

fur. They are now protected by law and can be hunted only during a particular season.

Beavers were once common in Asia and Europe too, but they were also over-hunted and are now found only in some places.

Beaver

Beavers are big RODENTS more than a metre long, including the tail, and weigh more than 25kg. They live at the edges of lakes and streams and are good swimmers. Beavers are able to stay under water for up to 15 minutes. They have a broad, flat tail covered with scaly skin. This is used for steering when they swim.

Beavers need pools in which to build their homes. Where no ready-made pool exists, they will dam streams with mud and sticks to make one. They cut down small trees with their sharp teeth to strengthen the dam.

Beavers build a home of mud and sticks by the side of the pool. This home, called a lodge, has an underwater entrance and an escape hole. Inside, there is a nest above water for the young beavers.

Beavers eat bark, mainly from alder and willow trees. They store twigs in their homes to feed on during the winter.

Beavers have thick fur which keeps them warm in the water. They live in many parts of North America where, for hundreds of years, hunters have trapped them for their

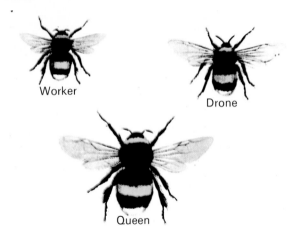

Above: The size of the queen bee compared with a worker and a drone.

Bee

There are many different kinds of bee, but the best known is the honeybee. Honeybees live in hives, or colonies, of about 50,000 worker bees. Worker bees are female but they do not breed. Each colony also has a queen bee which breeds, and a few hundred stingless drones which are male.

The worker bee's life is very short, usually about four weeks, so the queen has to lay many eggs to provide enough bees. She can lay up to 1500 eggs in one day. From time to time a new queen hatches. The old queen then leaves the hive with a *swarm* of about half the workers to seek another home.

The workers collect pollen and nectar from flowers. The nectar is made into honey. It is stored in the hive to feed the bees in winter. Beekeepers carefully remove the honey from the hive. They give the bees sugar syrup to replace the honey they take.

There are other types of bee that do not live in large colonies. These are called solitary bees. They produce a small family of a few hundred bees, most of which die when winter comes.

Ludwig van Beethoven, shown in this painting as a young man.

Beethoven, Ludwig van

Ludwig van Beethoven (1770–1827) was a German musician who composed some of the greatest music ever known. This included symphonies, concertos, and choral and chamber music. When he was young, Beethoven studied with both MOZART and Haydn. He became well known as a pianist and was admired by many famous people. He developed and extended such musical forms as the symphony and string quartet and experimented with new harmonies. Beethoven began to go deaf at the age of 30 but continued to compose music even when he was totally deaf.

Below: A worker bee gathers pollen. It stuffs the pollen into a sac on its hind legs to carry it back to the hive.

44

Beetle

Beetles are INSECTS. There are over 300,000 species of beetle known.

Some beetles are as small as a pinhead. Others are very large. The giant African goliath beetle measures up to 10cm long and can weigh 100 grams. It is bigger than a mouse.

In prehistoric times all beetles had two pairs of wings. But over millions of years the front pair changed, or *evolved*, into hard, close-fitting coverings for the second pair underneath. All beetles used to be flying insects, but now many of them live on the ground.

Beetles start their lives as eggs which hatch into grubs, or larvae. The larvae then turn into chrysalises, or pupae, before the adult beetles emerge.

Many beetles and their larvae are destructive pests. Woodworms, weevils, wireworms, cockroaches, and Colorado and flea beetles do great damage to crops, trees and buildings.

Some beetles can be very useful. Ladybirds are small beetles that eat harmful insects such as greenflies. Dung beetles and burying beetles clear away dung and dead animals.

Belgium

Belgium is a small country sandwiched between France, Germany and Holland. Its capital is Brussels. Belgium's population of 10,048,000 is made up of two main groups: the Flemings of the north, and the French-speaking Walloons of the south. Because of its central and strategic position, Belgium

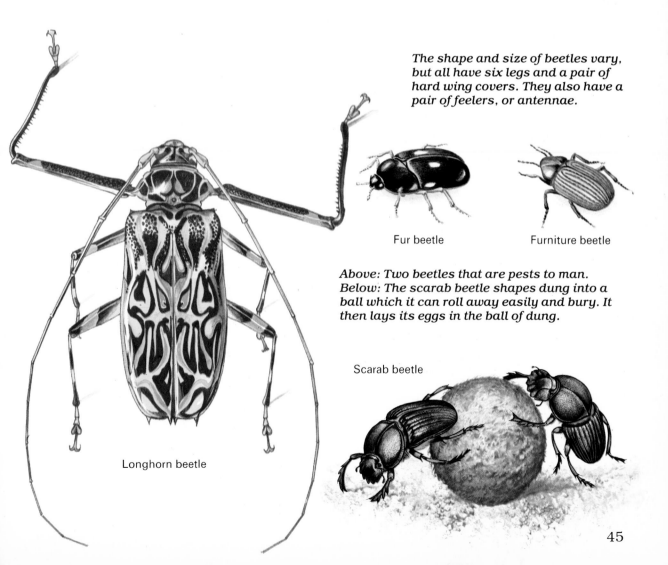

The shape and size of beetles vary, but all have six legs and a pair of hard wing covers. They also have a pair of feelers, or antennae.

Fur beetle

Furniture beetle

Above: Two beetles that are pests to man. Below: The scarab beetle shapes dung into a ball which it can roll away easily and bury. It then lays its eggs in the ball of dung.

Scarab beetle

Longhorn beetle

45

The main square in Antwerp, Belgium's chief seaport.

has been invaded and fought over throughout the course of European history. Today Belgium is an international centre. The headquarters of the EUROPEAN ECONOMIC COMMUNITY (EEC) and NATO are both in Brussels.

Bell, Alexander Graham

Alexander Graham Bell (1847–1922) is remembered as the inventor of the TELEPHONE. Bell was the son of a Scottish teacher who went to Canada with his family in 1870. Two years later Alexander set up a school for teachers of the deaf in Boston, Massachusetts. Through his work with devices to help the deaf, Bell became interested in sending voices over long distances. On March 10, 1876, the first sentence was transmitted by telephone. The historic words spoken by Bell to his assistant were: 'Mr Watson, come here; I want you'.

Bernhardt, Sarah

Sarah Bernhardt (1844–1923) was one of the most famous actresses of her time. Her excellent speaking voice and diction won her the admiration of audiences everywhere she went. She acted in many countries, though France was her home.

Sarah Bernhardt's real name was Rosine Bernard. After studying at the Paris Conservatory, her acting career began in 1862 at the Comédie-Française. She became best known around the world for her performance in *Camille*. She made a brief foray into the film world when she appeared in the motion picture *Queen Elizabeth* in 1912. When she died in 1923, much of Paris was in mourning.

In 1876 Alexander Graham Bell demonstrated the first practical telephone. In 1892 he personally opened the telephone link between New York and Chicago (right). Above right: an early Bell telephone.

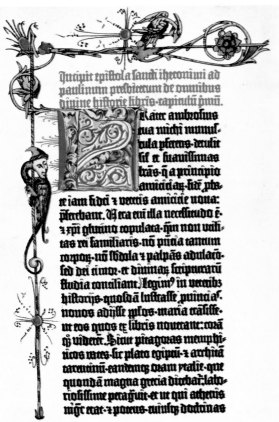

Above: The first printed Bibles were produced by Johannes Gutenberg in the 1400s.

Bible

The Bible is a sacred book. It is in two parts. The first is called the Old Testament and records the history of the Jewish people, or Hebrews, and the teachings of their prophets. The second part, the New Testament, records the birth of Jesus, his life and sayings and the sayings of his disciples.

Bicycle

The bicycle is a two-wheeled vehicle powered by its rider, who turns two pedals with his feet. The earliest bicycles, called 'dandy horses', were invented in the 1700s. They were simply two wheels joined by a rod, with a seat on top. The rider pushed it along the ground with his feet.

The first bicycle with pedals did not appear until 1865. These machines were known as 'bone-shakers' because the seats had no springs. The next important development was the 'penny-farthing', which had an enormous front wheel and tiny rear wheel. The modern style of bicycle appeared in the 1880s. It had a chain-driven rear wheel and air-filled tyres, and this basic style has changed very little since then. Today bicycle riding is a popular sport, both for serious competitors and for those who ride for fun and fitness.

The most famous bicycle race in the world is the Tour de France. The bicycles used have lightweight frames, no mudguards and special racing tyres.

Bird

Birds come in all shapes and sizes, but they all have wings and feathers. Some birds can fly thousands of miles. Others, such as the OSTRICH and the PENGUIN, cannot fly at all. The ostrich is the largest bird. It can weigh more than 150kg. The smallest bird, a HUMMINGBIRD, weighs less than 2 grams.

Birds developed from scaly REPTILES that lived about 180,000,000 years ago. Their scales changed over millions of years into feathers, and their front legs became wings. Birds have hollow bones for lightness in the air and strong breast muscles for working their wings. Large birds can flap their wings slowly and float, or hover, on air currents. Small birds have to flap their wings hard to stay in the air.

All birds lay eggs. Most birds are busy parents who work hard to rear their young. Some, like the cuckoo, lay their eggs in other birds' nests for foster parents to rear. Other birds bury their eggs in warm places and leave them. Most birds are wild but some, such as chickens, pigeons and canaries, have been tamed, or *domesticated*. Many birds are bred on farms for their eggs and meat.

There are many different kinds of bird. Tropical birds such as the toucan, bird of paradise and the parakeet, are brightly coloured. The woodpecker and the tree creeper build nests inside trees. The falcon hunts other birds and animals.

Above: The bones of a bird are strong but not heavy.

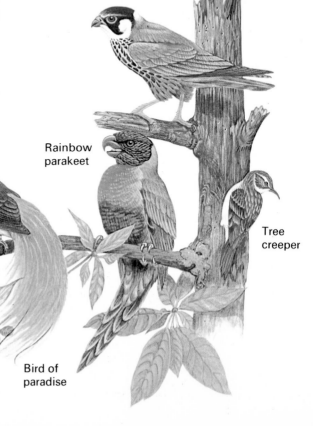

Great spotted woodpecker

Falcon (Hobby)

Rainbow parakeet

Tailorbird

Tree creeper

Bird of paradise

Toucan

Wood pigeon

Bison

Bison

The American bison, or 'buffalo', is a large mammal that lives on the plains of North America. Bison are often wrongly called buffalo because the first Europeans to see them thought they were a kind of ox. Huge herds of bison once roamed the plains. They were a source of food, clothing and shelter for the Indians who lived there. With the coming of white settlers, thousands of bison were wiped out. Today they are a protected species, living in special reserves.

A full-grown male bison may be nearly 4 metres from nose to tail and can weigh more than a tonne.

Blériot, Louis

Louis Blériot (1872–1936) was a famous French airman. He was a pioneer of aviation

Blériot takes off from Calais on his historic cross-Channel flight.

and designed and built a number of early aeroplanes. On July 25, 1909, he took off from Calais in one of his own AIRCRAFT. Thirty-seven minutes later he touched down at Dover, becoming the first man to cross the English Channel by air. Cooling rain had kept his engine working. He won a prize of £1000 offered by the London *Daily Mail* newspaper. Blériot went on to design other aircraft and became the owner of a large aircraft company.

Blood

Blood is the fluid that nourishes our bodies and removes waste products. It takes in food from the DIGESTIVE SYSTEM, and oxygen from the LUNGS, and carries them to all the CELLS in the body. Each cell takes exactly what it needs from the blood and the blood carries away cell waste, including water and carbon dioxide. Blood also carries special body chemicals to where they are needed. And it kills germs and keeps the body at the right temperature.

Blood is made in the marrow of the bones. The adult human body contains about five litres of blood. This blood is made up of a pale liquid called *plasma*, and millions of cells, or *corpuscles*. Most corpuscles are tiny red discs that give the blood its colour. The blood also contains white corpuscles. There are about 5 million red corpuscles and between 5000 and 10,000 white corpuscles in every cubic millimetre of blood.

Boer War

The Boer War (1899–1902) was fought in SOUTH AFRICA between the Boers—settlers of Dutch descent—and the British. The slow and badly-led British troops were no match for the fast and lightly-armed Boers in the early days of the war. The Boers used guerrilla tactics under their leaders Generals Smuts and Botha. But in the end Britain's overwhelming strength won. There were about 450,000 soldiers in the British armies during the Boer War, and only about 60,000 Boers.

Right: British troops during the Boer War, sometimes called the South African War. The British victory brought South Africa into the Empire as a British colony.

Bolivia

Bolivia is a land-locked country in central SOUTH AMERICA, west of Brazil. Most of Bolivia is an enormous plain stretching from the Brazilian border to the eastern foothills of the Andes Mountains. High in the Andes lies the great Bolivian plateau, over 4000 metres high. Two-thirds of Bolivia's people live here. The capital is La Paz, the highest capital in the world and Lake Titicaca, at 3812 metres above sea level, is one of the highest lakes in the world.

Above: A market in La Paz, Bolivia. La Paz is Bolivia's capital and seat of government, but the city of Sucre is also called the capital.

Spain ruled Bolivia from 1532 until 1825. It gained freedom from Spain with the help of Simón Bolívar, a Venezuelan general, after whom Bolivia is named. More than half the people are Indians, a third are *mestizos* (people who are part European, part Indian), and the rest are direct descendants of Europeans. Bolivia is the world's second largest producer of tin, and mining is the country's most valuable industry.

There are just over 6 million people in Bolivia and most of them speak Spanish.

Right: Simón Bolívar was a great leader who helped six South American republics to become independent. He became the first president of Colombia and Peru.

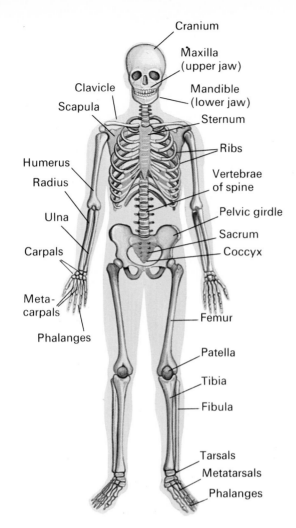

Cranium
Maxilla (upper jaw)
Clavicle
Mandible (lower jaw)
Scapula
Sternum
Ribs
Humerus
Vertebrae of spine
Radius
Pelvic girdle
Ulna
Sacrum
Carpals
Coccyx
Meta-carpals
Femur
Phalanges
Patella
Tibia
Fibula
Tarsals
Metatarsals
Phalanges

The human skeleton is built of more than 200 bones. The 26 bones of the spine are linked to one another and form the main framework of the body. They support the skull, the ribs, and the two bone 'girdles' that support the limbs—the shoulder blades and the pelvis. The arms are connected to the shoulder blades, the legs to the pelvis.

Bone

Bones make up the hard framework that supports the flesh and organs of all vertebrates (animals with backbones). All bones are made up of the same thing, mostly calcium. Bones are hard on the outside but soft on the inside. Bone *marrow*, in the hollow centre of the bone, is where new red BLOOD cells are made.

The human skeleton has four kinds of bones: long bones, such as arm and leg bones; flat bones, such as the skull; short bones, including the ankle and wrist bones; and irregular bones, such as those that make up the backbone. If bones are broken they will knit together again if they are rejoined, or *set*, properly. The cells in the broken ends of the bone produce a substance that helps the ends grow together again so that the mended bone is as strong as it ever was. But as human beings get older, their bones become more brittle and will break more easily.

Below: Where bones meet there is always a joint. There are immovable joints, as in the skull; slightly movable joints, as in the spine; and freely movable joints, as in the shoulder and hip. Where one bone rubs against another there is a tough substance called cartilage and the joints are lubricated by a special fluid called synovial fluid. Joints are held together by tough stretchy ligaments.

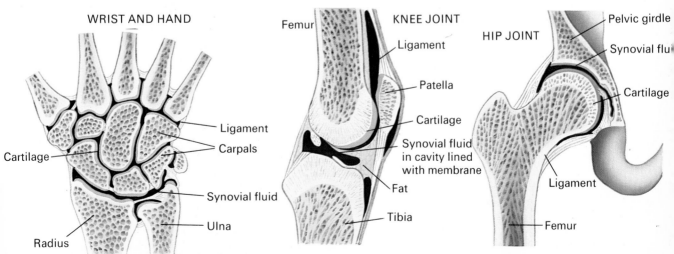

WRIST AND HAND
Ligament
Carpals
Cartilage
Synovial fluid
Ulna
Radius

Femur
KNEE JOINT
Ligament
Patella
Cartilage
HIP JOINT
Synovial fluid in cavity lined with membrane
Fat
Tibia
Pelvic girdle
Synovial flu
Cartilage
Ligament
Femur

Johannes Gutenberg with a sheet that has just come from his printing press. The metal letters have been arranged in the right order to make words. The pages of metal type are fixed in trays and inked. Paper is placed over the type and pressed down by the man on the right.

Book

Books are used for storing and passing on all kinds of knowledge, ideas and stories. Some of the earliest books were made by the ancient Egyptians. These were written by hand on rolls of paper made from the papyrus plant.

By the time of the Roman Empire many books were handwritten on parchment, or *vellum*. This material was made from animal skin. It was cut into sheets which were fastened together to look much the same as a modern book.

During the Middle Ages monks made many beautiful books. They were decorated, or *illuminated*, by hand with bright colours and sometimes gold and silver.

In the 1400s, PRINTING on paper began in Europe. When Johannes GUTENBERG invented movable type, words could quickly be made by using metal letters, and more books could be printed at a reasonable cost. Today millions of books are produced every year, in all the languages of the world.

Boomerang

The boomerang is a wooden throwing stick used mainly by the Australian ABORIGINES. There are two kinds. One is very heavy and is thrown straight at the target. The other is lighter. It is shaped in a special way so that when it is skilfully thrown it is possible to make it return to the thrower.

Botany

Botany is the study of plant life on earth. There are over 300,000 different kinds, or *species*, of plant, and new species are being discovered all the time. The variety of plants is almost endless. The smallest are one-celled plants, so tiny that they can be seen only with a microscope. The largest plants are the giant redwoods of North America, nearly 90 metres high.

Plants are the base of the food chain. Without them there would be no animals, for animals, even meat-eaters, depend on plants for food. A lion would find no grazing animals to prey on if there were no plants for those animals to eat.

Botanists study new plants to find out which group, or classification, of plants they belong to. They learn how best to cultivate plants that might be useful to

The main parts of a flower. The stamens are the male parts; the carpels are the female. Pollen from the stamens is carried down the style to fertilize the egg, or ovule, in the ovary. This turns into a new seed.

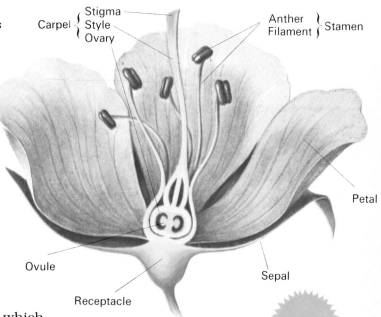

Carpel { Stigma
Style
Ovary

Anther } Stamen
Filament

Petal

Ovule

Sepal

Receptacle

carbon dioxide

sunlight

oxygen

water

people. By discovering the ways in which plants pass on certain qualities to the next generation, botanists have been able to grow bigger and better crops.

The first successful system for naming, or classifying, plants was developed by a Swedish botanist, Carolus Linnaeus. He gave every plant a name made up of two Latin words—one for its species and one for its group, or *genus*, within that species.

Braille

Braille is an alphabet for the blind. It is made up of raised dots which the reader can feel with the fingertips. Many books have been translated into braille for blind readers. Special braille typewriters make it easy to write braille. The system was invented by a Frenchman, Louis Braille, in the 1800s.

Above: The green chemical called chlorophyll in the leaves of plants takes in energy from sunlight. Water from the soil is sucked up by the roots and passes up to the leaves. Plants use water, energy from sunlight, and carbon dioxide from the air to make their food. They give out the oxygen we need to breathe.
Left: A braille reader scans a page with her fingertips.

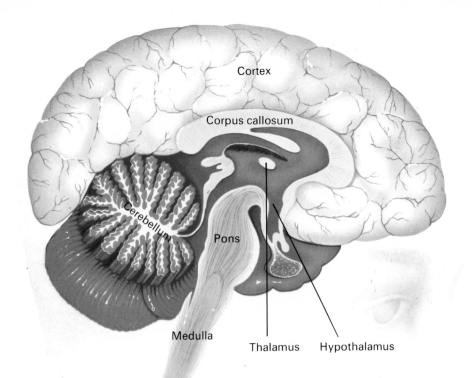

Cortex

Corpus callosum

Cerebellum

Pons

Medulla

Thalamus   Hypothalamus

Above: The main parts of the brain. The cortex makes up 80 percent of the brain.

Brain

The brain controls all the other parts of the body. In some tiny insects it is no bigger than a speck of dust. Even in some of the biggest dinosaurs it was no bigger than a walnut. But MAMMALS have big brains in relation to their size, and man has the biggest brain of all.

The human brain is largely made up of grey and white matter. Grey matter is NERVE cells, and white matter is the nerve fibres that carry messages from the nerve cells to the body. These nerve fibres leave the brain in large bundles like telephone cables and reach out to all parts of the body. Messages from the body are travelling back along the fibres to the brain all the time, even when we are asleep. A large number of blood vessels provide a continuous supply of oxygen to the brain.

Different parts of the brain control different parts of the body. For example, most thinking is done in the front part. Sight, however, is controlled from the back of the brain.

Brass

Brass is an alloy of zinc and copper. Small amounts of other metals may sometimes be added for special uses. Brass is often used for plumbing and electrical fixtures and for making delicate instruments.

The amount of copper in brass may vary from 50 percent to more than 95 percent. Brass with a large amount of copper in it is quite soft and is a reddish-yellow colour. Brass with a small amount of tin added is used for many of the fittings on boats and ships, as it does not rust.

Brazil

Brazil is by far the largest country in SOUTH AMERICA and the fifth largest country in the world. Much of Brazil is low-lying and contains the huge basin of the AMAZON River and the world's largest rain forest. The Amazon region is sparsely populated by Indians, blacks, mixed bloods and white settlers. Today, the government is trying to open up the region.

Over half of Brazil's 133,882,000 people

live in cities that include Rio de Janeiro, São Paulo, Belo Horizonte, and Recife. Brasília, a specially built modern city, has been the capital of Brazil since 1960.

Brazil was ruled by Portugal from the early 1500s until 1822, and most people still speak Portuguese. About three-quarters of the people are descended from Europeans; most of the rest are of mixed European, Indian and African ancestry. There are some pure Indians and blacks. Most Brazilians work on farms. The country leads the world in producing coffee, and oil is becoming more and more important. Brazil is also one of the biggest producers of beef, cocoa, cotton, corn, sugar cane and tobacco.

Breathing

Breathing is something we rarely have to think about. As soon as a baby is born, it starts to breathe, and we go on breathing all our lives. It is the OXYGEN in the air that we need. Like all other animals, we must have oxygen to stay alive. This oxygen is used with the food we eat to give us energy to move around and keep our bodies going.

We draw air into our LUNGS. From there it goes through tiny tubes which allow the oxygen to pass into the BLOOD vessels. The oxygen goes all around our bodies in the

Above: Rio de Janeiro, once the capital of Brazil, is now its second largest city. Above left: Brasília, the country's capital. By building the city in the interior, Brasília's planners hoped to open up the undeveloped heart of Brazil.

Below: Oxygen reaches the body through the lungs. When our chest expands, air rushes in through the nose or mouth. When our chest muscles relax, the lungs are squeezed and air is pushed out.

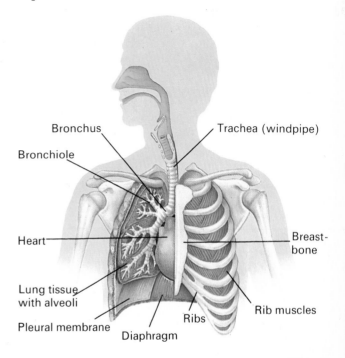

Bronchus

Bronchiole

Heart

Trachea (windpipe)

Breast-bone

Lung tissue with alveoli

Pleural membrane

Diaphragm

Ribs

Rib muscles

blood. We breathe out another type of gas called carbon dioxide.

An adult normally breathes in and out about 20 times a minute (children usually breathe faster than this).

Breathing is controlled by the muscles in the chest, especially the diaphragm muscle. When we breathe in, the diaphragm contracts downward. This lowers the air pressure inside the lungs, and air is sucked in to fill the space. When the diaphragm relaxes upward again, the space in the lungs decreases and the air is squeezed out.

Bridge

Bridges are used to take roads, paths, and railways over rivers, valleys or other obstacles. People have been building bridges for thousands of years.

The first simple bridges were probably fallen trees placed across a stream. Later, they may have been supported underneath by stones or logs. Another kind of simple bridge is a rope bridge.

The Romans were among the first great bridge builders. Some of their stone bridges are still standing today. In the Middle Ages bridges in towns often had shops and houses built on top of them.

Today, there is a great variety of bridges. They have to be carefully planned and built. The weight of the bridge must be balanced so that it does not fall down. It must also be strong enough to carry traffic and stand up to the force of the wind.

There are three main kinds of bridge. These are the *beam*, the *arch*, and the *suspension* bridge. Some are fixed and others can be moved.

Above: The Golden Gate suspension bridge in San Francisco was finished in 1937. It has a span of 1280 metres. Each cable is over 90cm thick, and is made up of 25,570 separate wires.

Suspension bridge   Arch bridge   Beam bridge

Right: The Romans were expert bridge builders. They built many arched bridges all over their empire. A number of these bridges still remain. This bridge has three arches and is built of stone. It crosses a river in Syria.

British Isles

A Scottish trawler

An oil-rig explores the British oil field in the North Sea.

ORKNEY ISLANDS

SHETLAND ISLANDS

John o' Groats

HEBRIDES

North West Highlands

Inverness
Loch Ness
Dee
•Aberdeen

▲ Ben Nevis
1347m

Grampians

Oban•
SCOTLAND
Dundee
•Perth
Tay

Loch Lomond
•Dunfermline

Glasgow
Clyde
Edinburgh

•Ayr

•Londonderry

NORTHERN IRELAND

Belfast

•Sligo

ISLE OF MAN

Tyne
Newcastle•
•Sunderland

P e n n i n e s

Lake District
Eden

•Middlesbrough and Teesside

N O R T H

S E A

Lough Mask

Central   Plains
•Galway

Dublin ■

I R I S H

S E A

Blackpool•
•Bradford
York•
•Leeds
Hull•

Manchester•

Shannon
Lough Derg
•Limerick

REPUBLIC OF IRELAND (EIRE)

Wicklow Mts

Barrow

Liverpool•
Sheffield•

▲ Snowdon 1086m

Nottingham•
•Stoke-on-Trent
•Wolverhampton
Dudley•
Walsall•
•Birmingham •Leicester
The Fens

•Norwich
•Great Yarmo

Mts of Kerry

Waterford•

•Coventry

Ouse
•Cambridge

Cambrian Mts

Avon
•Bedford

•Ipswich

•Cork

ENGLAND

Fishguard•

WALES

Severn

Oxford•
Cotswolds
Chiltern Hills

London ■

A T L A N T I C

O C E A N

•Swansea

Cardiff
•Bristol
•Bath

Thames

North   Downs
•Canterbury
•Dover

Exmoor

Southampton•
•Portsmouth
•Brighton
•Eastbourne

Bournemouth•
Isle of Wight

Exeter•
Dartmoor

•Plymouth

Kilometres
0 20 40 60 80 100

0   25   50
Miles

ISLES OF SCILLY

Land's End

E N G L I S H   C H A N N E L

FRANCE

CHANNEL ISLANDS

British Isles

The British Isles are made of two main islands, Great Britain and IRELAND, and more than 5,000 smaller ones. These range from large islands such as the Isle of Man, Shetland, Orkney and the Channel Islands, to bare rocks sticking out of the sea. (See map on page 57.)

Britain is divided into ENGLAND, Scotland and Wales. Ireland is divided into Eire (the Republic of Ireland) and Northern Ireland.

The British Isles are part of EUROPE. They are on the European CONTINENTAL SHELF. During the last ICE AGE Britain was joined to Europe by a wide stretch of land where the English Channel is now situated.

The climate of the British Isles is mild and quite wet. Most of the country is low-lying. There are some mountains and high ground in Scotland, Wales, the north of England and parts of Ireland.

Brontë Sisters

Brontë was the family name of three sisters, all of whom became famous writers. They were Charlotte (1816–1855), Emily (1818–1848) and Anne (1820–1849), and they were from Yorkshire.

The girls were daughters of a poor clergyman and had a strict upbringing. Their surroundings on the lonely Yorkshire moors and their somewhat lonely lives fired their imaginations and they began to make up stories and poems. Under masculine pen names they published a joint volume of poems in 1846, and soon all three had novels published. Charlotte's most famous work was the partly autobiographical *Jane Eyre*. Emily wrote just one novel, *Wuthering Heights*, which, like *Jane Eyre*, is today a classic. Anne, who died at the age of 29, wrote *Agnes Grey* and *The Tenant of Wildfell Hall.*

Buddha

The word Buddha means 'Enlightened One'. This name is given to great teachers of the Buddhist religion.

The first Buddha was Siddhartha Gautama. He was born about 563 BC in northern India. For most of his life he travelled around India teaching people. Buddha taught his followers that the only way to true happiness was to be peaceful and kind to other people and animals, and to avoid evil.

Like the Hindus, Buddhists believe that

Below left: A large statue of Buddha lying down. Other statues of Buddha (right) show him sitting with his legs crossed.

after they die they are born again as an animal or human being. If they are very good, they are not born again but live in a kind of heaven called *Nirvana*.

Building

Early man built with the materials he found around him—stones, branches, mud and turf. In Europe, poor people usually lived in houses made of wattle and daub. Wattle was a wickerwork of branches, and this was plastered over with a daub of wet mud. When this hardened it made quite a strong wall.

Because in some areas certain materials were easily available, buildings look quite different in different places. Where there was plenty of clay, people built with bricks; where there was plenty of wood, limestone or sandstone, people built their houses with those.

Today houses being built everywhere look very much the same. Large buildings have a framework of steel girders or reinforced concrete which takes all the weight of the building. The walls can be light and there can be plenty of windows.

All buildings, especially high ones, have to be built on firm foundations. If they are not they may collapse or sink into the ground, like the Leaning Tower of Pisa.

Bulb

Many PLANTS, such as tulips, daffodils and onions, grow from bulbs. The bulb is the underground part of the plant where food is stored during the winter months. When the plant has finished flowering, the bulb begins to grow under the ground. Then the leaves above the ground wither away, leaving only the bulb. It is made up of fleshy scales packed tightly together. The scales feed the bud as it grows.

In cold climates, bulbs are dug up in the autumn and replanted in the early spring.

Bulgaria

Bulgaria is a country in eastern EUROPE (see map on page 123). It belongs to a group of countries which are all communist. This means that their governments practise the beliefs of COMMUNISM. Much of the land and most industries are owned by the government.

Bulgaria has 8,990,000 people and covers 110,912 square km. Its capital city is Sofia.

In the north are the Balkan Mountains. To the east is the Black Sea where many people spend their vacations. In the centre of Bulgaria is a big valley with many farms. The farmers grow fruit, flowers, vegetables, grain and tobacco. There are also many factories and mines in Bulgaria.

The Romans were great builders. Their stone-masons cut and carved blocks of stone with many tools, and we still use the same types of tool today.

Butterflies and Moths

Butterflies are flying INSECTS. There are about 12,000 kinds of butterfly. They are related to moths. They live in most parts of the world, even as far north as the Arctic Circle.

Butterflies come in many colours and sizes. One of the smallest, the dwarf blue of South Africa, has a wingspan of only 14 mm. The largest, the Queen Alexandra birdwing, has a wingspan of 28 cm.

All butterflies begin their lives as caterpillars, which hatch from eggs. The caterpillars spend their lives eating the plant they were hatched on. They change their skins several times as they grow. When a caterpillar is full-grown it changes into a chrysalis with a hard skin. Inside this the chrysalis changes into an adult butterfly. When it is ready, the butterfly breaks out and flies away to find a mate and lay eggs.

Moths are closely related to butterflies. In general, though not always, moths fly at night and butterflies fly by day. Some moths are helpful to people; many are harmful. The larva of the silk moth, for example, spins the silk we use for fine cloth. The clothes moth, whose larvae eat wool, is the best known moth pest.

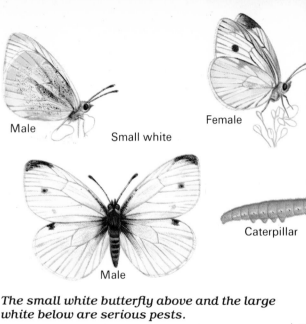
Male Small white Female

Male

Caterpillar

The small white butterfly above and the large white below are serious pests.

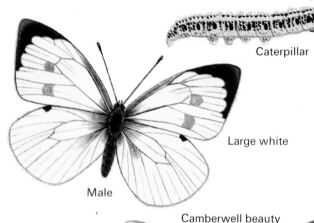
Caterpillar

Large white

Male

Broad-bordered bee hawkmoth

Left: A magnified photograph of part of a butterfly's wing.

Peacock

Camberwell beauty

Peacock caterpillar

Red admiral

today France, the Netherlands and Germany. In 55 BC, he invaded Britain. By 48 BC, Caesar had become the sole ruler of Rome.

Caesar made many enemies who hated what he was doing to the republic. A group of them plotted to kill him. On the 'Ides of March' (the 15th of the month), in 44 BC, they stabbed him to death in the Roman forum.

Julius Caesar, Rome's first emperor, was also a major historian.

Cactus

Although there are dozens of different cacti, they are all able to grow in hot DESERT climates. Cacti can do this because they store water in their fleshy stems. They are covered with prickly spines instead of leaves. The spines protect the plant's store of water from desert animals.

Below: Barrel cacti swell up with water when it rains. During droughts they lose water and shrink in size.

Caesar, Julius

Julius Caesar (about 100–44 BC) was a great leader of the ROMAN EMPIRE. He is most famous for his part in turning the Roman Republic into an empire ruled by one man.

He first became powerful when he commanded an army that conquered what is

Calculator

Calculators are not new inventions. The first mechanical calculator was built by Pascal, a French scientist, in 1642. Today modern electronic calculators can do in just one second what a mechanical calculator would take a year to do.

The secret of the speedy pocket calculators is a tiny silicon chip no bigger than a shirt button. This is the calculator's 'brain'.

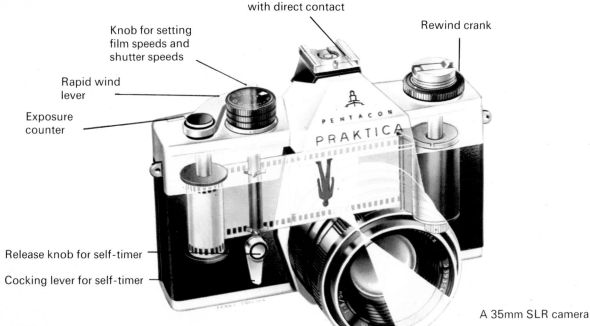

Accessory shoe
with direct contact

Knob for setting
film speeds and
shutter speeds

Rewind crank

Rapid wind
lever

Exposure
counter

PENTACON
PRAKTICA

Release knob for self-timer

Cocking lever for self-timer

A 35mm SLR camera

Camel

With their wide splayed feet, gangly legs, humped bodies and long, thick necks, camels look as if they have been made up from the parts of half a dozen other animals. But if it were not for camels, life in some desert regions would have been almost impossible.

Camels are one of the few creatures that can stand up to extreme heat and still do work carrying heavy loads. Their wide, padded feet grip well on loose desert sand. They are powerful and swift and can go for days without eating or drinking, living off the fat stored in their humps. Camels will eat almost anything. As well as desert shrubs and thistles, they will chew their way through tent cloth, mats and even baskets.

Camera

Modern cameras work in much the same way as the box cameras of a hundred years ago. A shutter opens for a fraction of a second—just long enough to let light from the scene being photographed pass through the glass LENS to fall on the film. The light forms an upside-down image of the scene

on the film. The film is then developed, that is, treated with chemicals to fix the image. The image on the piece of developed film is printed onto a special type of paper. The result is a photograph.

Today most cameras have a lot of different parts to help us to take photographs in many kinds of light and from close up or from far away.

Right: The single-humped camel on the right is an Arabian. The two-humped one on the left is the Bactrian camel of Asia.

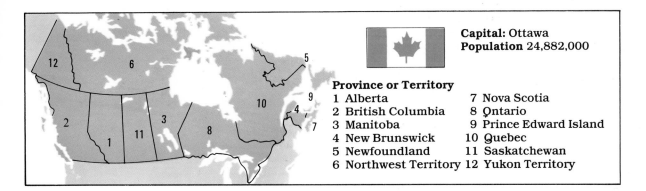

Capital: Ottawa
Population 24,882,000

Province or Territory

1	Alberta	7	Nova Scotia
2	British Columbia	8	Ontario
3	Manitoba	9	Prince Edward Island
4	New Brunswick	10	Quebec
5	Newfoundland	11	Saskatchewan
6	Northwest Territory	12	Yukon Territory

Canada

Canada is second only to the Soviet Union in size. It stretches from the Atlantic to the Pacific over a distance farther than that from North America to Europe. It covers an area of nearly 10 million square kilometres. But compared with its size, Canada has very few people, and most of them live in a narrow strip just north of the United States' border.

The Great Plains and the Rocky Mountains cover much of central and western Canada. Most of the country's wheat crop is grown on the plains. In the east are the Great Lakes that lie on the border with the United States. These huge inland seas empty into the St Lawrence River, which links them with the sea. To the north is a vast area of lakes and forests where few people live.

In the eastern part of Canada and along the fertile St Lawrence valley are many farms. The centre of government and finance is in Ontario, as are many of Canada's industries. The farmlands to the west in Alberta are also rich in oil.

Canada is part of the British Commonwealth and the official head of state is Queen Elizabeth of the United Kingdom. But the country is really governed by the prime minister and by Parliament.

Above right: Farms in central Canada can cover vast areas.

Right: Banff National Park in the Canadian Rockies is popular for its dramatic scenery and outdoor sports.

The English explorer John Cabot first sighted Newfoundland in 1497. But it was the French who first settled Canada. The explorer Jacques Cartier discovered the Gulf of St Lawrence in 1534, and Quebec City was established in 1608. Britain gained control of Canada in 1763 after the Seven Years' War. In 1867 the country became a self-governing dominion.

Canal

Any man-made waterway could be called a canal, but we usually mean one that is built to carry water traffic.

Canals have been in use for thousands of years. In ancient Egypt and Babylon they were used to irrigate farmland. One of the oldest canals still in use is the Grand Canal of China. It was opened in the 600s AD.

Until the 1500s, canals could only be built across flat country. With the invention of canal locks, however, they could be built across high ground too. The locks allowed boats to sail over hills by lifting them in a series of steps from one level to another.

Early canals could only be used by narrow, shallow-bottomed boats. These boats were pulled along by horses that walked on towpaths running alongside the canal. Modern canals, like the SUEZ CANAL and the PANAMA CANAL, are big enough to let ocean liners pass through them.

Cancer

Cancer is one of the most dangerous diseases in the world today. It is second only to heart disease as the leading cause of death. Cancer takes many forms, but all cancers spread by means of the uncontrolled growth of body cells.

Scientists all over the world are studying ways of fighting cancer. They are also trying to find out what causes it in order to cure and prevent the disease. Although there is still no absolute cure for cancer, scientists have made much progress. In 1900 almost every case of cancer was fatal. Today, educating people to spot cancer symptoms early has saved millions of lives. Cancer can be treated by surgery, by radiation or by chemotherapy.

Carbon

Carbon is an important ELEMENT that is found in every living thing—both plant and animal. Many of the things we use every day have carbon in them, such as sugar and paper. Forms of carbon also exist as COAL, OIL, graphite (the 'lead' in our pencils is graphite) and DIAMONDS.

Below: One form of carbon is graphite. The name 'graphite' comes from a Greek work meaning 'to write'. What we call the 'lead' in our pencils is actually graphite.

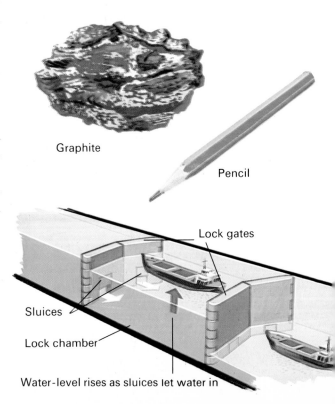

Graphite

Pencil

Lock gates

Sluices

Lock chamber

Water-level rises as sluices let water in

Right: A canal lock is like a step. A ship travelling upstream enters the lock through lock gates that close behind it. Sluices let water in and the water-level in the lock rises. When it is the same level as the canal beyond the lock, the farther gates are opened and the ship moves forward.

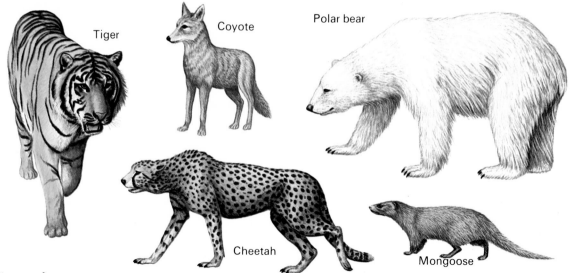

Tiger

Coyote

Polar bear

Cheetah

Mongoose

Carnivore

Carnivores are a group of MAMMALS that feed mainly on the flesh of other animals. They do not include birds of prey or people.

Although carnivores live mostly on meat, they will sometimes eat insects and plants. But what they all have in common is a set of very powerful jaws for chopping up their food, deadly curved claws for tearing, and long sharp teeth for seizing, stabbing, and killing their victims.

Carnivores include CATS, DOGS, BEARS, RACCOONS, weasels and hyenas. All have good eyesight, smell and hearing and are fast, intelligent and skilled at hunting down other animals. Some carnivores, such as wild dogs and hyenas, hunt in packs. In this way they can kill animals much larger than themselves. Other carnivores, such as the leopard and the jaguar, hunt alone.

Below: A piece of cartoon film seen frame by frame. Computers now speed up the laborious process of drawing the frames.

Some of the best-known carnivores belong to the cat and dog families. Bears eat plant food as well as meat.

Carpets and Rugs

As long as 2000 years ago, handwoven woollen carpets were being made in Turkey and the Middle East. But until the 1500s, they were very rare in Europe. In those days, people put their carpets on walls and over tables rather than on the floors.

Today most carpets are machine-made of wool, cotton or synthetic fibres. The most valuable carpets and rugs are still made by hand.

Cartoon

Most people think of short, funny films with talking creatures and plants when they speak of cartoons. But originally, cartoons were rough sketches of the design for a PAINTING or a TAPESTRY. These sketches were drawn to the same size as the finished thing. Comic strips in newspapers are called strip cartoons.

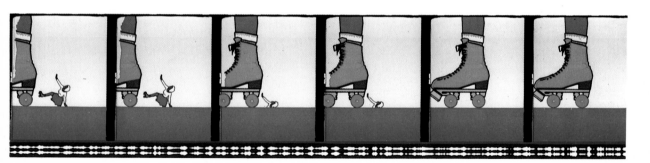

Cartoon films, or animations, are made from a series of drawings. Each drawing is a little different from the one before. When they are shown one after another at a very fast speed it looks as if the scene is moving.

The first castles the Normans built were motte and bailey castles like this one. A wooden fort was built on the motte (mound) and the garrison lived in the bailey (enclosure).

Bottom: Harlech Castle in North Wales, one of Edward I's castles. Fourteen castles were built at key points along the coast and garrison towns for English troops grew up around them.

Castle

One of the few places where kings and lords in the Middle Ages could feel safe was behind the thick stone walls of their castles. There, they and their men could fight off attacks by roving bandits and sit out long sieges by invading armies.

As castles developed they became larger

and more comfortable. Instead of having all the living quarters crowded into the main keep, small 'villages' of huts and buildings sprang up inside the castle walls.

Castles had high, thick, stone walls. A walk ran along the top of the walls and through each tower. The rounded towers could stand up to battering rams and hurled rocks much better than square ones could. The towers also jutted out from the main wall. This let the defenders fire on the attackers from three sides, and stopped them from reaching the foot of the walls.

All the members of the cat family have agile bodies, strong cutting teeth, and sharp claws which are particularly useful for climbing. Cats are mainly creatures of the night. Their eyes are adapted to seeing in dim light. All cats are fast runners over short distances.

Cat

A cat belongs to a group of MAMMALS called the feline family. Although the cat family ranges in size from domestic breeds to TIGERS, they all have many things in common. Cats have short, rounded heads, long face whiskers, sharp teeth that serve as deadly weapons for grabbing and biting their prey to death, and powerful claws. All cats except the cheetah can pull their claws back into a sheath of skin when they are not in use. Their long tails help them to balance and make them superb at jumping and climbing. LIONS and cheetahs live in families. All other cats live mostly alone.

All cats are CARNIVORES (meat-eaters). In fact, wild cats eat only freshly-killed meat. They do not eat fruit or insects, as many other carnivores do.

mestic cat   Caracal   Lynx   Leopard (black form)   Snow leopard

Cathedral

Cathedrals are CHURCHES—only bigger. They are the grandest and most impressive kinds of Christian churches ever to be built. A cathedral is the home church of a bishop. It is the centre from which he looks after all the other churches under his care.

Cathedrals are also places of worship. They can hold large numbers of people, as well as having room for choirs, organs, chapels and countless statues, paintings, stained windows and other religious items of decoration. Cathedrals were built with great splendour as they were seen as being built in honour of God. There are many styles of cathedral ARCHITECTURE.

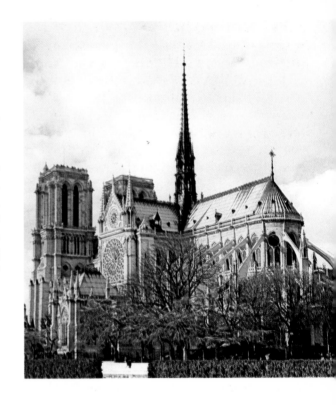

Right: Notre Dame cathedral in Paris was begun in 1163. It was a model for many later French churches.

Cave Dweller

Anybody who lives in a cave could be called a cave dweller. But what we usually mean are people who were the ancestors of modern man. Caves are natural places in which to shelter. They were some of the first dwelling places used by human beings.

The mouth of a cave is often dry, and it is possible to build a fire inside when the weather is cold. In hot weather, caves give shelter from the sun. Also, with walls all around them, cave dwellers could fight off dangerous animals from the cave mouth. The remains of ancient cave dwellers have been found in sites all around the world—in China, southern Asia, Europe and Africa. Here, tools and weapons have been dug up along with bones of the animals that were captured. Remains of their fires have also been found. Deep toward the back of the caves, graves of cave people have been unearthed. From all these things, archae-ologists have been able to piece together a great deal about the way of life of these people of long ago.

Below: Some tools fashioned by early men from the stones around them. The earliest ones were crudely chipped, but later ones were shaped by skilfully tapping away thin flakes of the stone. All sorts of shapes were produced from large all-purpose hand-axes to delicate arrowheads.

Caxton, William

In the 1400s, PRINTING was just becoming known in Europe. William Caxton (about 1421–1491) was the man who brought the new invention to Britain.

Caxton learned the art of printing in Belgium and Germany. In 1476 he set up a wooden press in England and the next year produced the first printed book in that country. In all, Caxton printed about 100 BOOKS, of which about a third can still be seen today. These include editions of the work of CHAUCER.

Caxton's books look very different from modern ones. They are quite difficult to read, as they have very little punctuation.

Cell

Cells are the smallest living parts of plants and animals. Single cells can be seen only under a MICROSCOPE. Even a tiny bit of human skin contains millions of them.

Cells are usually round in shape. A few are spiralled and some, like nerve cells, have sprawling, treelike branches.

In 1665, a scientist named Robert Hooke looked at a piece of cork under a microscope and saw that it was made up of many tiny compartments. He named them cells.

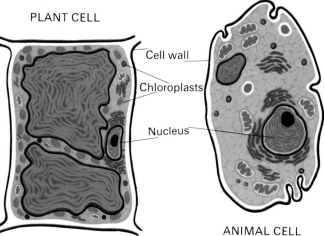

PLANT CELL

Cell wall

Chloroplasts

Nucleus

ANIMAL CELL

Plant cells are different from animal cells. They have an extra-thick cell wall. This gives plants their stiffness as they do not have bones to support them. Animal cells have only a thin cell wall. Plants also have chloroplasts. These give them their green colour and help them to use sunlight for growing. At the heart of all cells is a nucleus. The nucleus controls all of the cell's actions.

Caxton first saw printing, which was invented by the Chinese, at work in Germany. He set up this press in Westminster in 1476. His books, chiefly written in English, were printed on paper.

Central America

Central America forms a land bridge between the continents of North and South America. It consists of the independent republics of Costa Rica, El Salvador, Guatemala, Honduras, Nicaragua, Panama, Belize and the US-administered Panama Canal Zone.

This land bridge was created many millions of years ago by volcanic activity. To the east of Central America, the coast is flat and covered with jungle. Central America is a hot area. Most of the large cities are in the cooler highlands.

Central America, along with Mexico and the West Indies, is said by many people to be the tropical part of North America. Also, most of this 'tropical' area, along with much of South America, is often called Latin America. This is because the people there speak Spanish or Portuguese, which come from ancient Latin.

Most of the people of Central America are of Indian, Spanish or mixed origin. Spanish is the main language, but many Indians still speak their native language. Central Americans farm tropical crops such as sugar, bananas, cotton and coffee.

Above: Tikal, in Guatemala. These ruins are of the ancient ceremonial centre of the Mayan civilization, which flourished in Central America around AD 500–1,000.

Charlemagne

Charlemagne (AD 742–814) was a great military leader. In the eighth century he founded an empire that covered most of western Europe.

In the year 768, Charlemagne became the king of the Franks, a people who lived in the country we now call France. Through his skill in war he soon took over northern Spain, Italy and Germany. He fought for the Church in Rome, and in return, the Pope crowned him Holy Roman Emperor on Christmas Day, in the year 800.

Charlemagne wanted to build another

Above: Central America, Mexico, and the northern part of South America.

Right: The Panama Canal, the world's most famous ship canal, is 82 km long. It crosses Central America to link the Atlantic and Pacific oceans.

This magnificent crowned bust of Charlemagne was made to hold parts of his skull.

ROMAN EMPIRE, but after his death his sons fought among themselves, and his empire was slowly broken up.

Charles (kings)

Charles was the name of two British kings who ruled in the 1600s. Between their reigns, Britain was ruled by Parliament under its leader, Oliver CROMWELL, as a result of a bitter CIVIL WAR (1642–1649).

Charles I (1600–1649) is known in history as the only British king to have caused his people to rebel and execute him. He came to the throne in 1625, but he made enemies almost everywhere, and in 1642 the country was split by civil war. He was beheaded in 1649, after being sentenced to death by Parliament.

As King of Britain, Charles II (1630–1685) was liked as much as his father was hated. He spent most of his youth in exile in Europe.

In 1660, after being ruled by Cromwell for eight years and his son for two years, the English invited Charles II to return and take back the crown. He was a wise ruler, and he was very careful in the way in which he treated his people and parliament. His court was very lively and gay, and his personal charm won him many friends.

Charles I painted from three different angles by the Dutch portrait painter, van Dyck.

The pilgrims in Chaucer's Canterbury Tales *include all kinds of people—a knight, a nun, a lawyer, a prioress, a doctor, a sailor and a miller. The poem gives a vivid picture of Chaucer's times.*

Chaucer, Geoffrey

Geoffrey Chaucer (1345–1400) was a great English poet. He was one of the first people to write in the ENGLISH LANGUAGE rather than in Latin. His best-known work is the *Canterbury Tales*. It is a collection of stories told by an imaginary group of pilgrims (shown in the picture above), as they travelled to Canterbury Cathedral.

Below: Some of the items found in a chemistry laboratory: They are: 1. Chemical balance; 2. Bottles with ground glass stoppers; 3. Centrifuge; 4. Microscope; 5. Burette; 6. Conical flask; 7. Filter funnel; 8. Measuring cylinder; 9. Long-necked flask; 10. Pipette; 11. Flat-bottomed flask; 12. Beaker; 13. Test tube and holder; 14. Bunsen burner; 15. Mortar and pestle; 16; Condenser; 17. Tripod stand.

Chemistry

Chemistry is the study of materials—solids, liquids and gases. A chemist finds out what things are made of and how they are joined together. If a piece of wood is burned in a fire, this is a *chemical reaction.* The wood turns to ash and, at the same time, heat and light are given off. It took chemists a long time to find out that burning is the joining together of the wood with the gas oxygen from the air. There are lots and lots of chemical reactions.

The true science of chemistry as we know it began only in the 1600s. Chemists at this time began to find out how chemicals really work. Then they discovered the *elements,* simple substances which make up all the millions of different substances on earth. There are only about a hundred elements, each of them made up of tiny ATOMS. The atoms of elements often join together to make different substances. The salt you put on your food is made up of atoms of the elements sodium and chlorine. An atom of sodium joins with an atom of chlorine to make a *molecule* of salt, like this:

Sodium atom	Chlorine atom	Salt molecule

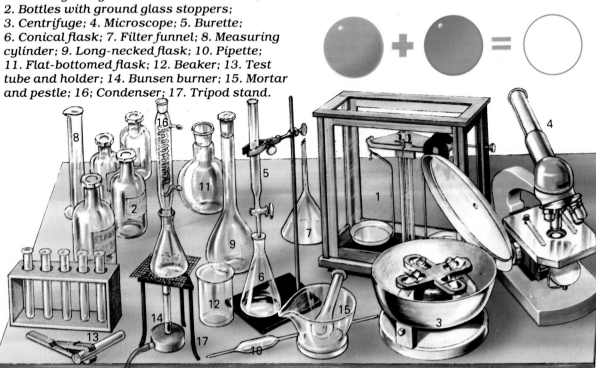

Chemistry is today a very important science, and chemists are employed in a vast number of industries.

Chess

Chess is a game that has been played for hundreds of years. It is played by two people on a board with 64 black and white squares. Each player has 16 pieces which he lines up on either side of the board (shown below). Each piece is moved around the board in a special way. The pieces are used to attack and retreat, and to defend each other; they can be captured and taken out of play. The most important piece for each player is the 'king'. The game is won when one player manages to capture the other player's king.

Black

White

Chile

Chile is a narrow country that lies along 4,265 km of the western coast of South America. It is made even narrower by the great Andes Mountains, which lie along its eastern border.

Chile has over a quarter of the world's copper resources, as well as other minerals. Its people are Spanish-speaking and are mainly Roman Catholics. The capital city is Santiago, with over four million people.

A military government seized power in Chile in 1973, and still rules the country today.

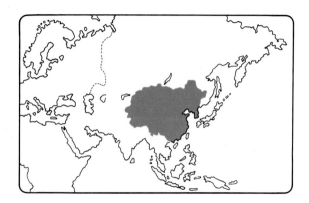

China

China is the third biggest nation in the world, and it has a population larger than that of any other country. A fifth of all the people on earth are Chinese—over one billion.

To the north and west, China is cut off from the rest of Asia by great deserts and by the Himalayas. To the east lies the Pacific Ocean and Japan. The Chinese have ruled within this area almost without a break for the past 3500 years.

The first real Chinese civilization grew up in the great river valleys of the Hwang-Ho in the north and the Yangtze in the south. Today, more Chinese live crowded close to these rivers than in any other part of the country.

In the dry Atacama Desert in Chile, the first rain in 400 years fell in 1971.

CHINA
Capital: Beijing (Peking)
Area: 9,560,000 square km
Population: (1983 est.): 1,022,054,000
Government: Republic
Currency: Renminbi, or Yuan
Official Language: Chinese

By far the greatest number of Chinese are farmers. In modern China, the farmers do not own their farms. Each village, or commune, owns its own land. Everyone works on it together, and the harvest is shared among them.

Hot summers and cool or cold winters with plenty of rainfall all year round make the heart of China a good farming region. But much of China cannot be farmed, and growing enough food for the many people who live there is still a great problem. The main crops that are raised are rice in the south and wheat and millet in the north. Silk, tea and cotton are also important, and there is a large fishing industry.

The biggest cities of China are the great

The Great Wall of China was built over 2,000 years ago to keep out enemies. It is 3,460km long.

port of Shanghai—near the mouth of the Yangtze—and Tientsin. The capital is Beijing, a fine old city. For centuries the Chinese emperors lived in great splendour in the Forbidden City in the centre of Beijing.

In 1949, China was greatly changed when the civil war which had been raging since the 1920s came to an end. The Communist Party led by Mao Zedong came into power. Mao Zedong persuaded the Chinese people to give up many of their old ways of life. He set out to make China an important industrial centre, and today China is as powerful as the other large nations.

Chocolate

Chocolate is made from the beans of the cacao tree. The beans grow inside pods which hang from both the trunk and the branches of the tree (below).

To make chocolate, the beans are first roasted, then ground up to give an oily

Hard work by people and machines has made China into a modern power.

liquid called 'chocolate liquor'. Other things may then be added to the liquor. The milk chocolate we buy in shops, for example, has milk and sugar added to it.

Christianity

Christianity is one of the world's great religions. More than one billion people call themselves Christians. These are people who follow the teachings of JESUS and who believe that he is the son of God who came to earth in human form.

Christianity is almost 2000 years old. In fact, we date our calendar from the year in which it was thought that Jesus was born. Christians accept the BIBLE as their holy book, and Sunday is their holy day, when they go to church to worship as a commun-

ity. The most important festivals are Christmas, which marks the birth of Jesus, and Easter, which marks his death and rise to heaven.

In some ways Christianity grew out of the religion of Judaism. But the teachings of Jesus upset the Jewish and Roman leaders of the time, and in AD 29 he was crucified. After his death, the followers of Jesus, the disciples, spread his teachings far and wide. Today there are many different forms of Christianity.

Church

Christian churches are as varied as the countries in which they are found. They come in all shapes and sizes—from tents and tiny wooden huts to towering stone

The inside of a large Christian church or cathedral, showing the bell tower, the nave, the altar and the transepts.

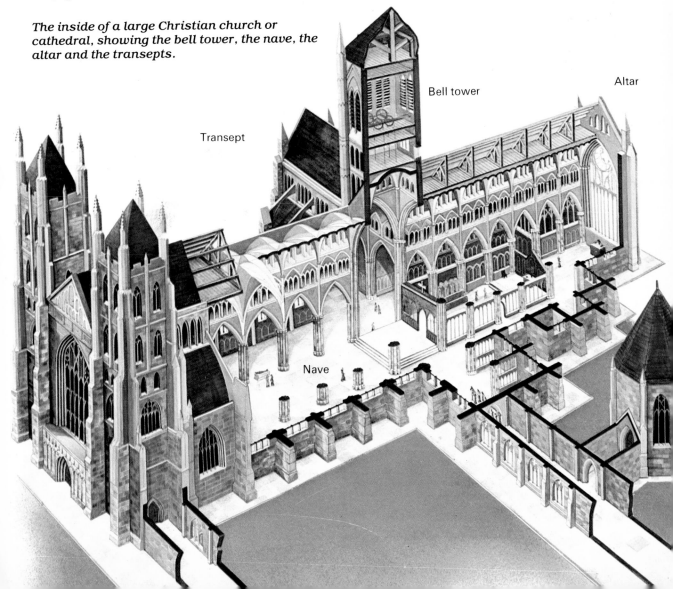

Transept

Bell tower

Altar

Nave

cathedrals. But all churches are used for the same purposes. They serve as places of prayer, as settings for holding religious services and as places that house all kinds of religious objects.

Larger churches, especially traditional Catholic ones, were usually built in the shape of a cross. In most, the altar is built at the east end. It is found at the end furthest away from the main door.

Most cathedrals were laid out in the same way on the inside. The worshippers sat in the centre, in a section called the *nave*. They faced toward the altar and the place where the choir sang. On either side were the wings, called *transepts*, which gave the church its cross shape.

Churchill, Winston

Sir Winston Churchill (1874–1965) was a great British Prime Minister, war leader, and writer. Although he was a senior minister in Parliament before and during World War I, he was not very powerful. But in 1940, when World War II threatened Britain, the country chose him as their Prime Minister. As a leader during wartime he showed great courage and determination. His rousing speeches helped the people of Britain to fight on when they stood alone against Germany and her allies.

Cinema

The art of making moving pictures came from an invention called the *kinetoscope*, built by an American, Thomas EDISON, in 1891. Soon after Edison's machine became known, two brothers, Auguste and Louis Lumière, built a similar machine of their own called a *cinématographe*. This machine projected pictures from a piece of film onto a screen. The pictures were shown one after the other so quickly that the images on the screen appeared to move. In 1896, in Paris, the Lumière brothers gave the world's first public film show. Soon, people all over Europe and North America were making films.

These early films did not look much like the ones we are used to seeing today. They were only in black and white, the movements were very jerky and they had no sound. At first, films were made to show news and real events, but by 1902 filmmakers began to make up their own stories, using actors to play the parts of imaginary people. These films were very popular in

A movie camera has a film like an ordinary camera. But instead of taking just one picture at a time, it takes many pictures every second. As the film moves past the lens in the camera, a shutter continually opens and closes to give a long line of pictures on the film. Then the film is developed and shown on a screen.

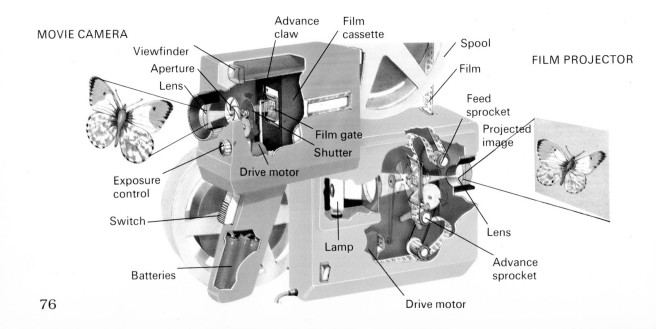

MOVIE CAMERA

Advance claw
Film cassette
Viewfinder
Spool
Aperture
Film
Lens
FILM PROJECTOR
Feed sprocket
Film gate
Projected image
Shutter
Drive motor
Exposure control
Switch
Lens
Lamp
Advance sprocket
Batteries
Drive motor

Many films made today, like Star Wars, *use a lot of equipment to create special effects.*

France and the United States, and Hollywood in California became the film-making centre of the world. The first 'talkie', or moving picture with sound, was shown in America in 1927. It was called *The Jazz Singer*.

America remained the leader in the film world. Huge amounts of money were spent on films that used hundreds of actors, singers and dancers, lavish costumes and specially designed 'sets' or backgrounds. But Europe too produced many important films, and after World War II, a more realistic type of film became popular, telling stories of everyday life.

Civil Rights

Civil rights are the rights people have to decide certain things about the way they live. The most important of these are the freedom to follow your own religion, to voice your opinions in speech or in newspapers, and to be treated by the law in the same way as everyone else. In the United States civil rights became an important issue in the 1950s and 1960s when black Americans fought for equal treatment as American citizens. The United Nations adopted a Universal Declaration of Human Rights in 1948. It said that all persons are born free and are equal in rights.

Civil War

Civil war happens when a whole country is divided into two or more groups who fight each other over their different political or religious beliefs. In England, the last civil war lasted from 1642 to 1649 and was fought between the king, CHARLES I, and Parliament.

Up to this time it had been agreed that although the King ruled the country he could only tax money from the people if Parliament agreed. Charles believed that God had given him the right to do this alone. So in 1629 he got rid of Parliament and ruled without it, taxing the people whenever he needed money.

People became very unwilling to pay their taxes to Charles. In 1640 Charles was forced to recall Parliament because he needed more money. Instead of giving him money, Parliament argued with the King and said he could not rule on his own. Charles angrily dismissed Parliament and later tried to arrest some of its leaders.

In 1642 the King called his friends to arm themselves. They were called Royalists. Parliament had its own army. They were called Roundheads because they had short hair. The Roundheads had a great general called Oliver CROMWELL. He was very strict and trained his army carefully.

After several battles the Royalist forces lost the war and the King was captured. Charles was put on trial and in 1649 he was executed. Parliament began to rule without a king, with Cromwell as its leader.

Civil War, American

The American Civil War was fought from 1861 to 1865 between the northern states (the Union) and those of the South (the Confederacy). The war was fought over the states' rights issue, in particular, the right of each state to make its own decisions about slavery. In 1860 the southern states

Right: The battle of Williamsburg, May 5, 1862. The Confederates withdrew after heavy fighting.

thought that the new president, Abraham Lincoln, would abolish slavery. This would mean that the big farms, or plantations, of the South would be ruined.

In 1861 eleven southern states under Jefferson Davis decided to break away, or secede, from the Union. They formed the Confederate States of America. As president, Lincoln would not allow the southern states to secede. War broke out in April 1861 when the Confederates fired on Fort Sumter in the harbour of Charleston, South Carolina.

The Confederate army was led by Robert E. Lee, a brilliant commander. He won the South's first victory at the Battle of Bull Run in July 1861. At first things went well for the South. But in 1863 Lee was beaten in a bloody battle at Gettysburg, in Pennsylvania, and the strength of the South was broken. In 1864 General Ulysses S. Grant took command of the Union armies, and in April 1865 he accepted Lee's surrender.

With the end of the war, the slaves were freed and the southern states rejoined the Union. But more than 600,000 lives had been lost, and the war gave rise to many new problems that stayed with the United States for many years.

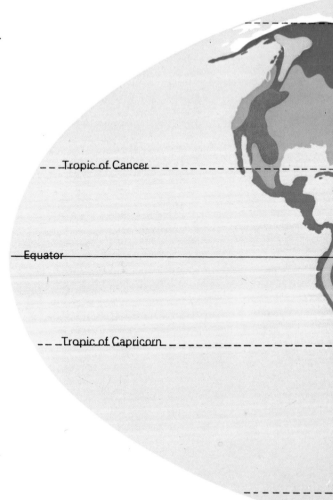

Climate

Climate is the usual WEATHER of a place over a long period of time. The weather can change from day to day, but the climate stays the same.

The sun has the greatest influence on the climate. It heats the land, the seas and the air. Countries near the equator get more of the sun's rays and usually have a hotter climate than places farther north or south. The sun's rays do not get to the Arctic and the Antarctic easily. They have very cold climates.

When the sun heats the air it causes winds which can make the climate hotter or colder. The winds may also carry rain or dry air which can make the climate wet or dry.

Together with the winds, the sun's heat

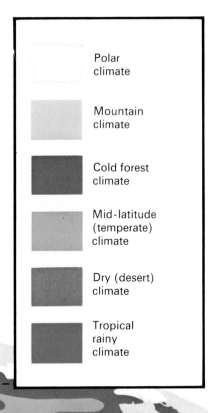

Polar climate

Mountain climate

Cold forest climate

Mid-latitude (temperate) climate

Dry (desert) climate

Tropical rainy climate

Arctic Circle

Antarctic Circle

makes ocean currents. The Gulf Stream is a current which travels from Mexico to north-western Europe. In winter the warmth from its water makes the climate of this part of Europe milder.

Mountains also affect the climate. The air high in the mountains is thinner. It does not soak up the heat of the sun as much as air at the bottom of mountains or in valleys.

Clocks and Watches

Long ago people measured time by putting a stick in the ground and watching its shadow move with the sun. Sundials work in the same way. But sun clocks work only when the sun is shining, so people began to

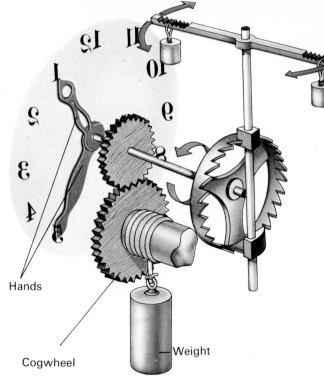

Hands

Cogwheel

Weight

Right: A simple weight drives this clock. The weight hangs from a cord wound around a spool. As the cord unwinds it sets the gears in motion to work the hands.

Below: A watch is driven by a coiled main spring. A hair spring turns the balance wheel and rocker to and fro. The rocker turns the escape wheel slowly and the escape wheel turns the hands round.

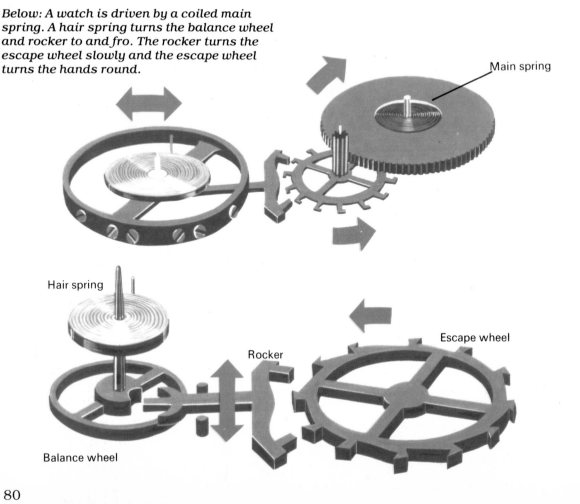

Main spring

Hair spring

Rocker

Escape wheel

Balance wheel

measure time by watching how long it took a candle to burn or a tank of water to empty.

The first mechanical clocks were made in Europe in the 1200s, although the Chinese probably had clocks as early as the 600s. European clocks were first used in abbeys and churches to mark the time of services. A clock in Salisbury Cathedral dates from 1386.

Early clocks like these were bad timekeepers and could lose or gain an hour a day. In 1581 the great astronomer GALILEO discovered that a PENDULUM could be used to measure time. This helped people to make much more accurate clocks. From then on improvements were made, and ordinary clocks are now accurate to within a few minutes a year.

Today's scientists need very accurate clocks. They invented first the electric and then the quartz crystal clock. Now there are atomic clocks that are accurate to less than one thousandth of a second a year.

Cloud

Clouds are great clusters of tiny water droplets or ice crystals in the air. A cloud may float more than 10,000 metres up, or drift so low that it touches the ground, when it is known as a mist or fog.

There is always a certain amount of water *vapour* in the air. It is made up of tiny specks of water. Warm air that contains water vapour often rises and cools. Since cool air cannot hold as much water as warm air, the vapour particles start to form droplets (condense) around bits of dust, pollen and salt that the wind has carried into the sky.

As more water vapour condenses, the droplets grow in size and clouds begin to form. At first they are white and gauzy. As they become heavy with water they become thick and grey. Finally the droplets become so heavy that they clump together and fall to the earth. If the temperature is high enough they come down as rain. Otherwise they fall as hail or snow.

Below you can see the main kinds of clouds. Clouds are made of water droplets. Cirrus *are wispy clouds high in the sky. They are made of water droplets frozen into tiny ice crystals.* Cirrostratus *clouds often mean rain is on the way.* Cirrocumulus *is often called a 'mackerel' sky. The low clouds are* Stratocumulus, Cumulus, Nimbostratus, Stratus *and* Cumulonimbus, *a dark thundercloud.*

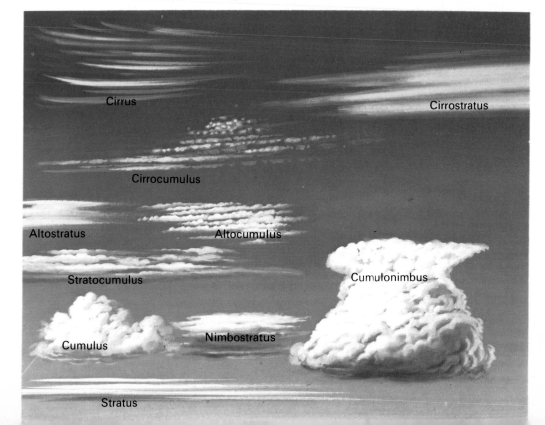

81

Right: A coal mine. The workings may stretch for miles underground.

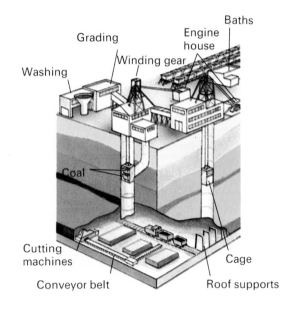

Coal

Coal is fuel which is found in layers, or *seams*, under the ground. It is known as a FOSSIL fuel because it was made millions of years ago from dead plants. Coal is used for heating and in making electricity, gas and chemicals. It is also made into another fuel called coke.

Coffee

Coffee is a drink made from the beans of the coffee plant. The beans are dried and roasted until they are brown, and then ground. Boiling water is passed through the ground coffee to make the drink.

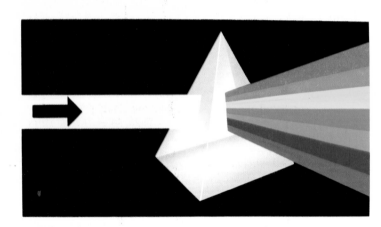

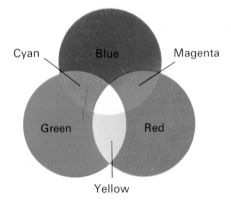

Colour

The first man to find out about coloured light was Isaac NEWTON. He shone sunlight through a piece of glass called a *prism*. (You can see one above.) The light that came out of the prism was broken up into all the colours of the rainbow—red, orange, yellow, green, blue and violet. Newton had found out that ordinary white light is made up of many colours added together.

When sunlight falls on rain or spray from a garden hose, we sometimes see a rainbow. Rainbows are caused by the drops of water behaving like tiny prisms. They break up the sun's light into colours.

Above: Red, blue, and green light can be mixed to make any other colour. Red and green light mixed give us yellow light. If we add blue to the yellow light, we get white light. Below: Mixing paints is quite different. Yellow and blue paint mix to make green. But you cannot make white paint by mixing different colours.

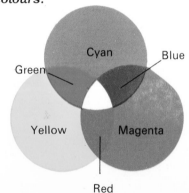

A red flower is red because it takes in all the other colours and throws back only red. A white flower gives back to our eyes all the colours of light. We know that all the colours added together make white. You can see this for yourself by making a paper circle with the colours as shown on the right. Spin the paper quickly and it looks almost white. When you look at white light you are seeing a mixture of colours.

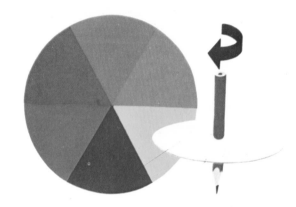

Columbus, Christopher

Christopher Columbus (1451–1506) was a sailor and explorer. He discovered America for Spain in 1492, though he believed that the land he had reached was Asia.

Like many people of his time, Columbus believed that the earth was not flat but round. Sailors from Europe used to sail east to bring back the riches of the 'Indies' (Asia). Columbus thought that sailing west would be quicker. Queen Isabella and King Ferdinand of Spain gave him ships and money to make this voyage.

In 1492 Columbus sailed west with three small ships—the *Niña*, the *Pinta* and the *Santa María*. For three weeks he and his crew saw no land. Then, on October 12, they reached an island near America. Columbus named it San Salvador. When he returned to Spain, Columbus had a hero's welcome.

Comet

Comets travel around the SOLAR SYSTEM in long paths, or ORBITS. Sometimes they pass close to the sun. At other times they move far beyond the path of Pluto, the outermost planet. A complete orbit by a comet is called its period. Encke's Comet has the shortest period of all. It is three and a half years. Others have periods of centuries or even thousands of years.

Comets are clouds of frozen gases, ice, dust and rock. The biggest are only a few kilometres across, but their bright tails may be millions of kilometres long.

Most of the time comets cannot be seen, even through the biggest telescopes. But whenever their orbits bring them back into the middle of the solar system they flare up and look very bright.

As a comet travels toward the sun, the sun's rays knock particles out of the comet and push them away to make a long tail. The tail is made of glowing gas and dust. But the tail is so fine that a space probe passing through it is not harmed. Much information about comets was obtained by sending probes to observe Halley's Comet in 1986.

Below: Only the brightest comets can be seen without a telescope. They are seen as they move past the sun, when their tails are at their longest and brightest. The best known of all is Halley's Comet. It appears in the sky every 76 years and is next due in 2062. Ikeya-Seki (below) was first seen in 1965. It is not due back for 880 years.

*Above: China became a
communist country in
1949. Left: Lenin was the
leader of the Russian
communists when they
took power in 1917.*

Communism

Communism is a set of ideas about the way a country should be run. The main idea of communism is that people should share wealth and property. This makes people more equal because nobody is very rich or very poor. In most communist countries the people own the factories and farms, but it is usually the government that runs them. People who believe in communism are often called Marxists. This is because they follow the ideas of Karl MARX, a thinker, or *philosopher*, of the 1800s.

Many countries have become communist in the 1900s. They include Russia, China, Cuba and some countries in Eastern Europe and the Far East. LENIN and Mao Zedong were among the great communist leaders of this century.

Compass

A compass is an instrument for finding the way. A magnetic compass always points to the earth's magnetic poles, which are close to the North and South Poles. The magnetic compass has been used for centuries by sailors and explorers to find the right direction to travel in.

A magnetic compass works by MAGNET-ISM. It has a magnetic needle fixed to a pivot so that it is free to swing around. The needle always points north and south when it is at rest. With a compass showing where north and south are, it is easy to travel in a straight line in any direction you wish to go.

The needle always points north and south because the earth itself is a big magnet. The compass lines up parallel with the earth's magnetic field.

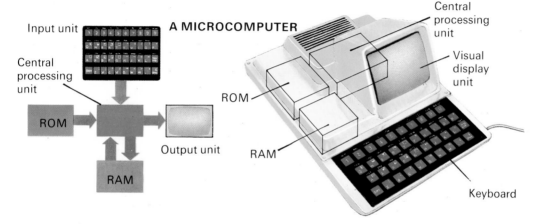

A MICROCOMPUTER

Input unit
Central processing unit
ROM
RAM
Output unit

Central processing unit
Visual display unit
ROM
RAM
Keyboard

Computer

Computers are playing a bigger and bigger part in all our lives. They can play a game of chess with you, guide a spacecraft, check fingerprints and draw a map of Australia. They can do all these things and many more merely because they can add, subtract and compare one number with another. Computers are special because they can do millions of calculations in a second.

Although the computer works with numbers, the information it uses does not have to start off as numbers. We can feed almost anything into it, but the first thing the computer does is to turn everything into numbers. But the numbers it uses are not quite the same as ours. We use the numbers 0 to 9. All the computer needs is 0 and 1. In fact, it can only count up to 1! This is called the binary system. The computer uses the binary system because it has been designed to work with electrical currents. It can recognize the difference between a big current and a small current flow. If there is a big current, it registers 1; if there is a small current, it registers 0. When we type on the keys of a computer keyboard, we are making little electrical currents flow through tiny circuits in microchips. It is these tiny currents that give us the answers we need.

One of the first modern computers, known as ENIAC, was built in the United States in 1946. It was so big that it filled a large room. Today a tiny microchip such as the one shown above right can do the work of ENIAC.

Above: Every computer contains four basic units. These are the input, memory, central processing, and output units. Below: The microchip has revolutionized computers. Bottom: Using a computer in a geometry class.

Congo

The Congo is a country in the west of central AFRICA. It used to be enormous, about the size of western Europe. Now it is much smaller. It has an area of 342,000 square km.

The Congo is a hot, wet country. It has great forests and swamps, and a low grassy plain on the coast. The capital is Brazzaville. The Congo produces a lot of timber, but it also has diamonds, sugar, oil, cocoa and coffee. The Zaire River, once called the Congo, flows through the country. It is 4,700km long and is one of the longest rivers in the world.

Conifer

Conifers are TREES and shrubs which have cones instead of flowers for making pollen and seeds. There are about 600 different kinds of conifer. Many of them are found in the cool parts of the world. Some even grow north of the Arctic Circle.

Conifers include pines, firs, spruces, larches and cedars. Most have needle-like leaves which they do not lose in winter.

All conifers have two kinds of cones, male and female. The male pollen cones and the female seed cones usually grow on the same tree. Conifers are fast-growing and their wood is widely used for building and furniture. It is also pulped for use in papermaking. The resins from some conifers are processed into creosote, naphtha, turpentine and other products.

Spruce

Scots pine

Yew

Juniper

Stone pine

Giant Sequoia
or Wellingtonia
or Big Tree

Cedar of Lebanon

Continental Shelf

Continents do not end where their coasts meet the sea. Their true edges lie far out under the sea. Each continent is ringed by a gently sloping shelf of land under the sea called the continental shelf. This shelf sometimes stretches for hundreds of kilometres from the shore. Beyond the continental shelf is the deep ocean floor.

In the past, the sea level was lower and much of the continental shelf was dry land. Rivers flowed through it to the sea and made valleys or canyons. These canyons are now under the sea.

Most sea life is found on the continental shelf. Sunlight shines through the water, helping plants, fish and other animals to grow.

Most of the continental shelf lies under about 140 metres of water. At its edge, the seabed falls steeply to the deep ocean floor. Here, the water is usually about 4,800 metres deep. The ocean floor is not flat but has big mountains and valleys.

Continents

Continents are large areas of land. The earth has seven continents: Africa, Antarctica, Asia, Australia, Europe, North America and South America.

The continents are not fixed. They are made of lighter rock than the rock on the ocean floor. The great heat in the centre of the earth has made the surface rocks break into huge pieces called *plates*. When the plates move they move the continents with them. This movement is very slow. A continent moves only a few centimetres in a century.

A few hundred years ago some people saw that the shapes of America, Europe and Africa looked like jigsaw pieces that would fit closely if they were pushed together. This gave them the idea that the continents used to be one big piece of land which broke up. This idea is called continental drift. Today, people who study GEOLOGY believe this idea is true.

Geologists think that the movements of the continents pushed up some pieces of land to make mountains such as the Alps and the Himalayas.

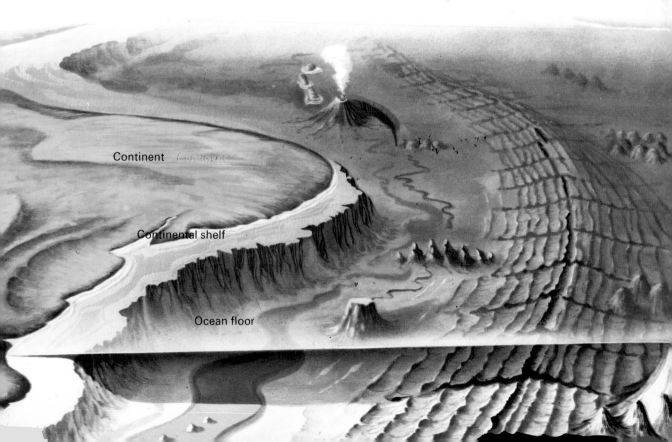

Continent

Continental shelf

Ocean floor

Cook, James

James Cook (1728–1779) was a famous British sea captain and explorer. His expeditions took him around the world and all over the Pacific Ocean. Cook's discoveries led to Australia, New Zealand and many South Pacific islands becoming British colonies.

After serving in the Royal Navy for 13 years, Cook was put in command of an expedition to Tahiti in 1768. After Tahiti, Cook sailed on to New Zealand and Australia. Cook landed in Botany Bay in 1770 to claim the continent for Britain.

On his second voyage (1772–1775), Cook set off to look for the 'southern continent', which many people believed lay south of Australia. He explored the edges of Antarctica. He also charted many previously unknown Pacific islands.

Cook's third and last voyage began in 1776. He left England with two ships—the *Resolution* and the *Discovery*—to try to find a route around North America. Again he sailed to the Pacific. In early 1778 he discovered the Hawaiian Islands. From there Cook sailed north along the west coast of North America. He got as far as the Bering Strait off Alaska before being forced back by ice. Returning to Hawaii, he was killed in a scuffle with natives. Today Cook is remembered as a skilled navigator and a great explorer.

When Cook landed in New Zealand he was met by the warlike Maoris. They paddled war canoes with carved prows. Cook got along well with them, and they let him map their islands. The map (below) shows Cook's voyage to Australasia (Australia, New Zealand and the islands in the Pacific).

Coral

Coral is a kind of limestone found mostly in warm, shallow seas. It is made by tiny animals, called coral polyps, that build

Below: A coral atoll.

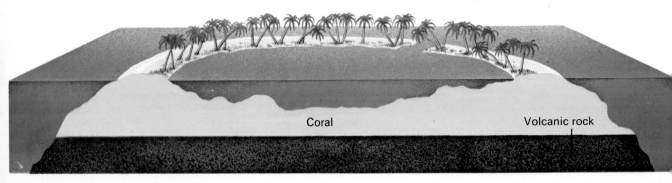

Coral

Volcanic rock

limestone 'shells' around themselves for protection. Most coral polyps live in groups, or colonies. These may take many shapes, from lacy fans to stubby branches, all in beautiful colours. Other colonies form thick underwater walls known as reefs.

Along some reefs waves may throw up bits of sand and coral which gradually build up the reef until it is above water. The reef then becomes an island. One kind of coral island is the atoll (opposite page), a ringed reef with a central lagoon.

Right: The coral polyp on the left is open, showing its mouth fringed with tentacles. The polyps on the right are closed.

Cork

The cork that is used to make bottle stoppers comes from the smooth bark of the cork oak tree of the Mediterranean. It is a light, spongy material that forms a thick layer about 3 cm deep around the trunk of the tree. It gives the tree protection against the weather and against harmful insects and fungi.

Cork is stripped from cork oaks once every nine or ten years until the trees are about 150 years old. It is also used in machinery and to make floor tiles.

Workers in Portugal gather bark from cork trees to make cork.

Cortés, Hernando

Hernando Cortés (1485–1547) was a Spanish soldier and explorer who landed on the coast of Mexico in 1519. With a force of only 600 men and a few horses he conquered the great AZTEC empire. Cortés' horses and guns helped convince the Aztecs he was a god. He captured the Aztec emperor Montezuma and by 1521 had taken control of Mexico.

Cotton

Cotton grows in warm and tropical places all around the world. It is one of the most important plants grown by people. Its fibres

The cotton gin was invented by Eli Whitney in 1793. In it, the cotton bolls were fed into a toothed cylinder which was turned to pull the fibres away from the seeds.

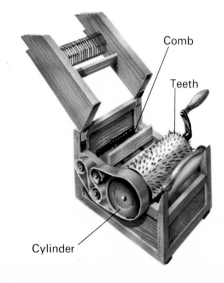

Comb

Teeth

Cylinder

89

are made into cloth, and the seeds are used for oil and cattle food.

Cotton has green fruits called bolls. When they are ripe, the bolls split open. Inside them is a mass of white fibres and seeds. The fibres are separated from the seeds, spun into yarn, and then woven into cloth.

A cow suckles its calf.

Cow

The cow that gives us milk is a member of the cattle family. Cattle are large grass-eating animals. Grass is difficult to digest, and all cattle have four stomachs to make digestion easier. During digestion the food is returned to the cow's mouth to be chewed and then swallowed again. When a cow does this we say it is 'chewing the cud'. The farm cow comes from an extinct wild cow called an *auroch* and has been tamed by people for about 6000 years.

Cowboy

People everywhere know the cowboy from the Hollywood western. But the cowboy, in history and today, is a man who rides horses and herds cows. The great days of the cowboys lasted only about 40 years, from 1860 to 1900.

During the heyday of the cowboy, grassland stretched from the Mexican border to Canada. Large herds of cattle grazed there before being driven to the railheads, where they were taken to market.

The cowboy led a simple and difficult life. He spent most of his time on horseback and was out in all kinds of weather.

Today, cowboy skills such as roping and branding are still celebrated at rodeos.

A cowboy rounds up a calf. The cowboy depends as much on the skill and intelligence of his horse as the shepherd does on his sheepdog.

Crete

Crete is a mountainous island in the Mediterranean. It lies to the south of Greece. Today it is a poor land, the home of half a million people who are mostly Greek and live mainly by farming. About 5000 years ago a great civilization began in Crete. It lasted for more than a thousand years.

The civilization was forgotten about until 1900 when Arthur Evans, a British archaeologist, rediscovered it. He began digging, or *excavating*, the ruins of a palace at Knossos.

Soon Evans found more remains which told him about the old civilization. It had busy towns and traded with ancient Egypt. The people had well-built homes and some of the houses had beautiful wall paintings, or *frescoes*. Evans called this civilization Minoan, after a legendary king of Crete called Minos. The Minoans also had an alphabet and could write. They may have been the first people in Europe to do this.

Suddenly, in about 1400 BC, many of the palaces and cities were destroyed. This may have been caused by an earthquake.

The palace at Knossos probably looked like this (below). It had many buildings, gardens, staircases and courtyards. Minoan craftsmen had great skill.

Crimean War

The Crimean War (1854–56) was a struggle between Russia on one side and Turkey, France and Britain on the other. At that time the Turkish Empire was very weak. Russia hoped to make its power greater in the eastern Mediterranean by taking Constantinople (now called Istanbul).

The British, French and Turks pushed the Russian army back into the Crimean peninsula, where the war was fought. There was much misery and suffering.

For the first time, newspaper reporters and photographers went to the battlegrounds. They reported the terrible conditions of the soldiers to the newspapers.

Cromwell, Oliver

Oliver Cromwell (1599–1658) and his son Richard were the only rulers of Britain never to have been a king or queen. He came to power after the civil war of the 1640s. Cromwell was a member of Parliament. He fought against CHARLES I with the army of Parliament and became its leader.

After Charles I was beheaded, Cromwell became the ruler of the country, but he never made himself king. The period of his rule is known as the Commonwealth, or the Protectorate. He was the only man ever to rule the country as leader of a republican government. He was called the 'Lord Protector'. After Cromwell died, his son Richard succeeded him, but he lacked support. In 1660 Richard was overthrown and Charles II became king.

Crusades

The Crusades were expeditions by Christians in the Middle Ages that led to wars with the Muslims in Palestine, the Holy Land. In 1087, the Turks captured the city of Jerusalem in Palestine. The Turks were Muslims and they stopped Christians from visiting the holy places in Palestine.

The Christian rulers in Europe were very angry about this. A few years later, the Byzantine emperor in Constantinople asked the Pope to help him drive the Turks from the Holy Land. The Pope started the first Crusade.

The armies of the first Crusade were successful. They took Jerusalem from the Turks in 1099. The Crusaders set up Christian kingdoms along the coast of Palestine and Syria and built strong fortresses to defend their new lands.

There were seven more Crusades after the first one. Many of them failed because the Crusaders quarrelled with each other. The Turks took back much of the Holy Land from the Christians. When the Turks took Jerusalem in 1187, the third Crusade set off from Europe. When they got to the Holy Land the Crusaders were defeated by the Turks who had a new general called Saladin.

Later, the Crusaders forgot that they were fighting for their religion. Many of them went to Palestine hoping to take the land and become rich. By 1291, the Turks took the last remaining Christian city at Acre.

During the Crusades European people learned more about the eastern parts of the world. When they returned to Europe they took back with them many new things including foods, spices, silk clothes and paper. They learned about medicine, mathematics and astronomy from the Arabs of the East, and trade between East and West began to grow.

The Crusader on the left is wearing a full coat of armour made from mail. The mail was metal chains or rings joined together. This figure comes from a tomb.

Saladin (left) was a famous Muslim general. He fought the armies of the third Crusade and took back many cities from the Christians.

Sometimes the Crusaders had to attack cities or castles with strong walls around them. They would use catapults and battering rams to break down the doors. They built tall towers so they could fire arrows into the enemy and climb over the walls.

Right: Make your own crystals. Dissolve some sugar in a little water, then pour it into a saucer and leave it (top). As the water evaporates, sugar crystals will form (centre). Use salt or borax to grow a perfect crystal (bottom). Stir into hot water. If you hang a thread in the liquid, crystals will form on the end of it as the water evaporates.

Above left: Six-pointed snowflake crystals. No two are alike. Above: Crystals of calcite. A clump such as this one can grow to a huge size.

Crystal

If you look closely at sugar through a magnifying glass, you will see that it is made up of thousands of tiny glassy pieces with flat sides. They are sugar crystals. Snow is made up of tiny crystals of frozen water. So are the beautiful patterns on a frosty window. Some crystals are so small they can be seen only through a microscope. Others can sometimes be as big as a man.

All crystals have a definite shape. They have smooth, flat sides that meet in sharp edges. The shape of any one type of crystal never changes, but there are many different crystal shapes. The differences between them are caused by the ATOMS in the crystals arranging themselves in different ways.

For example, the salt you eat is made up of two different kinds of atoms—sodium atoms and chlorine atoms. The tiny sodium and chlorine atoms are arranged in cube patterns. If you look at salt grains through a magnifying glass, you will see that most of them are little cubes. All salt crystals are built in the same way.

Cuba

Cuba is an island in the Caribbean Sea. It is part of the WEST INDIES. Cuba has 10,346,000 people and covers an area of 114,524 square km. The capital city of Cuba is Havana.

Part of the island is hilly, with high mountains in the south-east. In the centre are large cedar and mahogany forests. Cuba has big sugar-cane plantations and tobacco farms.

The climate is warm and pleasant, but Cuba lies in the path of hurricanes which blow through the West Indies every year. Hurricanes are very strong winds which can cause much damage.

Cuba was ruled by Spain after Christopher COLUMBUS went there in 1492. The United States took Cuba from Spain in 1898. In 1902 the island became independent. Cuba became a communist country in 1959 under its leader Fidel Castro.

Cube

A cube is an object with six square sides. All the edges are the same length. Sugar and ice are often made in cubes.

The space a cube fills is called its volume. You can find the volume of a cube by multiplying the length of a side by itself and then by itself again. If the length of a side is 3 centimetres, the volume of the cube is $3 \times 3 \times 3 = 27$ cubic centimetres.

Many kinds of CRYSTAL have a cube shape. This is because of the way their ATOMS are arranged.

Curie, Marie and Pierre

Marie Curie (1867–1934) and Pierre Curie (1859–1906) were scientists who studied RADIOACTIVITY and discovered the elements

The discoveries of the Curies were very important for medicine and science. In honour of their work, the unit for measuring levels of radioactivity was called the curie.

radium and polonium. They were married in 1895.

Because of their work on radioactivity and their discovery of radium in 1898, they were given the NOBEL PRIZE for physics in 1903. When Pierre was killed three years later, Marie took over his job as professor at the Sorbonne University in Paris. In 1911 she was given a second Nobel Prize, this time for chemistry.

Czechoslovakia

Czechoslovakia is a country in eastern EUROPE. It is surrounded by Germany, Poland, Russia, Hungary, and Austria. The country has 15,556,000 people and covers an area of 127,869 square km. (See map on page 123.)

Much of Czechoslovakia is covered in hills and mountains. Many of the people are farmers. Czechoslovakia also has coal and iron and an important steel industry.

The capital of Czechoslovakia is Prague. It is a medieval town, filled with churches and old buildings. Most of the people speak either Czech or Slovak, the two main languages of the country. The government has been communist since 1948.

Dam

Dams are walls built across rivers to hold back water. They are used for irrigation, to make electricity, or to provide water for towns. Dams are particularly useful in places where there is not much rain. They store the rainwater in large lakes and release it steadily over the whole year. Some dams are made of enormous quantities of earth and rock. Others are made of concrete and stone. Occasionally dams burst, causing severe flooding and disaster.

Dance

All through the ages dance has been important to people. Early prehistoric cave paintings show men dancing. Archaeologists think that the earliest dances were about the hunt. Men used to dress up as animals and make rhythmical movements. They believed this would attract the animals they needed for food and fur. These ancient ritual dances eventually developed into religious ceremonies. People danced to please their gods. They asked them for rain or for a good harvest. Sometimes they asked for success in the hunt or in battle. Dances like these still exist in many parts of the world.

In the Western world the religious meaning of dances disappeared many years ago. Today people dance only for pleasure or entertainment. In the 1920s and 1930s there were hundreds of dance halls. Dances like the foxtrot, quickstep, and waltz were popular. Some people still enjoy ballroom dancing, and it is popular at formal dances. But young people today prefer a freer form of dance. At dance clubs where rock music

There are different kinds of dams. A gravity dam (1) is a huge concrete or stone wall strong enough to hold back a great weight of water. Arch dams (2) are curved and are built across narrow canyons. Buttress dams (3) are strengthened by buttress supports. Embankment dams (4) are made by heaping earth and rock into a triangular shape.

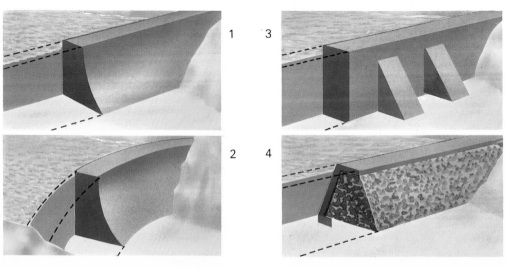

is played, dancers make up the steps as they go along.

Another kind of dance is the traditional folkdance. Most countries have their own typical dances, such as the flamenco, Spain's best-known traditional dance.

Classical BALLET, another major dance form, obeys certain rules of posture and motion. Many ballets are pieces of drama set to music, such as *Swan Lake* and *The Sleeping Beauty*. To become successful, a ballet dancer needs years of training.

People the world over have always danced. We have learned about ancient Egyptian and Greek dancing (1 and 2) from carvings on tombs and vase-paintings. The graceful minuet (3) was popular in the 1600s, while classical ballet reached its peak under Louis XIV of France (4). The dancers of Bali are famous for their graceful movements (5). Fred Astaire put ballet steps into his dancing (6).

In Africa, people keep alive the dances of the distant past. Many of these dances are a part of magic or religion. Today, African dancing is a popular form of entertainment.

Darwin, Charles

Charles Darwin (1809–1882) was an English biologist. In 1859 he published his great book, *On the Origin of Species.* Before this almost everyone believed that the world was created by God exactly as the Bible described. Darwin put forward the theory that all living things had evolved from earlier forms. They were alive because they had won the struggle to survive.

Darwin argued that within any species of living thing there would be small variations in shape, size or habit. Some of these variations would increase the living thing's chance of survival. For example, a giraffe with a long neck could reach leaves that a giraffe with a shorter neck could not. In times of famine, the taller giraffe would survive while the shorter one would die. The taller giraffe would, in time, replace the variety with the shorter neck.

This theory outraged many people. They thought it was against the teachings of the Bible. But today most people accept Darwin's theory. And many churches have decided that it does not conflict with their teachings or threaten religious beliefs.

Deer

Deer belong to the cow and antelope family. They are different from their relatives because they have antlers rather than permanent horns. Male deer grow new antlers every year. Female deer, except for reindeer, do not grow antlers. Deer are mainly found in the Northern Hemisphere.

Every year in early spring, a lot of blood starts to flow into two bony lumps on the male deer's forehead. The blood carries a bony substance that makes the antlers grow quite rapidly. At first they are covered with a soft, hairy skin known as velvet. In early summer the antlers are full grown. The blood supply is then cut off and the velvet dies. The male deer rubs off the velvet until his antlers are hard and shiny. Some antlers can be very big. One red deer's antlers have weighed as much as 35 kg. A moose's antlers have measured 2 metres.

At the age of 22, Darwin went on a five-year voyage on the Beagle to the South Atlantic and the Pacific. During the voyage he studied thousands of plants and animals and developed his theory of the survival of the fittest. The map shows the route followed by the Beagle, and Darwin's journeys into South America.

Male (right) and female red deer

Sharp ears

Keen sense of smell

Long neck helps the deer reach tasty leaves and shoots

The stag has six points on its antlers which shows he is full grown. He is called a royal stag

Mane grows long in the mating deason

Deer vary enormously in size. The biggest is the Alaskan moose, which stands up to 2.3 metres at the shoulder and weighs over 800 kg. The smallest is the pudu of Chile, which can measure as little as 33 cm at the shoulder and weigh as little as 8 kg.

Deer have provided people with meat and hides since earliest times. But they also damage the bark of trees. They are naturally wild animals but some of them, such as REINDEER, have been successfully domesticated.

Democracy

Democracy is a type of government that is organized by the people and for the people. In a democracy people elect their own government. Representatives of different political parties run for election and people vote for the one they prefer. The people can also dismiss their government if they want to. In a democracy people can say and read what they like. They cannot be put into prison without a fair trial.

There are many different kinds of democracy. The British form is a monarchy with an elected parliament. The American form is a republic with an elected president and an elected congress. There is no one perfect democracy in the world. But all free nations are trying to work toward a perfect democracy.

'Democracy' comes from a Greek word meaning 'rule of the people'. Pericles of Athens was a great democratic leader who lived in the 400s BC. He allowed the common people to hold any of the state posts. During Pericles' rule Athens reached the height of its fame.

Denmark

Denmark is a small Scandinavian country in the north of EUROPE. (See map on page 123.) It consists mainly of a peninsula called Jutland surrounded by 600 islands. To the south is West Germany. The capital is Copenhagen. Denmark is a flat country whose soil and climate are ideal for agriculture. Dairy and pig farming are especially important. Denmark is a member of the EUROPEAN ECONOMIC COMMUNITY. It exports a lot of butter and bacon. The Danes also make and export beer. There is little heavy industry. The Danes prefer to concentrate on high-quality goods such as china, furniture, and textiles.

The sculpture in Copenhagen Harbour is called the Little Mermaid after the fairy tale by Hans Christian Andersen.

Desert

Not all deserts are hot and sandy. Some are cold, and some are rocky. But all are very dry. Some scientists say that a desert is any area where less than 8cm of rain falls in a year. Other scientists call a place a desert when there is more rain than this but where it evaporates quickly in the sun or sinks rapidly into the ground.

Many big deserts are in the tropics, often inland on large continents where rainbearing winds cannot reach them.

There are three main types of desert. The first is rocky, where any soil is blown away by the wind. The second has large areas of gravel. The third is made up of great sand dunes, burning hot by day and bitterly cold at night.

It is difficult for plants and animals to live in such conditions. Some plants, like the CACTUS, store moisture in their fleshy stems. Others have seeds that lie apparently lifeless in the ground for long periods. When a shower of rain falls they burst into life and can flower and produce new seeds within weeks. Many desert animals shelter from the sun by day and come out only at night. Some never drink, but get all the moisture they need from their food.

The world's largest desert is the SAHARA in Africa. The driest desert is the Atacama in South America, where it may not rain for several years. There are also cold deserts. These include Antarctica and a large part of the Arctic.

Detergent

The word *detergent* means any substance that will clean things. SOAP is a detergent. But today the word detergent usually means synthetic, or man-made, detergents such as most laundry powders. Detergents are similar to soaps. But soaps leave filmy deposits behind, such as the familiar bathtub ring. Detergents can reach soiled areas better than soaps and do not leave deposits.

Diamond

Diamonds are CRYSTALS. They are harder than anything else in the world. They are formed by great heat and pressure deep beneath the surface of the earth. Diamonds are made of pure CARBON, the same mineral that is found in ordinary coal. They are usually colourless and have to be cut in a

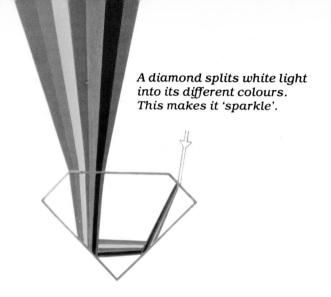

A diamond splits white light into its different colours. This makes it 'sparkle'.

Dictionary

A dictionary is a book that tells us what words mean. The words are arranged in alphabetical order from A to Z. Often the meanings, or definitions, include the history of the words and how they are used and pronounced. Dictionaries may vary in size from many volumes to dictionaries small enough to slip into your pocket. Dr Samuel Johnson was one of the greatest English dictionary makers.

Diesel Engine

Diesel engines are a type of INTERNAL-COMBUSTION ENGINE where fuel is burned inside the engine. Diesel engines are named after

Inside a diesel engine: (1) Air enters the cylinder. It is squeezed (2) until it is hot enough to burn the fuel (3), which pushes the piston down. The used-up gases are pushed out (4).

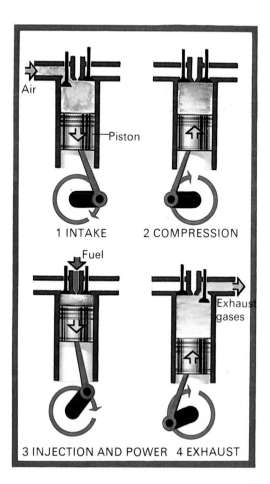

special way to catch the light and 'sparkle'. A diamond cutter is very skilled and uses tools tipped with diamonds, for only another diamond is hard enough to cut a diamond. Diamonds are used in industry for drilling and cutting.

Dickens, Charles

Charles Dickens (1812–1870) was a great English writer. His books give us a vivid picture of life in Victorian England in the middle 1800s. Many of his stories are about children, especially poor children and orphans. Dickens tried to improve the lives of the poor by making their suffering more widely known through his books. He also created some of the liveliest and best-known characters in English literature. Some of his most famous books are *Oliver Twist, David Copperfield, Great Expectations* and *A Christmas Carol.*

Dictator

A dictator is the leader of a country who rules with absolute power and authority. In ancient Rome a dictator was a magistrate who was given absolute power to deal with emergencies, when decisions had to be made quickly. Today the term is used to describe a tyrant who takes away people's rights and freedoms and rules by force. Often those who try to oppose a dictator are killed, imprisoned or forced to leave the country until such time as the dictator is overthrown.

their inventor, Rudolf Diesel, who built his first successful engine in 1897 to replace the steam engine. Diesel engines use a cruder, heavier fuel oil than petrol. They are cheaper to run than petrol engines, but they are heavier and more difficult to start, so they are not widely used in cars. They are more often used to drive heavy machines such as trains, tractors, ships, buses and trucks. A properly-working diesel causes less pollution than a petrol engine.

A diesel engine is similar to a petrol engine. But instead of using a spark from a spark plug to ignite the fuel, the diesel engine uses heat that is made by squeezing air in a cylinder. When air is very tightly compressed, or pushed, into a much smaller space than it filled before, it gets very hot. This heat sets fire to the diesel oil, which burns instantly, like a small explosion. The burning oil heats the air and forces it to expand again to push the piston and thus drive the engine.

Many RAILWAYS began using diesel engines after World War II. Railways badly damaged in the war took the opportunity to modernize their engines and replaced the old steam LOCOMOTIVES with diesel engines. Diesel engines were first used regularly on the railways of the United States in the 1930s. Today, diesel-electric engines are in use all over the world.

Digestion

Digestion is the way in which the food we eat is broken down into substances that can be used by the body. It takes place in the digestive tract, or *alimentary canal*, a long tube that runs from the mouth to the anus. Digestion starts in the mouth, where the teeth and special chemicals in the saliva help to break down the food. The food then passes down a tube called the *oesophagus*. Muscles in the oesophagus push and squeeze the food down into the STOMACH. There, acids and more chemicals help to turn the food into a creamy liquid. Then a muscle at the lower end of the stomach

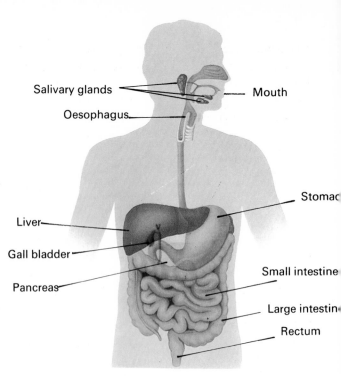

The human digestive tract.

opens from time to time to release food into the small intestine.

Inside the small intestine, bile from the LIVER and juice from the pancreas help to break down the food still further. Much of it passes through the thin walls of the intestine into the bloodstream. The remainder goes into the large intestine. There, liquids and salts are absorbed until only solid waste material is left. Bacteria in the large intestine digest any remaining food products. The final waste product is passed out of the body as *faeces*.

Dinosaur

The word *dinosaur* means 'terrible lizard'. These creatures lived between 65 and 225 million years ago. They developed from primitive REPTILES. Dinosaurs included some of the largest and most ferocious animals ever to live on earth.

There were two main groups of dinosaurs, the *saurischians* and the *ornithischians*. The ornithischian dinosaurs were all plant-eaters and most of them went around on all fours. Some of these, like

Stegosaurus and *Triceratops*, were large and lumbering but had bony armour and horns to protect them from the teeth and claws of the great meat-eating dinosaurs.

The second of the two main groups, the saurischians, contained both plant-eaters and meat-eaters. The plant-eaters included the largest dinosaurs, the biggest of which was *Brachiosaurus*. This huge creature was 24 metres long and weighed about 50 tonnes. *Brachiosaurus* had a long neck, a tiny head, a long tapering tail, and a thick body. *Brachiosaurus* and other similar dinosaurs such as *Apatosaurus (Brontosaurus)* and *Diplodocus*, ate the leaves at the top of trees.

Perhaps the most famous of the saurischian dinosaurs are the great carnivores, or meat-eaters. *Tyrannosaurus*, which was up to 14 metres from snout to tail, stood on its hind legs. Its forward-pointing toes bore claws as long as carving knives. Sabrelike

teeth—some nearly the length of a man's hand—lined the jaws. No flesh-eating beasts that ever lived on land were larger or more menacing than these monsters.

Disease

Diseases make us ill. Some are caused by bacteria, or germs, that invade our bodies. Others are caused by VIRUSES. Some diseases are passed down from parents to children in the genes they are born with.

The body resists diseases through its *immune system*. Special cells, such as white blood cells, fight the invading organisms. The body also produces antibodies to fight disease. Antibodies produced to fight

Tyrannosaurus, *the giant of the dinosaur carnivores,* **tears out the throat of a** Corythosaurus.

diseases such as measles or chickenpox stay in our systems and usually prevent us from having the disease again.

Doctors treat diseases with DRUGS, vaccines and INOCULATION.

Disney, Walt

Walt Disney (1901–1967) was an American film maker best known for his cartoons and films for children. Disney characters, especially Mickey Mouse and Donald Duck, are famous all over the world. Walt Disney began his work in the 1920s. His cartoon

Above: Walt Disney and his famous creation, Mickey Mouse, at Disneyland in Anaheim, California.

artists, or animators, produced characters and settings that moved realistically. Full-length cartoon features such as *Snow White and the Seven Dwarfs, Pinocchio* and *Bambi* are still popular everywhere.

Distillation

If a liquid is boiled, it becomes a gas, or *vapour*. If vapour is cooled, it condenses, and becomes a liquid again. If boiling and condensing take place in one piece of apparatus, the process is called *distillation*. Distillation has been used for centuries to make alcoholic beverages such as whisky, perfumes, flavourings, and to purify water.

Diving

People have been diving underwater for thousands of years. The first divers just

held their breath. This meant they could make only short, shallow dives.

Modern inventions allow divers to dive deeper and stay down longer. Scuba divers carry their own air supply with them. They wear rubber flippers and they can swim

Below: The bathyscaphe was developed by Auguste and Jacques Piccard to explore the seabed. Bottom: A diver helps raise the anchor of a sunken ship from the bottom of the sea.

freely. Helmeted divers breathe air pumped down through a tube. Heavy weights allow them to work on the seabed without bobbing up. All divers see through glass face masks and wear special suits to stay warm. Today's divers can study water life, build harbours and find sunken treasure.

Dog

People have been keeping dogs for perhaps 10,000 years. Most dogs are kept as pets, but some do useful work such as herding sheep or guarding buildings.

The first dog was probably descended from a WOLF and looked a lot like a wolf. Today there are more than 100 breeds of dog of many colours, shapes and sizes. The St Bernard is the largest breed. A St Bernard may weigh nearly twice as much as a man. The Yorkshire terrier is one of the smallest dogs. A full-grown Yorkshire terrier may weigh less than a small jar of jam.

Most of the breeds shown here were developed to be good at certain kinds of work. Airedales and some other kinds of terriers make fine rat hunters. Labrador retrievers bring back ducks shot by hunters. Collies round up sheep. Dachshunds were used for hunting badgers. Dobermans are ferocious guard dogs.

All puppies are born blind and helpless and at first feed only on their mother's milk. But small dogs are fully grown in a year or so. Most kinds of dog live for about 12 years.

Doll

Children play with dolls all over the world. Dolls may be made of wood, china, plastic or many other substances. The very first doll may have just been a forked twig that looked a bit like a human being. Homemade dolls can cost nothing. But doll collectors will pay a lot of money for rare old dolls.

Dolphin

Dolphins are small, toothed WHALES, with a long snout rather like a beak. The largest dolphins are twice as long as a man and five times as heavy. Most kinds live in the sea,

English setter   Cocker spaniel

Beagle

Three of the many breeds of dog that have been developed from the wolf over many thousands of years. This shows how the characteristics of a species can be changed by selecting which individuals breed together.

Below: Common dolphins can swim at a speed of 40km an hour. They are among the fastest animals in the sea.

Dolphins are sociable and playful mammals and really seem to enjoy leaping out of the water like this.

but two kinds live in rivers. Dolphins swim in groups called schools. They signal to each other by making whistling sounds.

Dolphins are playful and intelligent. Tame dolphins can learn many tricks. They will jump through hoops and snatch fish from a trainer's mouth. Dolphins can also learn to 'walk' across water on their tails.

Dragon

Dragons are storybook monsters, but once many people believed that they really lived. Artists showed them as huge snakes or lizards with wings of skin and terrifying claws. They were supposed to breathe fire and swallow people and animals whole.

Fighting dragons called for great bravery. Legends tell how Hercules, St George and other heroes killed these evil monsters.

Not everyone thought dragons were wicked. The Chinese looked upon the creatures as gods.

Dragonflies

These insects hatch from eggs laid in pools and rivers. The young are called nymphs. Dragonfly nymphs live in water for up to five years. Meanwhile they may shed their skin 11 times. At last they crawl out of the water, grow wings, and fly away.

Drake, Francis

Sir Francis Drake (about 1540–1596) was a sea captain who helped to make England a great sea power. In the 1570s he led sea raids against Spanish ships and ports in the Caribbean Sea. He also became the first Englishman to sail around the world. In 1588 he helped to destroy the Spanish Armada.

Many Spaniards thought Sir Francis Drake had a magic mirror in his ship's cabin which helped him to find Spanish treasure convoys.

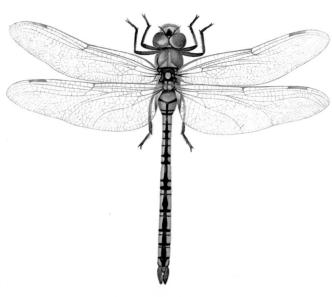

The male emperor dragonfly is 105mm long with a bright blue abdomen.

The Meeting of Jacob and Laban, *a pen-and-wash drawing by Rembrandt.*

cluded drawings in their best work. Some drawings are very precise and realistic. Every detail is picked out. In others, such as the drawing by REMBRANDT on the left, a powerful effect is produced by using very few lines and little detail. LEONARDO DA VINCI made scientific drawings and sketches for his paintings. Other painters who were also draftsmen include Pieter Bruegel (the Elder), Paul Cézanne and Pablo PICASSO.

Drawing

Drawings are pictures or designs usually made in line with pencil, pen or some similar material other than paint.

Drawing has been a natural human activity since prehistoric times, when people began to express their thoughts and ideas on the stone of cave walls. All children draw naturally. Many famous artists have in-

Dream

Dreams occur when our brains are active while we are asleep. Some dreams are of everyday occurrences. Others may be just a series of jumbled images. We may or may not remember what we have dreamed on

Our dreams often contain strange images mixed up together, as in this painting by Salvador Dali, Apparition of a face and fruit dish on a beach.

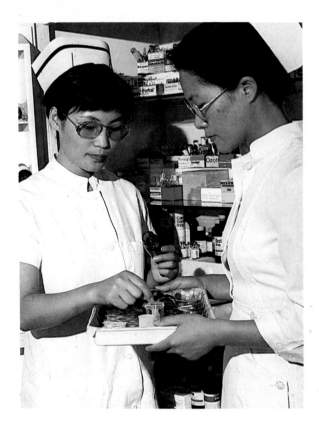

Left: Hospitals use a wide range of drugs to control and cure disease.

people need drugs containing VITAMINS or other substances their bodies must have.

Certain drugs come from plants or animals. For instance, the foxglove gives us a drug called digitalis. This makes weak hearts beat more strongly. Many other drugs are made from MINERALS.

Some people take drugs such as cocaine, cannabis or alcohol just because these give a pleasant feeling. Some of these drugs can cause illness and even death.

Drum

Drums are the most important of those MUSICAL INSTRUMENTS that are played by being struck. The sound is made by hitting a tightly stretched sheet of skin or plastic called a drumhead. A kettledrum has one drumhead stretched over a metal basin. A bass drum or a side drum has two drumheads, one across each end of a large open 'can'.

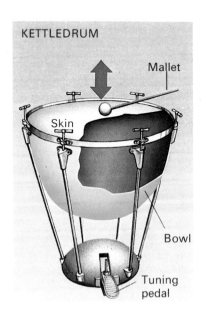

The drumhead of a kettledrum is stretched tightly over a deep bowl. It is tuned by loosening or tightening the skin with a foot pedal.

waking. A frightening dream is called a nightmare.

We do not know exactly why people dream. Dreams may be sparked off by indigestion or similar physical cause, such as a cramped sleeping position. External noises may also cause dreams. Some dreams are very common. These include dreams of falling, of being chased, of lakes or water.

People have always been fascinated by dreams. The greatest studies of dreams have been made by Alfred Adler, C. J. Jung and Sigmund Freud in their investigation into how our minds work.

Drug

Drugs are chemicals that affect the way the body works. Doctors give drugs to patients to help them fight disease. Antibiotics attack certain kinds of germs. These drugs help to cure people suffering from pneumonia and other illnesses. Drugs like aspirin help to deaden pain. The strongest painkillers are called anaesthetics. Some

Goldeneye   Tufted duck   Teal

Duck

These web-footed water birds are related to swans and geese. Ducks look rather like small geese with short necks.

The two main groups of ducks are dabbling ducks and diving ducks. Dabbling ducks feed at the surface of the water. They may put most of their body under the water, but they do not dive. Dabbling ducks include the mallards that swim on pools and rivers in the northern half of the world. (Farmyard ducks were bred from mallards.) Other dabbling ducks include teal and widgeon, and the pretty mandarin and Carolina ducks.

Diving ducks dive completely under water in their hunt for food. Most diving ducks live out at sea. These ducks include the eider duck from which we get eiderdown. Sawbills are also diving ducks. Their long, slim beaks have inside edges like the teeth of a saw. Sawbills are good at grasping fish. The longtailed duck is a diving duck that can fly at 110km/hr.

Three pairs of ducks of different kinds. The drakes (males) have brighter feathers than the ducks (females). Tufted ducks and goldeneyes are diving ducks. Teal are small dabbling ducks.

Dye

Dyes are substances that people use to colour TEXTILES and other materials. Some dyes come from plants. People used to obtain cochineal, a red dye, from the cochineal insect. Most dyes are made from chemicals. To dye an object you dip it in water containing dissolved dye. If the dye is *fast* the object will keep its dyed colour however much you wash it.

Topside of drake

Underside of duck

Strong wing feathers for flying

Preen gland

Webbed feet for paddling

A pair of mallards on land and in the air. In water they kick their webbed feet backward to swim forward.

Eagle

Eagles are large birds of prey. Most hunt small mammals and birds. Some catch fish or reptiles. The harpy eagle and the monkey-eating eagle catch monkeys. Each of these great birds measures more than 2 metres across its outspread wings. These eagles are the largest in the world.

Many eagles soar high above the ground. Others perch on a tree or rock. When an eagle sees its prey it swoops suddenly and pounces. It seizes its prey with its sharp claws and tears off pieces of flesh with its strong, hooked beak.

The bald eagle (below left) has a white head but is not really bald. This bird is the national emblem of the United States. It hunts fish in rivers, lakes and along the coast. The golden eagle (right) lives among mountains in northern lands. It hunts rabbits, hares and grouse.

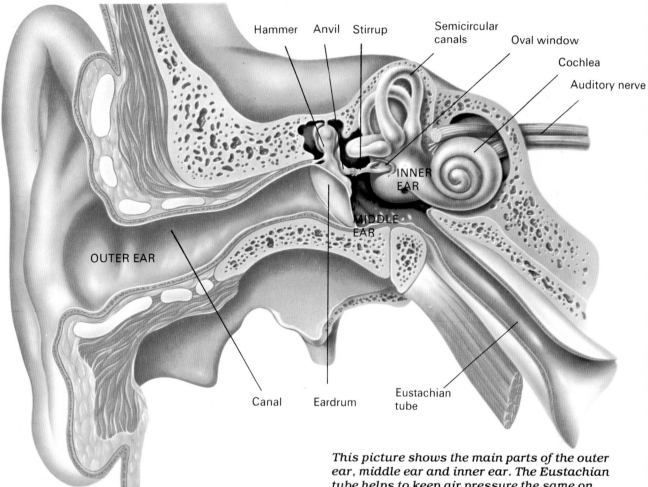

Hammer Anvil Stirrup Semicircular canals Oval window Cochlea Auditory nerve

INNER EAR

MIDDLE EAR

OUTER EAR

Canal Eardrum Eustachian tube

This picture shows the main parts of the outer ear, middle ear and inner ear. The Eustachian tube helps to keep air pressure the same on both sides of the eardrum.

Ear

Our ears help us to hear and to keep our balance. Each ear has three main parts. These are the outer ear, middle ear and inner ear.

The outer ear is the part we can see, along with the tube leading from it into the head. Sounds reach the outer ear as vibrations, or waves, in the air. The cuplike shape of the ear collects these sound waves and sends them into the tube.

Next, the sound waves reach the middle ear. Here, the waves make the eardrum move to and fro. The eardrum is a thin 'skin' across the entrance of the middle ear. The moving eardrum makes tiny bones vibrate in the middle ear.

The vibrations travel into the inner ear, where they set a liquid moving in the *cochlea.* This looks like a snail's shell. The nerves inside it turn vibrations into messages that travel to your brain. The inner ear also has three hollow loops containing liquid. These loops send signals to the brain to help you keep your balance. If you spin around and then stop, the liquid inside the loops swirls for a while. This confuses your brain and makes you feel dizzy.

Ears are delicate and easily damaged. Hitting or poking into an ear could cause an injury leading to deafness.

Earth, the

Our earth is the fifth largest of the PLANETS that move around the SUN. Seen from space the earth looks like a giant ball. Land and WATER cover the surface, and AIR surrounds the earth. The earth has three main layers.

The top layer is a thin crust of hard rock. The crust floats on a thicker layer of rock called the mantle. This is so hot that its rocks are at least partly melted. Below the mantle lies the core. Much of this is made of iron so hot that it is liquid.

All living things live on and just above the crust. (GEOLOGY tells us much about past life on earth.) Earth is the only planet in the SOLAR SYSTEM to have living things on it. Other planets are too hot or cold or are surrounded by poisonous gases.

The earth spins as it speeds through space. It takes a day and night to spin around once, and a year to travel around the sun. The earth spins in a tilted position. This causes the different seasons of the year.

Earthquake

People often use the saying 'safe as houses'. But in certain parts of the world houses sometimes topple over because the ground starts trembling. This trembling is called an earthquake. About half a million earthquakes happen every year. Most are so

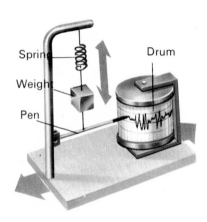

A seismograph records an earthquake's shock waves. It tells scientists how severe the earthquake is.

weak that only special instruments called *seismographs* show that they have happened. Only one earthquake in 500 does any damage. But some earthquakes can cause terrible damage and suffering. Three-quarters of a million people are thought to have died when an earthquake hit the Chinese city of Tangshan in 1976.

Small tremors can happen when VOLCANOES erupt, when there is a landslide, or when the roof of an underground cave falls

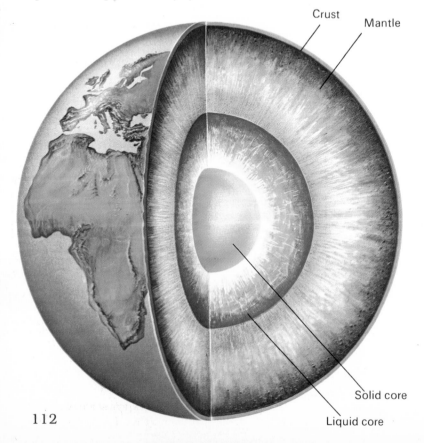

Crust

Mantle

A picture of the earth cut open to show its crust and inner layers. Most of the outer core is made of iron and nickel so hot that they are liquid. The inner core is even hotter. But the great weight of the rest of the earth pressing on it makes it solid.

Solid core

Liquid core

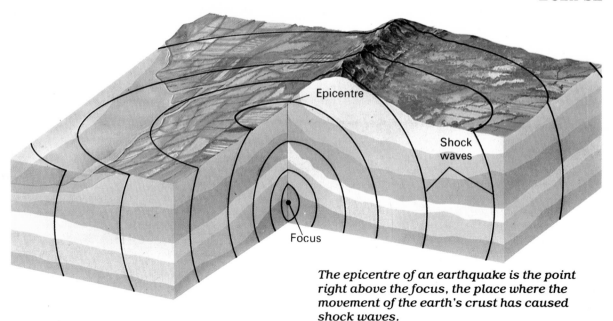

The epicentre of an earthquake is the point right above the focus, the place where the movement of the earth's crust has caused shock waves.

in. The largest earthquakes occur when one huge piece of the earth's crust slips suddenly against another piece. This slipping may take place deep underground. But the shock travels up through the crust and sets the surface quaking.

A seabed earthquake may set off a huge ocean wave called a tsunami or tidal wave. These can rise higher than a house and travel faster than the fastest train.

This diagram shows a solar eclipse caused as the moon's shadow falls on the earth, and a lunar eclipse as the earth's shadow falls on the moon. Only the umbra — *the dark middle part of each shadow — is shown.*

Easter

Easter is the day when Christians remember the resurrection of JESUS. Most Christians celebrate this on Easter Sunday. This is the Sunday following the first full moon after the first day of spring in the northern half of the world.

Eclipse

An eclipse happens when the shadow of one planet or moon falls on another. If the shadow hides all of the planet or moon then that is called a total eclipse. If the shadow hides only a part it is called a partial eclipse.

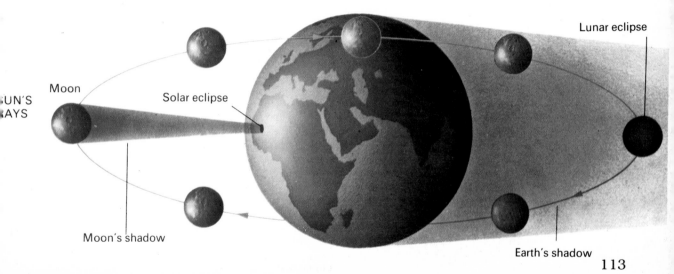

The only eclipses you can easily see without a telescope take place when the sun, moon and earth are in line. When the earth lies between the sun and the moon, the earth's shadow falls on the moon. This is an eclipse of the moon. When the moon lies between the earth and the sun, the moon's shadow falls on a part of the earth. An eclipse of the sun, or solar eclipse, can be seen from that part. Two or three of each kind of eclipse happen every year.

Ecology

Ecology is the study of living things and their surroundings. Scientists called ecologists try to find out how living things and their surroundings affect each other. Ecology shows us that most plants and animals can live only in a special set of surroundings such as a pond, field, forest or desert. In each place live plants that are suited to a certain soil, temperature and so on. All the animals living there eat the plants or one another. So the plants and animals are linked in what ecologists call a food chain. If some kinds die out, those that eat them lose their food and may die, too.

Every animal eats or is eaten by other living things. The picture shows some of the animals that may be involved in a community. The usual food eaten is shown by a solid line.

Edison, Thomas

Thomas Alva Edison (1847–1931) was an American inventor. As a boy he spent only three months at school, and his teacher thought that he was stupid. But he went on to produce more than 1000 inventions. The most famous were the electric light and the phonograph.

Edward (kings)

Nine kings of England were called Edward. Edward 'The Confessor' (about 1002–1066) founded Westminster Abbey. Edward I (1239–1307) brought Wales under English rule. Edward II (1248–1327) was the first English Prince of Wales. Edward III (1312–1337) began the Hundred Years' War. Edward IV (1442–1483) took the crown from Henry VI in the Wars of the Roses. Edward V (1470–1483) was murdered in the Tower of London. Edward VI (1537–1553) reigned as a boy king for only six years. Edward VII (1841–1910) was Prince of Wales for 60 years. Edward VIII (1894–1972) gave up the throne or *abdicated* so that he could marry Mrs Simpson, a divorced American.

Occasional food is shown by a dotted line. Plant-eaters eat plants. Some small mammals, birds and insects eat fruits and seeds. And all these creatures are preyed on by larger animals.

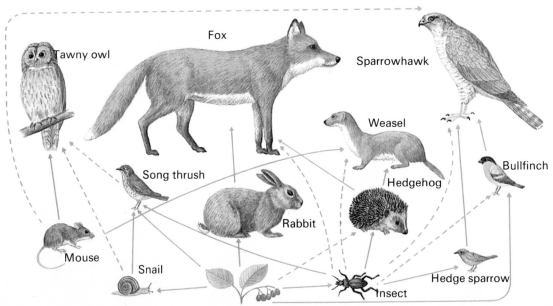

Tawny owl
Fox
Sparrowhawk
Weasel
Bullfinch
Song thrush
Hedgehog
Rabbit
Mouse
Snail
Hedge sparrow
Insect

Egypt

About 5000 years ago the Egyptians began to build one of the world's first great civilizations. For the next 2500 years, ancient Egypt was one of the strongest, richest nations on earth.

The people who made Egypt great were short, slim, dark-skinned men and women with black hair. They probably numbered no more than six million. Scarcely any of them lived in the hot sand and rock deserts that cover most of Egypt. Almost all the people settled by the river NILE which runs from south to north across the land.

Each year the river overflowed and left rich mud on nearby fields. Farmers learned to dig and plough the fields. They could grow two crops a year in the warm, fertile soil. The farmers grew more than enough grain, fruit and vegetables to feed themselves. The rest of the food helped to feed Egyptian craftsmen, miners, merchants, priests, noble families and the PHARAOHS who ruled over the entire land.

Most Egyptians were poor and lived in mud-brick huts with palm-leaf roofs. Rich Egyptians lived in large, well-furnished houses and had meat and cakes to eat. They wore fine clothes and jewels.

The most splendid buildings in the land were tombs and temples. Thousands of

Below: A scene showing how the ancient Egyptians lived by the Nile. They grew flax to make linen, and corn and barley for food. They also caught birds and fish, raised chickens and grew produce in their gardens. In the foreground, women are winnowing. Part of all produce was paid in taxes to the government.

workers toiled for years to build the mighty PYRAMIDS. In each such tomb, Egyptians would place the *mummy* (specially preserved body) of a pharaoh. They believed the dead went on living. So they buried food and furniture beside each mummy. Thieves later emptied almost all the tombs. Tutankhamun (1370–1352 BC) became pharaoh when he was just a boy. His tomb was discovered in Thebes, Upper Egypt. It tells us a lot about what royal burials were like.

The dry Egyptian air has preserved HIEROGLYPHICS written on fragile paper made from the papyrus plant. Paintings and hieroglyphics tell us a great deal about how the ancient Egyptians lived. The ancient Egyptians also left many fine statues. They may also have invented glass. They had a calendar, and they developed basic mathematics.

In time, foreign armies using iron weapons defeated the Egyptians. Their land fell under foreign rule after 525 BC.

Modern Egypt dates from AD 642 when Egypt was conquered by Muslim soldiers from Arabia. Egypt is now a Muslim, mainly Arab, country. It has about 48 million people, more than any other nation in Africa. No other African city is as large as Cairo, Egypt's capital. But Egyptians still depend upon the waters of the river that made old Egypt great.

Egypt is mainly an agricultural country. People raise cotton, wheat, barley, citrus fruits, dates and sugar cane. But industry is growing. The Aswan Dam irrigates thousands of hectares of land.

Einstein, Albert

Albert Einstein (1879–1955) was a great scientist who was born in Germany and became an American citizen. His theory of relativity was a new way of looking at time, space, matter and ENERGY. Einstein showed that a small amount of matter could produce a vast amount of energy. This made it possible for people to use ATOMIC ENERGY.

The Egyptian pyramids are tombs which housed the bodies of the pharaohs. As well as the huge pyramids of the kings, there are smaller ones for the pharaohs' wives.

Albert Einstein was one of the greatest scientists of all time. He was awarded the 1921 Nobel Prize for Physics. This was for work on theories that he had written about in papers published in 1905.

Electricity

Electricity heats and lights our homes. It is the kind of ENERGY that powers electric trains, vacuum cleaners, radios, televisions and many more devices.

The electricity that we use flows through wires as electric current. Current flows when tiny particles called electrons jump between the ATOMS that make up the metal in the wire. Current can flow only if a wire makes a complete loop called a circuit. If a gap is made in the circuit, the current stops flowing. Switches are simply devices that open and close gaps in circuits.

Batteries produce electric current that can be used to start cars, light torch bulbs and work radios. But most of the electricity we use is produced in power stations. In a power station generator, coils of wire are made to rotate between powerful magnets. This makes electric current flow through the coils of wire. This current then flows through other long wires to our homes.

Electricity flows easily only through metals such as copper. This is because the electrons on the outer part of the metal atoms are free to move. When there is electrical pressure in the wire, the electrons drift from one atom to the next. This makes an electric current flow along the wire. To make a bulb in a room light up, about two trillion (2, with 18 zeros) electrons flow every second.

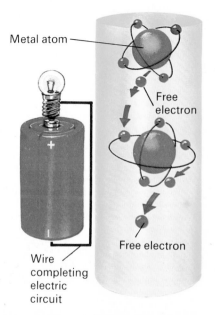

Metal atom

Free electron

Free electron

Wire completing electric circuit

Electronics

Electronics is an important part of the study of ELECTRICITY. It deals with the way in which tiny particles called electrons flow through certain CRYSTALS, gases or a VACUUM. Electronic devices like TRANSISTORS and SILICON CHIPS are used in such things as COMPUTERS, RADAR, TELEVISIONS and RADIOS. Electronics helps us to see the smallest living thing, to guide planes and to do difficult calculations instantly.

Above: The Space Shuttle's cabin is a mass of computerized electronics.

Below: Arcade games need electronics to achieve their special effects.

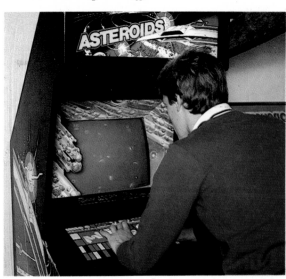

117

Elements

Your own body and everything you see around you is composed (made up) of chemical ingredients called elements. In each element all the ATOMS are of the same kind. You can join different elements to make more complicated substances called compounds. But you cannot break an element into simpler kinds of elements.

Chemists have found more than 100 different elements. Ninety-four of these occur naturally. Scientists have produced other elements in laboratories. At ordinary temperatures, some elements are gases, some are liquids and some are solids.

OXYGEN is the most plentiful element on earth. Half of the earth's crust and most of your body is made of oxygen.

Elements are each given a symbol. For instance, hydrogen is H, carbon is C, iron is Fe, Oxygen is O and gold is Au.

Below: An early list of elements made by John Dalton (1766–1844). He found that each element had its own kind of atoms.

Elephant

Elephants are the largest living land animals. They live in herds. A big bull (male) elephant may stand twice as high as a man and weigh as much as four cars. An elephant has larger ears, thicker legs, a longer nose and longer teeth than any other creature. Its skin is nearly as thick as the heel of a man's shoe.

Baby elephants stand no taller than big dogs. Elephants are fully grown after 20 years. They live almost as long as people.

People teach Indian elephants to move heavy loads. African elephants are harder to tame. Many thousands have been killed just for the ivory of their tusks. Today most elephants are protected by law.

An African elephant can stand 4 metres high and weigh up to 7 tonnes.

Elizabeth (queens)

Elizabeth I (1533–1603) was the daughter of King Henry VIII and one of the best known British monarchs. Hers was a reign of peace, but in 1588 her country beat off a Spanish invasion attempt—the great Armada. During Elizabeth's reign, the

country became a leading world power, and many great English playwrights, poets and scholars lived then. Elizabeth I never married, and she ruled England for 45 years.

Elizabeth II was born in 1926. She came to the British throne in 1952 after the death of her father, King George VI. Her son and heir is Charles, Prince of Wales.

Energy

Having energy means being able to do work. There are various kinds of energy. Muscles and machines have *mechanical* energy. They can move loads. A moving object has *kinetic* energy. Coal and food store *chemical* energy. If you burn coal or eat food they are chemically changed and give

The 'Armada Portrait' of Elizabeth I was painted to celebrate England's victory. Magnificently dressed, loaded with jewels, with a ruff of the most delicate lace, the Queen sits with her right hand on the globe. Behind her, scenes represent victory over the Armada. She was 56 at the time, yet appears eternally young, a symbol of her power to lead her people.

off *heat* energy. We can turn *electrical* energy into heat, light or sound.

Radiant energy from the sun gives us energy in the form of light and heat. Most of the energy on earth comes in some way from the sun. Coal, oil and gas—the fossil fuels—were formed from plants and animals which depended for their life on the sun's warmth and light.

Engineering

Engineers do a great many different types of jobs. Mining engineers find useful MINERALS and take them from the ground. Metallurgical engineers separate metals from unwanted substances and make them usable. Chemical engineers use chemicals to make such things as explosives, paint, plastics and soap. Civil engineers build bridges, tunnels, roads, railways, ports, airports, and so on. Mechanical engineers make and use machines. Such people design JET ENGINES and factory machinery. Electrical engineers work with devices that produce and use electricity. Others work in ELECTRONICS. Most of the main kinds of engineering fall into one or another of these groups.

Engineers design and make all kinds of machines. The mobile crane (top) is lifting a helicopter body. Both crane and helicopter are good examples of the engineer's skills. So is the big excavator above.

England

England is the largest country in the kingdom of Great Britain and Northern Ireland. If Great Britain were divided into five equal parts, England would fill three of them. England's neighbours are Scotland and Wales. But most of England is surrounded by sea. Green fields spread over the plains and low hills that cover most of the country. In the north and west there are mountains with moors and forests. Most English people live and work in big cities like London, Birmingham, Liverpool and Manchester.

England gets its name from the Angles, a group of the Anglo-Saxons who sailed to the island and settled there about 1500 years ago.

English Language

More people speak English than any other language except Chinese. English is the main language spoken in the United States, the United Kingdom, Ireland, Australia, New Zealand, Canada, and some other countries. Altogether more than 370 million people speak English as their everyday language. Another 100 million or more speak at least some English. Most English words come from old Anglo-Saxon, French or Latin words.

Equator

The equator is an imaginary line around the world, halfway between the North Pole and the South Pole. A journey around the equator covers 40,076 km.

The word 'equator' comes from an old Latin word meaning 'equalizer'. The equator divides the world into two equal halves. The half north of the equator is called the Northern Hemisphere. The half south of the equator is the Southern Hemisphere. Distances north and south of the equator are measured in degrees of latitude. The equator itself has a latitude of 0 degrees. (See also LATITUDE AND LONGITUDE.)

On the equator, nights are always as long as days. At midday the sun always shines from directly or almost directly overhead. So all places on the equator except high mountains are warm all through the year.

Eskimo

Eskimos are hardy people who live in the cold, ARCTIC lands of Greenland, North America and north-east Asia. They have slanting eyes, a wide, flat face, and a short, thick body with short arms and legs. This shape helps to keep them warm in the cold, Arctic climate.

Eskimos wear fur clothes. Some still live in tents in summer and build igloos for the winter. All Eskimos once killed for food. They used bows and arrows and harpoons, and hunted seals, whales, fish, seabirds and deer. Eskimos paddled skin boats. Dogs pulled their sleds overland. Most Eskimos no longer lead this kind of life. They now live and work in towns. The Eskimos call themselves *Innuit*, meaning 'men'.

When the sun's rays reach the poles they are more thinly spread than at the equator. They have also had to travel through more air. This is why it is hotter at the equator than in the polar regions.

This Eskimo girl has the typical straight black hair, prominent cheekbones and yellow-brown skin of her people.

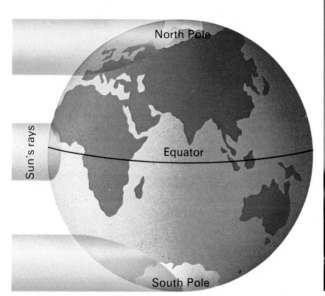

Europe

Europe is a peninsula sticking out from the western end of Asia. Other small peninsulas jut from the main one, and there are many offshore islands. Australia is the only continent smaller than Europe, but Europe holds more people than any continent except Asia.

European people have settled in the Americas, Australia, New Zealand, South Africa and Siberia. European ideas and inventions help shape the way of life of many people in lands all around the world.

Mountains cross the countries of southern Europe. From west to east there are the Pyrenees, Alps, Apennines, Balkans, Carpathians, Caucasus and other ranges. The Caucasus range has Mt Elbrus, Europe's highest peak.

In northern Europe low mountains cover much of Iceland, Ireland, Scotland, Wales, Norway and Sweden. Between the mountains of the north and south lies a great plain. Here flow Europe's longest rivers. The Volga in the USSR is the longest of them all.

All Europe lies north of the hot tropics and most of it lies south of the cold ARCTIC. So most of Europe is neither always hot nor cold. But Mediterranean lands have hot summers, and countries in the north and east have long, cold winters.

Shrubs and flowering plants grow in the far north. Next come the great northern

Europe is quite a small continent, but it has far more people than there are in all of North America. It has an average of 63 people per square kilometre. The United States has only 24.

forests of CONIFERS. Farther south lie most of Europe's farms and cities.

Much of Europe's wealth comes from its factories, farms and mines. Europe's richest nations include West Germany and Switzerland. The largest European country is the USSR. The smallest European country is Vatican City in Rome. There are 34 countries in Europe.

Europe is separated from Asia by the Ural Mountains in the USSR. The seas around Europe have many islands, all part of the continent — even far-off Iceland. Between the mountains in the north and the Alpine chain in the south lies a great wide plain. This plain stretches from southern Britain all the way to the Urals. It has some of the richest farmland in the world. Most of Europe's big cities are also in this area.

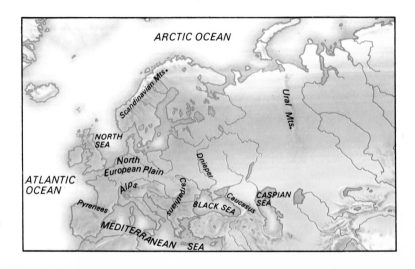

European Economic Community (EEC)

This is a group of western European nations that work together to help goods, people, and money travel between countries in the community. Its members are Belgium, Denmark, France, Ireland, Italy, Great Britain, Greece, Luxembourg, the Netherlands, Portugal, Spain and West Germany. People also call the community the European Common Market.

Everest, Mount

Mt Everest is the world's highest peak. It rises 8848 metres above sea level. The mountain stands in the HIMALAYAS on the borders of Nepal and Tibet. Gales and falling masses of rock and snow sweep the steep, cold slopes. Many climbers tried to reach the top before two finally succeeded in 1953. They were the New Zealander Edmund Hillary and Tenzing Norgay, a Nepalese Sherpa tribesman.

Mount Everest is the highest point on the earth's surface.

Evolution

The theory of evolution states that today's plants and animals are descended from other forms that lived long ago. This slow process of change has been going on for millions and millions of years—ever since life first appeared on earth—and is still happening. Much of the evidence for evolution comes from FOSSILS. Rocks contain the remains of extinct plants and animals and so help to build up a family tree for species now living.

The theory of evolution says that plants and animals must adapt to their surroundings if they are to survive. Those which adapt best are most likely to survive.

Charles DARWIN, an English naturalist, first put forward the theory of evolution in a book entitled *On the Origin of Species*.

Explorer

Explorers are people who travel to find out about unknown places. There have always been explorers. The Stone Age men and women who wandered across continents were in a way explorers. Phoenician seamen sailed the Mediterranean about 2,600 years ago. In the Middle Ages MARCO POLO reached China from Europe. But the great age of exploration began in the 1400s. Sailors such as Vasco da GAMA, Christopher COLUMBUS, Ferdinand Magellan, and James COOK discovered the shape, size and position of continents and oceans. Later, men like David Livingstone and Roald Amundsen explored wild, untamed continents. SPACE EXPLORATION now takes people beyond the earth.

Vasco da Gama's voyage to India gave the Portuguese the monopoly of the route to the East via Africa. For the Spaniards, Magellan tried to reach the East by sailing south of South America.

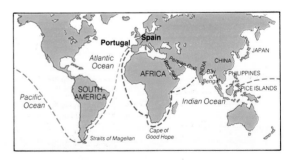

---- **Magellan**

---- **da Gama**

Eye

Our eyes show us the size, shape and colour of objects in the world around us. Your eyes can see something as small and near as a tiny insect crawling on this page, or as far off and large as the moon or stars.

A human eye is much larger than the part you can see. The eye is a ball bigger than a marble. It works much like a camera. Both bend LIGHT rays to form a picture of the object that the rays come from.

Light rays enter the eye through a layer of transparent skin called the *conjunctiva*. The rays pass through a hard, transparent layer called the *cornea*. This bends the rays. The LENS brings them into focus on the *retina* at the back of the eye. But you do not 'see' the picture formed here until light-sensitive nerve endings on the retina send the brain a message along the *optic nerve*.

To see properly, all the parts of the eye have to work correctly. For example, the *iris* (the eye's coloured part) can open and close to let more or less light enter through the *pupil*.

Sometimes eyes don't work correctly. For example, a person with a thin lens cannot see nearby objects clearly. Such conditions can be helped by wearing glasses or contact lenses.

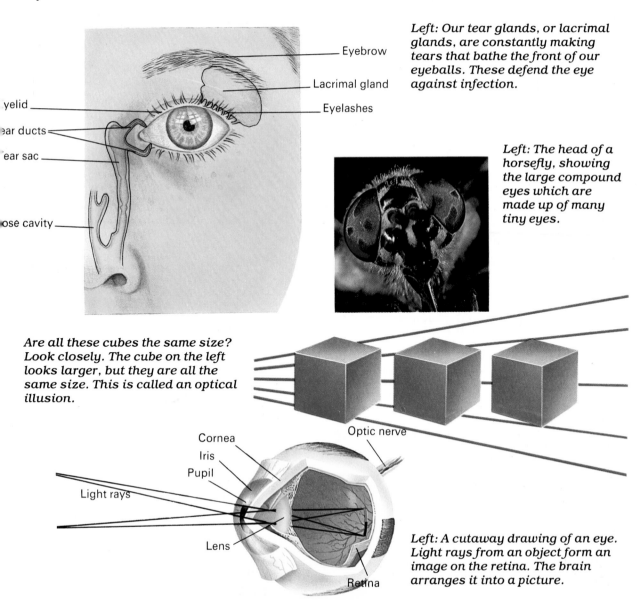

Eyebrow

Lacrimal gland

Eyelashes

Eyelid

Tear ducts

Tear sac

Nose cavity

Left: Our tear glands, or lacrimal glands, are constantly making tears that bathe the front of our eyeballs. These defend the eye against infection.

Left: The head of a horsefly, showing the large compound eyes which are made up of many tiny eyes.

Are all these cubes the same size? Look closely. The cube on the left looks larger, but they are all the same size. This is called an optical illusion.

Cornea

Iris

Pupil

Light rays

Lens

Optic nerve

Retina

Left: A cutaway drawing of an eye. Light rays from an object form an image on the retina. The brain arranges it into a picture.

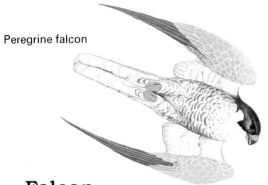

Peregrine falcon

Falcon

Falcons are a group of birds of prey that are found all over the world. They can be recognized by the dark markings around their eyes and by their pointed wings. Falcons use their large, hooked beaks for tearing flesh. But they kill their prey with their sharp claws. Falcons swoop down on their victims from above, hitting them with their claws. This act is called 'stooping'. It is used to kill smaller birds in mid-flight and also to take RODENTS and other small animals on the ground.

The biggest of all falcons is the gyrfalcon of the Arctic. It may reach over 60 cm in size. The smallest is the pygmy falcon of southern Asia. It is less than 15 cm long and feeds mainly on insects.

The peregrine falcon is one of the fastest flyers in the world. In a fast dive, it can reach 280 km/hr.

Faraday, Michael

Michael Faraday (1791–1867) was a brilliant English scientist. His studies of chemistry and physics made him world famous. Faraday is best known for his experiments with ELECTRICITY. He showed that it could be made to flow in a wire when the wire was passed between a set of magnets. Today this is how most electricity is produced in big generators.

Farming

Farming is man's most important activity. More people work at it than at any other job. And in all, about a third of the land on our planet is farmed.

Farmers grow hundreds of different kinds of crops. But a few, such as WHEAT, RICE and barley, and beans and peas are by far the most important. They are grown almost everywhere that farmers plough the soil.

The kinds of crops that are raised in one region depend on several things. The climate, altitude (the height of the land above sea level), and the fertility of the soil are the most important. For example, rice, oranges

Modern machines such as these combine harvesters have increased farm production in many countries.

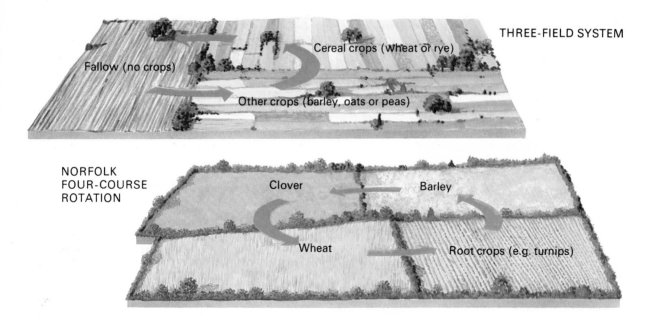

THREE-FIELD SYSTEM

Cereal crops (wheat or rye)

Fallow (no crops)

Other crops (barley, oats or peas)

NORFOLK FOUR-COURSE ROTATION

Clover

Barley

Wheat

Root crops (e.g. turnips)

All crops take goodness out of the soil. Farmers can improve their soil with fertilizers, by resting the soil or by growing different crops after each other. The top picture shows the medieval three-field system. Each year, two fields are cultivated and the third left fallow. The other diagram shows a newer system of crop rotation, with no fallow field.

and coconuts all need a warm, tropical climate in which to grow. COFFEE needs warmth, but does best at a high altitude.

Farmers do not grow only our food. They also raise crops such as hay and clover to feed animals. Some plant TOBACCO, COTTON or sugar cane. Others raise animals for meat.

Fat

Fat is an important food for animals and plants. The tissues of these living things contain fat. Fat in a pure state can take the form of a liquid, such as vegetable oil, or a solid, such as butter or lard.

Fat is a store of energy. A unit of fat contains twice as much energy as the same amount of PROTEIN or starch. Fats play an important part in our diet, although too much animal fat is not good for us. In animals and human beings fat is stored in tiny 'droplets' in a layer under the skin and in the CELLS of the body. Fats are also important in making SOAPS.

Fertilizer

Fertilizers are chemicals. They are dug into the soil to nourish it. In this way fertilizers help plants to grow bigger and healthier by giving them the chemical 'foods' they need. The most important fertilizers are calcium, phosphorus, potassium and sulphur.

Fertilizers are usually added to soils that do not contain enough nutrients. This can happen if the same crops have been planted in the soil year after year, or if the rain has washed all the nutrients out.

A person who eats too much stores the extra in fat cells all over his body.

Fingerprints

Fingerprints are marks we leave behind whenever we touch something. You can see them by pressing your fingertips into an ink pad and then onto a sheet of white paper. Everybody has patterns of lines and swirls on their fingers. But each person's fingerprints are different from everybody else's. Because of this, police officers use fingerprints to help identify criminals. They keep files of millions of different prints. By comparing those on file with those found at the scene of a crime, they can often trace the guilty person.

No two people in the world have the same fingerprints. Even the fingertips of identical twins are different. The patterns of ridges and whorls follow exactly irregularities in the underlying dermis. Even if the outer skin is damaged, the pattern does not change.

Finland

Finland is a country in northern EUROPE tucked between Scandinavia and the USSR. Northern Finland stretches north of the Arctic Circle. (See map on page 123.)

The thousands of lakes and rivers that dot the Finnish landscape form a great inland waterway. About 75 percent of the land is covered by thick forests of spruce, pine and large trees. The main industries of Finland are logging and the making of wood products, such as paper.

Just under five million people live in Finland. The capital, Helsinki, has a population of about 485,000.

Fiord

Along the coasts of NORWAY and Greenland are a series of steep-sided valleys called fiords. Here the sea has invaded the land. Narrow tongues of water wind inland for miles in narrow mountain gorges.

Fiords were formed when the great glaciers of the ICE AGES gouged out valleys as they flowed to the sea. When the ice melted, the sea flooded the valleys. Fiords are very deep and make perfect shelters for large ocean-going ships.

The spectacular scenery of the Norwegian fiord (below) is typical of the region. Here the slopes of mountains plunge straight into the sea in an unbroken drop.

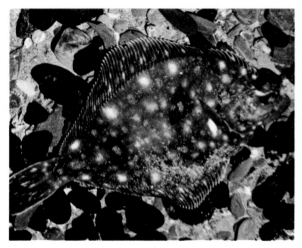

Left: This colourful angelfish lives among coral in the Caribbean. Above: The colours of the plaice hide it on the sea floor. It can change colour to match dark or light surroundings. Above left: The porcupine fish blows itself up into a spiky ball when danger threatens.

Fire

The ability to make and use fire is one of the great advantages people have over animals. Primitive people found fire frightening, just as animals do. But once they learned to make and control fires, they became a necessary part of life. They kept out the cold, lit up the dark, cooked food, kept them warm and kept away wild animals. But even today fires that get out of control cause terrible damage and suffering.

Firs

Firs are an important group of CONIFERS. They are found mostly in cool climates. Forests of fir trees grow all over northern Asia, Europe and North America. Firs are often found in mountainous areas.

The leaves of fir trees are short, thin and needlelike. They grow separately along the twigs, unlike pine needles, which grow in clusters. The fruit of the fir tree is a scaly cone. The tall Douglas 'Fir' is not really a fir—it belongs to a different group of evergreens.

Fish

There are more fish than all the other backboned animals put together. The fish shown on this page are just a few of more than 30,000 different kinds. Fish are also the oldest backboned animals. The ancestors of modern fish first appeared on the earth over 500 million years ago.

Fish range in size from tiny gobies less than 13 mm long to the great whale SHARKS, up to 15 metres long. Their shapes vary from the snakelike eels to the flatfish that lie on their 'sides' on the seabed. The SEA HORSE looks nothing like a fish at all. And a few fishlike creatures are not fish. WHALES and DOLPHINS are really mammals—they give birth to live young and feed them on milk.

Fish are cold-blooded. They live in fresh and salt water, and are found everywhere from the tropics to the poles. They breathe through gills, and move by bending their bodies from side to side. Their fins and tails help them to swim well. Over short distances, fish can swim with surprising speed.

The record is 70km/hr for the bluefin TUNA.

Most fish lay eggs in the water. This is called *spawning*. A few, such as some sharks and rays, give birth to live young. Egg-laying fish release millions of eggs into the water. But only a few of them will survive to become adults. Some fish, such as bass, SALMON and sticklebacks, protect their eggs by building nests. Because more eggs will survive, fewer are laid. Male sea horses and pipefish have a pouch into which the female lays her eggs. The male carries them until they hatch.

Fishing

Fishing is one of the world's most important activities. In one year, about 60 million metric tons of fish are taken from the seas, rivers and lakes.

Although fish are a good source of food, much of the catch ends up as animal feed or FERTILIZER. Oil from fish is used to make SOAPS or for tanning—turning animal skins into leather.

Often the catch is made far away from home port. The fish must be preserved or they will quickly spoil. In the past fish were often dried, smoked or salted, because there were no refrigerators. Today they are packed on ice or frozen. Some fishing fleets include large factory ships. These take

Trawl nets are great funnel-shaped 'sacks' that are dragged along the seabed. They are used to catch bottom-feeders such as cod and haddock. A purse seine net is used for catching surface-swimming shoals of fish. Gill nets are floating traps which tangle fish that try to swim through. They are used in shallow waters. Long-lines have many baited hooks. They are set along the sea floor to catch large fish such as halibut. Lobster pots are baited wooden traps laid on the sea floor.

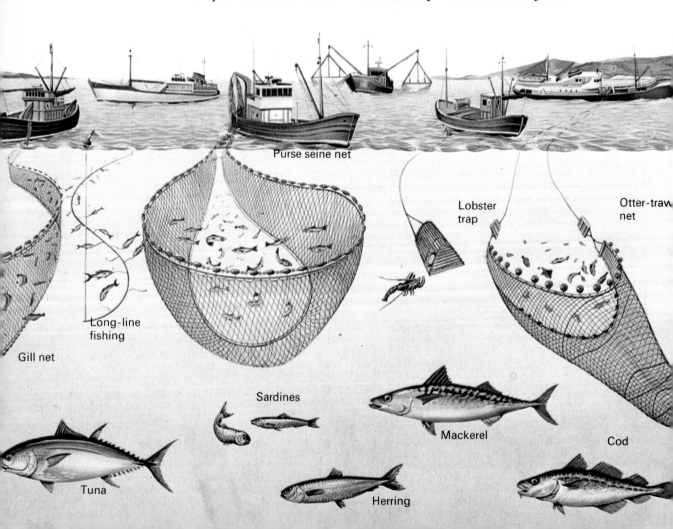

Purse seine net

Lobster trap

Otter-trawl net

Long-line fishing

Gill net

Sardines

Mackerel

Cod

Tuna

Herring

fresh fish straight from the other ships, and people on board can the fish or package them on the spot.

The best places to fish at sea are where the sloping sea bottom is no more than 180 metres deep. Here, fish can be found feeding in huge numbers. The Grand Banks off the coast of Newfoundland is one such region. It has been fished for hundreds of years.

Flag

Flags are pieces of coloured cloth, often decorated with bold markings. They have special fastenings so that they can be flown from masts and poles. Flags are used by countries, armies, and groups such as sports teams.

Flags have been used as emblems since the time of the ancient Egyptians. Their flags were flown on long poles as battle standards, held by 'standard-bearers'. Flying high in the air, flags helped soldiers to find their companions as they plunged into battle. And they showed which soldiers belonged to which king or general.

Today, national flags are flown as a symbol of a country's history, its power and its importance, or *prestige*. They are also a symbol of people's loyalty to one nation and one government.

Flags are also used for signalling. Since 1857 there has been an international code for flag signals. It is used by ships. A yellow flag, for example, means that a ship is in

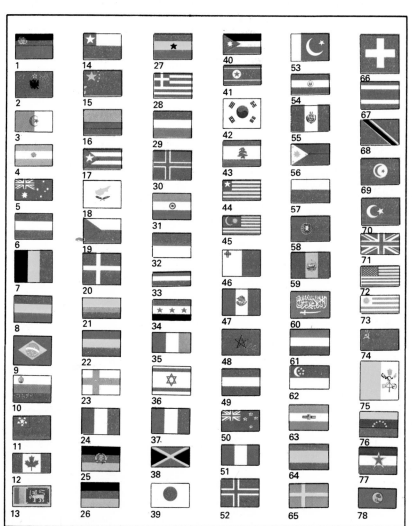

1. Afghanistan 2. Albania
3. Algeria 4. Argentina
5. Australia 6. Austria
7. Belgium 8. Bolivia
9. Brazil 10. Bulgaria
11. Burma 12. Canada
13. Sri Lanka 14. Chile
15. China 16. Colombia
17. Cuba 18. Cyprus
19. Czechoslovakia
20. Denmark 21. Ecuador
22. Ethiopia 23. Finland
24. France 25. E. Germany
26. W. Germany 27. Ghana
28. Greece 29. Hungary
30. Iceland 31. India
32. Indonesia 33. Iran
34. Iraq 35. Ireland
36. Israel 37. Italy
38. Jamaica 39. Japan
40. Jordan 41. N. Korea
42. S. Korea 43. Lebanon
44. Liberia 45. Malaysia
46. Malta 47. Mexico
48. Morocco 49. Netherlands
50. New Zealand 51. Nigeria
52. Norway 53. Pakistan
54. Paraguay 55. Peru
56. Philippines 57. Poland
58. Portugal 59. Romania
60. Saudi Arabia
61. Sierra Leone 62. Singapore
63. South Africa 64. Spain
65. Sweden 66. Switzerland
67. Thailand 68. Trinidad & Tobago
69. Tunisia 70. Turkey
71. United Kingdom 72. USA
73. Uruguay 74. USSR
75. Vatican City 76. Venezuela
77. Yugoslavia 78. Zaire

quarantine because of illness on board. For thousands of years flags have been important as a way of identifying ships at sea.

Other well known signals are a white flag—a sign of truce—and a flag raised to half-mast—a sign that people are mourning someone's death.

Flame

When something is heated enough to make it burn, it will also often burst into flames. These flames are gases that are given off during burning. Bright flames that give off plenty of light, such as those of candles, wood or coal, have tiny CARBON particles in them that glow brightly. Flames are not all equally hot. Wood fires burn at about 1000°C. The flames of acetylene welding torches are about 3000°C.

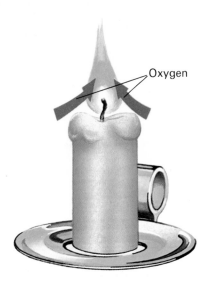

As a candle burns, it takes up oxygen from the air and gives out heat and light. When you strike a match, friction with the rough surface of the box makes the head hot and special substances in the match burst into flame.

Rough surface   Heat generated   Match lights

Flower

There are about 250,000 different kinds of flowering plants in the world. Their flowers come in a dazzling array of colours, sizes and shapes. Some grow singly. Some grow in tight clusters. Many have showy colours, a strong scent and produce a sweet nectar. Others are quite drab and unscented.

Whatever they look like, flowers all have

Flowers are the reproductive parts of plants. Below are two familiar flowers, both members of the rose family.

Wild strawberry

Dog rose

the same part to play in the life of the plant. Flowers help plants to reproduce themselves. Inside a flower are male parts, called *stamens*, and female parts known as *pistils*. The stamens contain hundreds of powdery grains of pollen. These fertilize the pistil. Then a FRUIT begins to form and grow. Inside the fruit are the SEEDS for a new generation of plants. The seeds are scattered in different ways. They may be blown by the wind, or carried off by birds and animals. From them new plants will grow.

Fly

Flies are winged insects. They are one of the largest groups of insects in the world. There are more than 750,000 different kinds of flies. They have two pairs of wings, one pair for flying and a smaller set behind the main pair to help them to balance in flight.

Many flies are dangerous. They spread deadly diseases such as cholera and dysentery. They pick up germs from manure and rotting food and carry them into homes where they leave them on our fresh food.

Some flies bite and feed on the blood of animals.

Flies have three pairs of legs, a pair of antennae and two huge 'compound' eyes, made up of many tiny 'eyes'.

Fog can form over land that is cooling quickly during a clear winter night. It can also form on the cold tops of hills and mountains, and roll down into the valleys.

Fog

What we call fog is simply a low-lying bank of CLOUD. Fog forms when warm, moist air comes into contact with cold ground. As the air cools, the moisture it contains forms the tiny droplets that make up any cloud.

Fog may form when warm air currents blow across chilled water or land. This kind is common around the coast. Another kind occurs on still, clear winter nights when the cold ground chills the air above it and there is no wind to blow the resulting fog away.

Football

There are several kinds of football. They differ in the shape of the ball, the size of the teams and the rules.

Soccer is played all over the world. The ball is round, the field anywhere from 90 to 118 metres long, and each team has 11 players. Teams score by kicking the ball into the goal at the opposite end of the field. The ball may not be carried.

American football uses an oval ball. The game consists mostly of tackling, passing and running, with very little kicking. The players—11 on each side—are protected by helmets and pads. This type of football is sometimes very violent.

Rugby football is played in Britain, the Commonwealth and parts of Europe. The ball is oval, and each team has 15 players. The ball may be kicked or carried.

133

Above: Conifers, or cone-bearing trees, are the main trees of cold forests.

Below: This diagram shows how a creature such as this fishlike reptile could become a fossil. When it dies, its body sinks to the seabed (1). Its bones are covered with silt (2), which gradually turns to rock (3). Later the seabed becomes dry land and the rocks above the fossil slowly wear away, exposing the fossil (4). Fossils of small snaillike sea creatures are quite common and can be found in layers in rocks by the shore.

Forest

Forests are large areas of tree-covered land. Tropical rain forests are found near the EQUATOR. In their hot and steamy climate many kinds of tree and plant grow very quickly. In some places the trees grow so closely together that the sunlight cannot reach the dark, bare forest floor.

Coniferous forests are nearly always found in cold northern lands. These forests are mostly made up of one kind of tree, such as spruce, FIR or pine. Few other plants grow there. In temperate lands like Europe, the United States, and the cooler parts of Australia and Africa, there are deciduous forests with trees like oak and beech.

Fossil

Fossils are the hardened remains or impressions of animals and plants that lived a very long time ago. A fossil may be a shell, a bone, a tooth, a leaf, a skeleton or even sometimes an entire animal.

Most fossils have been found in areas that were once in or near the sea. When the plant or creature died, its body sank to the seabed. The soft parts rotted away but the hard skeleton became buried in the mud.

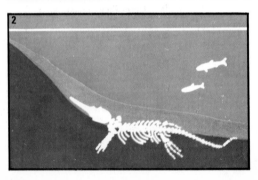

Ears are large to pick up as much sound as possible. A fox can hear even better than a dog.

Nose The fox's sense of smell is very keen. With its wet nose it can tell which way the wind is blowing, so it knows exactly where any smell is coming from.

Teeth Long ones at the front for tearing meat and sharp side ones for slicing it.

The body of a red fox

Eyes are not as important as the nose and ears, but foxes can see well at night.

Tail The fox's tail is called a brush. It helps it to balance; to signal to other foxes; and to keep warm, curling it round like a scarf.

Legs Strong legs and feet for running. The fox does not run very fast, but it can run for a long time at the same speed.

Over millions of years more and more mud settled on top of the skeleton. Eventually these layers of mud hardened into rock, and the skeleton became part of that rock. Water seeping through the rock slowly dissolved away the original skeleton. It was replaced by stony MINERALS which formed exactly the same shape.

These fossils lay buried until movements in the earth's crust pushed up the seabed and it became dry land. In time water, ice and wind wear away the rock and the fossil is exposed. The oldest known fossil is over three billion years old.

Fox

Foxes belong to the same animal family as dogs. The most common kind is the red fox, which is found in Europe, North America, North Africa and parts of Asia. It eats small birds, animals and insects, and occasionally poultry or lambs. Although the red fox prefers wooded country, some live in towns and cities. They eat mice, rats and food from dustbins.

Foxes are seldom seen because they are shy and mostly come out at night. They live in holes called 'earths' which they either dig themselves or take over from rabbits.

Foxes are very cunning animals. Sometimes they catch rabbits and other prey by chasing their own tails very fast. This fas-

cinates the rabbit, who watches without realizing that the fox is gradually getting nearer and nearer. When the fox gets close enough, it suddenly straightens out and grabs its dinner.

Fraction

If you cut a cake into equal parts, each part is a fraction of the whole cake. We can write this as a number, too. If the cake is cut into two, each half can be written like this: $\frac{1}{2}$. If the cake is cut into four, each quarter is written $\frac{1}{4}$. The number above the dividing line in a fraction is called the *numerator*. The number below is called the *denominator*.

Until fractions were invented, people had to manage with just *whole* numbers. It was not possible to express a length or weight between two whole numbers. The Egyptians invented a symbol to describe a part of a number. A Hindu astrologer, Bhaskara, invented another symbol that looked like the one we use today: $\frac{1}{2}$. By the time this symbol reached Europe, a line had crept in between the numerals: $\frac{1}{2}$.

Fractions help us to divide things. They can be used to mean a part of one: a half of one is a half ($\frac{1}{2} \times 1 = \frac{1}{2}$). They can also be used to divide numbers greater than one. A box of eggs has 12 eggs in it. Half the box has 6 eggs ($\frac{1}{2} \times 12 = 6$).

France

France is the largest country in western EUROPE. (See map on page 123.) It has a population of 55,000,000. In ancient times France was inhabited by Celts, but Julius CAESAR conquered it and for 500 years it was part of the Roman Empire. The Franks, from whom the country got its name, invaded in the 400s AD. France was divided into hundreds of small parts. There was no standard language until the founding of the French Academy in the 1630s.

France is a very varied and beautiful country. It has a temperate climate and is very fertile. Farmland covers about half the country and many of the people are employed in farming, fishing or forestry. France produces a lot of grain, fruit and vegetables, and it is famous for its WINES.

The history of France is long and turbulent. For centuries the French and English were enemies and fought many wars. The French people suffered under the rule of greedy kings and nobles. Then in 1789 the people started the FRENCH REVOLUTION. They overthrew their king and made France a republic.

But the country was soon taken over by NAPOLEON, who made himself Emperor. He went to war and conquered most of Europe before he was finally defeated at Waterloo in 1815. Since then France has fought three wars against Germany.

Today France is one of the wealthiest nations in Europe. It was one of the first members of the EUROPEAN ECONOMIC COMMUNITY.

Painters and writers from all over the world have lived in Paris, the French capital. Many tourists go there to see its historic buildings, which include the Louvre and Notre Dame Cathedral.

Above: Inside a French classroom. The Ministry of Education in Paris decides what subjects must be taught and how much time will be spent on each subject in every public school in the country.

The Eiffel Tower in Paris is 300 metres high. It was built in 1889, when it was the highest structure in the world.

In 1789 the people of Paris attacked the Bastille, a prison, in an attempt to capture weapons and free political prisoners. The fall of the Bastille marked the beginning of the French Revolution.

Franklin, Benjamin

Benjamin Franklin (1706–1790) was a gifted politician and scientist. He was born in Boston, the youngest of 17 children. Franklin became a printer and then went on to publish a yearly almanac which made him his fortune.

He became involved in the REVOLUTIONARY WAR, which brought America freedom from British rule. He helped draw up the peace treaty at the end of the war and was one of the men who signed the Declaration of Independence.

His scientific inventions include bifocal spectacles, and a rod that protects buildings from being struck by lightning.

French Revolution

For many centuries the poor people of FRANCE suffered under the rule of their kings and nobles. Rich people built themselves lavish palaces and mansions while others starved in misery. French kings forced the peasants and shopkeepers to pay taxes to support their extravagant way of life, and for the wars they were always fighting.

There was no parliament to stop the king from treating his subjects badly and eventually, in 1789, the French people exploded into revolution. King LOUIS XVI was imprisoned but tried to escape. Violent leaders like Danton and Marat directed the Revolution, and the king and queen and many nobles were beheaded.

Then followed the 'Reign of Terror', when the Revolutionary leaders began to quarrel among themselves, and many of them were beheaded too. The people tired of bloodshed and in 1795 they set up a government called 'The Directory'. But it ruled the country badly, and in 1799 it was overthrown by NAPOLEON.

Freud, Sigmund

Sigmund Freud (1856–1939) was a Viennese doctor who made a great contribution to our understanding of the human mind.

Freud received a degree in medicine from the University of Vienna in 1881 and began to devote himself to the study of mental illness. He taught that the *subconscious*—the thoughts and memories we are not aware of—held the key to a person's mental state.

137

Friction

When two things rub together it causes friction. Friction makes it hard to move something across a surface. Smooth objects cause much less friction than rough objects, so when things need to go fast we try to reduce friction. This is why the wheels of a train and the rails of the track are smooth. When we want things to slow down we add friction; for example, putting on the brakes in our cars. If two things rub together at great speed the friction produces HEAT. If you rub your hand very fast against your leg you can feel the heat made by the friction.

Frog

Frogs are amphibians. This means that they can live both on land and in water. Frogs are found all over the world except in very cold lands that are always frozen. There are hundreds of different kinds. The biggest is the Goliath frog of Central Africa. This frog can be over 80 cm long (with its legs extended) and weigh over 3 kg. The smallest is a tree frog from the United States, which is less than 2 cm long.

Frogs breathe through their skins as well as their LUNGS. It is important that frogs keep their skins wet, because if the skin became too dry the frog could not breathe and it would die. This is why you will never find a frog very far away from water.

Common frogs feed on insects, grubs and slugs. They catch their food with a long sticky tongue which is attached to the front of the mouth. A frog can flick its tongue in and out in a fraction of a second. Really big frogs eat snakes, small animals and other frogs, as well as insects. Tadpoles eat small water creatures, although they themselves often make a tasty meal for adult frogs.

Fruit

To most of us 'fruit' means juicy foods which grow on certain plants and trees. Apples, oranges and pears are three examples. These fruits taste good and are important in our diet. They give us mineral salts, sugar and VITAMINS. The water, skins and seeds of fruit help our DIGESTION.

To scientists who study plants, fruits are the ripe SEED cases of any flowering plant. The fruits protect the seeds as they develop

Xenopus, the clawed frog from South Africa, can change its colour to match its surroundings.

and help spread them when they are ripe. Some fruits scatter seeds. Others are eaten by birds and animals that spread the seeds. Fruits come in all shapes and sizes. Some have only one seed, most have more.

Fungus

A fungus is a simple PLANT with no true roots, stems or leaves. Fungi do not have the chlorophyll that helps green plants to make food. So fungi have to find a ready-made supply of food. Some feed as parasites on living plants or animals. Others feed on animal and plant remains.

There are more than 50,000 kinds of fungus. Some have only one CELL. Other fungi are chains of cells. These produce tiny, threadlike growths that spread through the substance they feed on. Many fungi grow a large fruiting body which sheds spores that produce new fungus plants. The mushrooms we eat are the fruiting bodies of a fungus. Some fungi are useful. Penicillin, the antibiotic DRUG, and YEAST are both fungi.

Above left: Bracket fungi growing from a tree trunk. Above: Fly agaric, also called fly Amanita, is a very colourful fungus, but it contains a poison. Below: Some edible fungi. Although many fungi can be eaten, many others are deadly, so it is unsafe to eat any without the advice of an expert.

Parasol mushroom

Fairy ring champignon

Field mushroom

Shaggy ink cap

Cep

Giant puffball

Chanterelle

Oyster mushroom

Truffle

Galaxy

Someone once called galaxies 'star islands in space'. A galaxy is made up of a huge group of STARS. Our SUN is just one star of about 100,000 million stars that belong to the Milky Way galaxy. A beam of light would take about 100,000 years to shine from one side of the Milky Way to the other. Yet the Milky Way is only a middle-sized galaxy.

Beyond our galaxy there may be as many as 10,000 million more. The nearest large galaxy is the Andromeda. The light we see it by took more than two million years to reach us.

Some galaxies have no special shape. Others have spiral arms made up of many millions of stars. The Milky Way and Andromeda galaxies both look like this. There are also galaxies that look like saucers or balls. Astronomers used to think that these changed into galaxies with spiral arms. Now some astronomers believe that the spiral galaxies shrink into the other kind instead.

RADIO ASTRONOMY has shown that radio waves are sent out from many galaxies. Strong radio waves also come from strange starlike objects known as QUASARS. Quasars are very powerful energy sources. Some people think that a quasar may be the beginning of a new galaxy. Scientists think that galaxies may form where GRAVITY pulls huge clouds of gas together.

This is a picture of the Andromeda galaxy. Our Milky Way galaxy would look like this if seen from space.

MVM INDIÆ EMPORIVM.

Galileo

Galileo Galilei (1564–1642) was an Italian mathematics teacher who might be called the first true scientist. Instead of believing old ideas about the way the world worked, Galileo made careful experiments to find out for himself. He learned that a PENDULUM took the same time to make a long swing as it did to make a short one. He showed that light objects fell as fast as heavy ones when pulled toward the earth by GRAVITY. He built a TELESCOPE and became the first man to use this tool for studying the MOON and PLANETS.

What Galileo saw made him understand that the earth was not the centre of the UNIVERSE. The Church punished him for this belief. But later scientists including Isaac NEWTON built new knowledge on Galileo's discoveries.

Gama, Vasco da

Vasco da Gama (about 1469–1524) discovered how to sail by sea from Europe to India by way of southern Africa. This Portuguese navigator left Lisbon with four ships in July, 1497. In East Africa he found a guide who showed him how to sail across the Indian Ocean. Da Gama reached Calicut in southern India in May, 1498. But Arab traders who were jealous of the Portuguese tried to stop him from trading with the Indians. On the journey home, 30 of his 90 crewmen died of scurvy, and only two of the four ships got back to Lisbon.

This old picture shows Calicut in India. After Vasco da Gama's voyage Portugal set up a trading centre there.

Gandhi

Mohandas Karamchand Gandhi (1869–1948) is sometimes called the 'father of modern India'. This frail-looking Hindu lawyer helped to free INDIA from British rule by peacefully disobeying British laws. In 1920 he told the Indians to spin cloth for their own clothes instead of buying it from Britain. In 1930 he broke a British law by making salt from seawater instead of buying salt from the government.

People admired Gandhi's beliefs, his kindness and his simple way of life. In 1947 Britain gave India independence. Soon after, one of his fellow Hindus shot Gandhi for preaching peace to Muslims, people who follow the religion of ISLAM.

Gandhi, Indira

Indira Gandhi (1917–1984) was prime minister of India from 1966 until 1977 and from 1980 until her death. Her father, Jawaharlal Nehru, supported GANDHI and became India's first prime minister after independence. In 1942, Indira married a lawyer, Feroze Gandhi. For years she helped her father, then went into politics herself. When in power, Mrs Gandhi fought for economic progress, social reforms and national unity. In 1984 she was killed by two Sikhs, members of an Indian religious group who want their own state.

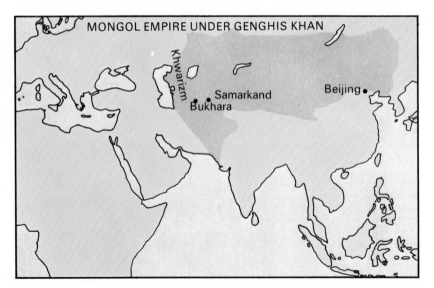

MONGOL EMPIRE UNDER GENGHIS KHAN

Gem

Some rocks hold hard CRYSTALS that can be cut to show clear, brilliant colours. These gems are often used in making jewellery. DIAMONDS are among the rarest, finest gems. But red rubies, blue sapphires and green emeralds are also much sought-after. Pearls are gems produced by oysters. Today cheap artificial gems are made from coloured glass and plastics.

Genghis Khan

Genghis Khan (1167–1227) was a Mongol chief who cruelly attacked many Asian peoples and won a mighty empire. His real name was Temujin ('ironsmith').

At 13 he took his dead father's place as chief of a small Mongol tribe of nomads. He soon won power over nearby tribes as well. In 1206 he became known as Genghis Khan, 'Very Mighty King'. Genghis Khan formed a huge army of tough, hard-riding nomads on the great grasslands of central Asia. Then he set off to conquer the lands around him. His troops pushed south-east to Peking (Beijing) in China, and south into Tibet and what are now Pakistan and Afghanistan. In the south-west they invaded Iran and southern Russia.

After he died, other Mongol rulers won more land and made the empire even larger.

This map shows the empire won by the cruel Mongol leader Genghis Khan (above). After his ambassador was killed in Khwarizm, he spent three years smashing all of that kingdom's biggest cities. Samarkand and Bukhara as well as Peking in China suffered horribly from Mongol armies.

Geography

Geography is the subject we study when we want to learn about the surface of the EARTH. Geographers study everything on the earth—the land, sea, air, plants, animals and even people. They explain where different things are found, how they got there, and how they affect one another.

There are many different areas, or branches, of geography. Physical geography describes things like MOUNTAINS, valleys, LAKES and RIVERS. Meteorology describes WEATHER. Economic geography deals with FARMING, mining, manufacturing and trade. Maps and charts are the geographer's most useful tools.

Geology

Geology is the study of the EARTH itself. Geologists discover what things the earth is made of, where they are found and how they got there. Geologists study rocks and MINERALS. They also try to find out how rocks are formed, and how they are changed by movements beneath the surface of the earth. VOLCANOES and EARTHQUAKES give us useful clues about underground movements.

Geologists also study the history of the earth. They have found rocks that are nearly four billion years old, and FOSSILS showing that EVOLUTION began about $3\frac{1}{2}$ billion years ago.

Geologists help engineers to choose where to build a road or tunnel. They help miners to find coal, oil or gas. By studying rocks brought back by astronauts, geologists hope to be able to tell us what the moon is made of.

Geometry

Geometry is a branch of MATHEMATICS. It can help you to find out the shape, size and position of an object. People draw lines and measure ANGLES so that they can solve geometric problems.

George (kings)

Six British kings were called George.

George I (1660–1727) was a German ruler who inherited the British throne.

George II (1683–1760) was the last British king to lead troops into battle.

George III (1738–1820) ruled as the INDUSTRIAL REVOLUTION began. He lost what became the UNITED STATES.

George IV (1762–1830) was a spendthrift who loved to be in fashion. As prince regent he took his father's place from 1811.

George V (1865–1936) was a naval officer. He reigned during WORLD WAR I.

George VI (1895–1952) reigned during WORLD WAR II. He was the father of ELIZABETH II.

Geographers study deserts, rivers and other things on the earth's surface. Geologists study rocks on and under it.

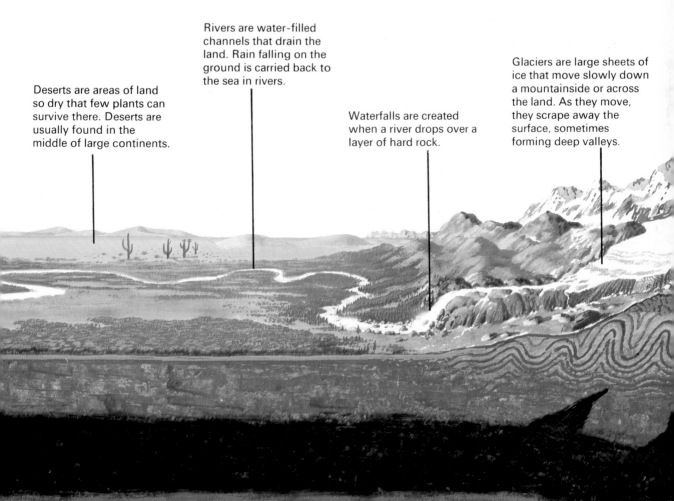

Rivers are water-filled channels that drain the land. Rain falling on the ground is carried back to the sea in rivers.

Glaciers are large sheets of ice that move slowly down a mountainside or across the land. As they move, they scrape away the surface, sometimes forming deep valleys.

Deserts are areas of land so dry that few plants can survive there. Deserts are usually found in the middle of large continents.

Waterfalls are created when a river drops over a layer of hard rock.

Germany

Germany used to be one great nation. After WORLD WAR II the land was divided into two nations: West Germany and East Germany. Both lie in the middle of EUROPE. (See map on page 123.)

West Germany is about the same size as the United Kingdom, and has more people than any other nation in western Europe. Farms and cities stand on the low plain in the north and in the valley of the river Rhine. The south has low, wooded mountains and sharp, tall peaks belonging to the Alps.

West Germany's farms produce more pigs and barley than any other western European nation. No other western European country produces so much coal or steel, or so many cars and televisions. West Germany's mines and factories make it the richest nation in Europe. The capital is Bonn.

East Germany is less than half the size of West Germany. There are nearly four West Germans for each East German. Like West Germany, East Germany has low, flat land in the north and forested mountains in the south. The Elbe and Oder rivers flow north toward the Baltic Sea. East Germans mine more soft brown coal than any other nation. East Germany is a communist country. The capital is East Berlin.

Geyser

Geysers are hot springs that now and then squirt out steam and scalding water. They work like this. Water fills a deep crack in the ground, often near VOLCANOES. Hot rock heats the water deep underground, but the weight of the water above it keeps the hot water from boiling until it is much hotter still. Then it turns to steam that forces the water upward, emptying the crack.

There are geysers in parts of Iceland, the United States and New Zealand. The tallest geyser ever known was the Waimangu geyser in New Zealand. In 1904 this squirted steam and water nearly 460 metres into the sky.

Hamburg is a major docking point in the North Sea.

Barges travel down the Rhine in West Germany past lovely towns and castles, green fields and vineyards.

Ghana

Ghana is a nation in West AFRICA. It is about the size of the United Kingdom. The country is hot, with plenty of rain in the south where Ghana meets the Atlantic Ocean. The land here is low, with tropical forests and farms. The north is drier and grassy.

Most of Ghana's 12 million people are blacks. They grow cocoa and mine DIAMONDS and GOLD. Electricity comes from

Cocoa trees grow on plantations in Ghana. Their huge pods are cut off with large knives. The beans inside are used to make chocolate and cocoa.

Lake Volta. This man-made lake covers more land than any other man-made lake in the world.

Giraffe

Giraffes are the tallest animals. They have long legs and a long neck. Yet this neck has only seven bones, the same as any other MAMMAL. Giraffes live in the hot grasslands of Africa where they feed on shrubs and trees.

A giraffe has two short horns between its ears. Its nostrils can shut to keep out dust. Inside its mouth is a long tongue that tears leaves from twigs.

Glacier

Glaciers are rivers of ice. Most form high up in the mountains where snow falls and never melts. As snow piles up, the lower layers are crushed and turn to ice. This begins to flow slowly downhill through valleys. Most glaciers take a year to flow as far as you can walk in five minutes. The rocks they carry grind against the sides and floor of each valley until they make it deep and wide.

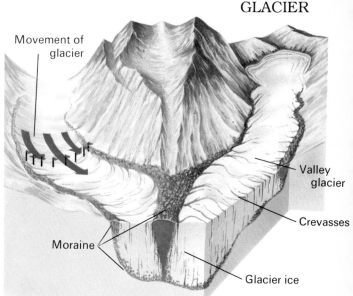

The movement of a glacier can be observed by putting a line of stakes across it. The stakes at the centre move fastest. Rocks and stones (moraine) are picked up by the ice at the bottom of the glacier. The movement of the glacier often causes big gaps called crevasses.

During ICE AGES, glaciers spread beyond the mountains. When the weather warms up they melt and go back. Many valleys in the ALPS and ROCKY MOUNTAINS once held glaciers.

145

Gland

Glands are organs that produce special substances needed by the body. There are two kinds—*endocrine* and *exocrine* glands. Endocrine glands send their substances, called *hormones*, directly into the bloodstream. One main endocrine gland is the *thyroid*. Its hormone controls the rate at which the body uses energy.

Exocrine glands release their substances through tubes either into the intestines or onto the skin. Sweat, tears and saliva all come from exocrine glands.

Glass

People use glass in windows, spectacles, mirrors, tumblers, bottles, electric light-bulbs and many other objects.

Glass is made of sand mixed with some lime, soda and other chemical ingredients. Then the mixture is melted in a furnace. When it flows, it is often called molten glass. Workers can shape the molten glass in several ways. They may pour it into a mould, or shape it by blowing through a tube into a blob of molten glass stuck to the far end. If they pour molten glass onto a bath of molten tin, the glass forms a smooth sheet that is used for windows.

Most glass is brittle and breaks easily. But some kinds are so tough that you could use them to hammer nails into wood.

Three different glass products being made: bottles (top); plate glass for windows (centre); and thick polished sheets called float glass (bottom).

The Rocky Mountain goat, like most goats, is a nimble, sure-footed climber.

Goat

Goats belong to the cattle family. They are taller, thinner, and more agile than their close relative, the SHEEP. Goats have hooves and hollow horns; the male has a beard.

Wild goats, found in the mountains of central Asia and the Middle East, live in herds and eat grass and leaves. Domestic goats are kept in many lands. They provide milk, meat, hair and skins. Two kinds, Angora and Cashmere goats, are famous for their silky wool which is woven into fine cloth.

Gold

Gold is a lovely yellow metal that never rusts. It is so soft that you can beat it into thin sheets, or pull it out into a wire. Half of the world's gold is mined in just one part of South Africa. Because gold is beautiful and scarce, it is also very valuable. Most gold is kept in banks.

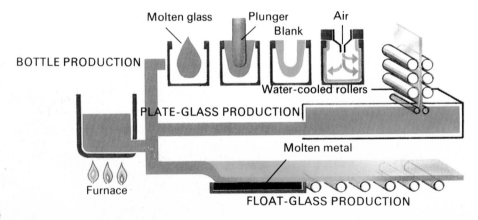

Gorilla

Gorillas are the largest of the APES. A big male may be as tall as a man. Gorillas live in family groups in the warm forests of central Africa. They eat fruit, roots, bark and leaves. At night they make beds of twigs in the low branches of trees.

Granite

Granite is a hard rock made largely of CRYSTALS of quartz and feldspar. Quartz is transparent, like glass. Feldspar is pink, white or grey. Granite also has specks of dark MINERALS in it.

Granite was once a mass of hot, melted rock underground. As the rock cooled it hardened. Then movements of the earth's crust forced it up to the surface. The weather very slowly breaks down granite into sand and clay.

Builders use granite when they need a hard, strong stone. People also use granite to make polished stone monuments because they last longer than those made of limestone.

Gorillas are huge, heavy animals and can weigh three times as much as a man. They walk on all fours and spend most of their day on the ground looking for food.

Grape

People grow grapes to make WINE or for eating. They can also be dried and turned into raisins, currants and sultanas. Grapes grow on vines and need long, dry summers to grow well. Most grapes come from France, Italy and Spain. There are more than 8000 different kinds.

Grapes are widely grown in Crete, a large Greek island in the Mediterranean Sea. The flavour of a wine depends on the soil of the vineyard where the grapes are grown, and the amount of sun they get.

147

Graph

A graph makes facts easier to understand. It is a simple drawing that helps you compare either amounts of different things or the same thing at different times. For example, a pie graph shows different amounts as different sized slices cut in a pie. Bar graphs use long and short bars to show different amounts. Line graphs show temperature and other changes by a line that rises and falls.

Grass

Grasses are flowering plants with long, thin leaves growing from hollow stems. There are about 5000 kinds of grass. BAMBOO is as tall as a tree but most grasses are short. Sheep and cattle eat grass. We eat the seeds of cultivated cereal grasses such as WHEAT, maize and RICE.

Below: Three types of cereal grass.

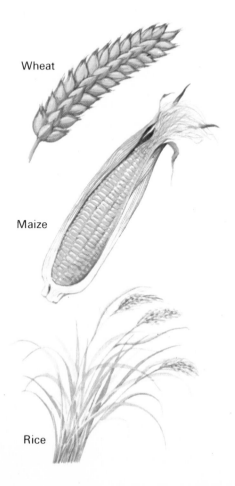

Wheat

Maize

Rice

A Lesser Marsh grasshopper, which lives by rivers and in wet meadows.

Grasshopper

These insects have feelers, wings and long back legs. Although most kinds of grasshopper can fly, they move mainly by jumping. Some can jump 20 times their own length. Grasshoppers eat leaves and those called LOCUSTS damage crops. Many males 'sing' by rubbing their back legs on their wings.

Gravity

Gravity is the pull that tries to tug everything toward the middle of the EARTH. It is gravity that makes objects fall, stops us from flying off into space and keeps the MOON circling the earth. When we weigh something, we are measuring the force with which gravity pulls that object down. The more closely packed the substances in an object are, the heavier it seems.

A large body has more gravitational pull than a smaller body.

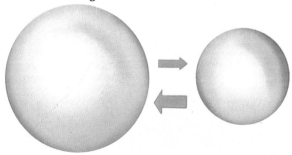

All PLANETS and STARS exert a pulling force. Scientists call this gravitation. The larger and denser a star or a planet is, and the closer it is to other objects, the more strongly it pulls them toward it. The SUN is far from the planets, but it is so huge that its gravitation keeps the planets circling around it. The moon is small and its gravitation is weak. An astronaut on the moon seems to weigh far less than he weighs here on earth.

Great Lakes

The Great Lakes are the world's largest group of freshwater lakes. Together, they are as big as the United Kingdom. Lake Michigan lies in the UNITED STATES. Lakes Superior, Erie, Huron and Ontario are shared by the United States and CANADA. The largest lake of all is Lake Superior. The lakes were formed when a huge sheet of ice melted 18,000 years ago.

Rivers and canals connect the lakes to each other and to the Atlantic Ocean. Ships can reach the sea from lake ports that lie 1600km inland. Lots of factories are built around the lakes to take advantage of the water supply. Most of the goods that the factories produce are taken to other parts by boat.

Great Wall of China

More than 2000 years ago the first emperor of CHINA, Ch'in Shi Huang Ti, built this wall to keep out China's enemies from the north. The Great Wall is the longest wall in the world. It stretches 3430km from the Yellow Sea in the east toward central Asia in the west.

The wall is made of earth and stone. Watchtowers were built every 180 metres along it. Chinese sentries sent warning signals from the towers if anyone attacked the wall. The signal was smoke by day and fire at night.

Part of the Great Wall of China. In places it stands wider and taller than a house.

Greece

Greece is a country that lies in south-east EUROPE. Mountains cover most of the land, and peninsulas poke out into the sea like giant fingers. Greece includes the island of Crete and many smaller islands in the Aegean and Ionian seas. Greek summers are hot and dry. Winters are mild and wet.

Almost ten million people live in Greece. Many work in the capital city, Athens. Greek farmers produce lemons, grapes, WHEAT and olives.

Greece, Ancient

The first great people in GREECE were the Minoans and the Mycenaeans. The Minoans lived in Crete. They had rich cities and farms and led a peaceful life. The Mycenaeans lived on the mainland of Greece. They were warriors and sailors. The heroes of HOMER's poems were probably Mycenaean. Both these civilizations ended about 1200 BC.

Around this time, new groups of people began to move into Greece. They came from the north and spoke Greek. Instead of making Greece one kingdom, they built separate cities. They often fought wars with each other. Sometimes they joined together to fight other enemies, such as the Per-

sians. Two of the strongest cities were Athens and Sparta. In the 400s BC Athens was ruled by a DEMOCRACY. It became very powerful.

The Greeks loved the THEATRE, ART and POETRY. They had many great thinkers, or *philosophers*, including ARISTOTLE, Plato, and Socrates. Greek cities had many graceful buildings. They were decorated with

Two ancient Greek soldiers arming themselves for battle. They are putting on bronze helmets with horsehair crests, leather breastplates with shoulder pieces and waist flaps, bronze greaves for the shins and large round shields.

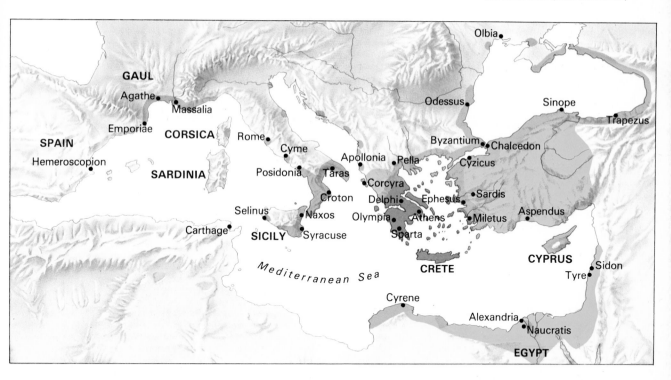

beautiful SCULPTURE. The Greeks also started the first OLYMPIC GAMES. In 339 BC
Greece was conquered by Philip, the father
of ALEXANDER THE GREAT.

*Above: Ancient Greece was about the same
size as Greece is today, but Greek settlers
spread out from the mainland (orange) to
many other parts of the Mediterranean (beige).
The map shows several colonial cities. Later,
after Alexander the Great had conquered the
Near East, Greek influences and settlers
spread even further (yellow).*

*A Greek house of the 5th century
BC. The main entrance is hidden
on the left. On the right is a shop,
opening onto the street. The
citizen's wife worked with the
female house-slaves, cooking
and weaving. The main room in
the house is the dining room,
with four or five couches and
small three-legged tables. Part
of the house is given over to
women's rooms.*

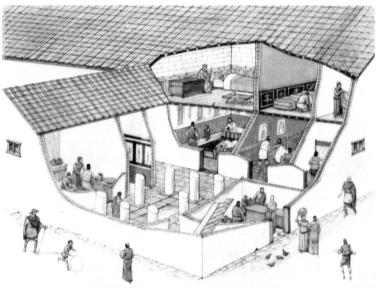

151

Greek Mythology

The ancient Greeks, like all peoples who lived thousands of years ago, invented gods and goddesses to explain the world around them. Stories about these *deities* are called *myths*. In Greek mythology, many of the gods lived on Mount Olympus. There they ate a special food called *ambrosia* and drank *nectar* to make them immortal. The greatest god was Zeus. When he was angry he made thunder. Zeus had many children. One, Athena, was the goddess of wisdom. The city of Athens is named after her. Another, Apollo, was the sun god. He drove the sun's chariot across the sky each day.

Cannon, 1460

Vigilant rocket

Gun

Guns are weapons that fire bullets or other missiles from a tube open at one end.

Guns were probably invented in the 1200s. By the 1300s guns were firing missiles that could pierce armour and break down castle walls.

Early guns were large weapons, far too heavy for one man to carry. The first gun was a big bucket with a small hole in the bottom. Soldiers put gunpowder into the bucket. Then they piled stones on top. They lit the gunpowder through the hole. When the gunpowder exploded, the stones flew out. The large, long guns called cannons were first used about 1350. Cannons fired big metal cannonballs. In the 1800s came guns which fired pointed shells that exploded when they hit their target. A spiral groove cut in the gun barrel made the shells spin as they flew through the air. Soldiers could fire such shells farther and hit their targets more often than with cannonballs.

Troops first used small arms in the 1300s. Small arms are guns that one man can carry. Inventors developed short-barreled pistols and revolvers for firing at nearby targets. They developed muskets, rifles and machine guns for long-distance shooting. In modern guns a hammer sets off an explosion that drives a shell or bullet from the barrel.

Tank gun, 1917

Four artillery officers stand around a small cannon. This type of gun was used in the American Civil War in the 1860s.

Gutenberg, Johannes

Johannes Gutenberg (about 1397–1468) was a German goldsmith sometimes called the father of PRINTING. In his day, people slowly copied books by hand or printed them from wooden blocks where each letter had to be carved separately. About 1440, Gutenberg learned to make metal letters called type. He could pick them up and place them in rows to build pages of type. Each page was held together by a frame. Gutenberg put the frame into a press, and quickly pressed the inked surface of his type onto sheets of paper. In this way, Gutenberg could make copies of a book faster and more cheaply than ever before.

Gymnastics

Gymnastics are exercises that help to make and keep the body fit. The OLYMPIC GAMES have separate gymnastic exercises for men and women. Women perform graceful steps, runs, jumps, turns and somersaults on a narrow wooden beam. They hang from a high bar and swing to and fro between it and a lower one. They leap over a vaulting horse. Women also perform floor exercises.

Men hang from a high bar and swing up and down, to and fro, and over and over in giant circles. Using two raised, level bars, they swing, vault, and do handstands. They grip hoops that jut up from a leather-covered pommel 'horse', and swing their legs and body. They leap over a vaulting horse. Some of these exercises are done by children and adults in gymnastics classes. Men also perform floor exercises.

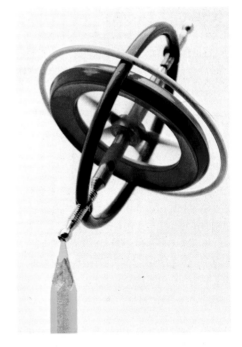

This toy gyroscope is tilted, yet balances on the tip of a pencil. It seems to defy gravity.

Gyroscope

A gyroscope is a wheel that spins in a special frame. No matter how the frame tilts, the wheel's axle points in the same direction. Even the pull of GRAVITY and the earth's MAGNETISM do not affect the axle.

On a ship or aircraft, a COMPASS made from a gyroscope always points to the north. Gyroscopes can also keep an aircraft on course without the pilot steering.

The backward roll is one of the floor exercises.

Hannibal

Hannibal (247–183 BC) was a Carthaginian general who invaded Italy. In 218 BC he left his base in Spain and marched an army over the Alps into Italy. He fought the Romans for 15 years but never quite crushed them.

Above: This old painting of musicians shows what harps looked like in Egypt more than 3000 years ago. The harpist twisted pegs on the frame to tighten or loosen the strings.

Hair

Hair grows like threads from the skins of most MAMMALS. It has the same ingredients that make nails, claws, hooves, feathers and reptiles' scales. Hair helps to keep the body warm, and protects the skin. There are several kinds of hair. Cats have plenty of soft, thick fur. Porcupines are protected by sharp, stiff hairs called quills.

Oriental people have straight hair. Caucasian (white) people usually have wavy hair. Black people have hair that is coiled like a spring. A cross-section of each type of hair under a microscope also looks different.

Harp

This musical instrument has long and short strings stretched over a tall frame that stands on the floor. One side of the frame is hollow. This helps to give the harp

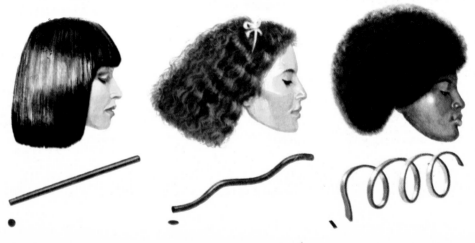

its special sound. A harpist plays by pluck-ing the strings with fingers and thumbs. Harps are the oldest stringed instruments. People made harps in Iraq more than 4000 years ago.

Harvey, William

William Harvey (1578–1657) was an Eng-lish doctor who showed that BLOOD flows around the body in an endless stream. Harvey proved that a beating heart squeezes blood through arteries and flaps in the heart, and that veins stop the blood flowing back. He worked out that the amount of blood pumped by a heart in an hour weighs three times more than a man.

Hastings, Battle of

In 1066 this battle made Norman invaders the masters of England.

WILLIAM THE CONQUEROR sailed 7000 Nor-man troops and some war horses from France to England in about 450 open boats. Meanwhile, ANGLO-SAXONS under King Harold were defeating Norse invaders in northern England.

Harold quickly marched south. He met William at Senlac near Hastings. The Anglo-Saxons defended a hilltop with axes, spears, swords and shields. The Normans attacked with arrows, lances, spiked clubs and swords. The battle lasted all day. Then the Normans pretended to run away. When some Anglo-Saxons followed, Norman cavalry cut them down. Then the Normans showered arrows on the rest and attacked once more. By evening, Harold was dead and his army was beaten.

Hearing

Hearing is the sense that allows us to pick up SOUND. The sense organ making this possible is the EAR. Some people cannot hear; they are *deaf*. Either they were born without hearing or, at some time, their ears became damaged by an illness or accident.

Towards the end of the Battle of Hastings the Norman cavalry overpowered the less well trained English soldiers. When the English were tricked into breaking ranks they were mown down.

Deaf people can 'talk' to each other by using a special sign language.

Like people, all animals with backbones have hearing organs. Some can hear much better than people. Cats and dogs, for example, pick up more sounds than we can. Tigers hunt by sound, and some owls also hunt in this way.

Heart

The heart is a muscle in the body. It pumps BLOOD around the body through veins and arteries. In an adult person, the heart goes on working at between 70 and 80 beats a minute until death. It was the English doctor William HARVEY (1578–1657) who discovered how the heart works.

The blood carries oxygen from the LUNGS and energy from the food we eat. Arteries carry this rich, red blood to feed the body. Veins carry away waste products and return the dark 'tired' blood to the heart.

When the heart stops beating, the body is starved of oxygen and quickly dies. But doctors can sometimes massage a stopped heart back to life. People with diseased hearts can be given 'spare parts' to repair them and even a new heart, transplanted from someone who has just died.

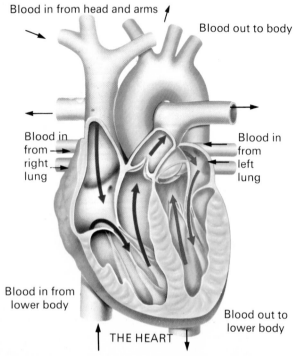

Blood in from head and arms

Blood out to body

Blood in from right lung

Blood in from left lung

Blood in from lower body

Blood out to lower body

THE HEART

Heat

Heat is a form of ENERGY. We can feel it but we cannot see it. We feel heat from the SUN, or when we sit in front of a fire. When something burns, heat is produced. The sun gives out enormous amounts of heat, which is produced by atoms joining together or 'fusing' inside the sun. This same kind of energy can be released by a hydro-

Water will take up heat until it boils. More heat is needed to keep it boiling and then to change it into steam.

1   2   3

gen bomb on earth. It is because we get just the right amount of heat from the sun that our earth and ourselves are what they are. A few degrees less heat from the sun and our world would be a lifeless frozen waste. A few degrees more heat and life as we know it could not exist.

Most of the heat we use comes from burning fuels. But heat can also be made by FRICTION, or rubbing. Heat is also produced when electricity travels through a coil of wire. This is what makes the bar of an electric fire glow red.

We can measure how hot a thing is by finding its temperature. This is done with a THERMOMETER. When a substance gets hot, the molecules, or tiny particles, of which it is made move around more quickly. Often the substance expands (gets bigger) as this happens. Metals expand the most.

Helicopter

The helicopter is an unusual and useful aircraft. It was invented in the 1930s and today is used for all kinds of jobs, especially rescue work. This is because helicopters can land in areas too small for ordinary aircraft. Helicopters can fly in any direction and hover in mid-air. Instead of fixed wings they have a moving wing called a rotor which acts as a wing and a propeller. A smaller rotor on the tail stops the helicopter from spinning round and is also used for turning.

Helicopters have dozens of important uses. They are used for passenger and airmail transportation, photography, prospecting, search and rescue, forest fire control and crop spraying. They are also used more and more by armies and navies to pick up wounded, to transport troops and to serve as fireships.

Russian Mi-10

American Boeing-Vertol 107–11

German FW-61

The German FW-61 had two rotors fixed side by side. It was the first successful helicopter. Some modern helicopters, like the Boeing-Vertol, have a rotor at each end of the fuselage. But the huge Russian Mi-10 relies on one big rotor.

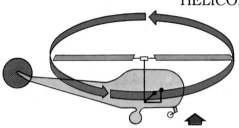

To fly upward, the rotor blades are kept at the same angle.

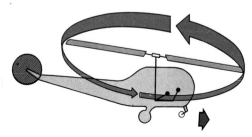

To fly forward, the blades tilt forward to 'bite' into the air.

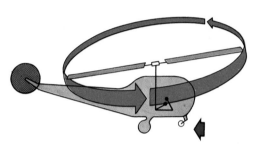

To fly backward, the blades tilt in the opposite direction.

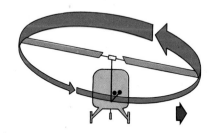

To fly sideways, the blades tilt either to the left or the right.

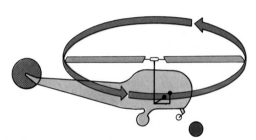

To hover, the blades are angled to balance up and down forces.

Henry VIII was a skilled statesman, scholar, musician and poet. But he was also selfish and ruthless.

Henry (kings)

Eight English kings have been named Henry. Henry I (1068–1135) was the youngest son of William the Conqueror. Henry II (1133–1189) was the first of the Plantagenet line of kings. He quarrelled with Thomas à Becket, Archbishop of Canterbury, who was then murdered by the king's knights. His grandson, Henry III (1207–1272), was a weak king who was ruled by the powerful barons.

During the Wars of the Roses, the families of York and Lancaster fought for the English throne. Three Lancastrian kings were called Henry: Henry IV, or Henry Bolingbroke (1367–1413), Henry V (1387–1422), and Henry VI (1421–1471). Henry V was a brilliant soldier. He is famous for leading his army to victory against the French at the battle of Agincourt.

The first Tudor king was Henry VII (1457–1509), who restored peace. His son, Henry VIII (1491–1547), was clever and popular, but also ruthless. He was married six times and broke away from the Roman Catholic church to divorce his first wife, Catherine of Aragon. Three of his children reigned after him: EDWARD VI, Mary I, and ELIZABETH I.

Herb

Herbs are plants with soft, rather than woody, stems. But the name 'herbs' is also given to certain plants that are added to food during cooking. They are valued for their scent and flavour.

Common herbs used in cooking include sage, thyme, parsley, garlic, mint, rosemary, basil, fennel and chives. Most can be grown quite easily, although they came originally from the warm, sunny lands of the Mediterranean region.

Herbs can be used fresh from the garden, or they can be cut and dried for storage. People have grown and used herbs for hundreds of years. In the days before modern medicine, herbs were used to treat many illnesses. Even today some herbs are still used in this way.

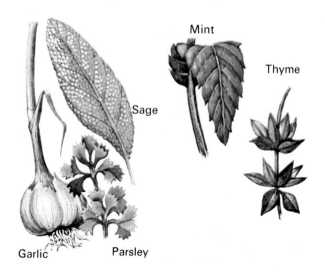

Hercules

Hercules is one of the great heroes of ancient mythology. Called Hercules by the Romans and Heracles by the Greeks, he was the son of Jupiter (Zeus) and an earthly princess. In a fit of madness, sent to him by a jealous goddess, Hercules killed his wife and children. To make up for this dreadful crime, he was ordered by Apollo to perform Twelve Labours: terrible tasks that mostly involved killing monsters. After many dangers, Hercules carried out all twelve labours

This picture on a Greek pot shows Hercules wrestling with a monster. He is wearing the skin of a lion which he killed in his first Labour.

and was rewarded with immortality. Today the word 'Herculean' is used to describe something very difficult.

Hibernation

When an animal hibernates, it goes to sleep for the winter. It does this because in winter food is scarce. Going to sleep during the cold weather saves animals from starving to death.

Before hibernating, animals eat as much food as they can find. The dormouse, for example, stuffs itself until it is fat and round. As autumn approaches, it makes a snug nest, curls into a ball and falls into a sound sleep. In fact, its heart beats so slowly the dormouse looks dead. Its body uses hardly any energy while in hibernation, in order to make its store of fat last as long as possible. In spring, a thin and hungry dormouse wakes up and comes out of its nest to look for food.

In cold countries many animals hibernate. Not all sleep right through the winter. Squirrels wake up on mild days and eat food they had hidden away in the summer. But all hibernating animals find a warm, dry place to sleep, where they are safe from hungry enemies.

Some hibernating animals (from top, left to right): newt, natterjack toad, adders, green toad, common toad, tortoise and woodchuck.

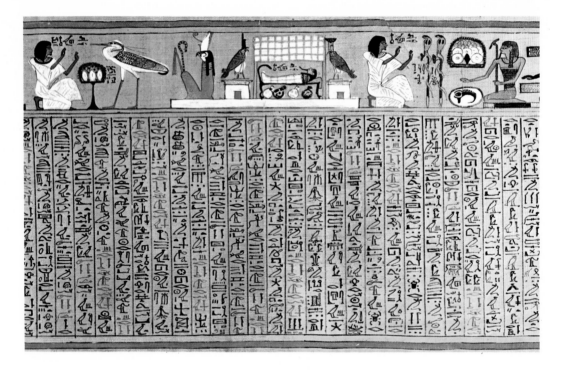

Egyptian hieroglyphics written on papyrus. Papyrus was a kind of paper made from a type of reed. The reeds were cut, beaten into thin strips and pressed together into sheets.

Hieroglyphics

Hieroglyphics were an ancient form of writing. Our alphabet has 26 letters. However 5000 years ago the ancient Egyptians used picture-signs instead of letters. Later these signs became hieroglyphics—marks that stood for things, people and ideas. Egyptian hieroglyphics were written from right to left.

Hieroglyphic writing was very difficult and only a few people could do it. When the Egyptian empire died out, the secret of reading it was lost. No one could understand the hieroglyphics carved on stones and written on papyrus scrolls. Then, in 1799, a Frenchman found the Rosetta Stone, which is now in the British Museum in London. On it was writing in two known languages, and also in hieroglyphics. By comparing the known languages with the hieroglyphics, experts were at last able to understand the signs.

Himalayas

The highest range of mountains in the world is the mighty Himalaya. The name means 'land of snow'. The Himalayas form a great barrier range across Asia, dividing India in the south from Tibet (part of China) in the north. Many of Asia's greatest rivers

Most peaks in the mighty Himalayas are snow-covered all year round.

rise among the Himalayas, fed by the melting snows.

Until aircraft were invented few outsiders had ever been into the Himalayas. There are no roads or railways. The only way to travel is on foot, over steep mountain tracks. Horses, yaks, goats and even sheep are used to carry heavy loads.

The highest mountain in the world lies in the Himalayas. This is Mount Everest, 8848 metres high.

Hinduism

Hinduism is one of the world's great religions. Most Hindus live in Asia, and particularly in INDIA. Their religion has grown over a period of 4000 years.

Hindus believe that God is present in all things. Only priests or Brahmins can worship the supreme God. Ordinary people worship other gods, such as Vishnu, God of Life. The most important holy books of the Hindus are the *Vedas*. Hindus believe that certain animals, such as the cobra and the cow, are sacred and must never be killed or eaten.

Hippopotamus

The name hippopotamus means 'river horse', but in fact the hippo is related to the pig, not the horse. It is a huge, heavy animal and lives in Africa. Of all land animals, only the elephant is bigger.

Hippopotamuses live near rivers and lakes. They spend most of their time in the water and are good swimmers. In spite of its fearsome-looking jaws, the hippopotamus eats only plant food. It browses on water weeds and grasses, and at night often comes ashore to feed.

These animals are not usually dangerous if left alone. But they can inflict serious wounds with slashes from the tusks in their lower jaws.

History

History is the story of the past. The people who write down history are called historians. They usually write about important

The hippopotamus's eyes and nostrils are on top of its head. In this way it can see and breathe with ease while almost hidden in the water.

events such as wars, revolutions and changes in government, because these kinds of events affect nations. However, historians are also interested in the lives of ordinary people and in what they did each day and thought about.

Today we think of history as being written down in history books. But in earlier times, before books and printing, history was passed on by word of mouth. People told stories about their kings, their wars, their adventures and also about their own families. It was in this way that the stories of ancient Greece were collected by the poet HOMER to form the *Iliad* and the *Odyssey*. Some early stories such as these were made up in verse and sung to music. This made it easier for people to remember the stories correctly.

In ancient Egypt, scholars recorded the reigns of the PHARAOHS, and listed the victories they won in battle. Often these accounts were written in HIEROGLYPHICS on stone tablets. The Chinese, Greeks and Romans were also very interested in history. It was they who first took the writing of history seriously, and they wrote of how

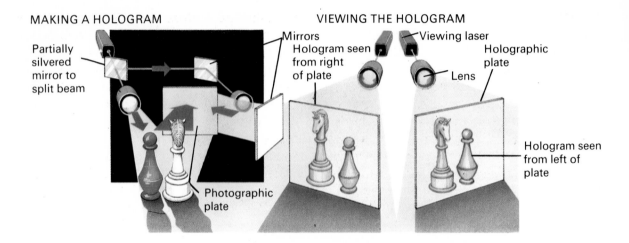

MAKING A HOLOGRAM — Partially silvered mirror to split beam — Mirrors — Photographic plate

VIEWING THE HOLOGRAM — Hologram seen from right of plate — Viewing laser — Holographic plate — Lens — Hologram seen from left of plate

their civilizations rose to power. During the Middle Ages in Europe, it was priests and monks who preserved ancient books and kept official records. These records include the *Domesday Book*, which tells us much of what we know about Norman England. History became an important branch of study in the 1700s and 1800s. Famous historians were Edward Gibbon (1737–1794) and Lord Macaulay (1800–1859).

Historians get their information from hidden remains such as things found buried in old graves, as well as from old books. The study of hidden remains is called ARCHAEOLOGY. But history is not just concerned with the distant past. After all, history is *our* story. What is news today will be history tomorrow.

Hitler, Adolf

Adolf Hitler (1889–1945) was the 'Führer', or leader, of GERMANY during WORLD WAR II. An ex-soldier, born in Austria, he became leader of the Nazi Party which took over Germany in 1933.

Germany was still weak after its defeat in WORLD WAR I. The Nazis promised to avenge this defeat and create a new German empire. In 1939 Hitler led Germany into World War II and conquered most of Europe. Millions of people were killed in Nazi death camps. But by 1945 Germany had lost the war. Hitler killed himself in the ruins of Berlin to avoid capture.

A split laser beam transforms the image of the chess pieces into a hologram. When viewed by laser light, the hologram shows the chess pieces in 3-D, but makes them blue, not red and white.

Holography

Holography is a way of making very realistic three-dimensional pictures called *holograms*. It does this by using LASER light instead of a camera.

To make a hologram, a laser beam is split into two; one beam hits the object and is reflected onto a photographic plate; the other beam, angled by mirrors, strikes the plate directly. The photographic plate is developed and a black-and-white pattern, the hologram, appears. When the hologram is lit up by a laser beam and viewed from the other side, it produces a three-dimensional image of the original object. The image seems real, with width, depth and height, but it is not in the object's original colour. Instead, it takes its colour from the laser beam.

Holography was first discovered 40 years ago. But it was not developed until the 1960s when lasers were introduced. Scientists are now looking at practical uses for holography. They are investigating using holograms in medicine, to probe the human body; in land surveys, to decipher aerial photographs; and in scientific work, to make very precise measurements.

Homer

Homer was a Greek poet and storyteller. He probably lived around 800 BC, but we know nothing else about him. All we have are two great poems said to be by Homer: the *Iliad* and the *Odyssey*. These poems tell us much of what we know about ancient Greek history and legend. The *Iliad* tells the story of the TROJAN WAR. The *Odyssey* tells of the adventures of Odysseus, a Greek hero, as he made his long journey home after the war.

Hong Kong

Hong Kong is a tiny British colony on the coast of China. Part of it is a small island, and the rest is a narrow strip of land called the New Territories, which is actually part of mainland China. Hong Kong has been governed by Britain since 1842. It is due to be handed over to Chinese rule in 1997.

Hong Kong has a fine harbour surrounded by mountains. The capital is Victoria, and another busy city is Kowloon. Hong Kong is a fascinating mixture of East and West. The people live by trade, fishing and farming. Tall apartment buildings have been built to house them, but there is still not enough room for all the five million people who crowd this small colony.

Horse

The horse was one of the first wild animals to be tamed. Today there are very few wild horses left. Many so-called 'wild' horses are actually descended from domestic horses which have run wild.

Tiny Hong Kong, in spite of its many skyscrapers, is still so overcrowded that thousands of people have to live on boats in the harbour.

The horse is valued for its speed and strength. But the first horse was a small rather doglike creature, with a way of life quite unlike that of modern horses. Called *Eohippus*, or 'dawn horse', it lived millions of years ago. It had four toes on its front feet and three toes on its back feet, and it probably hid from its enemies in the undergrowth.

Later, horses came out to live on the wide grassy plains. There was no undergrowth to hide in, so they escaped from enemies by running away. Gradually, their legs grew longer, and they lost all their toes except one. Finally, after millions of years of evolution, the modern horse appeared. It, too, has only one toe, and actually runs on tiptoe. Its toe has become a tough nail, or hoof.

This picture shows the names given to different parts of the horse's body. Almost all the horses kept today are ridden for pleasure and sport. There are very few working horses.

Hospital

Hospitals are places where sick people, or patients, are cared for. Doctors and nurses look after the patients and try to make them better.

There are two types of hospital. One, the general hospital, deals with everything from accident injuries to contagious diseases. The other type of hospital specializes in certain conditions. For example, there are *psychiatric* hospitals for people who are mentally ill; *maternity* hospitals where women have their babies; and *geriatric* hospitals for the elderly. In hospitals attached to medical schools, student doctors can gain experience through treating real patients.

In the ancient world, temples dedicated to the gods of healing used to have a hospital area. Sick people came there to pray and be treated. Later, in the Middle Ages, hospitals were attached to monasteries and run by monks and nuns. But in the last 200 years,

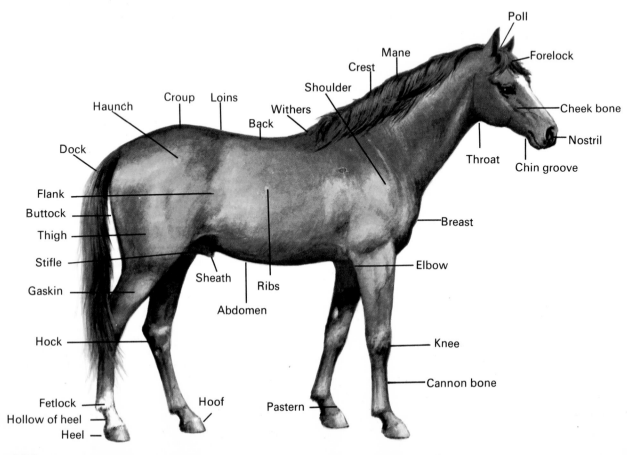

This baby, born too soon, is being kept alive in a warm, germ-free incubator. The nurse is checking the controls. Modern hospitals are full of special life-saving equipment.

non-religious hospitals have become the most common. In many countries, hospitals are now organized by the state and provide inexpensive or free medical treatment for all people. Modern hospitals have a wide range of technical equipment, such as X-RAY machines, heart-lung machines and LASERS.

House

Modern houses are airy, light and comfortable. Large windows, electricity, hot and cold running water and heating systems make them cosy to live in.

Houses date back to prehistoric times. Some of the first were built in the Middle East. They were simple little boxes with flat roofs. Often doors and windows were simply open spaces in the walls.

Houses in Greek and Roman times could be quite large. In towns they might be like apartments, perhaps five stories high. Wealthy Romans built themselves splendid villas that were even fitted with running water and heating systems.

In the Middle Ages houses were mostly crude wooden structures. They had just one or two rooms on a single level and everyone, including the animals, crowded into them to live, sleep and eat. Nobles' homes were more elaborate. They were often made of stone, and had several floors and many rooms.

As towns and cities grew in size, thousands of affordable flats and houses were built to house workers. Today houses are built from a variety of different materials and in many shapes and sizes.

Humidity

All air has some water in it, although we cannot see it. Humidity is the amount of water in the air. If the air contains only a little water vapour, the humidity is low. When air holds a lot of moisture, we say the humidity is high. The warmer the air, the more moisture it can hold. Humidity affects the way we feel. When the humidity is high we feel sticky and uncomfortable. This is because the sweat does not evaporate easily from our skin. But extremely low humidity is not very good for us. Some people use *humidifiers* in their homes to put more moisture into the air.

Hummingbird

These birds are among the smallest in the world. They are found only in the Western Hemisphere, from Canada to the tip of South America. The tiniest of the 320 known kinds lives in Cuba. It is less than 5 cm when fully grown, hardly bigger than a large bumblebee.

The feathers of hummingbirds are coloured in brilliant metallic hues of blue, green, red and yellow. When the colours flash in the sun, they look like glittering jewels.

Hummingbirds can beat their wings up to 70 times a second. This is what causes their distinctive humming sound. It also lets them hover in midair and fly backward and sideways like a helicopter. In this way, they dart from flower to flower and feed while flying. Hummingbirds take nectar and insects from deep inside flowers by rolling their tongue into a tube.

Hungary

This is a small, central European country with a population of less than 11 million. It covers an area of some 93,000 square km, slightly larger than Scotland. (See page 123.)

Hungary has no coastline. The mighty Danube River flows across the country on its way to the Black Sea, dividing it almost in two. Ships can sail upriver as far as Budapest, the capital of Hungary and its biggest city.

Hungary is low-lying and fairly flat. To the east it becomes a vast grassy plain. Here herds of sheep, cattle and horses are grazed. The climate is hot and dry in summer, and bitterly cold in winter. Agriculture is very important, and there are also rich sources of coal, oil, and bauxite for making aluminium.

After WORLD WAR I and the collapse of the Austro-Hungarian Empire, Hungary became an independent republic. Since WORLD WAR II it has had a communist government and has been closely linked with the SOVIET UNION.

A hovering hummingbird reaches deep into a hibiscus flower with its slender beak to suck up sweet nectar and tiny insects.

Hydrogen

Hydrogen is a gas. Scientists believe that it is the most abundant ELEMENT in the universe. It is the single most important material from which stars, including our SUN, are made.

Hydrogen is the simplest and lightest of all the elements. It is more than 14 times as light as air which is why it was formerly used to fill airships. It is also colourless, and has no smell and no taste. Hydrogen burns very easily, which explains its early name of 'inflammable air'. Great masses of hydrogen are always being burned in the sun. It is this fierce burning that gives us light and heat from the sun.

Coal, oil and natural gas all contain hydrogen. It is also a very important part of all plants and animals.

much of North America and Asia, and Europe as far south as London. In some places the ice piled up more than 1000 metres high. This made the sea level lower than it is today. A land bridge was formed between Asia and North America. The first people in the Americas came across this land bridge from Asia.

Iceberg

Icebergs are parts of glaciers and ice shelves that have broken away and float in the sea. They are found in the waters of the ARCTIC and the ANTARCTIC.

Icebergs can be very big. Some weigh millions of tons. Most of an iceberg is hidden under the surface of the sea. Some icebergs may be 145 km long. They can be 120 metres high above water. An iceberg this high would be about another 980 metres deep under water.

Icebergs are dangerous to ships. Some icebergs float south from the Arctic into the Atlantic Ocean. In 1912, a ship called the *Titanic* hit an iceberg in the Atlantic. It sank, and 1500 people were drowned.

Ice Ages

The Ice Ages were times when vast sheets of ice covered parts of the earth. Each period lasted for thousands of years. In between were warmer periods. The last Ice Age ended about 20,000 years ago.

During the Ice Ages the weather was very cold. Endless snow fell and glaciers grew and spread. At times the glaciers covered

Ice Hockey

Ice hockey is a team game played on ice. The players, six in a team, wear ice skates. They play on a *rink* that is 60 metres long and 26 metres wide, with a goal at either end. Each player has a long-handled stick with a curved blade at the bottom. He uses this to drive the *puck*, a rubber disc, around the rink. Both teams try to shoot the puck past the opposing team's defence and into their goal net. A game is divided into three periods; each period lasts 20 minutes.

Arctic icebergs

Tabular icebergs

The tallest icebergs break away from Greenland. The tallest ever seen was 167 metres above the water. The icebergs with the biggest area are the tabular icebergs that break away from Antarctica. The largest ever seen was bigger than Belgium.

Incas

The Incas were people who lived in SOUTH AMERICA. They ruled a great empire from the 1200s until the 1500s. The centre of their empire was in PERU. In the 1400s the empire grew. It stretched thousands of miles, from CHILE in the south to Ecuador in the north.

The Inca king and his nobles ruled over the people in the empire. They were very strict and told the farmers and craftsmen what to grow and make.

In the 1530s, Spanish soldiers led by Pizarro reached America. They captured the Inca king and said they would free him in return for gold. Incas brought their treasure to free the king, but the Spanish still killed him.

When the Spaniards arrived, the Incas had built about 16,000 kilometres of roads, many of them high in the Andes mountains. The roads zig-zagged up and down very steep slopes, and so steps were cut to make the going easier. Over deep ravines the Incas built suspension bridges made of ropes of twisted fibres or vines.

In the picture, trains of llamas carry packs, and a nobleman is carried in his litter. A relay runner prepares to hand over a *quipu*. The Inca people never invented writing, but used knotted cords called quipu to record numbers.

India

India has a population of 733 million. It has more people than any other country except China. India is part of ASIA. It is a large country with an area of 3,287,350 sq km.

To the north of India are the HIMALAYAS. Many people live in the fertile northern plains, which are crossed by the great Ganges and Brahmaputra rivers. The south is high, flat land, with mountains called the Ghats along the coast.

India is very hot and dry in summer. Parts of the country are almost DESERT. But winds called *monsoons* bring heavy rain to the north-east every year.

Most Indians are farmers. They live in small villages and grow rice, wheat, tea, cotton and jute. India is also a fast-growing industrial country. Cities such as Calcutta and Bombay are among the world's biggest. The capital is New Delhi.

Hindi and English are the two main languages, but there are hundreds of others. Most Indians are Hindus, but many follow the religion of ISLAM. There are also many other religions in India, including Buddhism and Christianity.

Below right: City streets in India are always full of noise and people. Below: These women are picking tea. India grows a third of the world's tea.

Indians, American

American Indians are the native peoples of the Americas—that is, the first people to live there. They are known as Indians because when Christopher COLUMBUS reached America in 1492 he thought he had arrived in India.

The Indians of the Americas are thought to have crossed to the North American continent from Asia about 20,000 years ago. Very gradually, over the centuries, they spread through North America and down into what is now CENTRAL and SOUTH AMERICA. They developed different ways of life according to where they lived. 'American Indians' now usually refers to the Indians of North America.

There, in the eastern woodlands, the Iroquois and Algonquin tribes hunted deer and built domed wigwams (huts) of wood and bark. On the Great Plains, tribes such as the Sioux and Cheyenne lived off the huge herds of BISON which they hunted. In the deserts of the south-west, the Acoma and Hopi tribes built villages of *adobe* (dried mud bricks). Along the coast of the Pacific north-west, tribes such as the Haida and Kwakiutl built huge totem poles of elaborately carved wood.

When Europeans began to settle in America, conflict broke out as they invaded the Indians' hunting grounds. Many Indians were killed or forced to move farther

Above: An old picture, from about 1585, of an Indian chief in ceremonial dress. Above right: An Indian from the Mojave Desert region in California.

west. By the late 1800s almost all the tribes had been given land on special reservations by the US government. Today many Indians are working to gain equal opportunities for themselves as American citizens.

Indonesia

Indonesia is a country in South-East ASIA. It is a chain of about 3000 islands around the EQUATOR. The islands stretch over a distance of 4800 km.

Indonesia has 160 million people. More than half of them live on Java, one of the biggest islands. The capital city, Djakarta, is in Java. Most Indonesians are farmers. They grow many things, including rice, tea, rubber and tobacco.

Industrial Revolution

The Industrial Revolution was a great change that took place in Europe and North America in the 1700s and 1800s. People began to make things on machines in factories. The new machines were run by STEAM ENGINES. They made things much faster than people could by hand. Mining and metals became more important and the RAILWAYS began to be built. Many people moved from the countryside to work in factories in the towns.

An old picture shows how women and children worked in coal mines during the Industrial Revolution. Others spent long hours in factories.

171

Inoculation

Inoculation protects people from diseases. It is also called *vaccination*.

Inoculation works by giving people a very weak dose of a disease. The body learns to fight the germs which cause the disease. In this way, the body becomes protected, or *immune*, from the disease.

Immunity from a disease may last from a few months to many years, depending on the kind of disease and vaccine. There are many kinds of inoculation. They are used against diseases such as typhoid, cholera, measles and polio. Many people used to fall ill and die from these diseases. Now more people are saved every year through inoculation.

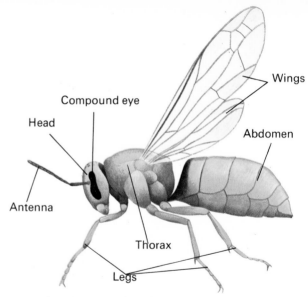

A typical insect, showing the clear division between the three parts of the body. Legs and wings are attached to the thorax.

Insects

There are about 35 million different kinds of insect in the world. Every year hundreds of new kinds are found. Some of the main kinds are BEETLES, BUTTERFLIES AND MOTHS, BEES, ANTS, GRASSHOPPERS and FLIES.

Insects do not have backbones. Animals without backbones are called *invertebrates*. Insects live everywhere except in the sea. Some insects live in hot, volcanic pools. Others live in the cold Antarctic. They can feed on almost anything: plants, animals, plastic and even chemicals. Some insects

Insects range in size from tiny fleas to goliath beetles as big as a human hand.

are very small. Tiny wasps called fairy flies are only about 0.25 mm long. Some insects grow very big. Giant stick insects may be 30 cm long.

The bodies of insects have three parts: the head, the *thorax* and the *abdomen*. The head has eyes and a pair of feelers, or *antennae*. It also has a mouth for biting or sucking. The thorax has three parts, each with a pair of legs. The thorax often has two pairs of wings as well. Inside the abdomen lies the gut.

Insects breathe through tiny holes in the sides of their bodies called *spiracles*. Tubes

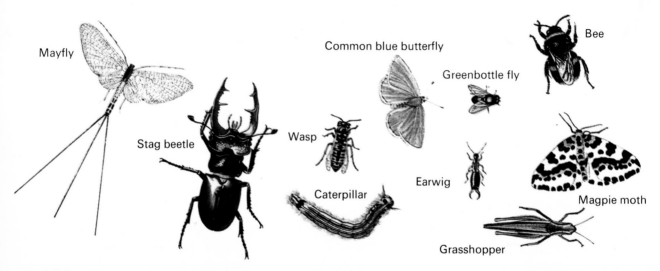

Mayfly

Common blue butterfly

Bee

Greenbottle fly

Stag beetle

Wasp

Caterpillar

Earwig

Magpie moth

Grasshopper

from the spiracles take air to all the CELLS of the body.

Many insects are pests. They damage crops and spread diseases. Some MOSQUITOS carry malaria. The tsetse fly spreads sleeping sickness. Flies and fleas also pass on diseases. Swarms of LOCUSTS can destroy tons of crops in a few hours. Some insects are useful. They eat harmful insects or lay their eggs inside them. Many insects help plants. They take pollen from one flower to another.

Many insects go through four stages in their lives. At each stage they are different. The insect is born as an egg. The egg hatches into a grub, or *larva*. After a while the larva stops eating and turns into a chrysalis, or *pupa*. The adult insect grows inside the pupa and breaks out of it when it is fully formed.

Adult insects do not live long. Most live for a few weeks. Adult mayflies live only a few hours. Some insects live longer. A queen bee may live for seven years. Termite queens live even longer.

Instinct

People have to learn to read and write, but bees do not learn how to sting. They are born to sting when there is danger. This kind of behaviour is called instinct. Instincts are inherited.

Animals do many things by instinct. Birds build their nests this way. Simple animals, such as insects, do almost everything by instinct. They have a set way of finding food, attacking enemies or escaping. Animals that act entirely by instinct do not have enough INTELLIGENCE to learn new ways of doing things.

Intelligence

When someone uses experience and knowledge to solve a new problem, he shows intelligence. Intelligence depends on being able to learn. Animals that act only by INSTINCT lack intelligence. People, apes, and whales are the most intelligent animals.

Internal-Combustion Engine

In internal-combustion engines, fuel burns inside the engines. The most common internal-combustion engines are petrol engines and DIESEL ENGINES. In the petrol engine, fuel mixes with air inside a cylinder. A spark sets the mixture alight and it explodes. This happens over and over again. Hot gases from the explosions push a piston to and fro inside the cylinder. Most engines have several cylinders. The pistons work very quickly in turn. They move the crankshaft. This movement turns WHEELS or propellers.

Petrol and diesel engines are used in MOTOR CARS and trucks, and in ships and planes with propellers.

How an internal-combustion engine works. 1. The piston draws fuel and air into the cylinder. 2. The piston rises and compresses the mixture. 3. The spark plug ignites the mixture. 4. The piston rises again and forces out exhaust gases.

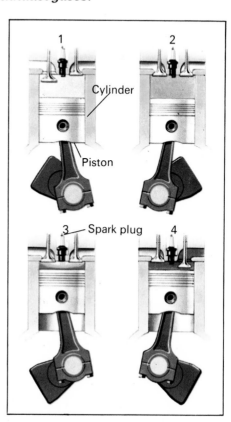

173

Iran

Iran is a country in ASIA. It lies between the USSR and the Caspian Sea in the north and the Persian Gulf in the south. Although the country is about seven times larger than the United Kingdom, it has fewer people living in it. Deserts, snowy mountains and green valleys cover most of the land. Much of Iran has hot summers and cold winters.

Iranians speak Persian. (Persia is the old name for Iran.) Their religion is ISLAM. Tehran is the capital city.

Many Iranians are nomads who travel around with flocks of sheep or goats. Each time they camp, the women set up simple looms and weave beautiful rugs by hand. Some Persian rugs and carpets take years to make. They are bought by people in many countries. Iran's most important product is oil. The country is one of the world's biggest oil producers.

Iran has a long history. In about 550 BC the Persians had a leader called Cyrus. Cyrus and his army made an empire that stretched from Greece and Egypt to India. The Persian empire was then the largest in the world.

ALEXANDER THE GREAT conquered Persia about 330 BC. Later, the country was ruled by ARABS and Mongols. During the twentieth century Iran was ruled by emperors, or *shahs*. In 1979 the government of Iran changed and the shah left the country. Iran became an Islamic Republic, ruled by a religious leader called Ayatollah Khomeini. Today Iran is unsettled politically. It has been at war with IRAQ since 1980.

Iraq

Iraq is an ARAB country in south-west ASIA. Much of Iraq is a dry, sandy and stony plain. It is cool in winter and very hot in summer. The Tigris and Euphrates rivers flow through the plain to the Persian Gulf. Their water helps the farmers to grow rice, cotton, wheat and dates. Iraq is also one of the biggest oil producers in the world. Pipelines carry the oil from the north of the country across the desert to ports in Syria and Lebanon.

Many Iraqis are nomads. They live in the deserts with their sheep and goats. But three million of the 15 million people work in the capital city of Baghdad.

Some of the first cities in the world were built near Iraq's big rivers. Ur was one of the earliest cities. It was built by a Bronze Age people called the Sumerians. The Bible says that Ur was also the home of Abraham. Later the Babylonians built their famous city, Babylon, in Iraq. The ruins of Babylon can still be seen.

Below left: This royal palace was built at Persepolis in Persia (Iran) 2500 years ago. It belonged to the Persian emperor Darius.
Below: This beautiful mosque is in Isfahan, Iran. A mosque is a Muslim place of worship.

Ireland

Ireland is the second largest island of the
BRITISH ISLES. It is formed like a saucer.
Mountains form the rim. The middle is a
low plain. Through this flows the Shannon,
the longest river in the British Isles. Irish
weather is often mild and rainy. Meadows
and moors cover much of the land. Northern Ireland is part of the UNITED KINGDOM of
Great Britain and Northern Ireland. Its
capital city is Belfast. Southern Ireland is
the Republic of Ireland, or Eire. Its capital is
Dublin. In 1973 the Republic of Ireland
joined the EEC.

The British and Irish governments are
trying to put an end to terrorism between
Catholics and Protestants in Northern Ireland.

Iron and Steel

Iron is the cheapest and most useful of all
metals. Much of our food, clothes, homes,
cars, tools and machines are made with
machines and tools made from iron.

Iron is mined, or *quarried* as iron ores, or
MINERALS. The ore is melted down, or *smel-
ted*, in a blast furnace. The iron is then
made into cast iron, wrought iron, or mixed
with a small amount of CARBON to form
steel.

Molten iron is poured into a furnace at an iron
and steel foundry in Canada.

Cast iron is hard but not as strong as
steel. Molten cast iron is poured into
moulds to make such things as engine
blocks. Wrought iron is soft but tough. It is
used for chains and gates. Steel is hard and
strong. Steel alloys containing metals such
as tungsten and chromium are used to
make many different things, from bridges
to nails.

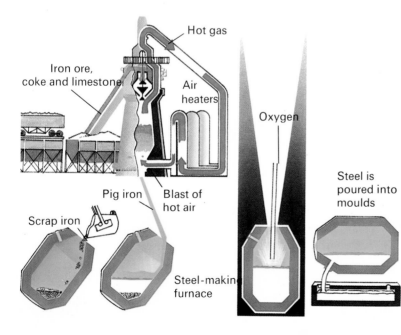

When iron ore is heated with coke and limestone in a blast furnace, a mixture of iron and carbon called pig iron is produced. The carbon comes from the coke. A blast of hot air is driven through the iron ore as it descends in the blast furnace. Molten pig iron is formed at the base of the furnace. Hot gases from the top of the furnace heat the air that is fed to the furnace.

The pig iron has too much carbon to make steel, so the extra carbon is burned off by blowing oxygen over it. Scrap iron may be added first. The molten steel produced is then poured into moulds to make steel blocks.

175

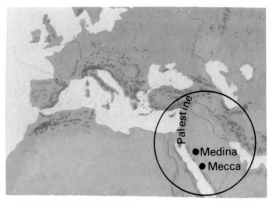

Above: Mohammed preached Islam in Mecca and Medina. Palestine is the home of Judaism and Christianity. Mohammed took ideas from these religions. All three teach belief in one God.
Left: This beautiful mosque is in Samarra, Iraq. The building behind is a minaret. Holy men stand on minarets to call Muslims to prayer.
Below: A 600-year-old painting of the angel Gabriel. Muslims believe he was the messenger of Allah (God).

Islam

Islam is a religion started in AD 622 by MOHAMMED. It has more followers than any other religion except Christianity. Islam means 'submission'. Its followers are called Muslims. Muslim means 'submissive one'. Muslims believe they must submit, or give in, to God's will. They believe in one God and in Mohammed as his prophet. Muslims pray five times a day and give gifts to the poor. They go without food until dark for one month a year and try to visit Mecca, Mohammed's birthplace, before they die. They also try to obey the rules for good living set out in the KORAN, the holy book of Islam.

Islam began in Arabia. Today it is the main religion in North Africa and most of south-west Asia.

Island

An island is a piece of land surrounded by water. Some islands are chunks of land that became separated from CONTINENTS. Other islands are VOLCANOES that have poked up above the sea. Yet others lie inland, in lakes and rivers. Greenland is the largest island in the world.

Israel

Israel is a country in south-west ASIA. It lies between the Mediterranean Sea, the Red Sea and the Dead Sea.

Farmers grow oranges, cotton and grain on fertile plains. More than half the land is dry mountain or desert. Summers are hot and winters are mild.

There are four million Israelis. One person in ten lives in JERUSALEM, the capital city. Most Israelis are Jews. There are also many ARABS. The main language of the country is Hebrew.

Italy

Italy is a country in southern EUROPE. It is shaped like a boot, with the toe pointed toward Sicily (see map on page 123). Sicily and Sardinia are big Italian islands.

Much of Italy is mountainous. The sharp, snowy peaks of the Alps cross northern Italy. The Apennines run like a backbone down the middle. Between the Alps and Apennines lies the plain of Lombardy. Italy is famous for its lovely mountain lakes and hot, sunny summers. Rain falls mostly in winter.

Crops grow on almost half the land. Italy produces more pears and olives than any other country. The farmers also grow a lot of grapes and lemons, as well as wheat, rice, apples and tomatoes.

Big factories in northern Italy make cars, chemicals, machines and textiles.

The capital is ROME. Many tourists visit Rome to see VATICAN CITY and the ruins of the ROMAN EMPIRE. Many of Italy's 57 million people are descended from the Romans.

Jerusalem, the capital, is Israel's second-largest city. It is sacred for Jews, Christians and Muslims.

Below: Venice is one of Italy's most beautiful medieval cities. It has many palaces and churches.

Jackal

Jackals are a kind of wild DOG. Some are brown or greyish and live in eastern Europe, Asia and North Africa. Africa has other kinds too. Jackals hide in bushes by day. At night they hunt small animals and find food in rubbish heaps.

Jade

Jade is a kind of MINERAL. It is a hard stone that is usually green, blackish green or white. Jade can be carved and polished to make delicate ornaments and jewellery. The Chinese have been making jade carvings for more than 3000 years.

People in many lands learnt to carve jade in STONE AGE times. They could not chip it into shape. Instead, they had to grind or saw it. To cut it they laid wet sand on the jade. They rubbed the sand grains to and fro with a slate or flat piece of sandstone. Then they shaped the jade with pieces of sandstone. To make holes in the jade they used sharp sticks or bones pressed on wet sand and twisted to and fro. Craftsmen still shape jade by hand. But now they use metal tools, and carborundum instead of sand.

Jaguar

No other American wild CAT is as heavy or perhaps as dangerous as the jaguar. From nose to tail a jaguar is longer than a man, and may be nearly twice his weight. The jaguar is yellow with black spots like a LEOPARD. But many of the jaguar's spots are in rings. Jaguars live in the hot, wet forests of Central and South America. They leap from trees onto wild pigs and deer. They also catch turtles, fish and alligators.

Jamaica

Jamaica is a tropical island in the Caribbean Sea. The name Jamaica means 'island of springs'. It is a beautiful island, with hundreds of streams flowing from springs on the sides of its green mountains.

There are more than two million people in Jamaica. Most of them are blacks of African ancestry. Many work on farms that grow bananas, coconuts, coffee, oranges and sugar cane. Jamaica also mines bauxite. Kingston is Jamaica's capital city.

This open ring was carved from jade in China about 2000 years ago. Old pieces of Chinese jade are very valuable.

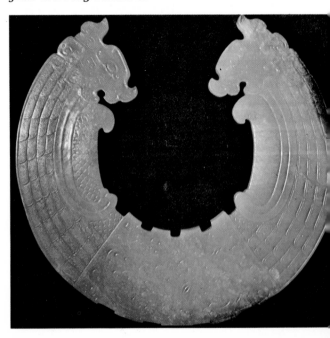

Japan

Japan is a long, narrow string of islands off the mainland coast of ASIA. Altogether they make a country larger than the British Isles.

Mountains cover most of Japan. The highest is a beautiful volcano. It is called Fujiyama, or Mount Fuji. Parts of Japan have forests, waterfalls and lakes. Northern Japan has cool summers and cold, snowy winters. The south is hot in summer and mild in winter.

Japan is a crowded country. It has more than 121 million people. To help feed them,

A street in Japan's capital, Tokyo. With almost 12 million people, Tokyo is one of the world's largest cities. It stands on Honshu, the biggest island. There are three other main islands — Hokkaido, Shikoku and Kyushu — and many small ones.

farmers grow huge amounts of rice and fruits. The Japanese also eat a lot of fish and seaweed. They catch more fish than any other country. Japan does not have many MINERALS. The Japanese buy most of their minerals from other countries. But no other country makes as many ships and television sets as Japan does. The Japanese also make a lot of cars.

Left: The opening of the first railway station in Japan. During the 19th century the Japanese copied everything Western — men wore top hats and women dressed in bustles. Knives and forks were used instead of chopsticks.

Jazz

Jazz is a kind of music; it is known for its strong rhythms. The leading players choose their own notes when they play a tune within the arrangement (often not written down), which is agreed with the rest of the band. In this way, jazz musicians often *improvise*, or make up music as they go along. Jazz began in the United States around 1900. It grew largely from songs sung by black slaves from Africa.

Jellyfish

A jellyfish is a sea animal. It is related to the sea anemone. The jellyfish looks like a bell made of jelly. To float upward, it pushes water down by squeezing the bell shut. Tentacles hang from the bell. These catch small animals. The jellyfish stings the animals. It then pushes the food into its mouth under the bell.

Jenner, Edward

Edward Jenner (1749–1823) was a British doctor. He inoculated a boy with cowpox germs. Cowpox disease is like smallpox but it is less dangerous. The boy did not catch smallpox. Jenner's INOCULATION made the boy's body strong against smallpox. As a result of Jenner's discovery, smallpox has disappeared.

Jerusalem

Jerusalem is the capital of ISRAEL. It is a holy city of the Jews, Christians and Muslims. David, Jesus and other famous people in the Bible lived or died here.

Jerusalem stands high up in hilly country. It has many old religious buildings. Huge walls surround the city's oldest part. In 1948 Jerusalem was divided between Israel and Jordan. But Israel took the whole city during a war in 1967.

Jesus

Jesus was a Jew. He started CHRISTIANITY. The New Testament of the BIBLE says that Jesus was God's Son.

Jesus was born in Bethlehem. His mother

Jenner at work. His process is called vaccination from 'vaccinia', another name for cowpox.

An old street in Jerusalem. In the distance is the Dome of the Rock, a Muslim shrine built on the spot where Mohammed is said to have ascended to heaven.

was called Mary. When he grew up he travelled about, teaching and healing sick people. Some Jewish priests were jealous of Jesus. They told their Roman rulers that he was making trouble. The Romans killed Jesus on a cross, but he came to life again and rose to heaven. Followers of Jesus spread his teachings through the world.

Jet Engine

A swimmer swims forward by pushing water backward. A jet engine works in a similar way. It drives an AIRCRAFT forward by pushing gases backward. Engines that work like this are called *reaction* engines. ROCKETS are also reaction engines. The main difference between jets and rockets is that jets take in oxygen from the air to burn their fuel, but rockets have their own supply of oxygen.

There are four main kinds of jet engine—turbojets, turboprops, turbofans and ramjets. Most modern jets are turbojets or turbofans.

Jet engines have replaced propeller-driven piston engines in many kinds of plane. There are many reasons for this. Jet engines weigh less than piston engines. They also break down less often. Their moving parts spin instead of moving to and fro. This stops the plane from shaking. Jet engines burn cheap kerosene instead of costly petrol. Jet engines can also carry planes faster and higher than piston engines can. Some jet fighters can travel at

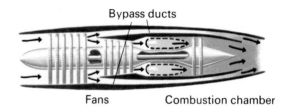

In a bypass turbofan engine, the incoming air is compressed by a system of fans. Another fan pulls in extra air which bypasses the combustion chamber. This makes the turbofan engine quieter and more powerful than other jet engines.

3400km/hr. Others can climb to about 30,500 metres.

Joan of Arc

Joan of Arc (1412–1431) was a French girl who believed that God told her to free France from its English invaders. At the age of 17 she left the farm where she worked, and persuaded France's King Charles VII to let her lead his army. She won five battles. Then she was captured and burned as a witch. But she had saved France. In 1920 the Pope declared her a SAINT.

In a turbojet, sucked-in air is squashed by spinning compressor blades. Oxygen and fuel burn in a combustion chamber. Hot gas rushes out, spinning a 'windmill' called a turbine. This works the compressor.

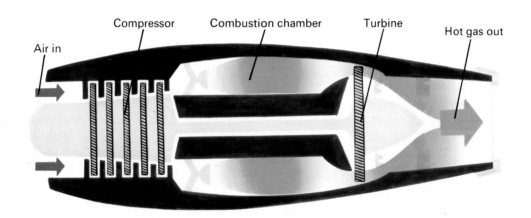

Johnson, Samuel

Samuel Johnson (1709–1784) was an English writer. He is still famous for the clever things he used to say. Johnson also wrote probably the first good English DICTIONARY. Many of the things we know about him come from a book written by his friend, James Boswell.

Judaism

Judaism is a religion that believes in one God and has as its holy book the Bible. The Hebrew Bible consists of the first five books of Moses (the Torah), historical accounts of the tribes of Israel and books written by prophets and kings. (Christians include all this material in their Bible, calling it the Old Testament.) Judaism's followers are called Jews. They observe the Ten Commandments. They believe God gave the Law to Moses on top of Mount Sinai after Moses led their ancestors out of Egypt, where they had been slaves. The commemoration of the Exodus from Egypt is one of Judaism's most important festivals and is called Passover. Today Jews live all over the world, but Israel is their spiritual centre and historical home.

Jupiter (planet)

Jupiter is the largest of the PLANETS in our SOLAR SYSTEM. It is twice the size of all the other planets put together. You could fit 1,300 planets the size of the earth into the space filled by Jupiter. Jupiter's force of GRAVITY is great. Anyone on Jupiter would weigh twice as much as on the earth. Astronomers believe that most of Jupiter is hot, liquid HYDROGEN. Jupiter is so hot that it would be a glowing star if it were ten times larger.

Jupiter spins so fast that a day and night last less than ten hours. But a YEAR on Jupiter is 12 times longer than one of ours. This is because Jupiter is farther from the SUN than we are.

A strange feature on Jupiter's surface is a great red spot that is always there. It is probably a huge storm.

Jupiter can be seen through a big telescope. Clouds hide the surface. Jupiter spins so fast that it pulls the clouds into dark and bright stripes. The strange red spot near the bottom of the picture is probably a storm. The storm has been raging for hundreds of years. The small, dark spot is a shadow. It is made by one of Jupiter's moons. Jupiter has 16 moons. The four largest are as big as Africa. One is covered with ice. Another has eight fiery volcanoes.

Kangaroo

Kangaroos are marsupials that live in New Guinea and Australia. Most of them live on grassy plains and all of them feed on plants. They move about in troops, springing along on their big, powerful hind legs and large feet. Their long tails help them to balance.

There are more than 50 kinds of kangaroo. Red and grey kangaroos are the largest. A red kangaroo may be taller and heavier than a man. Grey kangaroos can bounce along at 40km/hr if chased. Wallabies are smaller kinds of kangaroo. The smallest of all are rat kangaroos. They are about the size of a rabbit.

Kennedy, John F.

John Fitzgerald Kennedy (1917–1963) was the 35th PRESIDENT of the United States. He came from a wealthy Irish Catholic family and was born in Brookline, Massachusetts. During WORLD WAR II he served with the US Navy and received medals for courage.

During his presidency, Kennedy confronted the Soviet Union, forcing it to withdraw its missiles from Cuba. At home he set up the Peace Corps, improved welfare programmes, increased the minimum wage, and, against opposition from Congress, initiated civil rights laws.

In November 1963, Kennedy was shot dead in Dallas, Texas. His assassin, Lee Harvey Oswald, was murdered soon after.

The red kangaroo is the largest of all marsupials. It stands as tall as a man.

John F. Kennedy was the fourth American president to be assassinated.

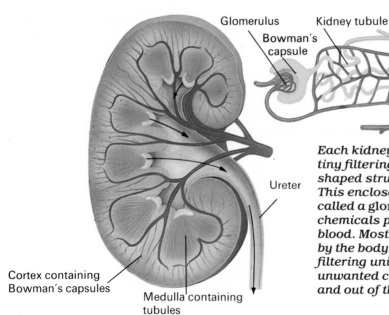

Glomerulus   Kidney tubule   Urine

Bowman's capsule

Filtered blood

Ureter

Cortex containing Bowman's capsules

Medulla containing tubules

Each kidney is made up of around two million tiny filtering units. Each unit has a cup-shaped structure called a Bowman's capsule. This encloses a bunch of blood capillaries called a glomerulus. Water and dissolved chemicals pass into the capsule from the blood. Most of the water and chemicals needed by the body pass back into the blood from the filtering unit's tubule. Urine containing unwanted chemicals passes into the ureter and out of the body.

Kenya

Kenya is a country in East AFRICA. It is just a bit larger than France. The south-west border touches Lake Victoria. The Indian Ocean is on the south-east. The EQUATOR goes across the middle of the country. Much of the land is covered by mountains and flat-topped hills. The rest looks like a huge, open park. It is a hot, dry country.

Kenya belongs to the Commonwealth. Most of the 19 million Kenyans are African. They belong to a number of different tribes. Many grow maize, tea and coffee. Kenya sells a lot of tea and coffee abroad. Tribes such as the Masai keep cattle. Many tourists visit Kenya to see the wildlife on the huge nature reserves. The capital city is Nairobi.

Kidney

All VERTEBRATES (animals with a backbone) have two kidneys. Kidneys look like large reddish-brown beans. Human kidneys are about the size of a man's fist. They lie on each side of the backbone, at just about waist level.

Kidneys clean the BLOOD. They filter out waste matter and strain off any water that the body does not need. Blood pumped from the HEART flows into each kidney through an artery. Each kidney contains tubes that act as filters. Blood cells, tiny food particles, and other useful things stay in the blood to be used by the body. Filtered blood flows out of the kidney through a vein. All the waste matter and extra water mix together to make urine. This drips slowly into the bladder.

King, Martin Luther, Jr

Martin Luther King Jr (1929–1968) was an American civil rights leader who worked for racial justice through peaceful means. He was born in Atlanta, Georgia, and became a Baptist minister like his father. It was in Montgomery, Alabama, where he was pastor, that he began his civil rights crusade. One of King's first actions was to

When Martin Luther King Jr was assassinated, President Johnson declared a day of national mourning.

organize a boycott of buses in Montgomery in 1956 as a protest against unfair treatment of black passengers. During the next ten years, he led many peaceful demonstrations and meetings all over the country. Success came when Congress passed civil rights laws in 1964 and 1965.

In 1964 King won the Nobel Peace Prize for his campaign of non-violence. In 1968 at the age of 39, he was assassinated in Memphis, Tennessee. The third Monday in January is now a US holiday in his honour.

Knot

Knots are a way of fastening rope, cord or thread. They are especially important for sailors and climbers. But everyone needs to tie a knot at some time.

Knots are used to make a noose, tie up a bundle or join the ends of small cords. There are also *bends* and *hitches*. A bend is used to tie the ends of rope together; a hitch is used to attach a rope to a ring or post. Common knots are the reef knot and bowline, both true knots; the clove hitch, half hitch and sheet bend. Rope ends can also be joined by weaving them together. This is called a *splice* and is not a knot. Knots can be a hobby. Many people make *knot boards* for displaying knots.

A reef knot ties together two cords of equal thickness; a sheet bend joins ropes of unequal thickness. A slip knot slides along itself and pulls tight around a post or other obstacle. Two half hitches make a quick fastening.

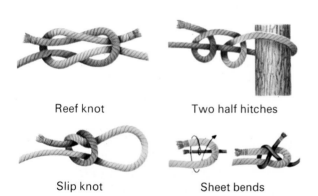

Reef knot   Two half hitches

Slip knot   Sheet bends

Koalas live in trees where they are safe from enemies. A mother koala carries her baby either in her pouch or on her back.

Koala

Koalas are marsupials that look like small, chubby bears. Koalas live in east and southeast Australia. They live much like SLOTHS. Koalas climb slowly among the branches of trees and hardly ever touch the ground. Their only food is eucalyptus leaves. Forest fires and hunting nearly made them extinct, but many koalas now live safely on reserves.

Koran

The *Koran* is the sacred book of ISLAM. Its name means 'a recitation'. It has 114 chapters of Arabic verse, and teaches that there is one God whose prophets (messengers) included Abraham, JESUS and MOHAMMED. The book teaches Muslims to be humble, generous and just. It is said that the Koran was revealed to Mohammed through the angel Gabriel. The way it is written has influenced Arab literature.

Korea

Korea is a peninsula that juts out from CHINA into the Sea of Japan. The land has many mountains and small valleys. Forests cover most of the country. Korean farms produce much rice and silk. Korean factories make steel and other products.

Korea was divided into two separate nations in 1945. They are now known as North Korea and South Korea.

Kremlin

This is the oldest part of MOSCOW. Some of its buildings date from the 1100s. The Kremlin was once the fortress home of Russia's *tsars*. Inside the high wall that surrounds it stand old palaces and cathedrals crowned by golden domes shaped like giant onions. For most of its history the Kremlin has been the seat of the Russian government; it still is today.

Kublai Khan

Kublai Khan (1216–1294) was the grandson of GENGHIS KHAN. Kublai became Great-Khan in 1259. Under his rule the Mongol empire reached its peak of power. He conquered CHINA and set up his capital at Cambaluc, modern Peking (Beijing). It was the first time that China had been completely overcome by outside forces. Neighbouring countries in South-east Asia, such as Burma, were forced to recognize Kublai as their ruler. He also tried to conquer Japan and Java, but failed. Kublai encouraged art, science and trade. Among his many foreign visitors was MARCO POLO.

Pusan is South Korea's second largest city. It is also a busy port.

The Kremlin, its domes shining in the sunlight, seen from the Moskva River.

Laboratory

A laboratory is a place where scientists work. Laboratory workers make experiments and test things to find out more about them. Some people now learn foreign languages in special rooms called language laboratories.

Lace

Lace is a delicate fabric. It is patterned with tiny holes. People make collars, shawls, scarves and tablecloths from lace. Lace is made from threads of cotton, linen, nylon or silk, and sometimes gold or silver. Lace-makers twist, knot or loop the threads in special ways. Lace made by hand is expensive. Much lace is now made on machines.

Lake

Lakes are large areas of water surrounded by land. The world's largest lake is the salty Caspian Sea. It lies in the Soviet Union and Iran. The largest freshwater lake is Lake Superior, one of the GREAT LAKES.

Many lakes were formed in the ICE AGES. They began in valleys made by glaciers. When the glaciers melted they left behind mud and stones that formed DAMS. The melted water from the glaciers piled up behind the dams.

Language

Language is what we use to talk to, or communicate with, one another. Many animals have ways of communicating. These may include special body movements and sounds. But the speaking of words is something that so far only humans can do. Spoken language came first; later people invented a way of writing it down. This is known as written language. Language is

Lake Moraine is high in The Rockies in Alberta, Canada.

The Lapps live with herds of reindeer. Lapps eat reindeer meat. They make their clothes and tents from reindeer skin.

always changing as some words are forgotten and others are added.

Today there are about 3000 languages in the world. They can be grouped into a number of language families. Some of the most widely spoken languages are English, French, German, Russian, Chinese, Hindi, Arabic and Spanish.

Lapland

Lapland is a place in the ARCTIC. It lies in the far north of Sweden, Norway, Finland and Russia. Lapps are short people. Many have straight, black hair and yellowish skin. They keep warm by wearing clothes made from wool and reindeer skins. Their clothes are brightly coloured.

Some Lapps are nomads. They travel the land with herds of REINDEER. They sleep in tents and eat reindeer meat. Other Lapps are fishermen or farmers. They live in small huts in villages. Lapps speak a language related to Finnish.

Laser

A laser is something that strengthens light and makes it shine in a very narrow beam. Many lasers have a ruby CRYSTAL or gas inside them. Bright light, radio waves or electricity are fed into the laser. This makes the ATOMS of the crystal or gas jump around very quickly. The atoms give off a very strong light.

The light of lasers can be used for many

A flash tube sets a ruby crystal glowing with a beam of light. The light bounces between mirrors and grows stronger. When it is very strong it shines through a mirror at one end as a laser beam.

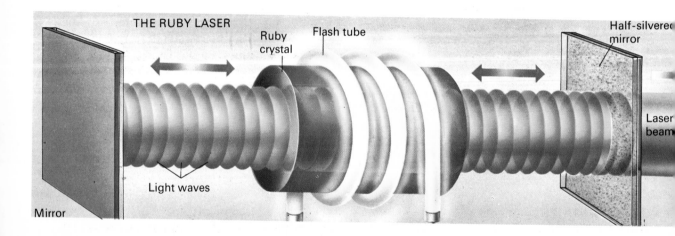

THE RUBY LASER

Ruby crystal

Flash tube

Half-silvered mirror

Laser beam

Light waves

Mirror

things. Doctors use small laser beams to burn away tiny areas of disease in the body. They also repair damaged eyes with laser beams. Dentists can use lasers to drill holes in teeth. Some lasers are so strong they can cut through DIAMONDS. Lasers are used in factories to cut metal and to join tiny metal parts.

Lasers can also be used to measure distance. The laser beam is aimed at objects far away. The distance is measured by counting the time it takes for the light to get there and back. Laser beams can also carry radio and television signals. One laser beam can send many television programmes and telephone calls at once without mixing them up.

Latitude and Longitude

Every place on earth has a latitude and a longitude. Lines of latitude and longitude are drawn on maps. Lines, or *parallels*, of latitude show how far north or south of the EQUATOR a place is. They are measured in degrees (written as °). The equator is at 0° latitude. The North Pole is at 90° north; the South Pole is 90° south.

Lines, or *meridians*, of longitude show how far east or west a place is. They are also measured in degrees. Greenwich, in London, is at 0° longitude. A place halfway around the world from Greenwich is at 180° longitude.

Lead

Lead is a soft, heavy, blue-grey metal. It does not RUST. Lead is used for many things, including pipes and roofs. Lead shields protect ATOMIC ENERGY workers from dangerous radiation. Lead is mixed with TIN to make pewter or *solder*. Solder is used for joining pieces of metal. Many things are now made without lead because lead can become poisonous when it is mixed with certain other things.

Leaf

Leaves are the food factories of green PLANTS. To make food, leaves need light,

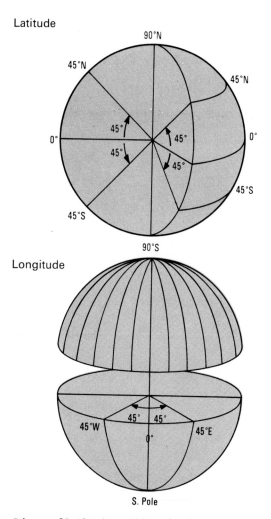

Lines of latitude and longitude are measured in degrees. Each measurement lies at a certain angle to the centre of the earth. Any point on the earth's surface can therefore be given a position in terms of latitude and longitude.

carbon dioxide and water. Light comes from the sun. Carbon dioxide comes from the air. Air enters a leaf through little holes called *stomata*. Water is drawn up from the ground by the plant's roots. It flows up the stem and into the leaf through tiny tubes called veins. Inside the leaf is a green colouring called chlorophyll. The chlorophyll uses light, water and carbon dioxide to make SUGAR. The way it does this is known as *photosynthesis*. The sugar then passes through tubes to the other parts of the plant.

In the autumn many trees lose their leaves. First they shut off the water supply

The sticky bud of a horse chestnut tree bursts open to let the leaves out.

to the leaves. This destroys the green colour and gives the leaves yellow, red and orange tints.

Leather

Leather is made from the skin, or hide, of animals. The skins are treated to make them strong and waterproof (for the soles of shoes) or flexible (for furniture and luggage). The process of treating them is called *tanning.* Before tanning, the skins are *cured* by being soaked in salt water. Then the remaining hair and meat is taken off. Next the skins are treated with a chemical called *tannin,* which comes from tree bark. Then the leather is oiled to soften it and dyed different colours. It is now ready to be cut, shaped and stitched or glued into the final product.

Lebanon

Lebanon is a Middle Eastern country bordering on the Mediterranean Sea. It is sandwiched between Syria and Israel. Lebanon's coast is flat, but most of the country inland is mountainous.

Lebanon has been a trading centre for centuries. Ancient Lebanon was part of the Phoenician empire. The Phoenicians were great traders all over the Mediterranean. Later, Lebanon became part of the Byzantine empire, ruled from Constantinople. It was famous for the fine cedar wood that came from its forests. The Arabs ruled Lebanon from the 800s AD, and during the CRUSADES it was occupied by the French. Because of its mixed history Lebanon is unusual for an Arab nation in that about half its people are Christians. In recent years the country has become a battleground for a number of religious and political opponents.

Lemming

The lemming is a small tubby RODENT. It belongs to the same family as the rat and mouse. There are several kinds of lemming. All have short tails. Most have brown or grey fur.

Lemmings live in northern forests and in the cold lands of the ARCTIC. They feed on leaves, stems, roots and berries. In winter, lemmings keep warm by living in tunnels underneath the snow. The tunnels are warm even on very chilly days.

In some summers lemmings breed very fast. They eat up all the food. Huge numbers of lemmings leave home to find more food. Many drown trying to cross rivers.

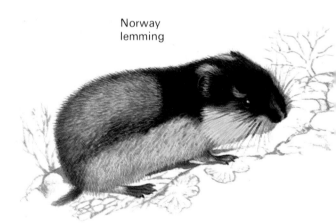

Norway lemming

Lemons

Lemons are oval yellow FRUITS. They have a sour taste. Their juice is used in drinks, to flavour food, and in perfumes. Lemon trees need a warm climate. The fruits are picked two or three times a year while still green. Most lemons come from the United States and Italy.

Lenin, Vladimir

Vladimir Ilyich Lenin (1870–1924) helped to make Russia the first communist country in the world. Before his time, Russia was ruled by emperors, or *tsars*. Like Karl MARX, Lenin believed in COMMUNISM. He wanted every country run by the workers and no longer split into rich and poor groups. For many years Lenin lived outside Russia. He wrote books, and articles for communist newspapers. In 1917 he went back to Russia. He became the leader of a group of communists called Bolsheviks, who overthrew the government. Lenin then ruled Russia until he died.

Lens

Lenses are used to make things look bigger or smaller. They are usually made of glass or plastic. The lens inside your EYE is made of PROTEIN. Sometimes eye lenses do not work properly. Then people cannot see clearly. The lenses in spectacles make people's eyesight better. Lenses are used for many other things. The lenses in MICROSCOPES, binoculars, and TELESCOPES make faraway things or small things seem much larger.

Each lens has two smooth sides. Both sides may be curved, or one may be curved and the other flat. There are two main kinds of lens. Lenses where the edges are thicker than the middle are called *concave* lenses. Concave means 'hollowed out'. When LIGHT rays pass through a concave lens, they spread out. If you look at something through a concave lens, it looks smaller than it really is.

Lenses where the middle is thicker than the edges are called *convex* lenses. Convex means rounded. When light rays pass through a convex lens, they come together. If you look at things through a convex lens, they seem larger.

Craftsmen who make lenses know exactly how to shape them for various uses. They may fit different lenses together, or shape each side of a lens differently. Short-sighted people use lenses with a concave and a

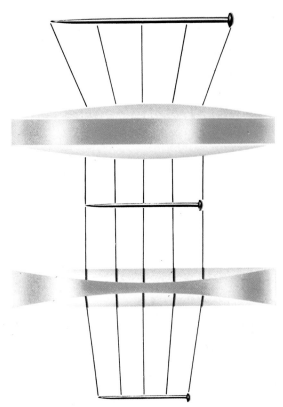

Above: The top lens is convex (thickest in the middle). The bottom lens is concave (thickest at the edges). The pin in between them looks larger through the convex lens, and smaller through the concave lens.

convex side. But the concave side is curved more than the convex side.

Leonardo da Vinci

Leonardo da Vinci (1452–1519) was an Italian artist and inventor. He lived during the Renaissance. One of his most famous paintings is the *Mona Lisa*. It is a picture of a woman who is smiling mysteriously. Many people have wondered what she is smiling at. Leonardo made thousands of drawings of human bodies, water, plants and animals. He wrote many notes on the things he drew.

Leonardo worked as an engineer for Italian nobles and for the French king, Louis XII. He designed forts and canals. The canals had locks so that boats could travel up and down hills. Leonardo also drew ideas for things long before they were invented. His drawings include a helicopter, a flying machine and a machine gun.

Leonardo was interested in many other things, including music and architecture. He was a good musician and singer.

Leopard

Leopards are large, wild cats just a bit smaller than LIONS. They live in Africa and southern Asia. Most leopards are spotted like jaguars, but some are nearly black. These are called panthers.

Leopards are very fierce, strong and agile hunters. They catch and eat antelopes, goats, dogs and sometimes people. They often hunt from trees, lying in wait on a branch. If they cannot eat all their catch at once, they may haul the carcass high up into a tree. This is to stop lazier hunters such as lions or hyenas from stealing it.

Leonardo da Vinci made this beautiful painting of the Virgin Mary and the baby Jesus.

Most leopards have blotchy spots called rosettes. Unlike jaguars, leopards have no spot in the middle of the rosettes.

Liberty Bell

The Liberty Bell is a famous symbol of American independence. It was rung at the State House, now Independence Hall, in Philadelphia when the Declaration of Independence was proclaimed in July, 1776. It rang at each anniversary of that event until 1835, when it cracked. Today visitors to Philadelphia can see the bell at Independence Hall.

Libya

Libya is a large country in North AFRICA. It is more than three times the size of France, but very few people live there. This is because most of Libya lies in the SAHARA.

Most Libyans are ARABS who farm the land. Libya is also rich in oil. The country became part of the Turkish Ottoman Empire in the 1500s, and was a colony of Italy from 1912 to the end of World War II. It became an independent monarchy in 1952 as the United Kingdom of Libya. In 1969 army officers overthrew the king and took control, and Colonel Mu'ammar al Qaddafi became head of the government. Since that time, Qaddafi has stirred up controversy worldwide by helping revolutionaries from other countries.

Lichen

A lichen is a simple PLANT. It has no roots, leaves or flowers. Some lichens grow as crusty patches on rocks, trees or walls. They grow very slowly. A patch no larger than your hand may be hundreds of years old. Other lichens grow as shrubby tufts. Lichens can live in places that are too bare, dry, cold or hot for any other plant.

Light

Light is a kind of ENERGY that we can see. Some objects—stars, lamps, certain chemicals—produce light. Most things do not produce light. We can see them only because they reflect light. For example, we can see the moon only because it reflects light from the sun.

Sunlight is the brightest light we normally see. Summer sunlight can be as bright as 10,000 candles burning close enough to touch. Bright sunlight seems white, but it is really made up of the colours of the RAINBOW. Isaac NEWTON showed this. He made a sunbeam shine through a specially shaped chunk of glass called a prism. Red, orange, yellow, green, blue, indigo and violet rays of light came out of the prism. The prism had split the sunbeam into separate beams, each with its own *wavelength*. This is easy to understand if you think of light travelling in waves. The distance between the tops of the waves is the wavelength. We see each wavelength as a different colour. Long waves are red, short waves are violet and wavelengths in between show up as the other colours.

Light travels very fast, more than 300,000km each second. Even so, it takes

Straight objects look bent in water because light rays bend when they pass from air to water.

A red flower is red because it reflects only the red colour in light and absorbs the others. Its black centre absorbs all colours.

eight minutes for the light from the sun to reach earth. A light year is the distance a beam of light travels in one year. Scientists use light years to measure how far away STARS are. Some are millions of light years away.

Lightning

Lightning is ELECTRICITY that you can see. It is a sudden flow of electric current between two clouds, between a cloud and the ground or between two parts of the cloud. There are three types of lightning. Streak lightning flashes in a single line from cloud to earth. Forked lightning happens when the lightning divides to find the quickest way to earth. Sheet lightning happens inside a cloud and lights up the sky, like the flashbulb on a camera.

Lincoln, Abraham

Abraham Lincoln (1809–1865) was president of the United States from 1861 to 1865. He grew up in a log cabin and had little schooling, but studied law by himself. 'Honest Abe', as he became known, was elected to the Illinois legislature in 1834.

In 1847 he became a Congressman, but instead of running for a second term, returned to his successful law practice in Springfield. His interest in politics began again when a law was passed in 1854 allowing people in new western territories

Overnight, Charles Lindbergh became a hero.

Lindbergh, Charles

Charles Augustus Lindbergh (1902–1974) was an American pilot who became the first man to fly the Atlantic Ocean alone. His single-engine aircraft, *Spirit of St Louis*, left New York on May 20, 1927. He landed on May 21 in Paris, $33\frac{1}{2}$ hours later, after flying about 5800 km nonstop. Lindbergh's flight showed people that air travel was possible. Later he helped to plan air routes to South America and over the Atlantic Ocean.

Lion

Lions are large, tawny-coloured wild CATS. An adult male weighs about 180 kg and measures about 2.7 metres from nose to tail. Females (lionesses) are slightly smaller and have no mane.

Lions usually live in family groups called

Lionesses resting after a meal. A large meal may satisfy a lion for several days.

to own slaves. In 1856 he joined the new, anti-slavery Republican Party and was elected president in 1860. Abraham Lincoln started a second term of office in 1865, just as he was trying to unite the nation at the end of the CIVIL WAR. But on April 14, 1865, on a visit to Ford's Theater in Washington DC, he was shot dead by John Wilkes Booth, an actor who supported the defeated South.

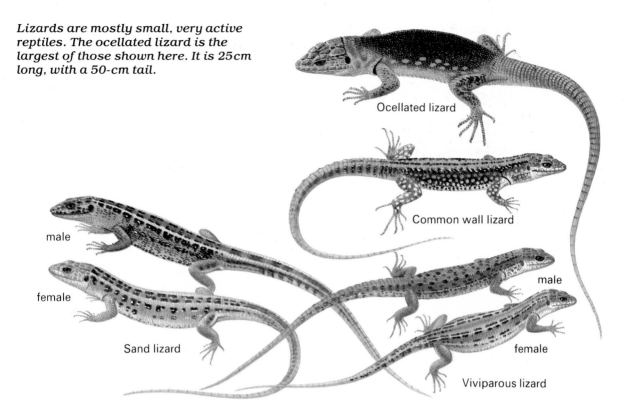

Lizards are mostly small, very active reptiles. The ocellated lizard is the largest of those shown here. It is 25cm long, with a 50-cm tail.

Ocellated lizard

Common wall lizard

male

female

Sand lizard

male

female

Viviparous lizard

prides. A pride has one male, one or two females, and all their cubs. Lions often hunt together. No other big cats seem to do this. They hunt mainly antelope and zebra. Lionesses do most of the hunting.

Lions used to roam wild over southern Europe, India and Africa. Now they live in South and East Africa and a tiny part of India. Many lions today lead protected lives on nature reserves.

Lister, Joseph

Joseph Lister (1827–1912) was an English surgeon who found a way to stop his patients from dying of infection after operations. He used antiseptics to kill germs on surgeons' hands and instruments.

Liver

Your liver is a flat, triangular organ tucked under your right ribs. It is larger than your stomach. The liver is a kind of chemical factory and storage cupboard. It produces the digestive juice that burns up the fat you eat. It makes the PROTEINS used in blood. It

gets rid of any poisonous substances in the blood or changes them so that they are harmless. Minerals and VITAMINS are stored in the liver until the body needs them.

Lizard

Lizards are REPTILES with dry, scaly skins and long tails. Most have four legs but some have none. These look like snakes. Some lizards are born live like MAMMALS, but most of them hatch from eggs.

There are about 3000 kinds of lizard. Most live in hot countries. Lizards that live in cooler places spend the winter in HIBERNATION. Lizards mainly eat insects.

Most lizards are only a few centimetres long. But the Komodo dragon is longer and heavier than a man.

Locks and Keys

There are two main kinds of lock. In the simplest kind, when the key is turned a piece of metal called a bolt moves out and fits into a slot. The key has a few notches that have to fit with similar notches in the

The French TGV stands for Train à Grande Vitesse, *which means 'high-speed train'. First tested in 1978, it quickly reached its design speed of 260 km/hr and even clocked up 314 km/hr with no problem.*

lock. The Yale lock was invented in 1860. In it the key can turn a cylinder when all the little pins in the lock are pushed to the right height by the notches on the key.

Locomotive

Locomotives are railway engines. They pull trains along RAILWAYS. Locomotives run on coal, oil, gas or electricity.

The first locomotives were STEAM ENGINES, which burned coal. In 1804 a British engineer, Richard Trevithick, built a steam locomotive, but it moved only at walking pace. Since then, engineers have built powerful locomotives that go much faster. One American locomotive was so strong it pulled 250 trucks. One modern French locomotive can travel at 314 km/hr. Most modern locomotives have DIESEL ENGINES or motors that run on electricity.

Locust

Locusts are GRASSHOPPERS that sometimes breed in huge numbers. They fly far across land and sea to find new feeding places. A big swarm may contain thousands of locusts. When they land, the locusts eat everything green. Swarms of locusts have destroyed many farms in warm lands.

Right: The locust has destroyed crops in warm countries since ancient times.

Locusts swarm only when there are too many of them. Farmers try to kill young locusts before they can fly.

London

London is the capital of the United Kingdom. It has about seven million people. The river Thames runs through London.

People from all over the world visit London to see Buckingham Palace, the Houses of Parliament, Westminster Abbey and the Tower of London. There are many museums, theatres and parks in London.

London began as a Roman settlement called *Londinium.* The Black Death came to London in the 1600s, followed by the Great Fire of 1666. The city was badly bombed in WORLD WAR II.

Louis (kings)

Eighteen French kings were called Louis.

The first was Louis I (778–840). Louis IX (1214–1270) led two CRUSADES. Louis XI (1423–1483) won power and land from his nobles. Louis XIII (1601–1643) made the French kings very powerful. Louis XIV (1638–1715) ruled for 72 years. He built a great palace at Versailles. All the French nobles had to live in his palace. Louis XVI (1754–1793) was beheaded after the FRENCH REVOLUTION.

Above: A painting of Louis XIV showing his pomp and wealth.

As you breathe in and out, your diaphragm contracts and relaxes, increasing and decreasing the volume of your lungs.

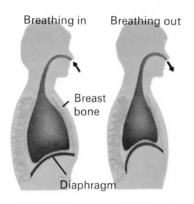

Breathing in   Breathing out

Breast bone

Diaphragm

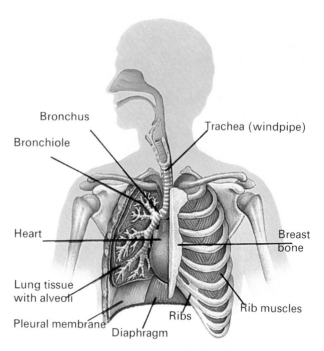

Bronchus

Bronchiole

Trachea (windpipe)

Heart

Breast bone

Lung tissue with alveoli

Pleural membrane

Ribs

Rib muscles

Diaphragm

Air is breathed in and passes down the windpipe into two bronchi. The bronchi enter the lungs and divide into small tubes called bronchioles. These divide into smaller alveoli. Each alveolus is surrounded by hundreds of tiny blood vessels. The lining of the alveolus is kept moist. Oxygen from the air dissolves in the moisture and passes into the blood.

Lung

Lungs are used for BREATHING. People have lungs, and so do many animals. Lungs take in OXYGEN from the air. They also remove waste carbon dioxide from the BLOOD.

Your lungs are two large, spongelike masses in your chest. They fill with air and empty as you breathe in and out.

You breathe in air through the nose or mouth. The air flows down the windpipe, or *trachea*. Where the lungs begin, the trachea divides into two hollow branches called bronchial tubes, or *bronchi*. Each divides into smaller tubes called *bronchioles*. These end in cups called air sacs, or *alveoli*. This is where the lungs give oxygen to the blood and take away carbon dioxide.

Lungs need clean air. Smokers and people who live in smoky towns, or work in some kinds of dusty air, may get lung diseases.

Malaria

Malaria is a tropical disease. It is carried by the *Anopheles* MOSQUITO, which can infect the humans it bites. Drugs are used to treat malaria. Scientists try to destroy the mosquitoes and the swamps in which the insects breed.

Malaysia

Malaysia is a country in South-East ASIA. It is in two parts, West Malaysia on the Malay Peninsula, and East Malaysia, which is part of the island of Borneo. The capital, Kuala Lumpur, is in West Malaysia.

Malaysia has about 15 million people, mostly Malays and Chinese. Its main exports are rubber, timber and tin.

A Malaysian rubber tree is tapped for latex, the liquid from which rubber is made.

Madrid

Madrid is the capital city of SPAIN. It was chosen by King Philip II (1527–1598) as his capital because it was in the middle of the country. Madrid is a dry, windy city, cold in winter and hot in summer. It is the centre of Spanish life, and the seat of the country's parliament. It has many fine buildings, including the Prado, a famous museum. More than three million people live in Madrid, which is the centre of Spain's road and railway network.

Magnetism

A magnet attracts some metals, particularly iron and steel. The earth is a huge natural magnet. Invisible lines of magnetic force spread out around the planet, joining the north and south magnetic poles. We call this the earth's *magnetic field*.

The needle in a COMPASS is a magnet. It always turns to face magnetic north. In ancient times people noticed that a kind of iron ore called a lodestone suspended from a string would always swing in the same direction. A lodestone is a natural magnet. Another name for it is magnetite.

An electromagnet is made by coiling wire around a metal core and passing electricity through the coil.

Malta

Malta is an island in the MEDITERRANEAN SEA. It lies south of Sicily. Since ancient times it has been a vital naval base, for it guards the Mediterranean trade routes to the East. For centuries Malta was ruled by the Knights of St John, but in 1813 it became British. During World War II, Malta survived heavy bombing raids and the whole island was awarded the George Cross medal.

Since 1962 Malta has been self-governing. Today, it is a republic. The capital is Valletta, with its splendid Grand Harbour.

Mammals

Mammals are not the largest group of animals on earth. But they are the most intelligent and show a greater variety of forms than any other group of animals.

All mammals have warm blood and a bony skeleton. Many have hair or fur on their bodies to keep them warm. Almost all female mammals give birth to live young, which feed on milk from special glands in their mother's body.

Mammals were the last great animal group to appear on earth. They came long after fish, amphibians, reptiles and insects. When DINOSAURS ruled the earth millions of years ago the only mammals were tiny creatures that looked like shrews. But after the dinosaurs died out, the mammals took over. Through EVOLUTION, the mammals multiplied into many different forms, which spread all over the world.

Scientists divide mammals into three families. The most primitive mammals still lay eggs, like the reptiles and birds. There are only two left—the echidna and the platypus. Then come the marsupials. These mammals give birth to tiny, half-developed young which have to be carried in their mother's pouch until they are big enough to look after themselves. The best known marsupial is the KANGAROO. Almost all the marsupials live in Australia.

The 'placental' mammals, the highest group of all, give birth to fully developed young. There are many different kinds, including flying mammals (BATS); gnawing animals or RODENTS; sea mammals (WHALES and DOLPHINS); and burrowing animals (for example, moles). There are insect-eaters, plant-eaters, and flesh-eaters. The flesh-eaters, or CARNIVORES, include the powerful CATS, WOLVES and BEARS. The most intelligent of all the mammals are the primates. This family includes MONKEYS, APES and humans.

Mammals are warm-blooded animals that feed their young on milk from the mother's body. All mammals have hair—but some, like people, do not have very much. Mammals are the most advanced of the animals. Here a pony feeds her foal. Mice (below) are among the most successful placental mammals.

Right: Bats are the only flying mammals.

Mammoth

During the ICE AGES, woolly mammoths roamed the plains of Europe and North America. They looked like shaggy-haired elephants, with long curling tusks. But they lived in much colder climates than the elephants of today.

Mammoths lived together in herds, feeding on plants, grass and leaves. Their enemies included the fierce sabre-toothed tiger, wolves and also CAVE DWELLERS, who hunted mammoths for food. Sometimes a group of hunters drove a mammoth into a pit, where it could be killed with spears.

The frozen bodies of mammoths have been dug up by scientists in the icy tundra of Siberia. Mammoth remains have also been found in tar pits in California. The last mammoths died out about 30,000 years ago.

Marconi, Guglielmo

Guglielmo Marconi (1874–1937) was the man who, most people say, invented RADIO. His parents were wealthy Italians. When he was only 20, he managed to make an electric bell ring in one corner of a room with radio waves sent out from the other corner. Soon he was sending radio signals over longer and longer distances. In 1901 he sent the first message across the Atlantic. In 1924 he sent signals across the world to Australia.

Marco Polo

Marco Polo (1254–1324) was an Italian traveller. He is famous for the long journey he made to faraway China at a time when the people of Europe knew little about the East. His father and his uncle were merchants from Venice and they decided to take the young Marco with them when they set out for the East in 1271. In 1275 they reached Peking (Beijing) and were welcomed by KUBLAI KHAN. The Polos stayed for many years, during which Marco travelled all over China. They left China in 1292 and arrived home in Venice in 1295. Later, Marco decided to write about his travels. His book, *Description of the World,* is one of the most exciting books ever written.

Part of a map of 1375 showing the Polos' caravan crossing Asia.

Below: Guglielmo Marconi with equipment similar to what he used to send the first radio signal across the Atlantic.

Marie Antoinette

Marie Antoinette (1755–1793) was the Austrian-born wife of LOUIS XVI of France. A beautiful and vivacious young woman, she found her husband dull and boring, and hated her duties as queen. Instead she spent money lavishly and cared little for the world outside the royal palace at Versailles. She became a symbol to the poor people of France of all they hated about the royal court. When the FRENCH REVOLUTION broke out in 1789, the king and queen were taken to Paris by force. They were executed on the guillotine in 1793.

Mars (god)

Mars was one of the oldest and most important of the Roman gods. He was the son of Jupiter and Juno and became the god of war. His son, Romulus, was supposed to have been the founder of ROME. The temples and festivals of Mars were important to the Romans. The month of March was named after him. It was the first month in the Roman year.

Mars (planet)

The planet Mars is only about half the size of the earth. It takes Mars about two years to travel around the sun. Most of Mars is covered with loose rocks scattered over a dusty red surface. This is why Mars is called the 'Red Planet'. It has a north pole and a south pole, both covered with snow or frost.

Seen through a telescope, the red surface of Mars is crisscrossed by thin grey lines. Some early astronomers thought that these lines were canals which had been dug by manlike creatures. But space probes to

Mars is much smaller that the earth, but, like our planet, it probably has a large iron core.

Mars in 1965, 1969 and 1976 found no trace of the canals. The American *Viking* spacecraft landed on Mars and took samples of the planet's soil. But it was unable to find any kind of life on Mars.

The planet has two tiny moons—Phobos and Deimos. Phobos, the larger of the two, is only about 24 km across.

Because Mars has a smaller mass than the earth, things on its surface weigh only about 40 percent of what they would weigh on earth. A day on Mars is about the same length as an earth day.

Below: The landscape of Mars is red and rock-strewn. The picture was taken by the Viking 1 *spacecraft. The surface of Mars has huge volcanoes and great gorges, far bigger than those on earth. Until recently, some people thought that the planet's 'canals' had been dug by manlike creatures to irrigate the soil. But space probes to Mars have found no canals and no sign of life on the planet.*

Martial Arts

The martial arts are various kinds of un-armed combat that come from the Far East. They include judo, karate and aikido—all from Japan—and kung-fu from China.

Judo, meaning 'easy way', is probably the most popular. It originally came from jujitsu, a violent practice that could maim or kill. Today judo is a safe sport practised by men, women and children, and has been an Olympic sport since 1964. It is used in many parts of the world for self-defence. A trained student of judo can quickly unbalance an opponent and throw him to the ground.

In karate and kung-fu, the hands, elbows and feet are used as weapons. Aikido, like judo, makes use of the opponent's strength to unbalance him. Kendo, another form of self-defence, is a kind of fencing using sticks instead of swords.

Marx, Karl

Many people think that Karl Marx (1818–1883) was the greatest political thinker and writer there has ever been. Marx was born in Germany and his ideas were the starting point of COMMUNISM. He believed that people who own property, the capitalist class, keep those who work for them down so the owners can become richer. He also thought that the workers would one day rise against the capitalists and take control. Marx's ideas later led to the Russian Revolution. Today he is studied as an economist as well as a revolutionary

Mary Queen of Scots

Mary Queen of Scots (1542–1587) was the last Roman Catholic ruler of SCOTLAND. The daughter of James V of Scotland, she was educated in France, and did not return to Scotland until she was 19. By that time she thought of herself as more French and Catholic than Scottish and Protestant.

Mary was the heir to the English throne after the Protestant ELIZABETH I. In 1567 Mary was forced to give up the Scottish throne. Later she was imprisoned for 20 years in England. People said she was plotting against Queen Elizabeth. She was executed on the Queen's orders in 1587.

Masks

The use of masks is very ancient. People wore masks on their faces as a kind of magic and in religious ceremonies. Masks were worn by actors in ancient China and Greece to show that they were a certain kind of character. They were also worn in religious plays in the Middle Ages and by medieval jesters. Nowadays masks are still worn by circus clowns, in modern dance, at parties, and during Mardi Gras carnivals in Latin America.

Matches

In the early 1800s matches were made by hand, often by children. They stuck the little wooden sticks into poisonous phosphorus paste. Phosphorus fumes often killed workers in match factories, and the early matches burst into flames too easily. The first 'safety' matches were made in the 1850s.

Mary Queen of Scots became Queen of Scotland when six days old, Queen of France at the age of 16, and spent 20 years as a prisoner in England. She was 45 when Queen Elizabeth ordered her execution.

Mathematics

We all use mathematics every day. We add up the coins in our pockets to find out how much money we have. We look at a clock and work out how much time we have left before going somewhere. In every business people are constantly using some kind of mathematics; often, today, with the help of calculators and computers. The branch of mathematics that deals with numbers is called ARITHMETIC. *Algebra* uses symbols such as x and y instead of numbers. GEOMETRY deals with lines, angles and shapes such as triangles and squares.

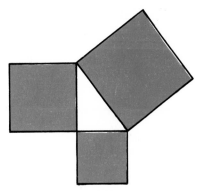

The Greek mathematician Pythagoras proved that the square on the longest side of a right-angled triangle equals the sum of the squares on the other two sides. This is one of the principles of modern geometry.

Maya

The Maya Indians first lived in Central America in the AD 400s. They grew maize and sweet potatoes and kept pet dogs. Later they built cities of stone, with richly decorated palaces, temples, pyramids and observatories. Even today many of these wonderful buildings are still standing, hidden in the jungle. The Maya were also skilled in astronomy and mathematics, and they had an advanced kind of writing.

The Maya people did not have any metals until very late in their history. They built only with stone tools. And they had no knowledge of the wheel.

Medicine

When we first think of the word 'medicine', we usually think about all the tablets, powders, pills and liquids that people take when they are not feeling well. But medicine also means the science of healing. It has taken a long time for medicine to become truly scientific. In the early days doctors relied mostly on magic cures, prayers and charms. But in the last few hundred years medicine has advanced faster than in all of human history. And in this century progress has been fastest of all. Scientists have found out about VITAMINS; they have made all kinds of wonder drugs such as penicillin;

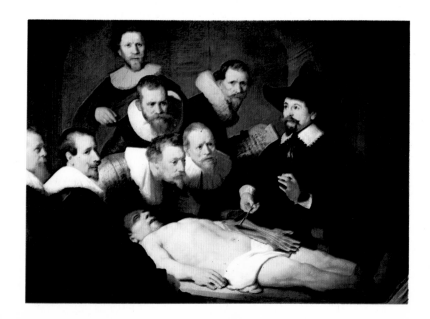

Early students of medicine often had to carry out dissections of the human body in secret. This was because the Church was opposed to the use of the dead for this purpose. But by the middle 1600s anatomy, shown here in Rembrandt's The Anatomy Lesson *(1632), was an accepted study.*

203

they have almost wiped out diseases such as tuberculosis; and they are finding out more and more about mental diseases. But perhaps the most important area of a doctor's job is still *diagnosis*, finding out what is wrong with a patient by studying the symptoms.

Mediterranean Sea

The Mediterranean is a large sea surrounded by three continents—Africa, Europe and Asia. It flows out into the Atlantic Ocean through the narrow Strait of Gibraltar. It is also joined to the Black Sea by a narrow passage.

In ancient times the Mediterranean was more imporant than it is now. In fact, it was the centre of the Western world for a long time. The Phoenicians were a seafaring people who travelled around the Mediterranean from about 2500 BC. Then the Greeks and Romans sailed the sea. The Romans were in control of the whole Mediterranean for nearly 500 years. They even called it *Mare Nostrum*, which means 'our sea'.

Today people know the Mediterranean best for its sunshine and its beaches.

Below: This Turkish trawler is harvesting sponges in the Mediterranean. The diver collects them.

Mendel, Gregor

Gregor Mendel (1822–1884) was an Austrian priest who became famous for his work on heredity. Heredity is the passing on of things such as eye colour, skin colour and mental ability from parents to their children.

Mendel grew up on a farm, where he

Mendel discovered that the gene for yellow in peas was stronger than that for green. Green and yellow peas produced all yellow, but green turned up in later generations.

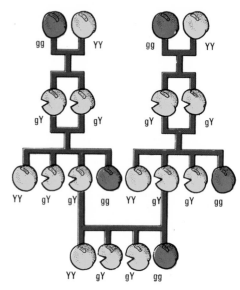

became interested in plants. When he entered a monastery he began growing peas. He noticed that when he planted the seeds of tall pea plants, only tall pea plants grew. Then he tried crossing tall peas with short peas, and found that again he had only tall plants. But when he crossed these new mixed tall plants with each other, three-quarters of the new plants were tall and one quarter were short. Mendel had found out that things like tallness or shortness are controlled by tiny *genes*, passed on from each parent. He also found out that some genes are stronger than other genes.

Mercury (planet)

The planet Mercury is the smallest planet in the SOLAR SYSTEM. It is also the closest to the sun. A day on Mercury lasts for 59 of our

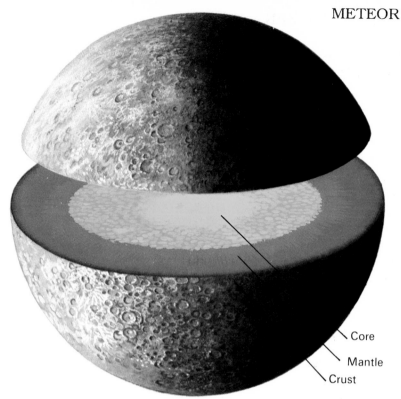

Right: Mercury's huge metal core makes it the densest planet in the solar system after the earth. Mercury travels very fast through space. Its great speed and its nearness to the sun give it the shortest year of all the planets (the time it takes Mercury to go around the sun once) — only 88 of our earth days.

Core

Mantle

Crust

days. During the long daylight hours the temperature on Mercury is so hot that lead would melt. During the long night it grows unbelievably cold. Little was known about Mercury's surface until the space probe *Mariner 10* passed within 800km of the planet. It showed that Mercury has a thin atmosphere and big craters like those on the moon. Mercury's year lasts only 88 of our earth days.

Meteor

A meteor is a tiny piece of metal or stone. It travels through space at great speed. Millions of meteors fall towards the earth every day. Most of them burn up before they reach the ground. The few that do land on earth are called meteorites.

Meteors sometimes travel in swarms. They circle the Sun in long orbits. Meteors are probably small pieces from comets.

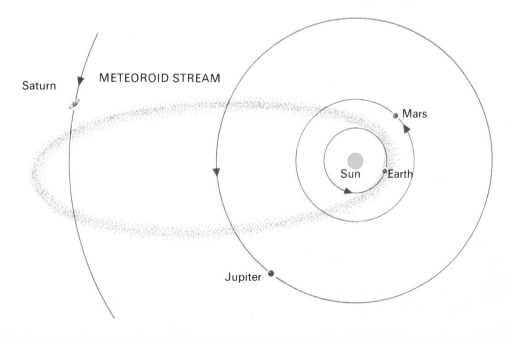

Saturn

METEOROID STREAM

Mars

Sun   Earth

Jupiter

Metric System

The metric system is used for measuring length, volume and weight. It is based on units of ten, or decimals. It was first used in France in the late 1700s. Now it is used all over the world.

Scientists everywhere use the metric system, based on the metre, the litre and the gram.

Mexico

Mexico is a country in NORTH AMERICA. It lies between the United States in the north and CENTRAL AMERICA in the south. To the east is the Gulf of Mexico, a big bay. On the west lies the Pacific Ocean.

Mexico has an area of 1,972,547 square km. Much of the country is hilly with fertile uplands. The highest mountains reach over 5700 metres. The low Yucatán peninsula lies in the south-east.

Mexico is a tropical country, but most of the land is high. This makes the climate cool and dry. There are deserts in the north.

The capital of Mexico is Mexico City. The population of Mexico is over 75 million. The first people in Mexico were Indians, such as the AZTECS.

Mexicans are descended from Mexican Indians and Spanish settlers. Most Mexicans are a mixture of both.

Michelangelo began carving this statue when he was only 23 years old. It shows the Virgin Mary holding Jesus. Jesus has just died on the cross.

Michelangelo

Michelangelo Buonarotti (1475–1564) was a painter and sculptor. He lived in Italy at the time of the RENAISSANCE. Michelangelo is famous for the wonderful statues and paintings he made of people. He spent many years painting pictures in the Sistine Chapel in VATICAN CITY. Many of his statues are large and very lifelike. His statue of David is over 4 metres high.

Microphone

A microphone is an instrument that turns the energy of sound waves into electrical

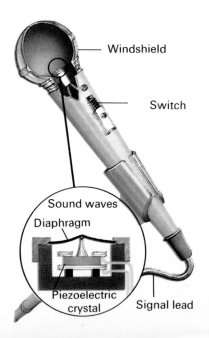

Windshield

Switch

Sound waves

Diaphragm

Piezoelectric crystal

Signal lead

currents. It works by producing an electric signal that goes to an amplifier or to a recording machine.

Inside the microphone, the sound waves strike a thin plate called a diaphragm. This vibrates at the same rate as the sound waves. It is connected to a device that produces an electric signal varying in strength at the same rate as the vibrations. In a crystal microphone, such as the one shown below left, a special type of crystal produces the electric signal when pressure is placed on it by the diaphragm.

Microscope

A microscope is an instrument used for looking at tiny objects. It *magnifies* things, or makes them look bigger. Things that are invisible to the naked eye are called *microscopic.* Many microscopic plants and animals, including bacteria, can be seen if you look at them through a microscope.

Microscopes work by using lenses. The simplest microscope is a magnifying glass. It has only one LENS. The lenses in many microscopes work by bending light rays. Small microscopes can magnify 100 times. Big microscopes used by scientists may magnify up to 2500 times. The electron microscope is much more powerful. It can magnify up to 2,000,000 times. Instead of bending light rays, it bends beams of electrons. Electrons are parts of ATOMS.

Anton van Leeuwenhoek was a Dutchman who lived in the 1600s. He made one of the first microscopes. Using his microscope, he showed that fleas hatch from tiny eggs. Before this, people thought fleas came from sand or mud. They could not see the eggs.

Optical microscopes cannot magnify more than about 2500 times because the light rays cannot produce a sharp image. Electron microscopes like the one on the right use beams of electrons instead of light rays. They work something like an optical microscope with a condenser and objective and eyepiece lenses. The lenses are powerful magnets or electrodes.

Middle Ages

The Middle Ages were a period of history in Europe which lasted for a thousand years. They began when the ROMAN EMPIRE collapsed in the 400s, and ended when the RENAISSANCE began in the 1400s.

During the Middle Ages, Europe was split into many tiny kingdoms and states. People lived under the feudal system. The feudal system divided everyone into groups. The king ruled the country. The nobles, or barons, had to swear loyalty to the king. In return, the king gave them land and power. The barons often lived in CASTLES. Each baron had knights who served him. The baron gave land to the knights in return for their help. Free farmers and craftsmen lived on the baron's land. They were called yeomen. The baron also ruled people called *serfs.* Serfs had to work hard for the baron. They were like slaves.

Most people farmed the land. Towns were small and trade was not important. The ROMAN CATHOLIC CHURCH was very powerful. It made its own laws and influenced the way people lived.

At the bottom of the microscope on the right, a mirror and condenser shine a beam of light through the object. The focusing knob is turned to bring the object into focus. The light rays go on to the eyepiece lens, which magnifies the image more.

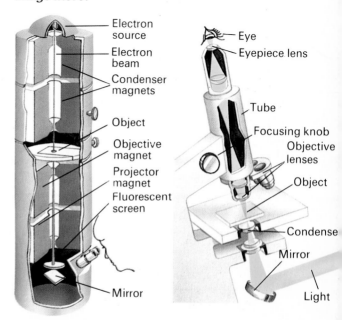

Electron source
Electron beam
Condenser magnets
Object
Objective magnet
Projector magnet
Fluorescent screen
Mirror

Eye
Eyepiece lens
Tube
Focusing knob
Objective lenses
Object
Condense
Mirror
Light

Migration

Many animals make long journeys to breed or find food. Most make the journey every year. Some make the journey only twice in their life. These journeys are called migrations. Animals migrate by INSTINCT.

Birds are the greatest migrators. Swallows leave Europe and North America every autumn. They fly south to spend winter in Africa or South America. The trip may be 10,000 km long. In spring, the swallows fly north again to breed.

But birds are not the only animals that make long trips. Butterflies, fish and mammals migrate too. Whales and fish make long journeys through the sea to find food and breed. Monarch butterflies of North America fly south for the winter.

Below: The monarch butterfly migrates in huge numbers from Canada to Mexico. Some wind up far out in the ocean.

Left: The Arctic tern migrates from the Arctic to the Antarctic and back again each year.

Milk

Milk is a food that all baby MAMMALS live on. It comes from the breasts, or mammaries, of the baby's mother. The baby sucks the milk from its mother's teat or nipple.

At first, the milk is pale and watery. It protects the baby from diseases and infections. Later, the milk is much richer and creamier. It contains all the food the baby needs. Milk is full of FAT, SUGAR, starches, PROTEIN, VITAMINS and MINERALS. After a while the baby grows teeth and starts to eat other kinds of food.

People use milk from many animals. These include cows, sheep, goats, camels and even reindeer. The animals are kept in herds. Sometimes they live on farms. Reindeer do not live on farms but wander about in the wild.

Milk is used to make many other foods. Cream, butter, yoghurt, cheese and some ice cream are all made from milk.

Milky Way

When you look at the sky on a clear, moonless night you can see a pale cloud of light. It stretches across the heavens. If you look at it through binoculars or a telescope, you can see that the cloud is really millions of stars. All these stars, and most of the other stars we see, are part of our GALAXY. It is called the Milky Way.

Astronomers think that the Milky Way has about 100,000 million stars like our sun. The Milky Way stretches over a distance of about 100,000 LIGHT years. Our own SOLAR SYSTEM is 30,000 light years from the centre of the Milky Way.

The Milky Way has a spiral shape. Its trailing arms turn slowly around the centre. They take 200 million years to make a full circle. From earth, we see the Milky Way through the arms of the spiral. Our sun and its planets, including earth, are a tiny speck way out on one of the Milky Way's long arms.

The Milky Way is not a special galaxy. There are thousands of other galaxies with the same shape. There may be millions and millions of other galaxies in the UNIVERSE.

Mineral

The rocks of the earth are made up of materials called minerals. There are many different kinds of mineral. Some, such as GOLD or platinum, are made up of only one ELEMENT. Others, such as QUARTZ and SALT, consist of two or more elements. Some minerals are metallic, such as copper or SILVER. Other minerals are nonmetallic, like sulphur.

Pure minerals are made up of ATOMS arranged in regular patterns known as CRYSTALS. Minerals form crystals when they cool from hot gases and liquids deep inside the earth. Crystals can grow very large if they cool slowly. But large or small, crystals of the same mineral always have the same shape. The exception is CARBON. It takes one crystal shape when it is DIAMOND and another when it is graphite. Another mineral with a name ending in *ite* is hematite, the most important source of iron.

The Milky Way galaxy has a spiral shape (below). The Solar System (below right) is shown in the little square as it travels round the galaxy.

Above: Quartz is the most common mineral in the world. Pure quartz is almost clear, such as the piece shown above, but impurities can give it many different colours.

Altogether there are over 2000 minerals. Yet most of the earth's rocks are made up of only 30 minerals. The most common mineral of all is quartz. Most grains of sand are quartz. Pure quartz is made up of large, well-shaped crystals and is a milky colour.

Mohammed

Mohammed (AD 570–632) was the founder and leader of the RELIGION known as ISLAM. He was born in Mecca in Saudi Arabia. At the age of 40 he believed that God asked him to preach to the ARABS. He taught that there was only one God, called Allah.

In 622 he was forced out of Mecca, and this is the year from which the Muslim calendar dates. After his death his teachings spread rapidly around the world.

Molluscs

Molluscs are a large group of animals. There are about 70,000 different kinds. After insects they are the most numerous of all animals. They are found everywhere, from deserts and mountains to the depths of the sea.

Molluscs have soft bodies and no backbones. Instead, a hard outer SHELL protects their body. Some molluscs, such as SQUID and cuttlefish, have their shell inside their

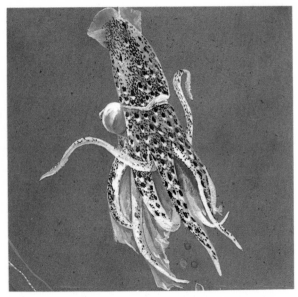

Squids swim in the sea and feed on shrimps. They are molluscs, as are snails, slugs, oysters, clams and mussels.

body. Certain kinds of slug have no shell at all.

Some shells are only a fraction of an inch wide. Others, such as the giant clam, are over a metre wide. As a mollusc grows, its shell grows with it. The shell is made of a hard limy material formed from the food the mollusc eats. Shells have many strange shapes and patterns and some of them are very beautiful.

The largest mollusc is the giant squid. This can grow to as much as 12 metres.

Money

We use money every day to pay for things we buy. We pay with either coins or paper notes. This sort of money is known as cash. There is also another kind of money. It includes cheques, credit cards and travellers' cheques.

Almost anything can be used as money. In the past people have used shells, beads, cocoa beans, salt, grain and even cattle. But coins are much easier to use than, say, cattle. For one thing, they do not die suddenly. They are also easy to store and to carry around.

Coins were first used in China. They were also used by the ancient Greeks as early as

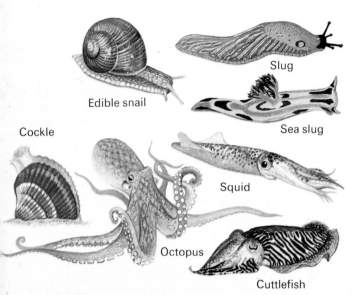

Edible snail

Slug

Sea slug

Cockle

Squid

Octopus

Cuttlefish

Above: An ancient Greek coin with the head of Apollo.

Below: The first British coin to show Britannia was made by the Romans.

Above: Coins and notes are only a small part of the money we use nowadays. In many countries, almost 90 percent of money is in the form of bank deposits. People pay each other by cheque and the banks simply move money from one account to another.

600 BC. They were valuable because they were made of either gold or silver.

Later, people began to use coins made of cheaper metals. The metal itself had no value, but the coins were still worth the amount stamped on them. They also started to use paper money. It no longer mattered that the money itself had no real value. It was backed by the government and banks, which people could trust. This is the kind of money we use today.

Monkey

Monkeys are MAMMALS that belong to the same group of animals as APES and humans. Most monkeys have a long tail and thick fur all over their body. A few have fur only on the rump. Monkeys are usually smaller than apes. Their hands and feet are used for grasping and are very similar to those of humans.

There are about 400 different kinds of monkey. Most live in the tropics, especially in forests, in Africa, Asia and South America. South American monkeys have long tails that they use like an extra arm or leg when swinging through the branches of trees.

On the ground monkeys usually move around on all four limbs. But when they are using their hands to hold something, they can stand or sit up on two legs.

Monkeys live in family groups known as troops. They spend a lot of time chattering, playing, fighting and grooming each other. Each troop of monkeys has its own special

Above: The mandrill comes from Africa. It spends most of its time on the ground.

Golden spider monkey

Black howler monkey

Long-nosed proboscis monkey

place where it lives and feeds. It will fight fiercely to defend this area against other invading groups. Most monkeys will eat fruits, leaves, buds, insects and sometimes birds' eggs, though some baboons will occasionally kill and eat young antelopes.

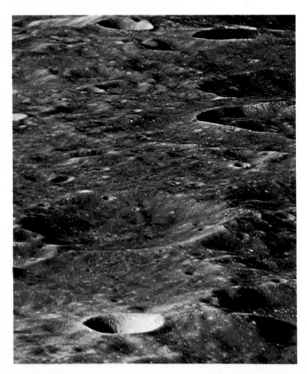

Moon

The moon is our nearest neighbour in space. It loops around the EARTH, never coming closer than 355,000 km. It travels at about 3600 km/hr, and takes $27\frac{1}{3}$ days to complete the circuit around our planet.

The first man-made object to reach the moon was a Russian spacecraft which landed on September 13, 1959. Ten years later, the American astronauts Neil Armstrong and Edwin Aldrin stepped onto the moon's surface.

What they found was a waterless, airless, dusty world. It was covered with thousands of craters, some as small as a footprint,

Left: The lunar highlands, photographed by the Apollo 8 spacecraft in December, 1968.

others stretching across 320km. The craters were holes made by meteorites. The astronauts brought back samples of moon rocks. The rocks show that the moon must be at least 4,600 million years old.

Below: The Moon as viewed from the earth through a telescope. The contrast between the smooth, low-lying parts and the rugged cratered highland parts is very clear. The smooth low parts may have been formed by the heat of gigantic meteorites striking the original surface crust.

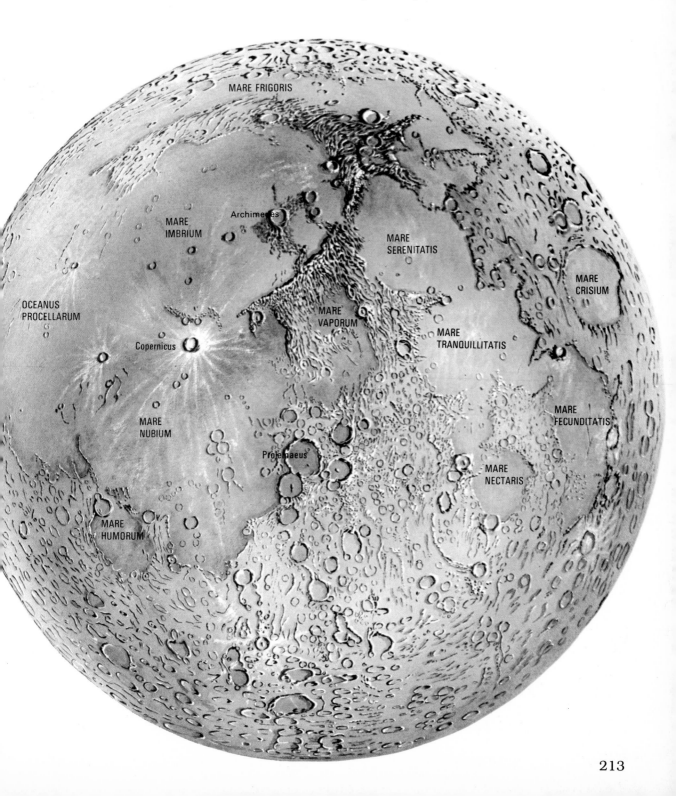

MARE FRIGORIS

MARE IMBRIUM

Archimedes

MARE SERENITATIS

MARE CRISIUM

OCEANUS PROCELLARUM

MARE VAPORUM

MARE TRANQUILLITATIS

Copernicus

MARE NUBIUM

Ptolemaeus

MARE FECUNDITATIS

MARE NECTARIS

MARE HUMORUM

Moore, Henry

Henry Moore (1898–1986) was one of the most famous British artists. He was a sculptor who worked in wood, stone and metal. His carvings are usually large and are easily recognised by their round, curving shapes and smooth lines.

Moore is also well known for his drawings. His pictures of people sheltering underground during the air raids of World War II are especially famous.

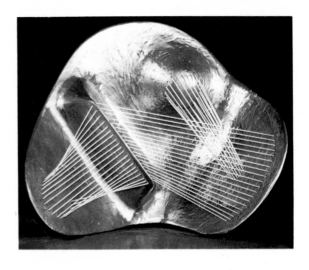

Right: A bronze sculpture by Henry Moore.

Morocco

Morocco is a country right at the top of north-west AFRICA. It is nearly twice the size of the United Kingdom and has two coastlines. On the west is the Atlantic Ocean and to the north is the Mediterranean Sea.

Most of Morocco's 22 million people are farmers. They grow wheat, corn, fruit, olives and nuts. Some keep sheep, goats and cattle. Most of the people are Muslims. The capital of Morocco is Rabat. The country is ruled by a king.

Moscow

Moscow is the capital of the SOVIET UNION. It is also the biggest city in the country. More than eight million people live there.

Moscow lies on a plain across the Moskva River. It is the largest industrial and business centre in the country. Everything is made in Moscow, from cars to clothes. It is also the political and cultural centre of the Soviet Union.

A market place in Morocco where farmers bring their produce to sell.

Red Square in Moscow is the scene of two enormous parades each year in May and November. Soldiers and the latest in military equipment are paraded before the Soviet leaders.

Moscow was first made the capital of Muscovy in 1547, during the reign of Ivan the Terrible, the first *tsar* (emperor) of Russia. It grew up around the KREMLIN, an ancient fort from which the Muscovy princes used to defend their country. Moscow remained the capital of the tsars until 1712, when Peter the Great moved it to St Petersburg. The city was nearly all burned down by NAPOLEON'S armies in 1812. After the Revolution of 1917, Moscow once more became the seat of government.

Mosquito

Mosquitos are a small kind of FLY. They have slender, tube-shaped bodies, three pairs of long legs, and two narrow wings. There are about 1400 different kinds. They live all over the world from the tropics to the Arctic, but must be able to get to water to lay their eggs.

Only female mosquitos bite and suck blood. They have special piercing mouths. Males live on the juices of plants. When the female bites, she injects a substance into her victim to make the blood flow more easily. It is this that makes mosquito bites itch.

Some kinds of mosquito spread serious diseases. Malaria, yellow fever and sleeping sickness are passed on by mosquitos.

Mosses

This is a very common kind of PLANT that grows in low, closely packed clusters. There are more than 12,000 different kinds. They are very hardy plants and flourish everywhere, except in deserts, even as far north as the Arctic. Most mosses grow in damp places. They spread in carpets on the ground in shady forests, or over rocks and the trunks of trees.

Mosses are very simple kinds of plants, like LICHENS. They were among the first to make their home on land. They have slender creeping stems that are covered with

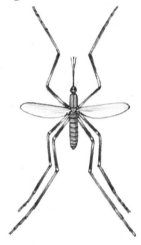

A male mosquito. The female is more dangerous as she bites and sucks blood.

Common hair moss

Motor Car

In about a hundred years the motor car has changed the world. It has also itself been changed. The clumsy 'horseless carriage' has become the fast, comfortable and reliable car of today.

In 1885 two German engineers, working independently, produced vehicles that were the forerunners of today's cars. These men, Karl Benz and Gottlieb Daimler, used INTERNAL COMBUSTION ENGINES fuelled by petrol.

In 1913 Henry Ford introduced the first successful way of producing cars quickly and cheaply. The cars moved down a line of workers who each assembled a certain part.

tiny leaves. Instead of proper roots that reach down into the soil, mosses simply have a mass of tiny hairs that soak up moisture and food. Mosses do not have flowers. They reproduce by spores, just like ferns. One kind, called sphagnum moss, grows in bogs and is the plant that makes peat.

Above: The Cadillac of 1930 was a high-powered luxury car. Below: The Model-T Ford was the first car that was both cheap and reliable. Over 16 million of them were sold between 1909 and 1927.

Cars are still made in this way except that it is now robots that do the assembling in many factories.

The power for the car comes from an internal combustion engine which burns a mixture of petrol and air in cylinders. Most engines have four or six cylinders. Inside the cylinders are pistons which are forced down by the burning gases and turn a crankshaft. At one end of the crankshaft is a heavy flywheel which smooths out the motion of the engine. From the crankshaft, the power goes to the transmission, which takes the power to the shaft that is made to drive the wheels. (The wheels that are driven can be either at the front or the back.) The driver can use gears to make the car go faster or slower for the same engine speed, and to reverse. Many cars have automatic transmission that changes gear automatically. All cars need a BATTERY

Above left: The Ford Fiesta. Above: The highly successful Rover SD1.

which is charged from the engine. The battery provides power for the starter motor, the lights, the horn and other accessories. Some cars and trucks have a DIESEL ENGINE which burns diesel oil.

Motorcycle

The first motorcyle was built in 1885 by the German Gottlieb Daimler. He fitted one of his petrol engines to a wooden bicycle frame. But today's motorcycles are very complicated machines. The engine is similar to that of a car, but smaller. (See INTER-

BMW, the German motorcycle company, began to produce motorcycles in 1923. Their latest machines are capable of over 220km/hr.

NAL COMBUSTION ENGINE.) It is either a two-stroke or a four-stroke engine, and it may have from one to four cylinders. The engine can be cooled by either air or water. It is started by pushing down a kick-starter. This turns the engine and starts it firing. The speed is controlled by a twist-grip on the handlebars. The clutch works from a hand lever. The gears are changed by a foot lever. Another foot pedal works the brake on the back wheel. A chain connects the engine to the back wheel and drives it round.

Mountain

A large part of the earth's surface is covered by mountains. The greatest mountain ranges are the Alps of Europe, the Rockies and the Andes of the Americas, and the Himalayas of Asia. The Himalayas have many of the world's highest peaks, including the biggest, Mount EVEREST.

There are mountains under the sea, too. Sometimes the peaks of undersea mountains rise above the sea's surface as islands. Mauna Loa, on the island of Hawaii, rises from the floor of the Pacific Ocean and is much higher than Everest.

Mountains are formed by movements in the earth's crust. Some mountains are formed when two great land masses move toward each other and squeeze up the land in between. Other mountains are VOLCANOES, built up from ash and lava.

But even the greatest mountains do not last forever. The hardest rock gets worn away in time by rain, wind, sun and frost. Rivers cut valleys, glaciers grind their way down, wearing away the mountains after untold centuries into gentle hills.

When the height of a mountain is given, it means the height above sea level. This can be a lot more than the height from the base.

In the far distance in this picture are the mighty Himalayas, the world's highest mountains. These great peaks were pushed up millions and millions of years ago when the whole of India moved slowly north and collided with the rest of Asia.

If we go up a high mountain in the tropics, it is almost like travelling at sea level from the equator to the polar regions.

Snow line

Tree line

Conifers

Deciduous forest

Tropical forest

Mozart, Wolfgang Amadeus

Wolfgang Amadeus Mozart (1756–1791) was an Austrian and one of the greatest composers of music that the world has known. He began writing music at the age of five. Two years later he was playing at concerts all over Europe. Mozart wrote more than 600 pieces of music, including many beautiful operas and symphonies. But he earned little money from his hard work. He died in poverty at the age of 35.

This unfinished portrait of Mozart was painted in the winter of 1782.

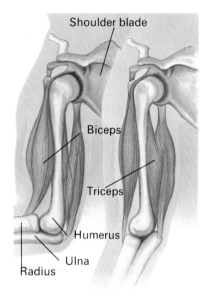

To bend your forearm, the biceps muscle contracts. It relaxes when you straighten your arm.

Muscles

Muscles are the things that make the parts of our bodies move. When you pick up this book or kick a ball you are using muscles. There are two different kinds of muscles. Some work when your brain tells them to. When you pick up a chair, your brain sends signals to muscles in your arms, your legs, and other parts of your body. All these muscles work together at the right time, and you pick up the chair. Other kinds of muscles work even when you are asleep. Your stomach muscles go on churning the food you have eaten. Your heart muscles go on pumping blood. The human body has more than 600 muscles.

Music

People have been making some kind of music all through history. The very earliest people probably made singing noises and beat time with pieces of wood. We know that the ancient Egyptians enjoyed their music. Paintings in the tombs of the pharaohs show musicians playing pipes, harps and other stringed instruments. The ancient Greeks also liked stringed instruments such as the lyre. But we have no idea what this early music sounded like, because there was no way of writing it down.

As instruments improved, new ones were added to the orchestra. BACH and Handel, who were both born in 1685, used orchestras with mostly stringed instruments such as the violin. But they also had flutes, oboes, trumpets and horns. Joseph Haydn was the first man to use the orchestra as a whole. He invented the *symphony*. In this, all the instruments blend together.

A new kind of music began with the great German composer BEETHOVEN. He began writing music in which some of the notes clashed. This sounded rather shocking to people who listened to his music in his day. Later musicians tried all kinds of mixtures of instruments. In the 1900s new kinds of music were made by composers such as Igor Stravinsky and Arnold Schönberg. Others since then have used tape recorders and electronic systems to produce new sounds which are often rather strange to our ears.

But music still has three things: *melody, harmony* and *rhythm*. The melody is the

Bassoon

Piccolo

Oboe

Flute

Clarinet

Cor anglais

Trumpet

Trombone

Double bass

Tuba

Cello

French horn

Cymbals

Triangle

Many sounds have no particular musical note. When a chair falls on the floor we hear a crash. This is an unpleasant sound. Pleasant sounds have a note — a definite pitch. That kind of sound is usually made by musical instruments.

tune. Harmony is the total sound when several notes are played together. A group of notes is called a *chord*. Rhythm is the regular 'beat' of the music. The simplest kind of music is just beating out a rhythm on a drum.

Musical Instrument

There are four kinds of musical instruments. In wind instruments, air is made to vibrate inside a tube. This vibrating air makes a musical note.

All *woodwind* instruments such as the clarinet, bassoon, flute, piccolo and recorder have holes that are covered by the fingers or by pads worked by the fingers. These holes change the length of the vibrating column of air inside the instrument. The shorter the column, the higher the note. In *brass* wind instruments, the vibration of the player's lips makes the air in the instrument vibrate. By changing the pressure of the lips, the player can make different notes. Most brass instruments also have valves and pistons to change the length of the vibrating column of air, and so make different notes.

Stringed instruments work in one of two ways. The strings of the instrument are either made to vibrate by a bow, as in the violin, viola, cello and double bass; or the strings are plucked, as in the guitar, harp or banjo.

In *percussion* instruments, a tight piece of skin or a piece of wood or metal is struck to make a note. There are lots of percussion instruments—drum, cymbals, gong, tambourine, triangle and chimes.

Electronic instruments such as the electric organ and the synthesizer make music from electronic circuits.

Above: Cats have claws that they can draw back, or 'retract', when they are not needed. This picture shows the bones and muscles in the cat's foot that make this possible.

Nails and Claws

Nails and claws are made of hard skin, like animals' horns. They grow at the end of toes and fingers. If they are broad and flat they are called nails, but if they are sharp and pointed they are claws. BIRDS, MAMMALS and REPTILES use their claws to attack and to defend themselves.

A close look at an animal's claws will tell you about its way of life. CATS and birds of prey have very sharp claws for seizing prey. ANTEATERS have long, strong, curved claws for tearing termites' nests apart.

Right: Different birds have feet and claws adapted for different purposes, from gripping prey (the osprey) to running (the ostrich).

Name

Names help us to identify people. A first name is a personal name chosen by our parents. Our last name, or *surname*, is a family name. It can often tell us something about our ancestors. The names 'Smith' and 'Shepherd', for example, are the names of jobs. Some people have names of places as surnames, such as 'Bedford'. Other surnames add 'son' to the father's name, such as 'Jackson' or 'Johnson'.

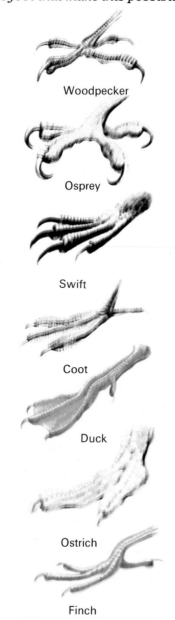

Woodpecker

Osprey

Swift

Coot

Duck

Ostrich

Finch

Napoleon Bonaparte was 36 when this portrait was painted.

French Empire
Areas controlled by Napoleon
Countries friendly to Napoleon

Napoleon was one of the greatest military leaders of all time. The map above shows the vast area conquered by 'the little corporal'.

Napoleon Bonaparte

In 1789 the people of FRANCE rebelled against the unjust rule of their king and his nobles. This revolution was supported by a young man who had been born in the island of Corsica 20 years before. His name was Napoleon Bonaparte (1769–1821).

Napoleon went to the leading military school in Paris, and by 1792 he was a captain of artillery. Three years later he saved France by crushing a royalist rebellion in Paris. Soon Napoleon was head of the French army and won great victories in Italy, Belgium and Austria. In 1804 he crowned himself emperor of France in the presence of the Pope. Then he crowned his wife, Josephine.

Napoleon tried, but was unable to defeat Britain at sea. He tried to stop all countries from trading with England, but Russia would not cooperate. So Napoleon took a great army into Russia in the winter of 1812. This campaign ended in disaster. His troops were defeated by the bitter weather. He met his final defeat at the Battle of Waterloo in 1815. There he was beaten by the British under Wellington and the Prus-

sians under Blücher. He was imprisoned on the island of St Helena, where he died in 1821.

Napoleon was a small man. His soldiers adored him and called him 'the little corporal'. His rise to power was helped by his wife Josephine. Napoleon drew up a new French code of law. Many of his laws are still in force today.

Navigation

Navigation means finding the way, usually in a ship or an aircraft. For hundreds of years, navigators at sea used the changing positions of the sun and stars to work out their LATITUDE. The difference between the time on the ship and the time set at 0° longitude at Greenwich helped them to work out their position.

Today many navigational instruments are electronic and are very accurate. Radio stations and satellites send out signals from which a ship can find its position. Then the navigator uses a COMPASS to keep his ship on the right course. A ship just leaving port relies on a pilot who knows the harbour, and then on coastal landmarks.

Accurate navigation is important in order to avoid dangerous rocks. At sea the ship depends on radio or celestial navigation. Aircraft depend mostly on radio navigation and on radar.

Neptune (god)

Neptune was the Roman name for the Greek god Poseidon, the god of the sea. People believed that when he was angry he sent storms and floods. He carried a three-pronged spear called a trident. The Romans believed that Neptune caused earthquakes by striking the ground with his trident, and that once when he struck the ground the first horse appeared.

Neptune (planet)

The PLANET Neptune is named after the Roman god of water and the sea. It is a large planet (much bigger than the earth) far out in the SOLAR SYSTEM. It is about 4493 million km from the SUN. Only PLUTO is farther away. It takes Neptune 165 years to circle the sun. (The earth takes 365 days.)

Being so far from the sun, Neptune is a very cold place. Scientists think its atmosphere is something like JUPITER's, which is mostly made up of the gas HYDROGEN. Neptune has two moons, Triton and Nereid. Triton is about the size of the planet MERCURY.

Early astronomers were unable to see Neptune, but they knew it had to be there. They could tell there was something affecting the ORBIT of the nearby planet URANUS.

In 1845 two astronomers, Adams in England and Leverrier in France, used mathematics to work out where Neptune should be. The next year Neptune was spotted.

Nerve

Nerves are tiny fibres made up of CELLS. They run all through the body. When a part of the body feels something, the nerves send a message through the spinal column to the BRAIN. If we feel pain, a message is sent back to make us move away from whatever is causing the pain. Nerves also carry the senses of sight, hearing and taste. The sense organs have special nerve endings that respond to heat, cold, light and other stimuli from the world around us.

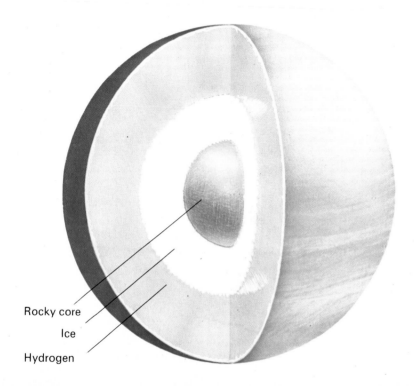

Rocky core

Ice

Hydrogen

If a piece were cut out of Neptune it would probably look like this. Scientists think the planet is made up of hydrogen surrounding a core of rock and ice. This core is probably about the same size as the earth.

Below: Because Neptune is so far away, no one knows its exact size. But we think it is about four times as wide as the earth.

In the 1700s many Amsterdam merchants made great fortunes because of the Dutch trading empire. These merchants' houses were built then.

Covered with mud and wearing frightening masks, New Guinea tribesmen perform a traditional ceremony.

Netherlands

The Netherlands, or Holland, as it is also known, is a low-lying country in western EUROPE. The sea often floods the flat land near the coast, so sea walls have been built for protection against storms. Living so near the sea, the people of the Netherlands (who call themselves the Dutch) have a long and successful history of seafaring, trade and exploring.

The Netherlands is a land of canals, windmills, farms and bulb fields which burst into colour in spring. It was once part of a group of countries called the Low Countries, but it became self-governing in 1759. Important cities are Amsterdam, the capital, and Rotterdam, which is the busiest port in Europe. The Netherlands is a prosperous country and one of the first members of the EUROPEAN ECONOMIC COMMUNITY.

New Guinea

New Guinea is one of the world's largest islands. It lies to the north of Australia. Most of its people are dark skinned with curly hair.

The island is divided into two parts. The west is called Irian Jaya, and belongs to INDONESIA. The east is called Papua New Guinea. About three million people live there. It used to belong to Australia but became independent in 1975. The capital is Port Moresby.

New Guinea's main exports are tea, cocoa, copra (coconut), copper and gold. The official language is English but some 700 different languages are spoken.

Newspaper

Newspapers are just what their name says they are—papers that print news. They first appeared in the 1400s, just after PRINTING began. Printers produced pamphlets telling people what was happening in the country and what they thought about it.

Modern newspapers first appeared in the 1700s. Today there are newspapers in almost every country in the world, in many different languages. Some are printed every day, some every week.

One of the oldest newspapers is *The Times* which is printed in London. It began in 1785 when it was called the *Daily Universal Register*. It changed its name to *The Times* in 1788. Other famous newspapers are *The New York Times* and *The Washington Post* in the United States, *Pravda* in the USSR, and *Le Monde* in France.

Newton, Isaac

Sir Isaac Newton (1642–1727) was an English mathematician and scientist who made some of the world's greatest scientific discoveries. He left Cambridge University in 1665 when plague shut the university. In the 18 months before the university re-opened, Newton did much of his most important work.

He invented a new kind of mathematics called *calculus*. Today calculus helps designers shape things such as aircraft wings.

Newton's experiments showed that white LIGHT is a mixture of all the colours of the rainbow (the spectrum). By studying the

Until the 1980s, newspapers were printed from curved metal plates. The plates were attached to a cylinder which rotated at a very high speed on a huge letterpress.

Below: Isaac Newton was one of the greatest of all scientists. In this picture he is seen making one of his experiments with light, which led to his discovery and description of the spectrum — that white light is really made up of many colours.

spectrum of light from a star or other glowing object, scientists can now find out what the object is made of. Newton's studies of light also led him to build the first reflecting TELESCOPE.

Newton also discovered GRAVITY. He realized that the same kind of force that makes apples fall from trees also gives objects weight and keeps PLANETS going around the SUN.

Modern JET ENGINES work in a way that was first described by Newton in 1687.

New Zealand

New Zealand is a remote island nation in the Pacific Ocean, south-east of Australia.

New Zealand is actually two main islands. North Island is famous for its hot springs and volcanoes. South Island has a range of mountains called the Southern Alps.

New Zealand also has plains and valleys, where farmers grow grains, vegetables and apples. New Zealand is also the world's third largest producer of sheep and wool.

There are over three million New Zealanders. Auckland is the largest city, but the capital is Wellington. Both are on North Island. New Zealand is a member of the Commonwealth. Many of its people are descended from British settlers. Others are Maoris, descended from Pacific islanders, who lived in New Zealand before the British came.

Above: The snow-crowned peaks of the Southern Alps rise beyond Lake Wakatipu on the South Island of New Zealand.

Nigeria

This nation in West AFRICA is named after the river Niger, which flows through it. Nigeria has more than 90 million people, more than any other nation in Africa. The capital is Lagos.

All Nigeria is hot. Dry grass and scrubby trees are scattered across the country. But swamps and forests line the coasts.

Nigerians are mainly black Africans. There are a great number of different tribes speaking many different languages. Half the people follow the religion of ISLAM. Most of the people grow maize, yams or other food crops. Nigeria is one of the world's main cocoa growers, and one of Africa's top two oil producers.

Nightingale, Florence

Florence Nightingale (1820–1910) founded modern nursing. She was wealthy and could have had an easy life, but instead she chose to work hard for the sick. In those days countless patients died in dirty hospitals run by untrained nurses. Florence Nightingale trained as a nurse, and ran a women's hospital in London.

In 1854 she took 38 nurses to Turkey to

tend British soldiers wounded in the Crimean War. Her hospital was a dirty barracks that lacked food, medicines and bedding. She cleaned it, found supplies, and gave the wounded every care she could. Her work saved many hundreds of lives.

Nile, River

The river Nile in Africa may be the longest river on earth. (Some people think that the AMAZON is longer.) The Nile was once shown to measure 6670 km. It rises in Burundi in central Africa and flows north through Egypt into the Mediterranean Sea. It is very important to the farmers who live around it.

Nobel Prize

These money prizes are given each year to people who have helped mankind in different ways. Three prizes are for physics, chemistry and physiology and medicine. The fourth is for literature. The fifth prize is for work to keep peace between peoples and the sixth is for economics. Money for the prizes was left by the Swedish chemist Alfred Nobel, who invented the explosive dynamite.

Below: Irrigation canals lead water from the river Nile to farmland alongside the river.

North America

North America stretches north from tropical Panama to the Arctic Ocean, and east from the Pacific to the Atlantic Ocean. Only Asia is larger than this continent.

North America has the world's largest island (Greenland), and the largest freshwater lake (Lake Superior). It contains the second largest country (CANADA), the second largest mountain range (the ROCKY MOUNTAINS), and the third longest river (the Mississippi River). North America's natural wonders include Niagara Falls and the Grand Canyon (the largest gorge on land).

The cold north has long, dark, frozen winters. No trees grow there. Farther south stand huge evergreen forests. Grasslands covered most of the plains in the middle of the continent until farmers ploughed them. Cactuses thrive in the deserts of the southwest. Tropical trees grow quickly in the hot, wet forests of the south.

Peoples from all over the world have made their homes in North America. First came the ancestors of the American INDIANS and ESKIMOS. Later came the Europeans, who brought black slaves from Africa. Most North Americans speak English, French or Spanish, and are Protestant or Roman Catholic Christians. They live in more than 30 nations. The UNITED STATES and Canada

are large, powerful and rich. But many of the nations of CENTRAL AMERICA and the WEST INDIES are small and poor.

Only one person in ten in the world lives in North America. Yet North Americans make half the manufactured goods on earth. This is because North America's farms and mines produce huge amounts of food and minerals to feed the workers and supply materials for factory machines.

Norway

Norway is Europe's sixth largest country. This long, northern kingdom is wide in the south but narrow in the centre and the north. (See page 123.) Mountains with forests, bare rocks and snow cover much of Norway. Steep inlets called FIORDS pierce its rocky coast.

Summers in Norway are cool and the winters long. It is very cold in the ARCTIC north, but the rainy west coast is kept fairly mild by the Gulf Stream.

Four million people live in Norway. Their capital is Oslo. Norwegians catch more fish than any other Europeans do.

Nuclear Energy

The nucleus, or 'heart', of an ATOM is made of tiny particles. Splitting nuclei (nuclear fission) and joining nuclei (nuclear fusion) give huge amounts of energy. Nuclear fission produces the ATOMIC ENERGY used in nuclear power stations and atom bombs. Nuclear energy is produced inside a nuclear reactor (below). There, fission produces energy in the form of heat. Nuclear fusion is used in hydrogen bombs. One day it may be used in power stations.

Number

In STONE AGE times people showed a number like 20 or 30 by making 20 or 30 separate marks. In certain caves you can still see the marks that they made.

In time people invented special signs or groups of signs to show different numbers. Such signs are called *numerals*. For centuries many people used Roman numerals. But these are rather clumsy. For example, the Roman numerals for 38 are XXXVIII. Our much simpler system uses Arabic numerals that were first used in India.

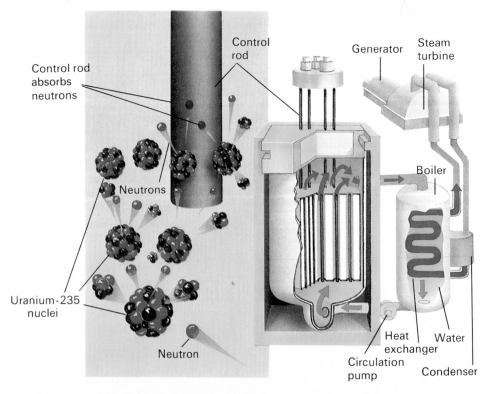

Control rod absorbs neutrons

Control rod

Generator

Steam turbine

Neutrons

Boiler

Uranium-235 nuclei

Neutron

Heat exchanger

Water

Circulation pump

Condenser

In a nuclear reactor the fuel is a metal called uranium-235. When the nucleus of a uranium-235 atom is struck by a neutron, it breaks into two smaller nuclei and several more neutrons. These strike other uranium nuclei and more neutrons are given out. The reactor's control rods keep the reaction going at a steady rate. The uranium gets very hot and a coolant — a liquid or a gas — moves through the reactor and is heated. Then the coolant goes to a boiler to make steam, which powers ordinary electricity generators.

Ocean

Oceans cover nearly three-quarters of the surface of the earth. If you put all the world's water into 100 giant tanks, 97 of them would be full of water from the oceans. The oceans are always losing water as water vapour, drawn up into the air by the sun's heat. But most of it returns as RAIN. Rain-water running off the land takes salts and other MINERALS to the oceans.

There are four oceans. The largest and deepest is the PACIFIC OCEAN. The second largest is the Atlantic Ocean. This is only half as large as the Pacific Ocean. The

Underwater explorers have found that the ocean floor has valleys, cliffs and volcanic peaks. In the deepest parts the floor is being pulled down inside the earth.

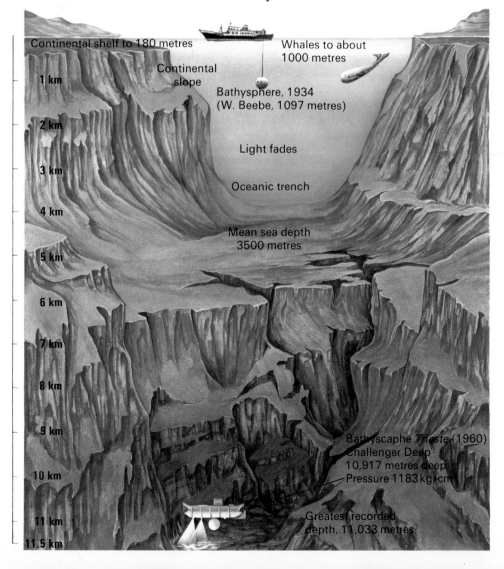

Continental shelf to 180 metres

Whales to about 1000 metres

Continental slope

1 km

Bathysphere, 1934 (W. Beebe, 1097 metres)

2 km

3 km

Light fades

Oceanic trench

4 km

Mean sea depth 3500 metres

5 km

6 km

7 km

8 km

9 km

Bathyscaphe *Trieste* (1960) Challenger Deep 10,917 metres deep. Pressure 1183 kg/cm²

10 km

11 km

Greatest recorded depth, 11,033 metres

11.5 km

Indian Ocean is smaller but deeper than the Atlantic Ocean. The Arctic Ocean is the smallest and shallowest of all.

The oceans are never still. Winds crinkle their surface in waves. Winds also drive the Gulf Stream and other currents. Every day the ocean surface falls and rises with the TIDES. In winter, polar sea water freezes over. ICEBERGS from polar seas may drift hundreds of miles.

Oceans are home to countless living things. The minerals in sea water help to nourish tiny plants at the surface. These animals and plants are called plankton. Small fish eat the plankton. In turn, small fish are eaten by larger hunters.

Octopus

There are about 50 kinds of octopus. They are soft-bodied MOLLUSCS that live in the sea. Octopus means 'eight feet' but the eight

tentacles are usually called arms. The largest octopus has arms about 9 metres across, but most octopuses are no larger than a man's fist. Suckers on the tentacles grip crabs, shellfish or other prey. An octopus's tentacles pull its victim toward its mouth. This is hard and pointed, like the beak of a bird.

Oil

Oils are FATS and other greasy substances that do not dissolve in water. But when we

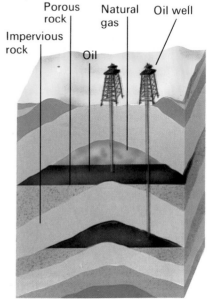

Oil and natural gas, trapped between layers of rock, are formed from plants and animals that lived a long time ago.

An octopus is seldom dangerous, but some are poisonous. A diver gripped by a big octopus may find it difficult to escape.

Each octopus hides in an underwater cave or crevice. It creeps about the seabed searching for food. Its two large eyes keep a watch for enemies. If danger threatens, the octopus may confuse its enemy by squirting an inky liquid. The inks hangs in the water like a cloud.

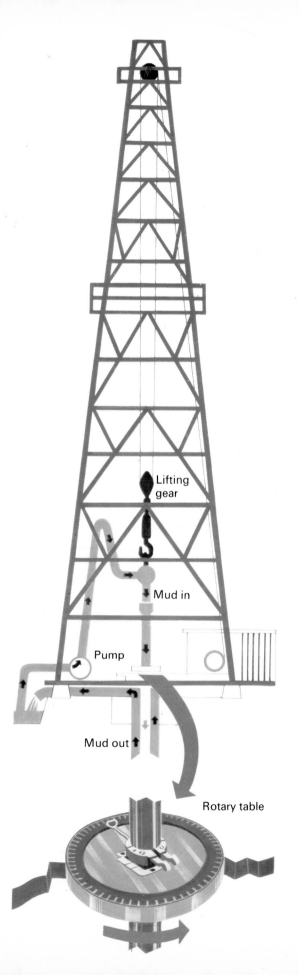

say 'oil' we usually mean petroleum oil. This oil was formed millions of years ago from dead plants and animals. The oil was trapped under rocks. Today engineers drill holes down through the surface rocks to reach the oil beneath.

Oil refineries separate the oil to make petrol, kerosene and lubricating oil. Oil is also used in making artificial fertilizer, many kinds of medicine, paint, plastics and detergent. We may run short of many of these things in the future, because the world's supplies of oil are running out.

Olive

These fruits grow on trees with slim, grey-green leaves and twisted trunks. Each FRUIT is shaped like a small plum. Farmers pick olives when they are green and unripe, or when ripe, they hit the trees with sticks to knock the olives onto sheets spread on the

Above: A 2500-year-old Greek vase shows men beating a tree to bring down olives.

Left: A drilling rig drills for oil with a steel 'bit' at the end of lengths of pipe. The pipe is lowered by lifting gear and turned by a rotary table. Soft mud pumped down the pipe comes back up outside it, bringing bits of rock.

231

ground. Olives taste bitter and have a hard stone in the middle. People eat olives and cook food in olive oil made from crushed olives.

Most olives come from Italy, Spain and other countries by the Mediterranean Sea.

Olympic Games

This athletics competition is the world's oldest. The first known Olympic Games took place at Olympia in Greece in 776 BC. The Greek Games ended in AD 394. The modern Olympic Games began in 1894. They are held once every four years, each time in a different country. Athletes from different nations compete in races, jumping, gymnastics, swimming and many more contests. The winners receive medals.

The Olympic Flame burns throughout the Games. It is a symbol of peace and friendship.

Onion

Onions are strong-tasting plants eaten as VEGETABLES and to add flavour to other foods. Most kinds of onion have a BULB made up of tightly packed layers of leaves. This is the part we eat. The leaves contain a special kind of oil. When you peel an onion, a vapour from the oil makes your eyes water. Onions are grown from seeds or from small, partly grown bulbs called *sets.* An onion plant lives for two years.

Opera

An opera is a play with music. The 'actors' are singers who sing all or many of their words. An ORCHESTRA accompanies them.

The first opera was performed in Italy nearly 400 years ago. Famous composers of serious opera include MOZART, Verdi, Puccini and Wagner.

Light, short operas are called operettas. Operettas of the 1800s gave rise to the tuneful musical comedies of the 1900s.

Opossum

Opossums are marsupials found in North and South America. Some look like rats, others look like mice. The Virginia opos-

sum is as big as a cat. This is North America's only marsupial. It climbs trees and can cling on with its tail. A female has up to 18 babies, each no larger than a honeybee. If danger threatens, the Virginia opossum pretends to be dead. If a person pretends to be hurt, we say he is 'playing possum'.

Sorting and packing freshly picked oranges in a Greek orange grove.

Orange

Oranges are citrus FRUITS, like lemons and grapefruits. Orange seeds lie in juicy segments surrounded by a soft rind with a shiny orange or yellow skin. Orange juice is rich in sugar and VITAMINS.

People eat more oranges than any other citrus fruit. Sweet oranges are eaten raw. Bitter oranges are used in marmalade. Half of the world's oranges come from the United States and Brazil. But orange trees grow in many of the world's warm countries.

Orang-utan

This big, red-haired APE comes from the islands of Borneo and Sumatra. Its name comes from Malay words meaning 'man of the woods'. A male is as heavy as a man, but not so tall. Orang-utans use their long arms to swing through the branches of trees as they hunt for fruit and leaves to eat. Each night they make a nest high up in the trees. A leafy roof helps to keep out rain.

Man is the orang-utan's main enemy. Hunters kill mothers to catch their babies and sell them to zoos. Orang-utans are already scarce. They could become extinct.

Orbit

An orbit is the curved path of something that spins around another object in space. Man-made satellites and the MOON travel around the earth in orbits. Each planet, including the earth, has its own orbit around the SUN. Most orbits are a loop or ellipse, rather than a circle. An orbiting object tries to move in a straight line but is pulled by GRAVITY toward the object that it orbits.

Orchestra

An orchestra is a large group of musicians who play together. The word *orchestra* once meant 'dancing place'. In ancient Greek theatres, dancers and musicians performed on a space between the audience and the stage. When Italy invented OPERA, Italian theatres arranged their musicians in the same way. Soon people used the word

A male orang-utan from Borneo. His cheeks have huge flaps of skin. Some males are almost too heavy to climb and spend a lot of time on the ground.

orchestra to describe the group of musicians, and not the place where they performed.

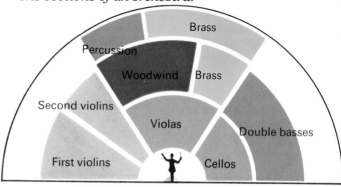

The sections of an orchestra.

The modern orchestra owes much to Haydn. He arranged its MUSICAL INSTRUMENTS into four main groups: string, woodwind, brass and percussion. Most orchestras have a conductor.

Ostrich

This is the largest living BIRD. An ostrich may weigh twice as much as a man and stand more than 2 metres high. Ostriches cannot fly. If attacked, they run away or kick hard enough to rip a lion open. Ostriches never hide their heads in sand, as people used to think.

Ostriches live in Africa. They roam in herds, led by a male. The females lay large, white eggs in a nest dug in the sand. Ostriches can live for 50 years or more.

Otter

Otters are large relatives of the weasel. They have long, low bodies and short legs. An otter is a bit heavier than a dachshund. It hunts in water for fish and frogs. Thick fur keeps its body dry. It swims by moving its tail and body like an eel, and using its webbed hind feet.

Otters are wanderers. By night they hunt up and down a river, or roam overland to find new fishing grounds. They love to play by sliding down a bank of snow or mud.

Owl

These birds of prey hunt mainly by night. They have soft feathers that make no sound as they fly. Their large, staring eyes help them to see in the dimmest light. Owls also have keen ears which help them to catch mice in pitch darkness.

When an owl eats a mouse or bird, it swallows it complete with bones and fur or feathers. Later, the owl spits out the remains in a pellet. You can sometimes find owl pellets on the ground.

Oxygen

Oxygen is a gas. It is one of the most abundant ELEMENTS on earth. It makes up one part in every five parts of AIR. Oxygen is found in water and in many different rocks. Most of the weight of water, and half that of rocks, comes from the oxygen.

FIRE needs oxygen to burn. Almost all living things need oxygen for BREATHING and to give them the energy just to stay alive. Animals need extra oxygen to move about. PLANTS give out oxygen into the air.

Owls include those below and the eagle owl (right).

Brown form

Tawny owl   Grey form

Pygmy owl   Little owl

234

Pacific Ocean

This is the largest and deepest of all the OCEANS. Its waters cover more than one-third of the world. All the CONTINENTS would fit inside the Pacific Ocean with room to spare. Its deepest part is deep enough to cover the world's highest mountain.

The Pacific Ocean lies west of the Americas, and east of Australia and Asia. It stretches from the frozen far north to the frozen far south. There are thousands of tiny islands in the Pacific. Most were formed when VOLCANOES grew up from the seabed. Sometimes earthquakes shake the seabed and send out huge tidal waves.

Painting

Painting is a form of ART in which people use coloured paint to make pictures on canvas, plaster, wood or paper. Today most people paint for their own pleasure. But this was not always so.

In the Middle Ages most artists worked for the Church. Their paintings showed scenes from Bible stories. Such paintings helped people who could not read to understand the Bible.

By the 1400s Europe's rich princes and merchants were paying artists to paint pictures to decorate their homes. The pictures might be family portraits, still-life scenes of flowers and fruit or landscapes showing cities and country estates.

In the 1800s many artists began trying out new ideas. For example, some tried to give a feeling of the light and shade in a landscape. Others used bright, flat colours to bring out the patterns in still-lifes and landscapes. In the 1900s Pablo PICASSO and other artists began to experiment with abstract paintings. These concentrate on the basic shapes, colours and patterns of the things painted.

Left: Vittore Carpaccio painted these Italian women and their pets nearly 500 years ago. Old paintings can show us how people used to dress and behave.

235

Pakistan

Pakistan lies between India and Iran. There are more than 94 million Pakistanis. Most of them follow the religion of ISLAM.

Much of Pakistan is hot and dry, but crops such as wheat and cotton grow with the help of water from the Indus River. The Indus flows from the HIMALAYAS to the Arabian Sea. The capital of Pakistan is Islamabad.

Palestine

Palestine is a land on the eastern shore of the Mediterranean Sea. Most of the stories in the BIBLE took place there. Palestine gets its name from the Philistines who once lived in part of it.

By 1800 BC the Hebrews had made Palestine their home. Later they ruled it as two nations, called Israel and Judah. Both of these nations were then taken over by foreign rulers.

Most of what used to be called Palestine now lies in the nation of Israel. Other parts are in Jordan, Lebanon and Syria.

Palm Tree

A palm tree has leaves that sprout straight out of the top of its trunk, rather like the fingers of an outspread hand. There are more than 1000 kinds of palm. Not all are trees. Some are shrubs and others are vines. Most palms grow in warm climates.

People make mats and baskets from palm leaves. We eat the fruits of some palms, such as coconuts and dates.

The date palm has a thick, rough stem covered with hard, brown fibres.

Panama Canal

The Panama Canal crosses Panama in CENTRAL AMERICA. Ships use it as a short cut between the Atlantic and Pacific oceans. Before the Canal was finished in 1914, ships from the United States' east coast had to sail all around South America to reach the west coast. Sets of locks on the canal raise and lower ships crossing the hills of Panama.

Panda

There are two kinds of panda. Both live in the forests of east Asia. The giant panda (above) looks like a black-and-white bear. It lives in BAMBOO forests in CHINA. Giant pandas are becoming very scarce. The red panda is not much larger than a cat. It has a bushy tail and reddish fur. Both kinds eat plants. Their nearest relatives are the raccoons of North and South America.

Paper

Paper gets its name from papyrus, a plant used by the ancient Egyptians to make a kind of paper. But the Chinese invented paper as we know it. About 1900 years ago they learned to separate the fibres from mulberry bark. They soaked, then dried them, making a flat sheet that they could write on. Paper is still made of plant fibres. Some of the best paper is made of COTTON. Newspaper is made from wood pulp.

Paris

Paris is the capital of FRANCE, and France's largest city. More than eight million people live there. The river Seine divides the city into the left bank and the right bank.

If you gaze down on Paris from the Eiffel Tower you will see many parks and gardens, fine squares and tree-lined avenues. Other famous landmarks are the Cathedral of Notre Dame, the Arc de Triomphe and the Louvre Palace, now a famous museum.

Below: Many artists live and work in a part of Paris called Montmartre.

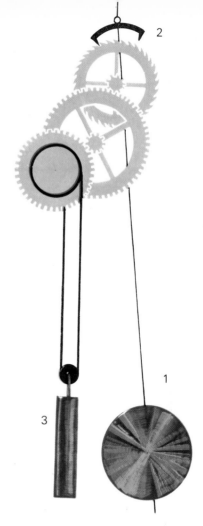

Inside this clock a pendulum (1) is swung by an escapement (2) that controls a toothed wheel turned by a slowly falling weight (3).

Pasteur, Louis

Louis Pasteur (1822–1895) was a great French scientist. He proved that bacteria and other germs cause diseases. Pasteur injected weakened germs into animals and people to stop them from catching the diseases those germs usually caused. He invented *pasteurization*—a way of heating milk and cooling it quickly to make it safe to drink. Pasteur also found out how tiny yeast cells turn sugar into alcohol.

Pendulum

This is a hanging weight that is free to swing to and fro in a curved path called an *arc*. Each swing takes the same amount of time, no matter whether the swing is big or small. This makes pendulums useful for keeping time in CLOCKS.

237

Right: The Emperor penguin is the largest of all penguins.

Emperor penguin

Chinstrap penguin

Macaroni penguin

Right: The Emperor penguin is the largest of all penguins.

Penguin

Penguins are swimming birds. They cannot fly, because their wings are shaped like flippers. Penguins use their wings to 'row' themselves through the sea. They swim and dive well. A penguin in the water can leap up nearly 2 metres to land on a rock or ice. Penguins are popular attractions in zoos.

All penguins come from the southern part of the world. Emperor penguins live in ANTARCTICA. In winter each female lays one egg on the ice. Her mate rolls the egg onto his feet and warms it with the lower part of his belly until it hatches.

Pepys, Samuel

Samuel Pepys (1633–1703) was an English government official who wrote a famous diary. This gives us a lively idea of what life was like in London in the reign of CHARLES II. Pepys wrote about the fire that burnt down much of London. He set down gossip about the king, described family quarrels, and told of visits to the theatre.

Pepys became Secretary of the Admiralty. He doubled the size of England's navy, and helped make it very strong.

Perfume

Certain substances that produce a pleasant smell are called perfumes. People use perfumes on their bodies. Factories add perfumes to soap, DETERGENT and other products. Natural perfumes are oils squeezed from flowers, leaves or stems and mixed with special animal substances like musk. Factories make synthetic perfumes from substances including coal tar.

Peru

Peru is the third largest nation in SOUTH AMERICA. You could fit more than five United Kingdoms inside Peru with room to spare.

Peru touches five other countries. West-ern Peru is washed by the Pacific Ocean. The sharp, snowy peaks of the high Andes Mountains cross Peru from north to south like a giant backbone. Between the mountains and the ocean lies a thin strip of desert. East of the mountains hot, steamy forests stretch around the Amazon River.

About 18 million people live in Peru. Many are Indians, or descended from Spanish settlers, or a mixture of the two. The

Above: A Quechua Indian woman of Peru carrying her child. Quechuas can work in thin mountain air that makes most people gasp.

A pharaoh, richly dressed in kilt and cloak. His double crown shows he ruled the north and south. His crook and flail show the care and power that he exercised.

capital is Lima, near the sea. Peruvians grow sugar cane and coffee. The sheep and llamas in the mountains produce wool. Peru mines copper, iron and silver. Its ocean fishing grounds yield some of the richest catches in the world.

People have been building towns in Peru for several thousand years. The most famous people were the INCAS, who had a mountain empire. In the 1530s the Spaniards seized Peru. Since the 1820s Peru has been an independent nation.

Below: These many-sided stone blocks were cut and put together by the Incas long ago.

Pharaoh

We use the word *pharaoh* to mean 'king' when we talk of the kings of ancient EGYPT. (The ancient Egyptians gave their kings other titles as well.) 'Pharaoh' comes from *peraa*, which means 'great house'. This was the royal palace where the pharaoh lived.

Egyptians believed that each pharaoh was the same god in the shape of a different man. He lived in certain ways said to have been fixed by the gods. The pharaoh was said to look after all the needs of his people. He was supposed to rule everything and everyone in Egypt. He owned all the land. All of Egypt's nobles, priests and soldiers were supposed to obey him. But in fact the priests and nobles largely ran the country.

Photography

The word *photography* comes from Greek words that mean 'drawing with light'. When you take a photograph, rays of LIGHT produce a picture on the film in your CAMERA.

What happens is this. First you look through a viewfinder at the subject you want to photograph. Then you press a button that lets light from the subject enter the camera. The light passes through a LENS that produces an image of your subject on the film. But the image shows up only when the film is developed (treated with chemicals). A developed film is called a *negative*. This shows black things white, and white things black. From negatives you can print *positives*, the final photos.

Right: One of the first kinds of camera. It used metal plates for making prints. These were called daguerreotypes, after their French inventor, Louis Daguerre.

Below: A group of photographers in the 1840s. These people are using the newly invented photographic paper to make prints.

Piano

A piano is a keyboard instrument with up to 88 keys. When you press a key a padded hammer hits two or three wires. These vibrate and produce a sound. Short wires produce high notes; long wires, low notes. The sounds can be long, short, loud or soft.

Picasso, Pablo

Pablo Picasso (1881–1973) was the most famous artist of this century. He was born in Spain but lived mostly in France.

People said Picasso (right) could draw before he learned to talk. He disliked paintings that looked like photographs, and admired the curving shapes of African sculpture. Picasso began painting people as simple shapes such as cubes. He also did sculpture and pottery.

Pig

These farmyard animals have a long, heavy body; short legs ending in hoofed toes; a long snout; and a short, curly tail. Males are called boars. Females are called sows. The heaviest boars weigh over a tonne.

Pigs provide us with bacon, ham, pork and lard. Different parts of a pig's body are used to make brushes, glue, leather and soap. Pigs are descended from the wild boar.

Picasso painted this nightmarish picture in 1937 to show the misery and horror of war. It is called Guernica, *after a town bombed in the Spanish Civil War.*

Pilgrims

The Pilgrims were the group of English settlers who founded the first permanent settlement in America in 1620. They were all English Puritans who had broken away from the official Church of England. In July 1620, led by William Brewster, they sailed from Plymouth in the ship *Mayflower*. Landing in America the following November, they founded the settlement of Plymouth, Massachusetts.

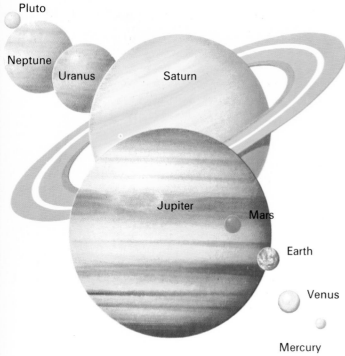

Pluto
Neptune
Uranus
Saturn
Jupiter
Mars
Earth
Venus
Mercury

animals, most plants cannot move about.

There are more than 300,000 kinds of living plant. The smallest are one-celled plants so tiny that you need a microscope to see them. The largest plants are TREES that can weigh as much as 2000 tonnes.

Plants are divided into different groups, designed for life in different places. A SEAWEED is an alga, a floppy type of plant found in water. LICHENS grow on bare rock, but mosses need wet soil. Most true land plants have stems strong enough to hold their leaves above the ground. These plants include plants that grow from SEEDS. Among these are the CONIFERS and plants producing FLOWERS.

Plants are perhaps the most important of all living things. They make the food all animals depend on. Plants also provide such useful substances as wood and cotton.

Planet

The word planet comes from a Greek word meaning 'wanderer'. Long ago, sky-watchers gave this name to 'stars' that appeared to move. We now know that planets are not STARS, but are heavenly bodies that travel around stars.

The EARTH and other planets of our SOLAR SYSTEM travel around the star we call the SUN. Each planet travels in its own ORBIT. But they all move in the same direction, and, except for Mercury and Pluto, they lie at about the same level.

Astronomers think the planets came from a band of gas and dust that once whirled around the sun. They think that GRAVITY pulled parts of this band together as masses that became planets.

The nine planets in the solar system are MERCURY, VENUS, EARTH, MARS, JUPITER, SATURN, URANUS, NEPTUNE and PLUTO.

Plant

Most living things are either animals or plants. Plants differ from animals in several ways. For example, green plants can make food with the help of chlorophyll. Each plant CELL has a wall of cellulose. But unlike

PARTS OF A PLANT

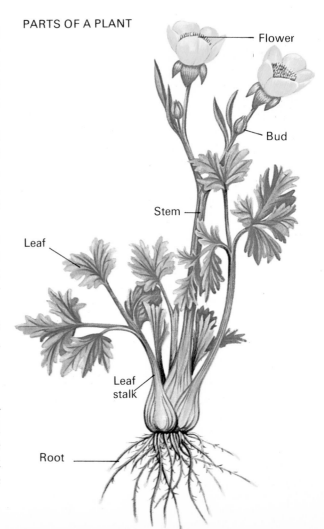

Flower
Bud
Stem
Leaf
Leaf stalk
Root

Plastics

Plastics are man-made substances and can be moulded into many different shapes. They are used to make anything from furniture and car seats to shoes and bags or cups and plates.

Most plastics are largely made from chemicals obtained from petroleum oil. Coal, limestone, salt and water are also used. Plastics can be hard, soft or runny. They can be made to look like glass, metal, wood or other substances.

Hard plastics are used in radio and camera cases. But fine threads of the hard plastic nylon make soft stockings.

Plastic bags and squeeze bottles are made of soft plastics like *polyethylene*. (Poly means 'many'.) Each particle of polyethylene is made up of many of the particles that form the gas called ethylene.

Pluto is probably made up in much the same way as the earth, with an iron core and a rocky surface. The red arrow (left) points to Pluto as seen from earth. It is so small and far away that it was not discovered until 1930.

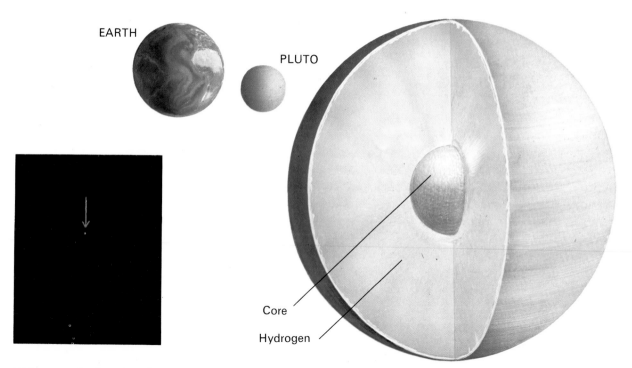

EARTH

PLUTO

Core

Hydrogen

Pluto (planet)

The planet Pluto is named after the Greek god who ruled the dreary world of the dead. Pluto must be bitterly cold, because it is farther away from the sun than any of the other PLANETS. It is almost 40 times farther from the sun than the EARTH is.

Pluto spins and moves around the sun much more slowly than the earth. A day on Pluto may equal nearly a week on earth. One year on Pluto lasts almost 248 of our years.

Pluto is only half as big as the earth, and weighs one-sixth as much.

Pocohontas

Pocohontas (about 1595–1617) was an American Indian princess, daughter of the chief Powhatan, who lived in Virginia when English settlers first arrived there. Legend has it that she saved the life of Captain John Smith, leader of the colony at Jamestown, when he was about to be clubbed to death by her father's warriors. Later she was taken hostage by the settlers and baptized with the name Rebecca. She married John Rolfe, a colonial leader, in 1614 and went to England, but she died of smallpox on the return voyage.

Poetry

Poetry is one of the oldest forms of writing. Poets choose words carefully, for their sound as well as their meaning. Poems are usually written in verses. The lines have a rhythm built up by strong and weak sounds. Sometimes rhyme is used for extra rhythm.

Poison

Poisons are chemical substances that kill or damage living things. Some poisons get into the body through the skin. Some are swallowed. Poisonous gases are harmful if someone breathes them in with air.

Different poisons work in different ways. Strong acids or alkalis 'burn'. NERVE poisons can stop the heart. Some other poisons can make the body bleed inside.

DRUGS called antidotes can cure people who are suffering from certain poisons.

Poland

This is the seventh largest country in EUROPE. Poland lies in eastern Europe, south of the Baltic Sea. (See page 123.) Most of Poland is low farmland, although forests sprawl across the Carpathian Mountains in the south. Poland's largest river is the Vistula. This rises in the mountains and flows into the Baltic Sea. Rivers often freeze in Poland's cold, snowy winters.

There are more than 36 million Poles. Most of them speak Polish, and most are Roman Catholics. Their capital is Warsaw.

Poland grows more flax and potatoes than almost any other land. Only three countries mine more coal than Poland. Its factories make machinery and ships.

Police

Police work for a government to keep law and order in their country. Their main task is to see that everyone obeys their country's laws. Part of this job is protecting people's lives and property. Police also help to control crowds. They help people hurt in accidents, and take charge of lost children.

A policeman in France stops traffic to let people cross a busy street. Police of different countries wear different uniforms but their tasks are very much the same.

Police officers try to prevent crime, and track down and capture criminals. This can be dangerous and sometimes officers are killed.

Polo, Marco See MARCO POLO

Pompeii

Two thousand years ago, Pompeii was a small Roman city in southern Italy. A sudden disaster killed many of its citizens and drove out the rest. But the same disaster preserved the streets and buildings. Today, visitors to Pompeii can learn a great deal about what life was like inside a Roman city.

In AD 79 the nearby volcano of VESUVIUS erupted and showered Pompeii with volcanic ash and cinders. Poisonous gases swirled through the streets. About one citizen in every ten was poisoned by fumes or burned to death by hot ash. The rest escaped. Ash and cinders soon covered up the

244

buildings. In time people forgot that Pompeii had ever been there.

For centuries Pompeii's thick coat of ash protected it from the weather. At last, in the 1700s, people began to dig it out. The digging has gone on until today. Archaeologists discovered buildings, streets, tools and statues. They even found hollows left in the ash by the decayed bodies of people and dogs killed by the eruption. The archaeologists poured plaster into these hollows. They let the plaster harden, then they cleared away the ash. They found that the plaster had formed life-size models of the dead bodies.

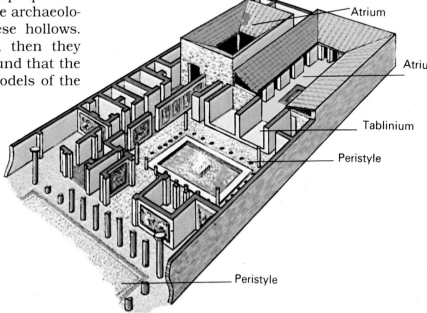

Right: The House of the Faun in Pompeii was a grand residence built in the 100s BC. It had twin entrance halls (atriums), and two colonnaded gardens (peristyles). Off one atrium was the tablinium — a bedroom, study and reception room. Below: Part of the excavated ruins of Pompeii as they are today.

The illustration below is from a guide book to Pompeii of 1881. It shows the uncovering of a bakery with the millstones for grinding the flour on the right and the oven in the background, complete with bread, which was ready for customers in the afternoon of 24th August AD 79.

Pond Life

At first glance a pond seems empty. But look closer, and you will see that it is a living world of plants and animals.

Tall plants such as reeds and arrowheads grow around the rim. Shallow water near the edge holds underwater plants like hornwort, Canadian pondweed and waterlilies.

Millions of algae and other tiny plants, as well as tiny animals like water fleas, make up the plankton drifting in the water.

Pond life is most plentiful where plants grow thickly just below the water's edge. Countless tiny crustaceans, INSECT larvae, worms and MOLLUSCS find food and shelter here. Frogs and newts lay eggs in spring. Here, too, water birds browse on water plants or hunt for small fish. Larger fish live in the deeper water farther out. Dead plants and animals sink to the bottom where worms and other creatures eat them.

Pope

'Pope' is a title of the head of the ROMAN CATHOLIC CHURCH. (The word 'pope' comes from *papa*, which means 'father'.) The Pope is also the Bishop of Rome. He rules the VATICAN CITY inside the city of Rome.

Roman Catholics believe that Jesus made St Peter the first pope. Since then there have been hundreds of popes. Each time one dies, churchmen choose another. The pope makes church laws, chooses bishops, and can declare people SAINTS.

Below: An aquarium for pond animals like small fish, caddis worms and water snails, needs sand, water plants, water fleas and pond water free from chemicals. The natural pond (bottom) is home for many kinds of creature. Grebes and coots nest here. Frogs and newts visit to lay their eggs. Fish, water spiders and various water insects swim beneath the surface in their search for food.

Portugal

This is a narrow, oblong country in south-west EUROPE. It is sandwiched between the Atlantic Ocean and SPAIN, a country four times the size of Portugal. (See page 123.)

Much of Portugal is mountainous. Rivers flow from the mountains through valleys and across plains to the sea. Portugal's mild winters and warm summers help its people to grow olives, oranges and rice. Its grapes produce port, a wine named after the Portuguese city of Oporto. Portugal's woods yield more CORK than those of any other nation. Its fishermen catch sardines and other sea fish. Portugal has mines that produce tungsten and uranium. Factories turn out textiles, shoes and fish products.

There are about 10 million Portuguese. They speak Portuguese, a language much like Spanish. Their capital is Lisbon.

Potato

Potatoes are valuable foods. They are rich in starches and contain PROTEINS and different VITAMINS. Potatoes must be cooked to give nourishment that we can use.

Potato plants are related to tomatoes. Each plant is low and bushy with a soft stem. Each potato grows on a root as a kind of swelling called a tuber. When its tubers have grown, the plant dies. But new plants spring up from the tubers.

Potatoes were first grown by South American Indians. Spanish explorers brought potatoes back to Europe. Today most are grown in Europe and Asia.

This potato plant has been removed from the soil to show its roots and tubers. The old, dark tuber fed the growing stem and roots. Then the leaves and roots made food to produce young tubers.

A fisherman mends nets at Nazaré in western Portugal. Fishing provides work for 30,000 people in Portugal. The country cans sardines for sale abroad.

Young tuber

Old tuber

Potter, Beatrix

Beatrix Potter (1866–1943) was a British writer who wrote the words and painted the pictures in a series of books for young children. The most famous one is probably *The Tale of Peter Rabbit*, but she wrote many others about different animals too.

Pottery

All kinds of objects made of baked clay are called pottery. Many cups, saucers, plates, bowls, pots, vases and other tools and ornaments are made of this very useful substance.

People have been making pottery for thousands of years. Early pots were thick and gritty. They leaked, and they cracked if heated. In time people learned to make pottery that was more useful and more beautiful. Today the two main kinds of pottery are porcelain and stoneware. Porcelain is fine pottery made of white China

Above: An elegant, two-handled pot from ancient Crete. The potter who made it used an octopus as the central part of his design.

Many potters use a wheel powered by a foot treadle. As the wheel spins, the pot is formed from soft clay. Later it is dried and baked.

Pot
Wheel
Bowl
Flywheel
Cam
Foot treadle

Below: A Chinese potter made this animal-shaped vessel about 4000 years ago. Early potters discovered how to make shaped pots and how to paint decorations on them.

clay. Thin porcelain lets the light show through. Stoneware is usually thicker than porcelain and it does not let the light show through.

To make a pot, a potter puts a lump of moist clay on a spinning disc called a *wheel*. He uses thumbs and fingers to shape the clay into a pot. He leaves this pot to dry. Next he may coat it with a wet mixture called a glaze. Then he fires (heats) the pot with others in an oven called a kiln. Firing makes the pots rock hard and turns their glaze into a smooth, hard, shiny coat. Different glazes produce different colours. Some glazes can even produce a metallic lustre on a pot.

Prehistoric Animals

Prehistoric animals are those that lived before recorded history began about 5000 years ago. We know about them from their FOSSILS found in rocks. Different kinds of creatures lived at different times. Each kind came from another through EVOLUTION.

The first prehistoric animals probably looked like little blobs of jelly. They lived in seas perhaps a billion years ago. By 600 million years ago there were jellyfish and sponges much like those alive today. There were also strange beasts with jointed

bodies. From these, much later, came crabs, insects, millipedes and spiders.

The first backboned animals were strange, armoured fishes that lived about

The longest known dinosaur is the largest land animal that has ever been found. Its name is Diplodocus, and from its head to the end of its tail, it measured 26.7 metres. Diplodocus was a plant eater and would not have been dangerous — unless it stepped on you.

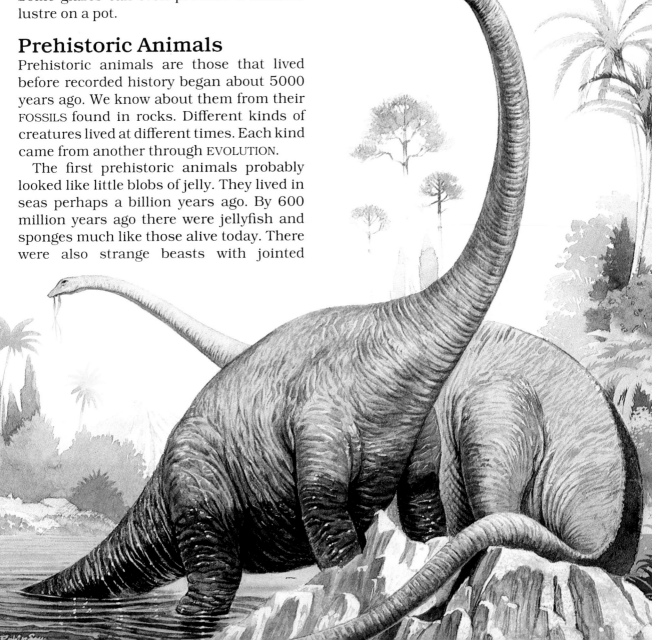

PREHISTORIC ANIMALS

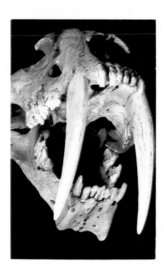 

Smilodon, a sabre-toothed cat that lived thousands of years ago.

500 million years ago. In time there were some fishes that could breathe dry air and crawl on land on stumpy fins. These fishes gave rise to prehistoric AMPHIBIANS. Some looked like salamanders the size of crocodiles. From amphibians came early REPTILES and all the other backboned animals.

About 200 million years ago the Age of DINOSAURS began. Some dinosaurs may have weighed 250 tonnes and were as long as several buses. These were the largest land animals ever. Above them flew the first

Careful use of the hammer and chisel bares the fossil backbone of a giant of the past. This fossil Tarbosaurus was found in east-central Asia. It is 60 million years old.

BIRDS. There were also pterodactyls, strange furry beasts with wings like bats. One kind was the largest animal that ever flew. Big reptiles with paddle-shaped limbs hunted fishes in the seas.

About 65 million years ago the dinosaurs, pterodactyls and sea reptiles died out. The new masters of the land were prehistoric birds and MAMMALS. Some gave rise to the birds and mammals of today.

Prehistoric People

Prehistoric people lived long ago before there were any written records of history. We know about them from the remains of their tools, weapons and bodies. Prehistory is divided into the STONE AGE, the Bronze Age and the Iron Age. The ages are named after the materials that people used to make their tools and weapons.

The Stone Age lasted for a long time. It began around $2\frac{1}{2}$ to 3 million years ago when humanlike creatures began to appear on the earth. They were different from the apelike animals which lived at the same time. They had larger brains, used stone tools and could walk upright.

Around 800,000 years ago, a more humanlike creature appeared. Scientists call this kind of early man *Homo erectus*. This means 'upright man'. *Homo erectus* is probably the ancestor of more advanced types of man, called *Homo sapiens*. This means 'intelligent man'. One kind of *Homo sapiens* was Neanderthal man, who appeared about 100,000 years ago. Modern man, called *Homo sapiens sapiens*, first appeared in Europe and Asia around 35,000 years ago.

Toward the end of the Stone Age, prehistoric people began to use metals. The first metal they used was copper. They made copper tools about 10,000 years ago. About 5000 years ago, people invented bronze. Bronze is a hard alloy of copper and tin. This was the start of the Bronze Age, when the earliest civilizations began. The Bronze Age ended about 3300 years ago in southeastern Europe, when people learned how to make iron tools. This was the start of modern times.

The pictures below show how the first people developed from our early ape-like ancestors. It took millions of years for this to happen.

25 million years ago

5 million years ago

1 million years ago

40,000 years ago

President of the United States

The President of the United States is the world's most powerful elected person. He is head of state, filling a role that in some other countries might be filled by a king or queen. He is also head of the government, like a prime minister. The president is also the commander-in-chief of the army, navy and air force.

The American people elect a president for a four-year term. A president may serve two terms. The president cannot make laws – that is done by Congress. But he has the power to veto laws. In the same way the president cannot declare war on another country, but he can send troops into trouble spots where they are needed. Nuclear weapons may not be used by the army without the permission of the president.

From 1789 to 1987 the United States has had 40 presidents. The first was George Washington. Other famous presidents of the past include Thomas Jefferson, Abraham LINCOLN, and John KENNEDY.

Postage stamp portraits of some 20th century US presidents.

Below: Abraham Lincoln was the 16th president of the United States. He served from 1861 to 1865. Lincoln increased the authority of the office of president when he took strong measures before and during the Civil War.

PRESIDENTS OF THE UNITED STATES

President	Party	Served
George Washington (1732–1799)	Federalist	1789–1797
John Adams (1735–1826)	Federalist	1797–1801
Thomas Jefferson (1743–1826)	Democratic-Republican	1801–1809
James Madison (1751–1836)	Democratic-Republican	1809–1817
James Monroe (1758–1831)	Democratic-Republican	1817–1825
John Quincy Adams (1767–1848)	Democratic-Republican	1825–1829
Andrew Jackson (1767–1845)	Democrat	1829–1837
Martin Van Buren (1782–1862)	Democrat	1837–1841
William H. Harrison (1773–1841)	Whig	1841
John Tyler (1790–1862)	Whig	1841–1845
James K. Polk (1795–1849)	Democrat	1845–1849
Zachary Taylor (1784–1850)	Whig	1849–1850
Millard Fillmore (1800–1874)	Whig	1850–1853
Franklin Pierce (1804–1869)	Democrat	1853–1857
James Buchanan (1791–1868)	Democrat	1857–1861
Abraham Lincoln (1809–1865)	Republican	1861–1865
Andrew Johnson (1808–1875)	National Union	1865–1869
Ulysses S. Grant (1822–1885)	Republican	1869–1877
Rutherford B. Hayes (1822–1893)	Republican	1877–1881
James A. Garfield (1831–1881)	Republican	1881
Chester A. Arthur (1830–1886)	Republican	1881–1885
Grover Cleveland (1837–1908)	Democrat	1885–1889
Benjamin Harrison (1833–1901)	Republican	1889–1893
Grover Cleveland (1837–1908)	Democrat	1893–1897
William McKinley (1843–1901)	Republican	1897–1901
Theodore Roosevelt (1858–1919)	Republican	1901–1909
William H. Taft (1857–1930)	Republican	1909–1913
Woodrow Wilson (1856–1924)	Democrat	1913–1921
Warren G. Harding (1865–1923)	Republican	1921–1923
Calvin Coolidge (1872–1933)	Republican	1923–1929
Herbert C. Hoover (1874–1964)	Republican	1929–1933
Franklin D. Roosevelt (1882–1945)	Democrat	1933–1945
Harry S. Truman (1884–1972)	Democrat	1945–1953
Dwight D. Eisenhower (1890–1969)	Republican	1953–1961
John F. Kennedy (1917–1963)	Democrat	1961–1963
Lyndon B. Johnson (1908–1973)	Democrat	1963–1969
Richard M. Nixon (1913–	Republican	1969–1974
Gerald R. Ford (1913–	Republican	1974–1977
James E. Carter (1924–	Democrat	1977–1981
Ronald Reagan (1911–	Republican	1981–

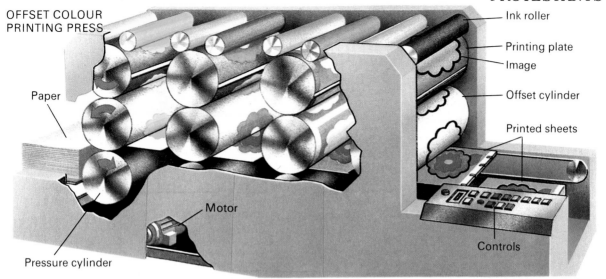

OFFSET COLOUR PRINTING PRESS

Ink roller — Printing plate — Image — Offset cylinder — Printed sheets — Controls — Motor — Paper — Pressure cylinder

Printing

Printing is a way of copying words and pictures by mechanical means.

In *relief* printing, ink is put onto raised images, such as letters. The letters are then pressed against paper. The most common method is called *letterpress* printing.

In other kinds of printing, the ink is put onto a flat surface. *Offset lithography* uses printing plates that are made photographically. The plates are treated with chemicals so that the greasy ink sticks only to the images to be printed.

The earliest printing, using wooden blocks, was done in China, probably as early as the 500s AD. Johannes GUTENBERG of Germany founded modern printing in the 1400s.

Proteins

Proteins are substances in food which are vital to life. They contain CARBON, HYDROGEN, OXYGEN and nitrogen. They build up body tissue, expecially muscle, and repair broken-down CELLS. They also give heat and energy, help us to grow, and help to protect us from disease. Our bodies do not store extra protein, so we must eat a regular supply.

Foods that come from animals provide most of our proteins. But some plant foods, such as peanuts, peas and beans, are also rich in protein.

To print in colour, the original colour picture has to be photographed to separate out the red, yellow, blue and black parts of the picture. The printing press has four rollers, each with a printing plate carrying one of the colours wrapped round it. As the paper passes through, it is inked with each of the colours, one after the other. This gives a full-colour picture on the paper. In offset printing, the image is transferred to an offset cylinder, which then prints it on the paper.

Protestants

Protestants are Christians who do not belong to the Roman Catholic or the Eastern Orthodox churches. Protestants believe that the things written in the BIBLE are more important than any rules made by church leaders. There are some passages in the Bible which can be explained in different ways. Protestants believe that people should make up their own minds about what these mean.

Protestantism began with the Reformation, when Martin Luther led a movement to change the ROMAN CATHOLIC CHURCH. In 1529, the Roman Catholic Church in Germany tried to stop people from following Luther's ideas. Luther's followers protested against this and were then called Protestants. Early Protestant groups included the Lutherans and Calvinists (Presbyterians). Later groups included the Baptists, Congregationalists, Methodists and QUAKERS.

Pulley

A pulley is a simple machine. It consists of a wheel on a fixed axle. A rope or belt passed over the wheel is tied to a load. When the rope is pulled, the load is raised.

A *movable pulley* runs along a rope. One end of the rope is fixed to a support. The load hangs from the pulley itself. When the other end of the rope is pulled, the pulley moves the load along the rope. Pulleys are used in machines such as cranes.

The invention of the wheel led to a useful lifting device, the pulley. The pulley was invented about 800 BC

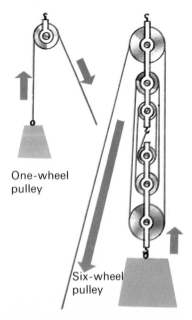

One-wheel pulley

Six-wheel pulley

An explorer and his wife stand with two African pygmies, who are sometimes called Negrillos. Pygmies are usually between 1.3 and 1.4 metres in height.

Puppet

Puppets are dolls or figures that are made to move. Some, such as marionettes, are moved with strings. Others, such as glove puppets, are moved with the hand. Puppets have been popular for over 2000 years. They are often used to 'act out' a story or a short play. Punch and Judy, popular puppet characters, originated in Italy.

Pygmies

Pygmies are small people. They are found in parts of central Africa, Asia and some Pacific islands. They are mostly nomads and live in bands. They hunt and gather plant foods. Today they are dying out as their homelands disappear.

The weight of the load that can be raised with a pulley depends on the number of wheels and the way in which they are connected. If the pulley has one rope, with a six-wheel pulley you can lift a load six times greater than you could without it.

Pyramids

Pyramids are huge, four-sided buildings. They have a square base. The sides are triangles that meet in a point at the top.

The Egyptians built pyramids as royal tombs. The first was built in about 2650 BC at Sakkara. It is 62 metres high. The three most famous pyramids are near Giza. The Great Pyramid, built in the 2600s BC by the PHARAOH Khufu, is 137 metres high. Khafre, who ruled soon after Khufu, built the second pyramid. It is 136.1 metres high. The third, built by Khafre's successor Menakaure, is 73.1 metres high. About 80 pyramids still stand in Egypt.

This is how the great pyramid at Teotihuacán, Mexico, would have looked. It was built of clay, and faced with limestone blocks jointed with mortar. The great stone blocks must have been hauled to the site by hand, since the people had no draught animals and the wheel was unknown.

Central and South American Indians also built pyramids as temples during the first six centuries AD. One huge pyramid is at Cholula, south-east of Mexico City. It is about 54 metres high.

Pyrenees

The Pyrenees are a chain of MOUNTAINS that lie between France and Spain. They stretch about 435 km from the Bay of Biscay to the Mediterranean Sea. Throughout history they have formed a natural barrier between France and Spain, so that most trade between the two countries has been by sea. Iron, lead, silver and cobalt are mined in the mountains, and the beautiful scenery attracts many tourists.

The peaks of the Pyrenees rise to over 3000 metres, though most average about 1100 metres. The highest is Pico de Aneto at 3404 metres. On the south slope of the eastern Pyrenees lies the tiny republic of Andorra.

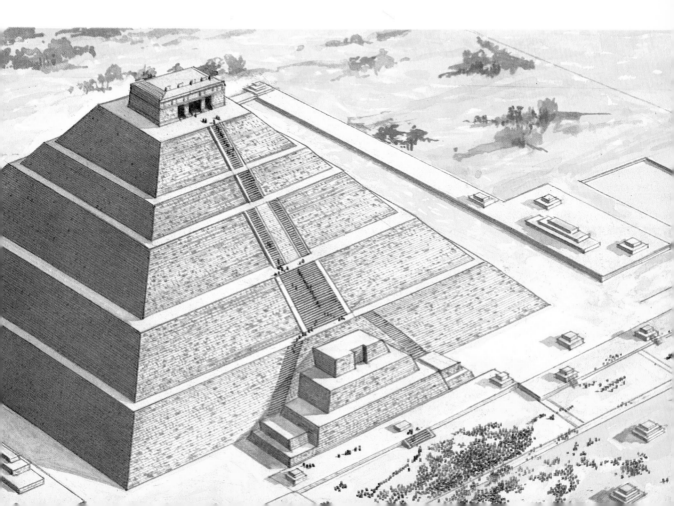

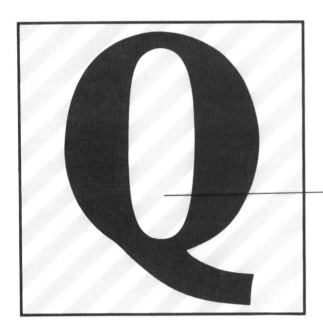

They were called Quakers because some of them shook with emotion at their meetings. Early Quakers were often badly treated because of their belief that religion and government should not be mixed. Quakers have simple religious meetings and do not have priests.

Quarrying

Quarries are huge pits where rocks are cut or blasted out of the ground.

As long ago as prehistoric times, people had quarries where they dug up flint to make into tools and weapons.

Today rock is quarried in enormous amounts. Explosives blast loose thousands of tons. This is scooped up by bulldozers and diggers, and taken to crushers. The rock is ground into stones for use in roads, railways, concrete and cement. Not all rock is removed in this way. Stone that is used in building and paving is cut out of the ground

Quakers

The Quakers are also known as the Society of Friends. They are a PROTESTANT group that began in England during the 1650s.

Marble, used by sculptors and for building work, is quarried by hand.

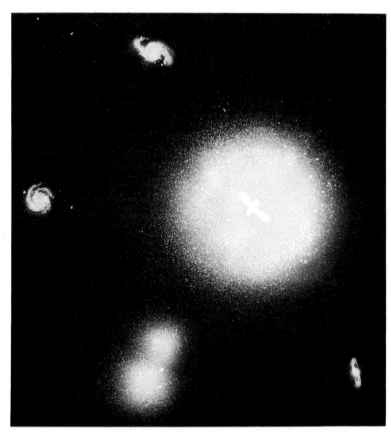

This is how a quasar might look, if viewed from nearby. At the centre of an elliptical galaxy, a brilliant point of light is surrounded by a spinning disc of shining material. The brilliance is believed to be caused by gas whirling faster and faster around a black hole until it is travelling almost at the speed of light.

Quasars seem to be huge but young galaxies that were formed soon after the birth of the universe. We only see them as young galaxies now because their light has taken thousands of millions of years to reach us on earth.

rather than blasted. Electric cutters, wire saws and drills are used to cut the rock.

Quartz

Quartz is one of the most common MINERALS in the world. It is found everywhere. Sand is mostly made of quartz, and many rocks have quartz in them.

Quartz forms six-sided CRYSTALS. It is very hard, harder even than steel. In its pure form it has no colour and is as clear as glass. But most is smoky white or tinted with various colours. Many semi-precious GEMS, such as agate, amethyst, opal and onyx, are quartz.

Quartz is an important mineral. It is used in many things, including abrasives (such as sandpaper), lenses and electronics.

Quartz is so hard it can cut glass. It often remains in the ground when other softer minerals have worn away.

Quasar

Quasars are very distant, very powerful objects farther out in space than the most remote GALAXIES. They may be galaxies with some extra-powerful energy source at their centre. Quasars send out strong radio waves and X-RAYS. From earth they look like very faint stars because they are so far away. All quasars are millions of light years away, and so we see them now as they were that length of time ago.

Raccoons eat a lot of water animals. They often play with their food in the water before they eat it.

Rabbit

Rabbits originally came from Europe. Today they are found all over the world. They are small MAMMALS with a short tail and long, pointed ears. Rabbits live in

Inside this rabbit burrow are a mother and her young (1), the main sleeping chamber (2), and a tunnel-digger at work (3).

burrows in the ground. Each one is the home of a single family. A group of burrows is known as a warren. Rabbits leave their burrows at dusk to feed on grass and other plants.

Raccoon

In North America, raccoons are common creatures of the wild. They have long grey fur, a short pointed nose, and a bushy tail ringed with black. They may grow to as much as 90 cm long.

Raccoons live in forests. They make their homes in tree holes and are good climbers. At night, they leave their hollows to hunt for

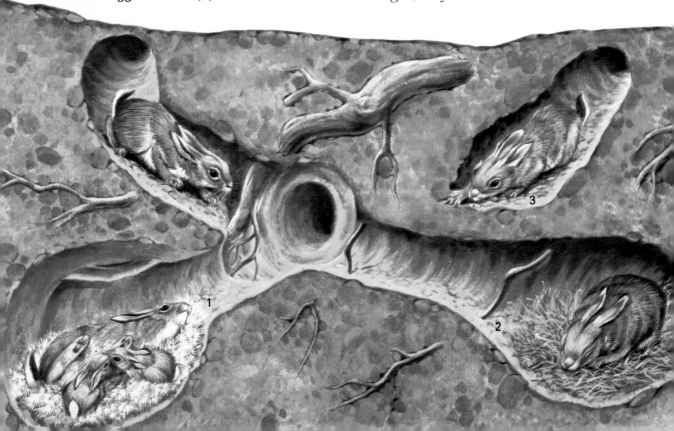

food. They will eat almost anything: fruit and plants, eggs, insects, fish, birds and small mammals. But their main food comes from rivers, so their tree holes are usually found close by.

Radar

Radar is a device for tracking objects by RADIO beams. Because these beams work in the dark, in fog, and over distances well out of eyesight, radar is an enormously useful invention. It can detect objects thousands of miles away.

Radar works by sending out a narrow, high-powered beam about 500 times a second. It travels at a steady 300 metres every millionth of a second. When the beam

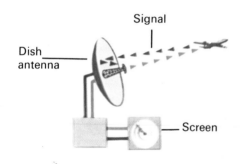

strikes an object a faint echo bounces back. The echo is picked up and turned into a light 'blip' on a screen. A radar operator can tell by studying the blip how far away the object is, in what direction it is moving, and at what speed.

Radar is used by air traffic controllers at airports, by the military to track missiles and planes, and by weather stations to find and follow the paths of storms. SATELLITES fitted with radar can map the ground.

Radio

The common household object we call a radio is only the receiving end of a great system of radio communications. Most of the system is never even seen.

A radio programme begins in a studio. There, voices and music are turned into electronic signals. These are made stronger (amplified), and then sent out from tall masts as radio waves. These are picked up by the radio in your home and changed back into sounds you can hear. Radio waves travel at the speed of light. This is so fast that a signal can circle the world $7\frac{1}{2}$ times in one second.

The first person to make radio waves was Heinrich Hertz in 1887. But it was Guglielmo MARCONI who sent the first messages in 1894. His first signals went a few feet. Seven years later he sent signals across the Atlantic.

Left: A radar station sends a high-powered signal. It hits the plane and its echo bounces back. The antenna picks it up and turns it into a 'blip' on a screen.

Below: Someone speaks into a microphone. The voice sounds are turned into electric currents. These are made stronger (amplified) and broadcast by radio waves from a transmitter. Inside the radio, the sound signals are separated from the carrier waves and amplified. They are turned back into sound waves that we can hear.

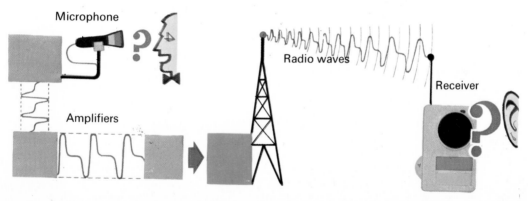

Radioactivity

The atoms of some substances are always shooting off tiny particles and rays that we cannot see or feel. This is called radioactivity. These strange rays were discovered in 1896. And it was found that nothing could be done to stop the rays from shooting out. It was also found that in time these radioactive substances changed into other substances, and that they did this at a steady rate. If a piece of radioactive URANIUM was left for millions of years it would turn into a piece of lead. Scientists use radioactive CARBON in the remains of animals and plants to find out how many thousands of years ago they lived.

This telescope at Jodrell Bank near Manchester uses its receiving bowl to focus weak radio signals onto the receiver stalk at its centre. It can detect stars that may not be seen by ordinary telescopes.

Radio Astronomy

A heavenly body such as a STAR does not only give off LIGHT waves. It sends out many kinds of radio waves too. Radio astronomers explore the UNIVERSE by 'listening' to the radio signals that reach earth from outer space. These signals are not made by other forms of life. They come from natural events such as exploding stars or heated clouds of gases. By studying these signals, radio astronomers can find out many things about different parts of the universe.

Radio telescopes have giant aerials that are often dish-shaped. They pick up faint signals that have come from places much deeper in space than anything ever seen by ordinary TELESCOPES. The first large radio telescopes were built after World War II. Today the biggest in the world is at Arecibo in Puerto Rico. Its huge receiving dish has been built across an entire mountain valley. It is 305 metres wide.

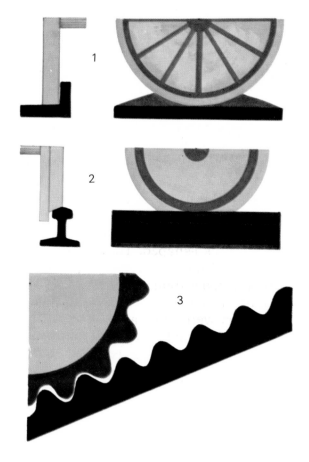

Railway

Railways have been in use since the 1500s. At first, rails were made of wood and wagons were pulled by horses. These railways were used to haul carts in mines. Railways are useful because heavy loads can be pulled along them very easily.

Steam LOCOMOTIVES came into use in the early 1800s. In 1825 the first steam engine to be used on a public railway began to run between Stockton and Darlington. The engine, called the *Rocket*, was built by George Stephenson. A few years later, the *Rocket* was hauling 20 tonne loads over a 56-km run in under two hours.

In the railway building boom that followed, tens of thousands of kilometres of track were laid down.

Today there are about 1,250,000km of railway lines in the world. The longest railway in the world is the Trans-Siberian line in the USSR. It runs from Moscow to Nakhodka, a distance of 9334km. The trains make 97 stops.

Above: Early railway wagons had flat wheels and rode on L-shaped rails (1). Modern wheels have flanges (projecting edges) (2), which hold the wheel on the rails. To climb steep slopes, wheels have special cogs (3).

Below: A section of modern railway line shows how the steel track is fixed onto sleepers with spikes. The sleepers rest on a bed of crushed stones.

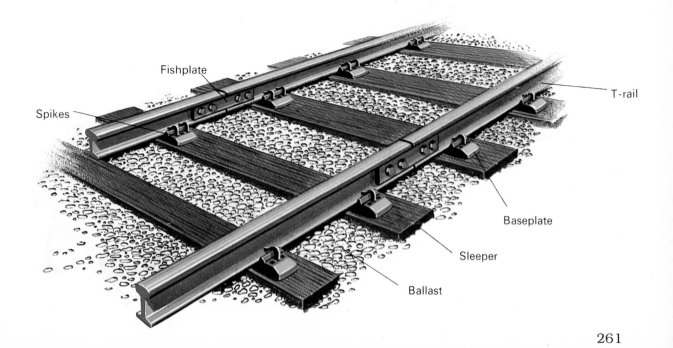

Fishplate

Spikes

T-rail

Baseplate

Sleeper

Ballast

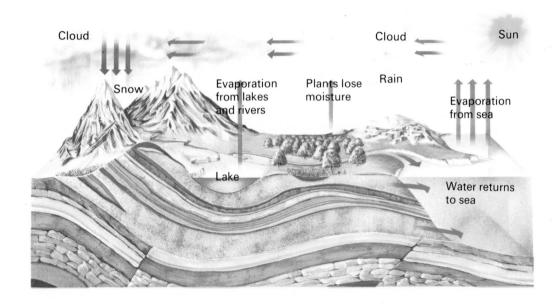

Cloud

Snow

Evaporation from lakes and rivers

Plants lose moisture

Cloud

Rain

Sun

Evaporation from sea

Lake

Water returns to sea

Rain and Snow

When rain pours down, it is only the sky returning the same water to earth that originally evaporated from the land and sea.

Rain forms when water vapour in the air starts to cool. As the vapour cools it turns first into tiny droplets, which form wispy CLOUDS. The droplets grow and the clouds thicken and turn a dull grey. At last the drops become so heavy that they start to fall. Depending on how cold it is, the drops hit the ground as either rain or snow.

The amount of rain that falls is widely different from place to place. In the Atacama Desert in Chile less than 25 mm of rain falls in 20 years. But in eastern India, the monsoon drops more than 1000 cm of rain every year.

Rainbow

The gorgeous colours of a rainbow are formed by sunlight shining on drops of rain. The best time for rainbows is right after a shower, when the clouds break up and sunlight streams through.

Rainbows can be seen only when the sun is behind you and low over the horizon. When the sun's rays strike the raindrops, each drop acts as a prism and splits the LIGHT into a spectrum of colours ranging from red to violet. The lower the sun, the higher the rainbow and the fuller its curved arch.

This diagram of the water cycle shows how evaporated water forms clouds and returns to earth as snow or rain.

According to legend, a pot of gold is found at the end of every rainbow. The reason the earth is not crowded with rich people is because rainbows never touch the ground.

Raleigh, Walter

Sir Walter Raleigh (1552–1618) was an English knight at the court of ELIZABETH I. He was a soldier, explorer, historian and poet. He tried unsuccessfully to set up a colony in Virginia, in the newly discovered land of North America. He introduced potatoes and tobacco smoking to the English. But his boldness and dashing way of life made him many enemies, and he was executed for treason during the reign of James I.

Rat

Rats are RODENTS. They are found all over the world in enormous numbers, and can live happily in towns and cities. They will eat almost anything. They are harmful to man because they spoil huge amounts of food and they spread diseases. Some rats carry a type of flea which can cause bubonic plague in human beings.

The common brown rat can be a serious pest. It will eat almost anything and breeds at an alarming rate. Rats are between 20 and 25cm long, not including their scaly tail.

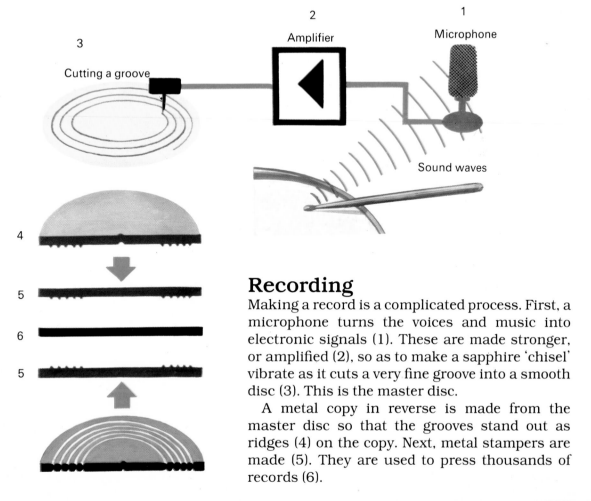

Recording

Making a record is a complicated process. First, a microphone turns the voices and music into electronic signals (1). These are made stronger, or amplified (2), so as to make a sapphire 'chisel' vibrate as it cuts a very fine groove into a smooth disc (3). This is the master disc.

A metal copy in reverse is made from the master disc so that the grooves stand out as ridges (4) on the copy. Next, metal stampers are made (5). They are used to press thousands of records (6).

Female, summer

Male

The reindeer is the only deer in which the females have antlers. They may be 120cm high at the shoulder, and adult males can weigh 100kg. Reindeer are very important to the Lapps of northern Europe because these animals provide clothing, meat and milk.

All religions have symbols (signs) by which their worshippers recognize them. The goddess is Hindu (1), the menorah is Jewish (2), the cross is Christian (3), the temple is Shinto, a Japanese religion (4), the crescent moon is Islamic (5), and the last is a statue of Buddha (6).

Reindeer

Reindeer are a type of DEER that live in the far north of Asia and Europe. They are a close relative of the North American caribou. Reindeer are tall MAMMALS with a brown coat and white belly markings. Both males and females have great branches of antlers.

Reindeer live in large herds. In their summer breeding grounds on the open tundra (treeless plains), they feed on grasses and other vegetation. At the end of the summer there is a huge MIGRATION farther south, where they spend the winter. Reindeer are hunted by ESKIMOS for their skin, meat and antlers. The Lapps keep reindeer herds.

Religions

The greatest religions of today are Buddhism (based on the teachings of the BUDDHA), CHRISTIANITY, HINDUISM (followed by Hindus), ISLAM, and JUDAISM (followed by Jews). All are very ancient. The most recent is Islam, which was founded about 1300 years ago. The largest, Christianity, has well over a billion followers.

There are also some people today who follow ancient religions based on the worship of many gods and spirits. Often these gods are part of nature. They may be rocks, trees or lakes.

The major religions of today are very grand, with magnificent shrines and temples as places of worship. Statues and works of art showing religious figures are common. Specially trained priests and holy men say prayers and lead religious ceremonies. They also study the laws and teachings of the religion. These are often written down in holy books, which have been passed down through the ages.

Rembrandt

Rembrandt Harmensz van Rijn (1606–1669) is one of the most famous of all Dutch painters. He and his helpers produced hundreds of paintings and drawings.

Rembrandt is best known for his portraits of the wealthy townspeople of Holland. Unlike many painters, he became very successful while he was still alive. However, later in his career, many of the rich people no longer bought his pictures because they did not like the way his style of painting had changed. Although he became very poor, this was the time when he painted some of his best works, such as this portrait of himself (above).

Renaissance

The Renaissance is the name given to a period of about 200 years in the history of Europe. The word means 'rebirth' in French, and the Renaissance was the time when people again became interested in every aspect of art, science, architecture and literature.

Since the times of the ancient Greeks and Romans there had been little interest in these things. Then, during the 1300s, Italian scholars began to take an interest in the past. They also looked for new scientific explanations of the mysteries of the world and the universe. During the Renaissance a great number of painters, sculptors and architects were at work in Italy. The works of art of LEONARDO DA VINCI and MICHELANGELO are among the most famous products of this time. From Italy, the ideas of the Renaissance quickly spread to the rest of Europe.

At the same time as all these artistic and scientific ideas, there was a great growth in trade. Later, there were voyages to explore Africa and India, and in 1492 America was discovered by COLUMBUS.

The Renaissance in the arts spread from Italy into France and Spain. In France, many of the great castles were built about this time. The castle pictured below is the graceful Château of Chenonceaux. The building of this castle began in 1515.

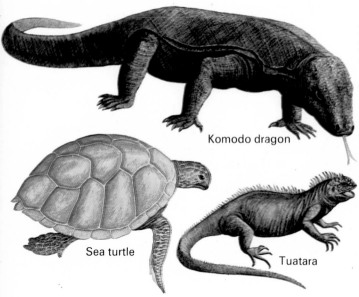

Komodo dragon

Sea turtle

Tuatara

The Komodo dragon (top) is the largest lizard. It can measure 3 metres in length. Sea turtles (left) leave the sea only to lay their eggs. The tuatara has survived for 150 million years. It now lives only on a few islands off New Zealand.

Reptiles

Reptiles are the most advanced of all cold-blooded animals. They live on land and in the sea.

Except for the North and South Poles, reptiles live in all parts of the world. Most, however, live in warm regions. This is because they are cold-blooded and must get their warmth from their surroundings.

When it is cold they become very sleepy and cannot move fast enough to catch food or escape enemies. Most reptiles that live in cold places spend the winter in HIBERNATION.

Reptiles played a very important part in the EVOLUTION of the earth. About 200 million years ago, the first reptiles left the water and began to roam over the land. They soon became the strongest form of life on earth. They ruled the planet for close to 100 million years. One group of reptiles, the DINOSAURS, were the most spectacular creatures ever to walk the land. The biggest weighed more than 50 tonnes.

Today there are four main groups of reptiles: ALLIGATORS AND CROCODILES, LIZARDS and SNAKES, TURTLES, and the rare tuatara. The biggest reptiles are the alligators and crocodiles. The estuarine crocodile of South-East Asia grows to 6 metres in length, and is the biggest of them all.

There are over 5,000 kinds of lizards and snakes. They live everywhere, from deserts to jungles and faraway ocean islands. Some have poisonous bites with which they kill their prey. Turtles are well protected by their hard shells. The biggest are the lumbering giants of the Pacific and Indian Ocean islands.

Revolutionary War, American

The Revolutionary War was fought between Britain and her 13 American colonies from 1775 to 1783. The colonies won their independence from Britain and became a new nation, the United States of America.

For many years before the war Britain and the American colonies had disagreed about a number of things, chief of which was taxes. The British tried to force the colonies to pay taxes, but would not allow the colonies any representation in the British Parliament. The colonies insisted on 'no taxation without representation'.

The first shot in the war was fired at Lexington, Massachusetts, on April 19, 1775. In July, George Washington was made commander of the American forces. On July 4, 1776, the colonies adopted the Declaration of Independence, written by Thomas Jefferson.

At first the war went poorly for the Americans. But in October 1777, the British were defeated at the Battle of Saratoga, in New York. This was the turning point. The victory helped to bring France into the war on the Americans' side. On October 19, 1781, a British army under Lord Cornwallis surrendered to Washington.

Backed by the French, the American army forced the British to surrender at Yorktown, Virginia, in 1781.

All rhinos are short-sighted, but their senses of smell and hearing are acute. There are five different species. The white rhino is the largest of all. Here a mother and young graze side by side.

Rhinoceros

The rhinoceros is one of the largest and strongest of all land animals. A full-grown male can weigh as much as 4 tonnes. This massive beast has a tough leathery skin and one or two horns on its snout. The horns can be up to 120 cm long.

The rhinoceros lives in Africa and in south-eastern Asia. There it feeds on leafy twigs, shrubs and grasses. Although an adult rhino has no natural enemies, it is so widely hunted for its horns that it is in danger of dying out completely.

Rice

Rice is a member of the GRASS family. Its grains are one of the most important cereal crops. It is the main food of more than half the people in the world.

Young shoots of rice are planted in flooded fields called paddies. Here they grow in 5 to 10cm of water, until they are ready to be harvested. Young rice has long narrow leaves and fine clusters of flowers. These turn into the grains that we eat.

River

Rivers are one of the most important geographical features in the world. They range in size from little more than swollen streams to mighty waterways that flow thousands of kilometres.

The greatest rivers in the world are the AMAZON, the Mississippi and the NILE. They all drain huge areas of land. The basin of the Amazon, for example, stretches over an area larger than all of western Europe.

Some rivers serve as roads that allow ocean-going ships to sail far inland. In tropical jungles they are often the only way to travel. Rivers with DAMS supply us with electric power. They are also tapped for water to irrigate farmland.

Road

The Romans were the first great road builders. Some of their long, straight roads still survive. The Romans made roads of gravel and stones. The surface paving stones were arched so rain ran off into ditches.

Above: Workers harvest rice in Japan. Rice grows well on flat land where there is heavy rainfall.

Modern road building began during the INDUSTRIAL REVOLUTION. In the early 1800s a Scottish engineer, John McAdam, became the pioneer of modern road-making. But the stony surfaces of his roads were not good for vehicles with rubber tyres. Later, macadamized roads were built. They are covered with tar or asphalt to make them smooth. Many roads, especially highways, are now made of concrete.

Below: The Romans built straight roads made from stones and gravel. John McAdam (1756–1836) built roads from layers of stones, with the largest stones at the bottom and the smallest on top. When pressed down by traffic, they had a hard surface.

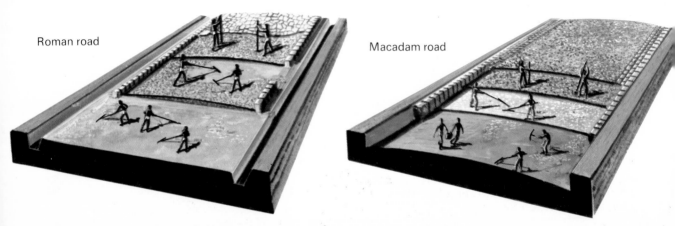

Roman road

Macadam road

Robin Hood

Robin Hood was an English hero who lived as an outlaw in Sherwood Forest, in Nottinghamshire. He and his band of men robbed the rich and helped the poor. He was supposed to have lived in the 1100s, but most historians think that he never really existed.

Robot

In films and books set in the future, robots often look like metal people and they can walk, talk and think.

Real robots are very different. They are machines with arms that can move in several directions. Robots are *programmable* machines. This means they can be instructed to carry out different tasks. The instructions, or programs, are stored in the robot's computer brain.

Most robots work in industry and do jobs such as paint spraying, welding and heavy lifting and loading. Some robots work in places that are dangerous for humans, such as nuclear power stations and outer space.

Below: These robot welders are putting together cars in a Japanese factory. Machines controlled by computers now do many such tasks.

The Daleks, from the TV series Dr Who, *are metal-clad visitors from outer space who wage war against humans.*

By moving several joints at the same time, the arm of the robot on the right can be placed in almost any position needed.

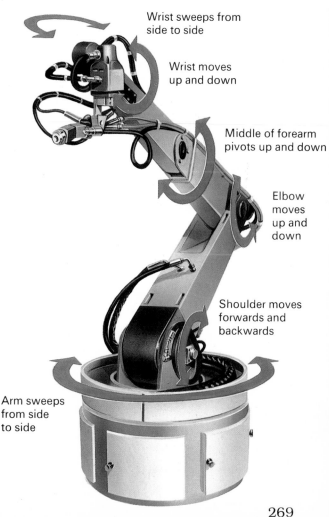

Wrist sweeps from side to side

Wrist moves up and down

Middle of forearm pivots up and down

Elbow moves up and down

Shoulder moves forwards and backwards

Arm sweeps from side to side

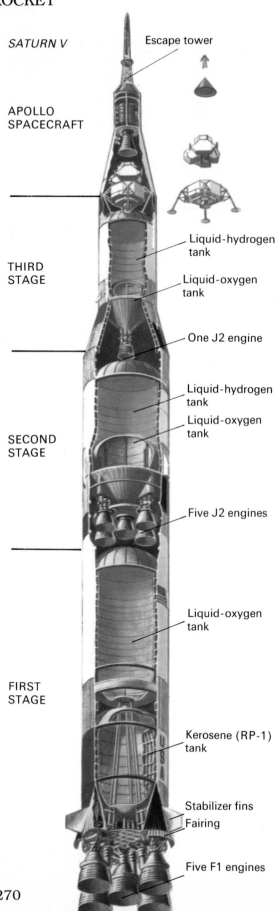

SATURN V

Escape tower

APOLLO
SPACECRAFT

Liquid-hydrogen
tank

THIRD
STAGE

Liquid-oxygen
tank

One J2 engine

Liquid-hydrogen
tank

Liquid-oxygen
tank

SECOND
STAGE

Five J2 engines

Liquid-oxygen
tank

FIRST
STAGE

Kerosene (RP-1)
tank

Stabilizer fins

Fairing

Five F1 engines

Rocket

A firework rocket and the rocket that took men to the moon work in much the same way. Both burn fuel to produce hot gases. The gases shoot out backward. This makes a pressure inside the rocket that thrusts it forward. The gases do not move rockets by pushing against the air, as happens in jet engines. This means that rockets can move in empty space.

Rockets used to launch SATELLITES and spacecraft were developed after World War II. They are *multistage* rockets, which means several rockets joined together. Each stage fires in turn. The Chinese used rockets as weapons as early as the 1200s.

Left: The Saturn V rocket was used for the Apollo flights. It is a three-stage rocket. Each stage drops away after use. Small rocket engines power the spacecraft after it is launched.

Rocky Mountains

The Rocky Mountains are a huge range of mountains in NORTH AMERICA. They stretch from Alaska through western CANADA and the USA as far south as New Mexico. The highest peak, Mt Elbert, is 4399 metres above sea level. The Rockies have several national parks, and many wild animals live there.

Rodents

Rodents are a group of gnawing animals. They have large, sharp front teeth that grow all the time. The animals wear down these

Bank
Vole

teeth by gnawing their food. They also use their teeth to dig burrows in the ground for their homes and nests.

The 2000 or so rodents also include mice, RATS, SQUIRRELS and VOLES. The South American capybara is the largest rodent. It grows to a length of 1.25 metres and weighs more than 45 kg.

Pope Paul VI (who was pope from 1963 until 1978) is seen here in St Peter's, the great church in Vatican City. This is the centre of the Roman Catholic Church.

Muskrat

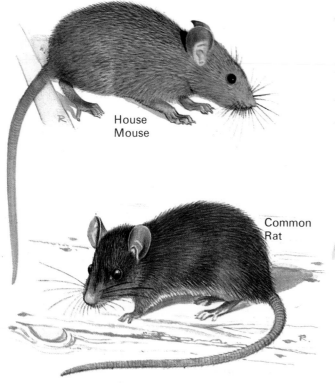

House Mouse

Common Rat

Roman Catholic Church

The Roman Catholic Church is the oldest and largest of all Christian churches. It has about 585 million members. The Pope is the head of the Church. He lives in VATICAN CITY.

Roman Catholics follow the teachings of JESUS Christ. The Church also helps its followers by giving them rules for good living. The main church service is called the Mass. Some Roman Catholics become nuns, monks and brothers. They devote their lives to their faith in orders (societies) such as the Franciscans or Benedictines.

Field Vole

Wood Lemming

Roman Empire

The ancient Romans built up a vast empire around the Mediterranean Sea. ROME, in Italy, was the centre of the empire. Legend says that Rome was founded in 753 BC. In the 500s BC, it was ruled by the Etruscans. It was not until 509 BC that Rome began to rule itself. Then it was run by officials, called consuls, and magistrates. The consuls shared power with the Senate, a council of men from important families.

In the 200s BC the power of Rome began to reach out to all Italy. It took over the island of Sicily from the powerful city of Carthage, and in 146 BC Rome completely destroyed Carthage. Roman power spread in all directions. But the Romans quarrelled with each other and fought civil wars between 133 and 27 BC. In 49 BC, Julius CAESAR became dictator. He ruled Rome until he was murdered in 44 BC. Another civil war followed, then Caesar's adopted son, Octavian, became the first Roman emperor. He was renamed Augustus, and made peace throughout the empire.

In the early days of Roman rule, many Christians were killed. But in AD 313, Emperor Constantine gave Christians freedom

The Colosseum in Rome was built in AD 72. It held 50,000 spectators and was famous for its combats between gladiators and the killing of many Christians.

of worship. He also set up the city of Byzantium, or Constantinople, in the east of the empire. In 395, the empire was split into two. The western half had its capital at Rome, and Byzantium was the capital of the eastern half. In the 400s, the western empire was attacked by tribes from the north. It collapsed and was split into small kingdoms. The eastern empire lasted until the Turks took it in 1453. But Roman architecture, art, engineering, law and literature greatly influenced European ideas.

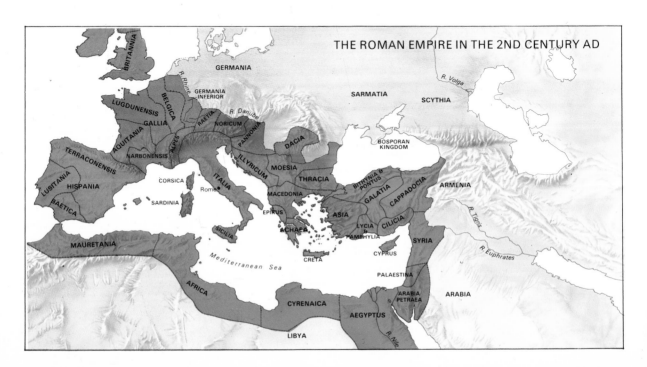

THE ROMAN EMPIRE IN THE 2ND CENTURY AD

In Rome itself, luxury and poverty lived close together. Wealthy citizens occupied large ground-floor apartments in blocks ('insulae'). But the upper floors were overcrowded with poor families.

Rome

Rome is the capital of ITALY. With a population of nearly four million, it is also Italy's largest city. Rome stands on the river Tiber, about 27km from the Mediterranean Sea. Many tourists visit Rome to see the great ruins of ancient Rome, and the beautiful churches, fountains, palaces and art galleries.

Rose

Roses are among the most popular of all FLOWERS. There are thousands of different roses. Many have been bred from the wild sweet-briar and the dog rose. Some roses flower only in early summer, but most garden roses now flower for many months.

This open-air market is in Rome, one of the world's most beautiful cities.

Rubber

Rubber is an important material with many uses in industry and in the home. Most natural rubber comes from the rubber tree. When the BARK of the tree is cut, a white juice called *latex* oozes out. The juice is collected and made into rubber. Today most natural rubber comes from Malaysia and Indonesia.

Scientists found ways of making synthetic rubber during World War I.

Rust

Rust is a brownish-red crust that forms on ordinary IRON AND STEEL when they are left in damp air. As rust forms, the surface of the metal is eaten away. Rusting is speeded up near the sea, where the air contains salt, or in cities where air pollution is severe.

To prevent rusting, iron and steel may be coated with such metals as tin or zinc. Grease, oil and paint also protect the metal.

The camel is still the best form of transport in the Sahara. It can travel for days without water.

Sahara

The Sahara is the world's largest hot DESERT. It covers about 8.4 million square km in North Africa. It extends from the Atlantic Ocean in the west to the Red Sea in the east. In the north, it stretches to the Mediterranean coast in Libya and in Egypt. Recently, the lands south of the Sahara have had very little rain. Because of this the desert is slowly spreading southward.

About a third of the Sahara is covered by sand. Other parts are covered by gravel and stones, or by bare rock. The Sahara is the hottest place on earth. The world's highest air temperature in the shade, 57.7°C, was recorded there.

Saint

Saints are holy people. Christian saints are people who have been *canonized* (named as saints) by the ROMAN CATHOLIC CHURCH or the Eastern Orthodox churches. Most saints are canonized long after their deaths.

When someone is being made a saint, the Church looks at the person's life to see if he or she was very good. The saint must also have taken part in a miracle.

Countries and even trades may have their own saints. These are called patron saints. The patron saint of travellers is St Christopher; of scholars, St Thomas Aquinas; of missionaries, St Francis Xavier. Many people believe that saints perform miracles, such as healing the sick.

Salmon

Salmon are fish which breed in shallow rivers. After the eggs hatch, the young fish

Salmon lay their eggs in river beds. The young feed on the yolk in the egg sac. After a while, the salmon leaves the river to live in the sea.

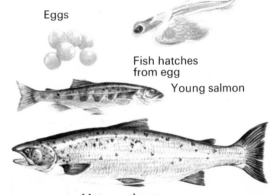

Eggs

Fish hatches from egg

Young salmon

Mature salmon

Salt can be made by flooding land with sea water. The sun dries up the water and the salt is left behind.

move down the river to the sea. They spend their adult life in the sea (about one to three years). Then they return to their birthplace to breed. This may mean a journey of hundreds of kilometres. Most salmon die after laying their eggs.

Salt
The chemical name for the salt we eat is sodium chloride. We need some salt to stay healthy. Salt is also used to preserve foods and it is important in many industries. Much of our salt comes from sea water, but some is mined from deposits in the ground.

Samurai
The Samurai were Japanese warriors. At first, only the emperor's guards were called Samurai. But from the 1100s to 1867, all the military people in Japan were called Samurai. They included warriors, lords and Japan's military ruler, the *shogun*.

The Samurai wore very decorative armour and headdresses, and carried two swords. They believed in a way of life called *Bushido*, which means 'the way of the warrior'. Samurai had to be very brave. They fought for honour, in much the same way as the knights of Europe. They did not like trade and profit-making. If a Samurai

did something dishonourable, he had to kill himself with his own sword. This was called *hara-kiri*.

The Samurai lost their power at the end of the 1800s. Changes in Japan meant that they were not so important any more. Even their name was changed. But today, many people in Japan and around the world are interested in the Samurai. There are many books and films about them. One popular film is *The Seven Samurai*, made in 1954. It has been shown in many countries. It tells the story of seven warriors who protected some poor farmers from fierce bandits.

Satellite
A body that moves in ORBIT around another body is called a satellite. The earth and the other planets are satellites of the sun. The moon is the earth's satellite.

But the earth has many more satellites. These are the artificial satellites launched

Below: An Intelsat communications satellite. The electrical power comes from solar cells around the outside.

by rockets into fixed orbits. Weather satellites have cameras trained on the earth and send down pictures of cloud and storm formations. Communications satellites relay television and telephone signals around the world. Each one has its own radio receiver and transmitter powered by batteries charged by the sun's rays. The satellites receive a signal from the transmitting station on earth, amplify it and beam it down to another earth station which may be thousands of kilometres away.

The first artificial satellite was *Sputnik 1*, launched by the USSR in 1957.

Saturn (planet)

Saturn is the second largest PLANET in the SOLAR SYSTEM after Jupiter. It is about 120,700 km across. Saturn is famous for the rings that circle it. These rings are made of billions of icy particles. The rings are more than 273,600 km across, but they are very thin. The frozen particles in the rings

This picture shows how Saturn would look if seen from its satellite Titan. The sky is blue because Titan has an atmosphere.

may be the remains of a moon that drifted too close to Saturn and broke up.

Photographs taken by the *Voyager* space probes in 1980 and 1981 showed that Saturn has many more rings than was thought.

To the naked eye, Saturn looks like a bright star. The planet is actually mostly made up of light gases, and it is less dense than water. But scientists think that it may have a solid core. Saturn has 23 satellites. The largest is Titan. It measures about 5200 km across—larger than Mercury. Titan is the only known satellite to have an atmosphere— a layer of gases surrounding it.

School

Nearly all countries try to provide enough schools to give their children some education. In many countries laws are passed by which children have to go to school between certain ages, such as between 5 and 16. But some poor countries do not have enough schools or teachers. They try to make sure that children go to school for long enough to learn to read, write and use numbers.

Science

The main kinds of science are ASTRONOMY, biology, CHEMISTRY, GEOLOGY, MATHEMATICS, MEDICINE and physics, which deals with types of ENERGY.

Scotland

Scotland is part of the United Kingdom of Great Britain and Northern Ireland. Most Scots live in a narrow belt in the south where most industry is. In this belt are Glasgow, Scotland's largest city, and Edinburgh, the capital. The Highlands of Scotland have very few people and many beautiful mountains and lochs. The highest mountain in Britain is Ben Nevis, 1343 metres high. There are many islands off the Scottish coast. These include the Hebrides, Orkneys and Shetlands.

Scotland joined with England and Wales in 1707, but the Scots have kept many of their own traditions. Some Scots want their own government.

Above: A lifelike head cast in bronze. It comes from Ife in Nigeria.

Sculpture

Sculpture is a way of making attractive models, statues and objects as works of ART. They may be carved from stone or wood, or they may be made by casting. In making a cast, the sculptor first makes a model in clay or wax. He uses this model to make a mould. He then pours hot molten metal, such as bronze, into the mould. When the metal has cooled and hardened, it is taken out of the mould. The metal 'cast' is a perfect copy of the original model.

Sculpture has been an important form of art since the early history of mankind. Much early sculpture was religious, but sculptors also carved people and animals.

Early Greek statues were models for RENAISSANCE sculptors such as MICHELANGELO, possibly the finest sculptor ever.

Modern sculptors have moved away from lifelike figures. Great artists such as Henry Moore make *abstract* figures and groups.

Left: This famous sculpture shows a legendary Greek called Laocoön and his two sons, who were said to have been killed by serpents. It dates from about 160 BC.

Right: The sea horse swims upright and is cased in rings of bony armour. It holds onto seaweeds by its tail.

Sea Horse

Sea horses are strange fish with delicate, bony bodies. They are called sea horses because of their horse-shaped heads, and they have a tube-like snout. Most are between 15 and 25 cm long.

Sea horses swim by waving their back fin. They often cling to seaweed with their tail. The males look after the eggs. They keep them in a pouch on their bellies until they hatch. Sea horses are found in seas in tropical and warm areas.

Seals and Sea Lions

Seals and sea lions are large sea mammals. Many of them live in icy waters. They spend most of their time in the sea, but sometimes come ashore to lie in the sun. They also have their young, called pups, on land. Seals have streamlined bodies and legs shaped like flippers for swimming. They also have a thick layer of fat, or blubber, under their skin to protect them from the cold. Seals and sea lions eat fish and other sea creatures.

Sea lions have small ears outside their heads and have fur all over their bodies. The males often have a shaggy mane. The Californian sea lion is the smallest. It is often seen in circuses and zoos.

Although they spend most of their lives in the sea, seals must come ashore to breed. A few species live in fresh water.

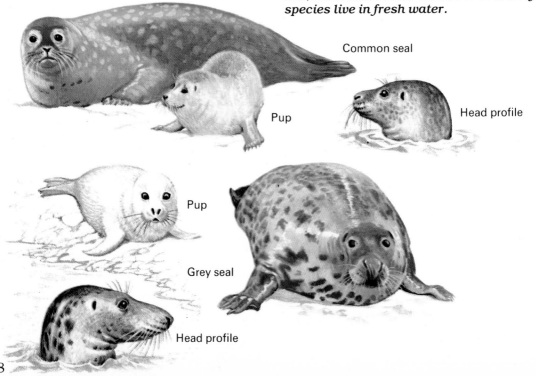

Common seal

Pup

Head profile

Pup

Grey seal

Head profile

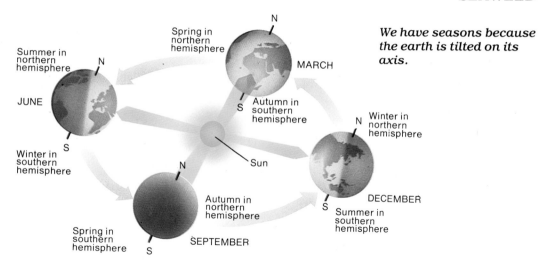

We have seasons because the earth is tilted on its axis.

Seasons

The year is divided into four seasons. They are spring, summer, autumn and winter. Each season has its own kind of weather.

In spring, for example, the days become warmer; plants begin to grow again after the winter cold and most animals have their young. In autumn, the days are cooler; leaves fall from the trees and many birds fly south for the winter.

Seasons happen because the EARTH is tilted on its *axis* (a line through the centre of the planet between the North and South Poles). As the earth travels around the SUN, first one pole, then the other, leans toward the sun. When the North Pole tips toward the sun it is summer in the northern half of the world and winter in the southern half. Six months later, it is the South Pole's turn to lean sunward, making it summer in southern lands and winter in northern ones. Spring and autumn, the halfway seasons between summer and winter, happen when the earth is between its summer and winter positions.

At the poles, there are only two seasons: summer and winter. During the polar winter the sun never rises and days are dark. In the summers the sun shines all the time and there are no real nights.

Farthest from the poles, at the EQUATOR, the earth's tilt has no effect. The four seasons do not exist.

Seaweed

Seaweeds are a group of plants that live in the sea. They grow on rocks or on the seabed. Like most plants, seaweeds need sunlight to make food. Because the sun's rays do not reach very far down into the sea, there are no seaweeds in deep water.

In some countries people eat seaweeds as vegetables.

Some seaweeds have little sacs of air. These sacs help the seaweeds to float in the water.

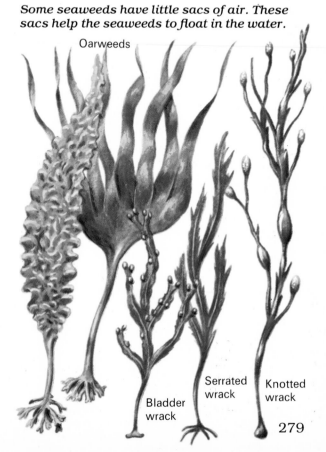

Oarweeds

Bladder wrack

Serrated wrack

Knotted wrack

279

Seed

Seeds are the most important part of a PLANT; they are the beginnings of new plants. A seed is formed when pollen reaches the female part of a FLOWER. The new seed grows inside a FRUIT, which protects it. In a grape, for example, the fleshy part is the fruit and the pips are the seeds.

Seeds have to be scattered to find new ground to grow on. Some fruits have wings and are carried by the wind. Others are prickly and stick to the fur of passing animals. Many seeds contain the baby plant and a little supply of food. When the seed begins to grow, the baby plant takes in this food until it has roots and leaves and can make its own food.

Seven Wonders of the World

The Seven Wonders of the World were seven outstanding man-made objects that were built in ancient times. Only one of these wonders, the PYRAMIDS, exists today. The others have all been destroyed. They were:

The Hanging Gardens of Babylon, which seem to have been built high up on the walls of temples. They were probably a gift from King Nebuchadnezzar II to one of his wives.

The Temple of Artemis at Ephesus (now in Turkey). This temple was one of the largest in the ancient world. Some of its marble columns are in the British Museum in London.

The Statue of Zeus at Olympia, Greece, which showed the king of the gods on his throne. It was made of gold and ivory.

The Seven Wonders of the Ancient World: (1) The Pyramids of Egypt. (2) The Pharos of Alexandria. (3) The Tomb of Mausolus at Halicarnassus. (4) The Hanging Gardens of Babylon. (5) The Colossus of Rhodes. (6) The Temple of Artemis at Ephesus. (7) The Statue of Zeus at Olympia.

The tomb at Halicarnassus (now in Turkey) which was a massive tomb built for Mausolus, a ruler in Persia. It became so famous that all large tombs are now called *mausoleums*.

The Colossus of Rhodes in Greece which was a huge, bronze statue of the sun god, Helios. It stood over the harbour entrance.

The Pharos of Alexandria in Egypt which was the first modern lighthouse. It was built in 270 BC on the island of Pharos outside Alexandria harbour. It had a wood fire burning on top.

Shakespeare, William

William Shakespeare (1564–1616) is England's greatest writer. He is most famous for his plays—about 40 altogether—which include *A Midsummer Night's Dream, Hamlet, Macbeth* and *Romeo and Juliet*.

Very little is known about Shakespeare's life. He was born in Stratford-upon-Avon and was the son of a glovemaker. When he was 18, he married Anne Hathaway, a farmer's daughter, and had three children. Then, at the age of 20, he left Stratford and went to London where he became an actor and playwright. At the end of his life he returned to Stratford. Many of the words and phrases we use today were first used by Shakespeare.

Shark

The shark family includes the world's largest and fiercest fish. Sharks have a wedge-shaped head, long body and a triangular back fin that often sticks out of the water. Their SKELETONS are made of rubbery gristle, not bone. Most sharks live in warm seas. They vary greatly in size. The dogfish, one of the smallest sharks, is only 60cm long. The largest fish in the oceans, the whale shark, measures over 15 metres—as long as two buses.

The whale shark is harmless to people and other animals because it lives on plankton. But many sharks are cruel killers with rows of razor-sharp teeth. Several are man-eaters. The greediest monster, the great

The thresher shark uses its huge tail to sweep its prey into a group. The hammerhead is named after its curious head.

white shark, swallows its prey whole. The remains of big animals, such as horses, seals and other sharks, have been found in its stomach.

Other man-eaters are the blue shark, the tiger shark and the leopard shark, which has leopardlike spots. The smell of blood in water causes sharks to attack anything near, even other sharks.

Sheep

Sheep have been part of people's lives for thousands of years. At first, sheep were kept for their milk and skins. Milk can be made into cheese and the skins were used for clothing. Then people discovered that the animals' thick coats could be *sheared* (shaved off) and the wool woven into cloth. Today sheep are kept mostly for wool and for meat (*mutton* or *lamb*).

Shells and Shellfish

Many animals live inside shells. This is because they have soft bodies that need protection. Shells are usually hard and are all sizes and colours. The shells of some sea snails are no bigger than a grain of sand, but the giant clam of the Pacific Ocean has a shell 120 cm across.

Some land animals such as SNAILS have shells, but most creatures with shells belong in the sea. Shelled sea animals include MOLLUSCS and crustaceans. Some of these, such as oysters, scallops and lobsters, can be eaten. These are often called shellfish although they are not really fish at all. Shellfish have been an important food for thousands of years. In some places, kitchen refuse of prehistoric people has been found that consists entirely of enormous mounds of shells, as high as a two-storey house.

Ship

Today most ships are cargo vessels. They are usually built for a certain type of cargo. *Tankers* carry liquids such as oil or wine. Some oil tankers are so long that the crew can ride bicycles around the deck. *Bulk carriers* take dry cargoes like coal and wheat that can be loaded loose. *Container ships* carry all kinds of goods packed in large boxes called containers. *Refrigerator ships* are for carrying fresh food such as fruit and meat.

Planes have replaced most passenger ships, but there are still many ferries that take people and cars across smaller stretches of water.

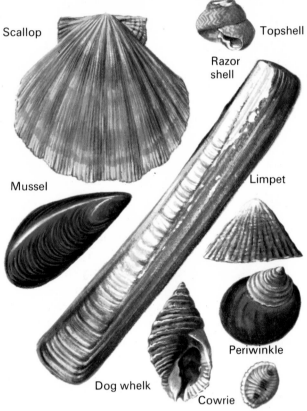

Scallop | Topshell | Razor shell | Mussel | Limpet | Dog whelk | Periwinkle | Cowrie

Above: Different mollusc shells found on the seashore.
Below: A bottle of champagne is broken across the bow of a new ship before it glides into the water.

Silicon Chip

Silicon chips are tiny pieces of the ELEMENT silicon. They can be made to carry very small electrical circuits, called micro-circuits. These are used in transistor radios, digital watches, electronic calculators and computers. Because the chips are so small, the objects they are used in can be small too.

Silk

Silk is a natural fibre made from the cocoon of one kind of moth. Silkworms, which are really caterpillars, are kept in special containers and fed on mulberry leaves for about four weeks. At the end of this time they spin their cocoons and start to turn into moths. Then they are killed and each cocoon is unwound as a long thread between 600 and 900 metres long. Several of these fine threads have to be twisted together to make a thread strong enough to use.

Silk was first used in Asia centuries ago, especially in China and Japan. Silk WEAV-ING in Europe began in the 1400s. Silk makes a very fine, soft material. It was used for stockings before nylon was invented. Silk can be made into other fabrics such as satin and chiffon, and can be dyed in beautiful colours.

Above: Part of a silk dress that was made in China 2000 years ago. Rich people wore clothes like this and sent silk cloth to Europe, where it was made into expensive clothes.
Below left: A picture from ancient China shows silk being spun into a thread for weaving.
Below right: A silkworm's cocoon with the animal inside, changing from a caterpillar into a moth. The animal has to be killed before the silk is unwound.

Cocoon ————

Silkworm in cocoon

Silver

Silver is a precious metal. It has been used by people all over the world for thousands of years.

Silver bends very easily, and can be beaten into many shapes and patterns. Like gold, it can be hammered out into thin sheets. It is used to make useful and decorative things such as spoons and forks, bowls and jewellery. Sometimes it is used as a coating on cheaper metals such as copper or nickel, to make them look like silver. It can also be mixed with another metal (usually copper), and then it is called *sterling* silver.

Silver used to be made into coins, but most of today's 'silver' coins are really made of a mixture of copper and nickel.

Silver carries electricity well and is used for this in industry. Some chemicals made from silver react to light and are used in photography. Another chemical, silver nitrate, is painted on the back of glass to make mirrors.

Silver is rare and expensive. It is mined in many parts of the world.

Above: This silver coffin was made for King Psusennes of Egypt about 3000 years ago.

Skeleton

Our skeleton is made up of BONES. If we did not have a skeleton, our bodies would be shapeless blobs. The skeleton protects our vital organs, such as heart, liver and lungs. It is also an anchor for our MUSCLES.

In humans and other animals with backbones (VERTEBRATES), the skeleton is inside the body, covered by the flesh and skin. In other animals, such as INSECTS and SPIDERS, the skeleton is like a hard crust on the outside of the body. It is called an *exoskeleton*. Some animals, such as the JELLYFISH and OCTOPUS, do not have a skeleton. Their bodies are supported by the water they live in.

There are more than 200 bones in the human skeleton. These include the bones of the spine, skull (which protects the brain), ribs, pelvis, breastbone and limbs. Joints are places where bones meet.

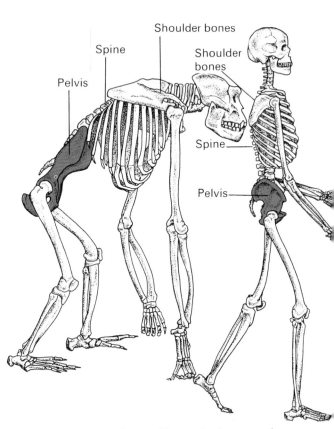

The skeletons of a gorilla and a human show how differently they walk. The shape and position of the pelvis and spine are important. The gorilla needs long arm bones because it walks mostly on all fours.

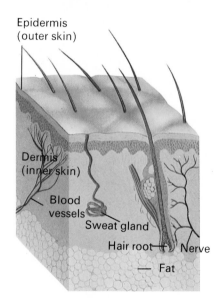

Your skin is a waterproof, elastic covering for your body. It helps to protect the body from damage and germs.

Skin

Skin is the covering on the outside of our bodies. It protects our bodies and is sensitive to heat, cold and pain. Human skin can be quite thick and hard on places that get a lot of wear, such as the soles of the feet. It can also be very thin on other places, such as the eyelids.

Our skin is in two layers. The outer layer, the *epidermis*, has a chemical called melanin which gives skin its colour. The inner layer, the *dermis*, contains nerves, blood vessels, sweat glands and the roots of hairs. The skin of an adult human covers about 1.7 square metres.

Slavery

Slavery means owning people to work for you, just as you would own a car. Slaves can be bought and sold. In ancient civilizations, prisoners captured in war were often made into slaves, and poor people sometimes sold their children as slaves.

From the 1500s, the Spanish took people from Africa as slaves for their colonies in America. By the 1770s, British ships were carrying slaves to America. Hundreds were packed tightly into ships. Conditions were terrible, and many slaves died on the way. Slavery was ended in the United States in 1865, after the CIVIL WAR.

Sleep

Sleep is a time when we are unconscious and resting. People and other animals need sleep to stay healthy. Without it, people become short-tempered and after a long time they may start having *hallucinations*—seeing things that are not there.

There are four different stages of sleep. At each stage the electrical waves given off by the BRAIN change. When we are deeply asleep, these waves are slow and large. When we are only lightly asleep the waves are faster. This is the time when we—and all mammals—dream.

Different people need different amounts of sleep. Babies need a lot. Adults need between six and nine hours a night.

Sloth

Sloths are a group of MAMMALS that live in South America. They move very slowly, usually at night. Sloths spend most of their lives hanging upside down in trees, as in the picture below. They eat leaves, buds and twigs. Their fur is often covered with

masses of tiny green creatures called algae. This makes the sloth hard to see among the leaves. A sloth's grip is so secure that it can even fall asleep without letting go of the branch it is hanging from.

There are two main kinds of sloth—the two-toed and the three-toed.

We call someone 'slothful' when we mean he is lazy and slow.

Smell

Smell is an important sense, like sight and hearing. Humans and other MAMMALS smell through the nose. We sniff the air, and the scents given off by the things around us are picked up by special cells in the nose. These cells send messages to the BRAIN.

Our sense of smell is useful when we are eating. It helps us to TASTE things. It can also let us know when food is bad. Most other animals have a much better sense of smell than humans. Dogs can use their sense of smell to track down and follow prey. Moths do not have noses, but they can still smell things. Some male moths can smell a female many miles away.

Smog

There are two kinds of smog. One is a very thick, smelly mixture of smoke and fog. It used to be very common in London. In the winter of 1952, there was a very bad smog and about 4000 people died of chest diseases. Since then, laws have been made to make sure there is less smoke in London and no more smog.

The other kind of smog is caused by air pollution from car exhausts and other fumes. These are changed by sunlight into a white mist that hangs over cities. Smog of this sort can be dangerous to the people who live in cities. It can hold chemicals that are harmful.

Snail

Snails are MOLLUSCS with a coiled shell on their back. There are more than 80,000 kinds in the world. Some live on land, some in fresh water and some in the sea. They are eaten by fish and birds, and some kinds are used as food for humans.

Most snails are less than an inch long. But one of the largest, the giant land snail, is about 20 cm long.

Snake

Snakes are REPTILES. They are long and thin and have no arms or legs. They move along by wriggling their bodies.

Snakes have a dry, smooth skin. Most live in warm places. Those that live in colder climates spend the winter in HIBERNATION.

A few snakes have poison glands. They inject this poison into animals that they bite. The rattlesnake and the cobra are both poisonous snakes.

Most snakes hatch from eggs. A female snake can lay up to ten eggs at a time. Others give birth to live young. The largest snakes are pythons and anacondas. These can grow to 10 metres long.

Right: Smoke like this from factories can cause smog when it mixes with fog. Sunlight shining on smoke makes a different kind of smog.

Soap

Soap is used for cleaning things. It is made by mixing FAT or vegetable oil with a chemical such as caustic soda. It loosens dirt in clothes and carries it away. Today chemical cleaners called DETERGENTS are often used instead.

Solar Energy

Solar energy is energy from the sun. It reaches the earth as light and heat. Without these things there could be no life on earth.

Only about 15 percent of the sun's energy that reaches the earth is absorbed by the earth's surface. Much of it bounces off the earth and back into space. Solar energy can be collected and used to make electricity.

This is the world's largest solar furnace. It is in the French Pyrenees. The curved mirror focuses the rays of the sun to make temperatures of up to 3000°C. Flat mirrors reflect sunlight onto the curved mirror.

Solar System

The solar system is made up of the SUN and the planets travelling around it. Mercury is the planet nearest the sun. Next comes Venus, Earth, Mars, Jupiter, Saturn, Uranus, Neptune and Pluto.

Until the 1500s, most people thought that the earth was the centre of the universe, and that the sun and planets travelled around it. In 1543 a Polish astronomer, Nicolaus Copernicus, discovered that, in fact, the earth moved around the sun.

Sound

Sound is made by vibrating objects that send sound waves through the air. When these vibrations reach our EARS, we hear them as sounds.

Sound travels through air at about 334 metres a second. This is slow enough for us to see something happen (if it is far enough away) before we hear it. The sound takes time to reach us.

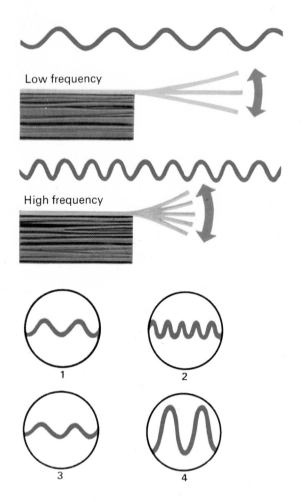

Low frequency

High frequency

1

2

3

4

Sound is made by vibrations, or 'waves', in the air. The slower the vibrations, the lower the sound. If sound waves go through a microphone they are turned into electrical waves. These can be seen on a screen like a television. The four sound wave pictures here show (1) a low sound, (2) a high sound, (3) a soft sound, and (4) a loud sound.

The speed of the vibrations makes a difference to the kind of sound we hear. If the vibrations are very fast, they are said to be 'high frequency' and the sound we hear is high-pitched. If they are slow, the sound is said to be 'low frequency' and the sound we hear is low-pitched.

South Africa

South Africa is a country in southern AFRICA. Most of the country is tableland, a high region of flat-topped hills. Around the coast is a narrow plain. The climate is hot and dry.

South Africa is a rich country. Factories make a wide range of goods. Mines produce gold, diamonds, uranium, copper, iron and other minerals. Farms grow big crops of maize, wheat and fruit. Millions of sheep graze on the grasslands in the centre of the country .

Just over 30 million people live in South Africa. Almost three-quarters of them are black Africans. There are fewer than 5 million whites. The whites, who are descended mainly from Dutch and British settlers, control the country's government and money. Since the 1940s, South Africa has had a policy of *apartheid*, or 'apartness'. This means that whites and non-whites live separately. Black protests against this system have been building up over several years. Today most of the world's nations think that apartheid should be ended.

South Africa produces about two-thirds of all the world's gold. Most of the gold is mined in the Transvaal, where this miner is working. Gold is South Africa's most valuable export. The country is also the world's biggest producer of diamonds.

Left: South America is a vast continent that stretches from north of the equator to the Antarctic. Above left: Bogotá is the capital and largest city of Colombia. Above: Quito, the capital of Ecuador, has a 17th-century cathedral.

South America

South America is the world's fourth largest continent. Lying between the Atlantic and Pacific oceans, it stretches from the EQUATOR in the north to ANTARCTICA in the south, from the Andes Mountains in the west to the wide AMAZON delta in the east.

The Andes are the longest mountain range in the world. They run along the Pacific coast for 8000 km. They are also the starting point of one of the world's greatest rivers, the Amazon. This huge waterway travels 6300 km across South America and empties 118 million litres of water into the ocean every second. The huge area drained by the Amazon is thick with jungle.

Two other great rivers are the Orinoco in the north and the Plate in the south. The land south of the Amazon jungle has swamps, lakes, grasslands and, near the continent's tip, the Patagonian desert.

There are 13 countries in South America. The largest, BRAZIL, takes up half the continent. Most South Americans speak Spanish. But in Brazil they speak Portuguese, in Guyana they speak English, in French Guiana, French, and in Surinam, Dutch. These different languages are the leftovers of history. South America was explored by the Spanish and Portuguese in the 1500s. Then Spain, Portugal, and other European countries set up colonies. In the 1800s, most of these colonies won their independence.

The first people of South America were Indians. Most of them, including the INCAS, were killed by foreign conquerors. Later the

289

SOUTH AMERICA

ATLANTIC OCEAN

Barranquilla
Caracas
Maracaibo
Orinoco
Georgetown
Medellin
Paramaribo
VENEZUELA
Cayenne
Llanos
GUYANA
SURINAM
Bogotá
FRENCH
Cali
COLOMBIA
GUIANA

Quito
ECUADOR
Manáus
Belém
Guayaquil
Amazon

GALAPAGOS IS.

Fortaleza

PERU
Chiclayo
Selvas
BRAZIL
Trujillo

Recife

Callão
Lima
Cuzco
Salvador
BOLIVIA
La Paz
PACIFIC OCEAN
Cochabamba
Brasilia
Oruro
Brazilian Highlands
Sucre

PARAGUAY
Paraná
Gran Chaco
Rio de Janeiro
Asunción
São Paulo

Pôrto Alegre
Córdoba
URUGUAY
Mt Aconcagua
Rosario
Valparaiso
Buenos Aires
Montevideo
Santiago
La Plata
ARGENTINA

CHILE
PAMPAS
Bahia Blanca
Colorado
ATLANTIC OCEAN

■ Capital Cities

0   500   1000 miles

0   500   1000   1500 kilometres

Chubut

Patagonia

FALKLAND IS.

Tierra
del Fuego
Cape Horn

ANDES

ATACAMA DESERT

MOUNTAINS

Europeans brought in African slaves. Today most South Americans come from European and African ancestors. There are still some Indians in the Andes and Amazonia.

South America is very rich. The rocks of the Andes are full of minerals. There is silver in Peru, tin in BOLIVIA and copper in CHILE. There are also huge amounts of oil in VENEZUELA in the north. The open grasslands of ARGENTINA, URUGUAY and Paraguay provide food for millions of sheep and cattle. Brazil's farmers produce a third of the coffee in the world. Peru's fishermen catch a fifth of the world's fish. So far this wealth has not been used properly. Most South Americans are poor. Many people still scrape a living from the land.

Soviet Union (USSR)

The USSR is the world's largest country, covering 22,402,000 square km. It lies in EUROPE and ASIA. USSR stands for Union of Soviet Socialist Republics. Many people still call it Russia, although Russia is really only one of the 15 republics that make up the country. Russia covers three-quarters of the USSR, and the Russian language is the most important of the 60 or so languages spoken. The capital of the USSR is MOSCOW.

Before 1917, Russia was a poor country ruled by *tsars*, or emperors. In 1917, there was a revolution. A COMMUNIST government took over, led by LENIN. Between 1918 and 1920 Russia was nearly destroyed by a civil war between the communists and their enemies. The communists won, and began

Above: These young Russians belong to the Young Pioneers, a group that is given some military training.
Below: A view of Red Square in Moscow, the Soviet capital. On the right is the Kremlin, a group of buildings in which the communist party leaders meet. On the left are the 'onion' domes of St Basil's Cathedral.

USSR

to turn Russia into a great industrial nation.

The land of Russia is varied. Large parts of it are cold or dry and have few people. More than 70 percent of the 273 million citizens live in the European part of the country, west of the Ural Mountains.

Russian farmers grow many crops, including wheat, rye and barley. They also grow vegetables, fruit, tea and cotton. The farms are owned or run by the government. Most of the farms are very big, and about a quarter of the population works on them.

Russia is rich in MINERALS. It has great deposits of coal, oil and natural gas, and

Above left: A troika, or sled drawn by three horses, is still sometimes seen in Russia. Above: A 13th-century monastery in the ancient city of Novgorod.

has more iron, chromium, lead and manganese than any other country. Fishing and forestry are also important industries.

At the beginning of the 1900s Russia was a country of farmers. There were few factories. Today Russia is a leading industrial country. The government runs the factories and tells the workers what to make.

During World War II Germany invaded the Soviet Union, but after fierce fighting the Soviet Army drove the Germans back. The Russians occupied Hungary, Romania, Czechoslovakia, Poland and part of Germany itself. After the war, communist governments closely tied to the Soviet Union were set up in these countries.

The United States and Russia grew to distrust each other and what was called the Cold War developed. US and Soviet leaders signed a treaty in 1987 to stop the spread of nuclear weapons, and to reduce the number of them held on both sides.

Russians are fond of sports, art and reading. The government helps sportsmen and athletes in their training. Many Russians win gold medals at the OLYMPIC GAMES. The Bolshoi ballet company of Moscow is world-famous. Russia also has some of the best CHESS players in the world. Some of the world's most famous writers, such as Tolstoy and Chekhov, were Russians.

A market in Tbilisi, the capital of the Georgian Soviet Socialist Republic.

Space Exploration

People have always gazed in wonder at the sun, moon and the stars. Yet for thousands of years, they had no means of studying the heavens above. Then, in the 1600s, TELE-SCOPES were invented and people were able to take a closer look at the universe. More recently, scientists have been able to discover a lot more about space. We are living in the Space Age.

The Space Age began in 1957 when the Russians sent the world's first man-made SATELLITE, *Sputnik I*, into ORBIT around the earth. Only a month later, they launched *Sputnik II* with a passenger, a dog called Laika. Instruments connected to Laika collected information about the animal's reactions to space travel. A year later, in 1958, the United States launched its first satellite.

Since then, Russia and the United States have taken giant steps forward in space. After the first satellites came the first probes. These probes were unmanned spacecraft sent to explore the moon. In 1961 the Russians sent the first man into space. Yuri Gagarin flew around earth once in his spacecraft *Vostok I*.

Above: The first two men to set foot on the moon can be seen in this picture. Neil Armstrong is reflected in Edwin Aldrin's space helmet. Below: This colour-enhanced picture of Halley's Comet was taken from the spacecraft Giotto as it flew close to the comet in March, 1986. From the colours scientists can tell what the comet is made of.

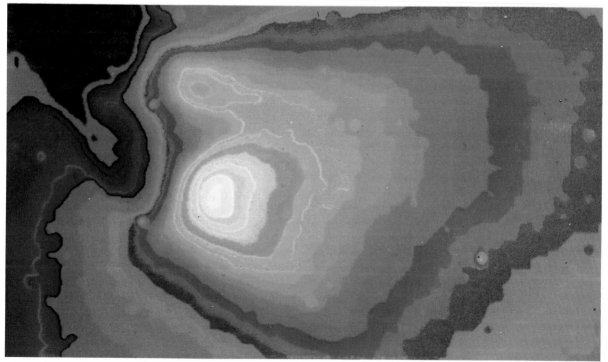

© Max-Planck-Institute für Aeronomie, Lindau, FRG

During the next few years, Russia and the United States continued to launch satellites, manned spacecraft and probes. Some of the probes went to the moon; others explored Mars and Venus. Then, in 1969, man reached the moon. Two American astronauts, Neil Armstrong and Edwin Aldrin, landed in their *Apollo* spacecraft.

In the 1970s, space exploration continued with more moon trips, more probes to other planets and space stations.

The Mariner 10 space probe was put into orbit around the Sun, and passed Mercury three times in 1974 and 1975. It gave astronomers the only close-up photographs of Mercury they have so far had before its instruments stopped working.

Mariner also discovered that Mercury has a huge iron core, probably about three-quarters of the size of the planet itself.

In the year AD 10,000,000, Voyager 2, battered by collisions with stray meteoroids, may drift into an alien solar system. What would happen if a strange spacecraft, also lost and drifting, was discovered in our solar system, perhaps heading towards the Earth?

In 1981 the space shuttle *Columbia* made its first flight. This was followed by many successful flights until tragedy struck in January, 1986 when the space shuttle *Challenger* blew up after launch.

The space probe *Voyager 2* passed close to Saturn in 1981 and sent back some beautiful pictures of the planet's rings. Then it flew on to Uranus, which it reached in 1986 to photograph that distant planet's moons.

Spain

Spain lies in south-west EUROPE, beyond the Pyrenees. Most of the country is covered by high plains and mountains, with a low plain around the coast. The highland has hot summers, cold winters and little rain. The coast is milder and wetter, especially in the north.

Half the people work on farms, growing potatoes, wheat, grapes, olives and fruits. Wine, olive oil and oranges are exported. Many Spaniards who live on the coast are fishermen. They catch sardines and anchovies. Others work in the tourist trade. Each year, millions of tourists visit Spain to

Many castles in Spain were built when the Moors occupied the land.

enjoy its sunny beaches. The two main industrial areas are around Bilbao in the north and Barcelona in the north-east. Madrid is the capital and largest city.

Speech

Once, the only sounds people could make were grunts, yells and other simple sounds. Then, over tens of thousands of years, they learned to form words. Languages slowly developed.

Speech sounds are made by air from our lungs passing around two membranes called vocal cords. We change the pitch of the sound by altering the tension of the vocal cords, just as we can alter the pitch of a guitar by tightening or slackening the strings. By changing the shape of the passages in our throat, mouth and nose, and by using our tongue, we can alter the sounds produced. We can make the words of speech.

Women usually have higher-pitched voices than men because their vocal cords are shorter.

Even people who speak alike have voice differences that can be detected electronically. The sounds they make can be printed as graphs called voiceprints. As with fingerprints, each person produces a different pattern. The voiceprint below is a graph of someone saying 'Where are you?' It took one second to record.

The best-known sphinx is this one at Giza in Egypt. It was built about 2600 BC and is about 21 metres tall.

Sphinx

The sphinx is a strange, imaginary beast with a human head and a lion's body. It belongs to the legends of ancient Egypt and Greece. In Egypt, the sphinx represented the power of the king, the PHARAOH. Sphinx statues often had a pharaoh's head.

Greek legends say the sphinx was a woman. She lived near the city of Thebes and asked passers-by a difficult riddle. When they could not answer it, she ate them. But one day, King Oedipus solved the riddle. The sphinx was so angry she killed herself.

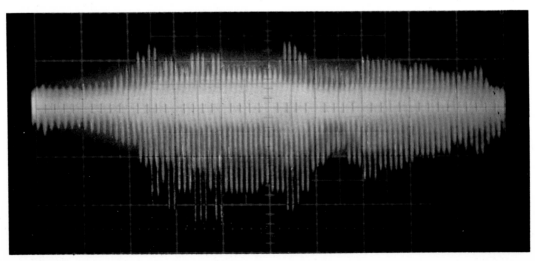

Spice

Spices have a strong taste and smell and are used to flavour foods and drinks. They are made from the dried parts of plants, usually ground into a powder. Most spice plants grow in hot countries such as Africa, India and Indonesia. Pepper, ginger, cloves, cinnamon and nutmeg are common spices.

Wolf spiders

Tarantula

Nutmeg   Cinnamon

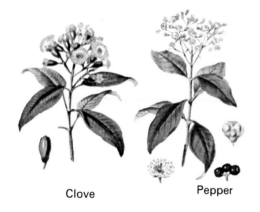

Clove   Pepper

Above: Like many other spiders, wolf spiders lay their eggs in silk cocoons. Female wolf spiders carry their cocoons with them. When the babies hatch they ride on their mother's back until they can look after themselves. Tarantulas are among the largest spiders.

bite. All spiders have poison, but in most cases it does not hurt people.

There are about 30,000 kinds of spiders. They are all sizes. The comb-footed spider is no bigger than a pinhead, but some bird-eating spiders can be 25 cm across. They have different life stories. Some live for only a year, others for 20 years. Some mate in winter, others in spring. Tiny spiders lay a few eggs, perhaps just one, but the largest lay up to 2000.

Some spiders, such as the garden spider below, build beautiful cartwheel-like webs. The webs are sticky. A small insect that flies into one of these cannot escape.

Spider

Spiders are small animals. Although they look like insects, they are not. Insects have six legs; spiders have eight. Insects have feelers and wings; spiders do not. Insect bodies have three parts; spiders' bodies have two.

All spiders spin silk threads. Many of them use the threads to make a sticky web for catching insects. Not all spiders trap their food in webs. Some are hunters and chase their prey; others lie in wait, then pounce. When a spider catches something, it stuns or kills it with a poisonous

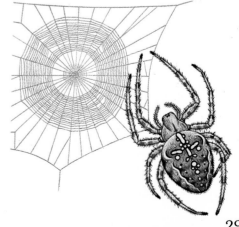

Left: Each of the squid's 10 arms has rows of sucking discs. These are used to seize and hold on to prey.

Squid

Squid are MOLLUSCS related to the OCTOPUS. Many live deep in the sea by day but rise to feed at night. A squid uses its 10 tentacles to catch fish and feed them into its beaklike mouth. Some squid are no bigger than a thumb. But the giant squid can grow to 12 metres long.

Squirrel

Most people think of squirrels as a kind of RODENT that is good at climbing trees. Tree squirrels are exactly that. They have sharp claws for climbing and a long, bushy tail that helps them to steer and keep their balance. Tree squirrels can leap 3 metres to reach one tree from another.

Flying squirrels jump 10 times farther than that. These little creatures have flaps of skin between their front and back legs. The flaps form a parachute when a flying squirrel jumps and spreads its limbs. Tree squirrels and flying squirrels feed on leaves, twigs or seeds.

Ground squirrels live in burrows under the ground. They include the chipmunks, prairie dogs and woodchucks.

The most common squirrel in Great Britain is the grey squirrel. There are more than 300 different kinds of squirrels.

The grey squirrel (right) has a reddish tinge to its coat in summer. The tail has light-coloured fringes. There are no ear tufts. This squirrel is a North American species that has become a pest in many countries. The red squirrel's summer coat is usually a rich red. The winter coat is greyish. It has ear tufts in the winter. The flying squirrel glides from tree to tree by using a fold of skin that extends between its front and back legs. This skin acts like a parachute.

Red squirrel

Grey squirrel

Flying squirrel

Stalin, Joseph

Joseph Stalin (1879–1953) ruled the USSR from 1929 to 1953. After LENIN died, Stalin made Russia one of the two most powerful nations in the world. He killed or imprisoned millions of Russians who disliked him or disagreed with his kind of COMMUNISM. The name Stalin is Russian for 'man of steel'.

Stamp

A stamp can be a special mark, or a piece of printed paper with a sticky back. A passport and many other kinds of documents must bear the correct government stamp. Postage stamps are stuck on letters and packages to be carried by the postal service. Each nation has its own postage stamps. Millions of people collect postage stamps. Some kinds are scarce and valuable. A very rare stamp can cost more than a house.

Above: Two US postage stamps and (top, right) the Penny Black of 1840, the first stamp with a sticky back.

Star

The stars we can see from earth are just a few of the many millions scattered through space. Stars look small because they are so far away. But most are huge, fiery balls of gas like our SUN.

Stars begin as clouds of gas. GRAVITY pulls the gas particles in toward the middle of each cloud. There the particles collide and grow hot, and other particles press in.

HYDROGEN atoms change into helium atoms by a process called nuclear fusion. That process gives off NUCLEAR ENERGY. This is what makes stars glow so brightly.

Stars swell as they use their hydrogen. Astronomers call such stars *red giants*. Red giants later shrink into tiny white-hot stars called *white dwarfs*. In time, these cool and fade into the darkness of space.

Right: Some of the stars in the Pleiades, a cluster of stars in the constellation Taurus. Only a few stars in the cluster can be seen with the naked eye.

Steam Engine

Boiling water turns into steam. Steam will fill 1700 times more space than the water that it came from. So if you squash steam into a small container it presses hard against the sides. If one side is free to move, the steam pressure will push it outward.

In the 1700s British inventors began to use this fact to build engines powered by steam. Early steam engines worked with a simple to-and-fro motion. In Thomas Newcomen's engine, a furnace heated water in a boiler. The water gave off steam that pushed a piston up inside a cylinder. When the steam cooled and turned back to water, air pressed the piston down again. Newcomen's engine was used to pump water from flooded mines.

James Watt built a more powerful engine where steam pushed the piston first one way and then the other. Rods from the piston spun a wheel. By the early 1800s, such engines were moving heavy loads faster than men or horses could. Yet, unlike men and horses, steam engines never tired.

Steam engines powered factory machines that made the INDUSTRIAL REVOLUTION possible. They also powered LOCOMOTIVES and steamships. For the first time, people travelled faster than horses.

Steam locomotives like the one above were called Big Boys. They were built in the US in the 1940s and were the biggest engines ever.

The INTERNAL-COMBUSTION ENGINE has largely taken the place of steam engines. But many ships' propellers and power station generators are worked by steam that spins wheels called turbines.

Stocks and Shares

A company must have money to start and carry on its business. It often gets this money by selling shares in the company. The people who buy *shares* become part owners of the company. They can, for example, vote for the directors of the company. If the company does well and makes a profit, the shareholders receive a share of the profit according to the number of shares they own.

Sometimes a company wants to borrow money, so it sells *stocks*. A stockholder receives interest at a fixed rate but has no say in the running of the company. However, if the company goes bankrupt, stockholders get their money back before the shareholders do.

Stocks and shares are bought and sold in stock exchanges.

Stomach

Your stomach is a muscular bag open at both ends and shaped like a fat letter J. It plays an important part in the DIGESTION of food.

When you eat a meal, food travels down your throat to your stomach. The stomach can store a large meal. Juices produced in the stomach kill germs in food. They also moisten and start digesting the food. Stomach muscles churn the mixture, then force it out into the small intestine.

Stone Age

The Stone Age was the great span of time before people learned how to make metal tools. Stone Age people used stone, wood and bone instead of metal. The Stone Age probably began more than three million years ago. It ended in Iraq and Egypt when the Bronze Age began there about 5000 years ago.

The Stone Age had three parts: Old, Middle and New. The Old Stone Age lasted until 10,000 years

Below: Part of a bison painted on a cave wall in south-western France. Stone Age artists drew the big animals they hunted.

Above: A Stone Age tool made from a deer's antler. It is decorated with a carving of a bison's head.

ago in the Middle East. When it began, hunters could scarcely chip a stone well enough to sharpen it. When the Old Stone Age ended, people had learned to chip flint into delicate spearheads, knives and scrapers.

In the Middle Stone Age, hunters used tiny flakes of flint in arrows and harpoons.

The New Stone Age began in the Middle East about 9000 years ago. New Stone Age people made smooth axe heads of ground stone. Farming replaced hunting in the New Stone Age.

Right: A thumb-sized carving of a woman's head made from a mammoth tusk over 20,000 years ago. The Stone Age carver may have lived like the people in the scene below.

Stonehenge

Stonehenge is a huge prehistoric temple on Salisbury Plain in southern England. The main part is a great circle of standing stones. Each is more than twice as tall as a man and weighs nearly 30 tonnes. Flat stones were laid across the tops of the standing stones to form a ring. Inside the ring stood smaller stones, and a great block that may have been an altar. The big stones were raised 3500 years ago. Other parts are older.

Right: The huge stones that form Stonehenge were dragged from a site more than 400km away. The task must have taken years.

Stork

These big birds have long beaks and legs. They can wade in swamps and capture fish and frogs. But some kinds prefer feeding on dead animals. More than a dozen kinds of stork live in warm parts of the world.

The white stork is the best-known kind. In summer, white storks nest in Europe and central Asia. In autumn, they fly south.

Flapping their wings soon makes storks tired. They prefer to soar and glide.

Stuarts

The House of Stuart was a royal family that ruled Scotland from 1371 to 1603, and England and Scotland from 1603 until 1715.

MARY QUEEN OF SCOTS was put to death by ELIZABETH I, who feared that Mary might replace her as the Queen of England. CHARLES I was executed in the English CIVIL WAR, and CHARLES II's son James II was forced to leave the country. The throne went to his sister Mary and her husband, WILLIAM OF ORANGE, then to James' sister Anne. Anne was the last Stuart ruler. She died in 1715.

Submarine

Submarines are boats that can travel under water. To dive, the crew of a submarine make it heavier than the amount of water needed to fill the space taken up by the submarine. To rise, the crew make the submarine lighter than that amount of water. When water and submarine both weigh the same, the boat stays at the same level under the surface.

In 1620 someone rowed a wood and leather submarine down the river Thames. But the first submarine that worked well was not built until the 1770s. Both these early submarines were worked by hand. They were slow and underpowered.

In the 1870s an English clergyman invented a submarine powered by a steam engine. But each time it dived the crew had to pull down its chimney and put out the fire that heated water to produce steam.

By 1900 the American inventor John P. Holland had produced a much better underwater boat. Petrol engines drove it on the surface. But petrol needs air to burn. Under water the boat ran on battery-driven motors that did not need air.

In 1955 came the first nuclear-powered submarine. Such boats can travel around the world without having to come to the surface. In 1958 the nuclear submarine *Nautilus* of the United States Navy made the first submerged crossing across the top of the world under the North Pole. These submarines are armed with nuclear missiles that can strike at enemy targets thousands of miles away.

Below: This cutaway view shows a nuclear submarine. Heat from its nuclear reactor turns water into steam. This spins turbine blades that drive the propeller.

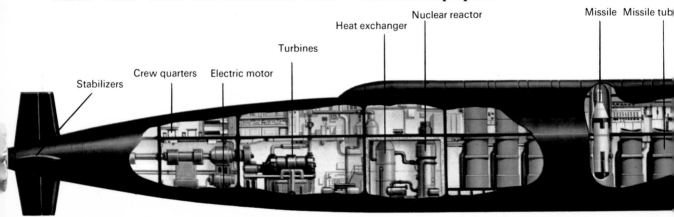

Stabilizers Crew quarters Electric motor Turbines Heat exchanger Nuclear reactor Missile Missile tube

Sudan

This is the largest nation in AFRICA. It is more than ten times the size of the United Kingdom.

Sudan is a hot country in north-east Africa. Desert sprawls across the north. There are flat grasslands in the middle. The south has forests and a huge swamp.

Sudanese people include Arabs and blacks. Most live near the NILE, which flows north across the country. The Sudanese raise cattle, grow crops such as sugar cane, or work in cities. Khartoum is the capital city.

Suez Canal

The Suez Canal crosses Egypt between Port Said on the Mediterranean Sea and Suez on the Red Sea. It is the world's longest canal that can be used by big ships. It measures 160km from end to end and 60 metres across its bed. Ships use it as a short cut on voyages between Europe and Asia. This saves them from sailing 9650km around southern Africa.

The canal was begun in 1859 by a French company run by the engineer Ferdinand de Lesseps. More than 8000 men and hun-

Egypt seen from a spacecraft. The Suez Canal crosses the narrow gap between the Mediterranean (top left) and the long thin Gulf of Suez, part of the Red Sea.

dreds of camels worked on it for 10 years. France and England operated the canal until Egypt took it over in 1956.

Sunken ships blocked the canal for eight years after Egypt's war with Israel in 1967. But dredging has now made it much wider and deeper than it was a century ago.

Sugar

Sugar is a sweet-tasting food. We eat it as an ingredient in ice cream, sweets and soft drinks. We use sugar crystals to sweeten cereals, coffee and tea.

Sugar gives your body energy more quickly than any other kind of food. But

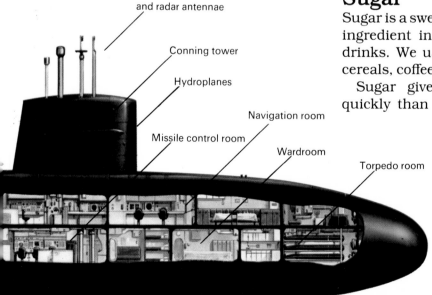

Periscopes, radio and radar antennae

Conning tower

Hydroplanes

Navigation room

Missile control room

Wardroom

Torpedo room

Left: When sugar beet is harvested it is sliced and soaked in water to make a syrup. This is boiled and dried to make pure sugar.

eating too many sugary things can cause your teeth to decay.

All sugar contains carbon, hydrogen and oxygen. Different groupings of these ATOMS produce different kinds of sugars. The kind we eat most of is known as *sucrose*.

Every green PLANT produces sugar. But most of the sugar that we eat comes from two plants. One is sugar cane, a type of giant grass. The other is sugar beet, a plant with a thick root rich in sugar.

Sun

The sun is just one of many millions of STARS in the Milky Way. But it is also the centre of the SOLAR SYSTEM. The PLANETS and their moons all whirl around it. The heat and light given out by the sun make it possible for plants and animals to live here on the planet that we call the EARTH.

The sun seems small because it is so far away. A spacecraft that took an hour to

Below: The sun shown as if cut open like an apple. The core holds helium, produced by nuclear reactions that send energy through the outer layers into space. The bright surface layer is the photosphere.

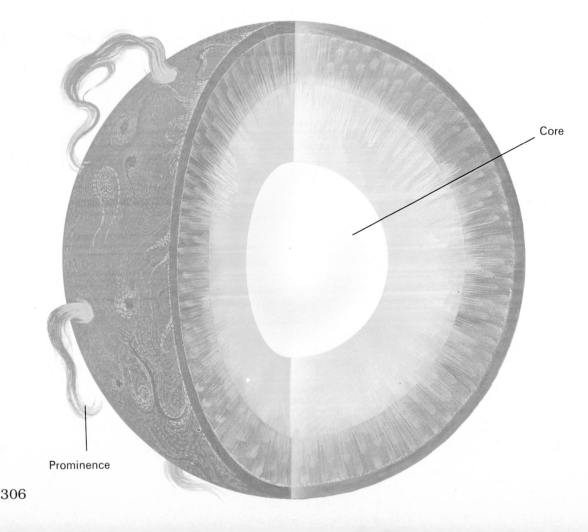

Core

Prominence

zoom around the earth would need five months to reach the sun. In fact, the sun is so big that you could fit a million earths inside it with room to spare. A bucketful of the sun's substance would weigh far less than a bucketful of rock from the earth. But the whole sun would weigh over 750 times more than all the planets.

Part of the sun seen through a specially darkened telescope. A loop of flaming gas thousands of miles long bursts from the surface. Such streamers are called prominences. You should never look at the sun through an ordinary telescope because you would do serious damage to your eyes.

The sun is a great glowing ball of gases. In the middle of the sun a process called nuclear fusion turns HYDROGEN gas into helium gas. This change releases huge amounts of NUCLEAR ENERGY. The sun beams out its energy in all directions as *electromagnetic waves*. Some of these waves give us HEAT and LIGHT. But there are also radio waves, ultraviolet rays, X-rays and others.

The sun was formed from a mass of gas and dust five billion years ago. It contains enough hydrogen fuel to keep it glowing brightly for another five billion years.

Surgery

Surgery is cutting someone open to remove or mend a damaged part of the body. Surgery is performed in a hospital by a specially trained doctor called a surgeon. He works in a specially equipped room. X-RAY and other tests may help to show the surgeon how best to operate. Before an operation, a patient is given an anaesthetic so that he or she sleeps and feels no pain.

The surgeon cuts the patient open with a sharp knife called a scalpel. Other tools help him prevent bleeding and hold back flaps of skin. After operating he closes the wound by sewing its edges together.

Surveying

Surveying means using measuring instruments and working out certain sums to find out the exact positions of places on the earth's surface. This kind of information makes it possible for people to make maps and charts and to build bridges, roads and buildings.

Above: A surveyor using an instrument that measures distances by timing radio signals sent from one place to another. Surveyors using it can work quickly, and even measure distances in fog.

Below: A patient undergoing surgery. To protect him from germs, the surgeon and his team wear gloves and masks, and use sterilized instruments and dressings.

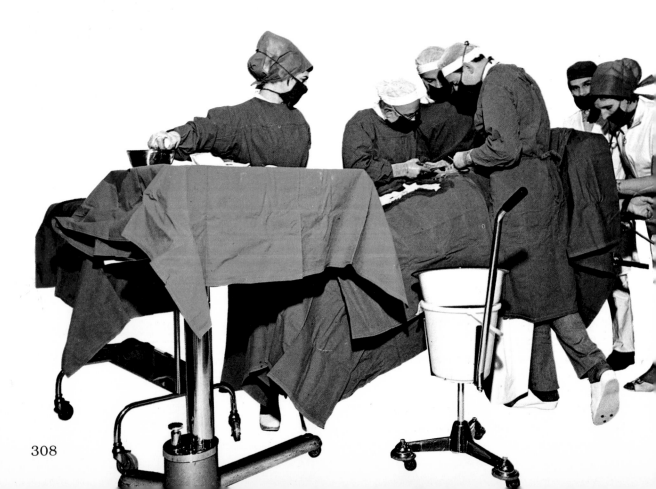

Swan

These big, graceful waterbirds are among the heaviest birds able to fly. To take off, they need a long, clear stretch of water.

Swans swim with webbed feet, lowering their necks to feed on underwater plants. They build bulky nests by pools or rivers. Their young are known as cygnets.

Some kinds of swan fly south in spring and autumn. They fly in V-shaped flocks.

Right: The swan is one of the biggest birds. The mute swan and the whooper swan can have bodies 1.5 metres long. The mute swan can be identified by its bulging forehead. The whooper swan and the Bewick's swan are winter visitors from the north.

Sweden

Sweden is the fourth-largest nation in EUROPE. The country lies in the north, between Norway and the Baltic Sea. Mountains cover most of the west, and forests take up more than half of the land. Their CONIFER trees yield much of the world's softwood. Most of Sweden's electricity comes fron rivers flowing down the mountains. Farmers produce milk, meat, grains and sugar beet on farmlands near the coast. The north is too cold for farming, but it has rich iron mines.

Most of the eight million Swedes live in the south. The capital, Stockholm, is there.

Above: A swan on her large nest. Nearby swim her brown cygnets.

Mute swan

Whooper swan

Bewick's swan

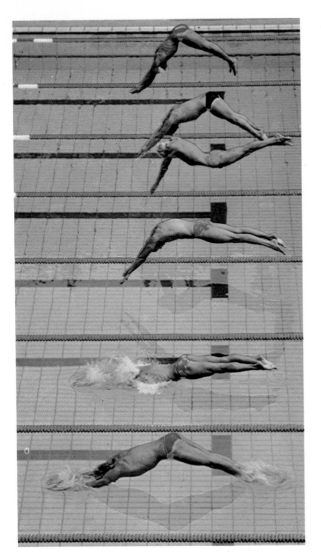

Left: The way a swimmer dives into the water at the start of a race can make a big difference to his chance of winning. There are different racing dives.

The crawl (above) is the fastest swimming stroke. It combines a flutter kick by the legs with a hand-over-hand arm stroke. The leg flutter is done almost entirely from the hips. Correct breathing is a vital part of the stroke.

Switzerland

This small, mountainous country lies in the south-central part of EUROPE. The sharp, snowy peaks of the Alps and their steep-

Below: Skiing in the Swiss Alps.

Swimming

Swimming is the skill or sport of staying afloat and moving through water. Swimming is healthy exercise, and being able to swim may save your life if you fall into water by accident. Many animals know how to swim from birth. But people have to learn, usually with help from a trained instructor.

Learners often start in a pool or at the edge of the sea. First they should float or glide. Then they can try kicking. Arm movements come last. Beginners must learn to fit in breathing with arm movements. Swimmers usually use one or more of five main strokes. These are called the breaststroke, butterfly stroke, backstroke, sidestroke and crawl.

sided valleys fill most of southern Switzerland. In summer, tourists pick wildflowers and watch dairy cattle grazing on the mountain meadows. Winter visitors to the many resorts ski down the snowy alpine slopes.

Most of the country's crops are grown where the mountains meet the lower land of the Swiss Plateau. Here, too, stand most of Switzerland's cities, including Bern, the capital. Swiss factories make chemicals, machinery, watches and chocolates.

Most of the six and a half million Swiss speak German, French or Italian. The Swiss people are among the most prosperous in the world.

Syria

This Arab country lies just east of the Mediterranean Sea. Much of Syria is covered by dry plains that are hot in summer and chilly in winter. There are nearly ten million people. Nomads drive flocks of sheep and goats over the dry lands. Farmers grow grains, grapes and apricots in areas where rivers or rain provide water.

Most Syrian towns grew up on the roads used long ago to bring goods from the East.

During the Arab-Israeli war of 1967,

Holiday resorts in Switzerland are well known for their fresh mountain air and clear lakes. In the summer, boating and mountain climbing are popular activities.

Syria lost the Golan Heights in the southwest of the country to Israel. Syria joined other Arab nations in a war against Israel in 1973. During the 1980s, Syria gave military aid to Lebanese Muslims fighting Lebanese Christians supported by Israel.

Left: The ruins of Palmyra in Syria. Under the Romans it became a very important city. In the late third century AD its queen Zenobia declared her country independent. She was captured by the Romans and the city was destroyed.

Taj Mahal

This is the world's most beautiful tomb. It stands on the Jumna River at Agra in northern India. The emperor, Shah Jahan, built it for his favourite wife, Mumtaz Mahal, who died in 1631. When the Shah died he was buried with his wife in her tomb.

Tape Recorder

A tape recorder turns sound waves into a magnetic pattern on tape. When played, the pattern changes back into sound.

A microphone inside or connected to the recorder changes sound into an electrical signal. This is amplified (made stronger) and fed to the recording head. The head produces a magnetic field which magnetizes the tape as it passes the head.

When playing the tape back, the magnetic field produces an electrical signal which goes to an amplifier and loudspeaker.

Tapestry

Tapestries are designs or pictures woven in cloth. It is a very old craft. The Egyptians made tapestries about 1700 years ago.

Tapestries are made by WEAVING coloured silk thread across rows of strong linen or wool threads held in a frame.

The tapestry design is drawn onto the linen threads with ink. The weaver works from the back of the tapestry.

Below: A simple tape recorder. A recording head consists of a wire coil wound around an iron ring. The ring has a gap in it.

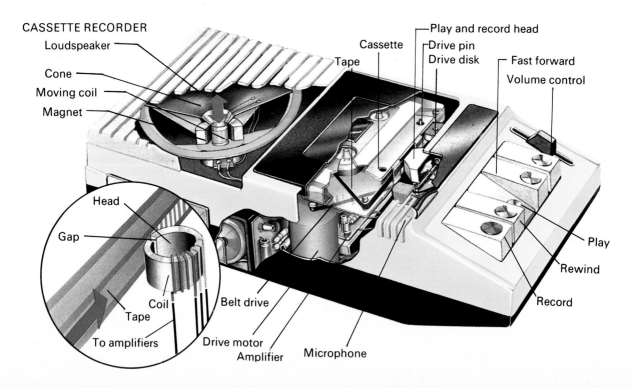

CASSETTE RECORDER

Loudspeaker — Cone — Moving coil — Magnet — Head — Gap — Coil — Tape — To amplifiers — Belt drive — Drive motor — Amplifier — Microphone — Tape — Cassette — Play and record head — Drive pin — Drive disk — Fast forward — Volume control — Play — Rewind — Record

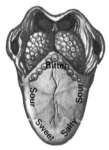

**THE ORGANS OF
SMELL AND TASTE**

*Above: Each patch of
taste buds picks up one
kind of taste. Bitter
tastes are picked up at
the back of the tongue,
sour tastes at the side,
and sweet and salty at
the front.*

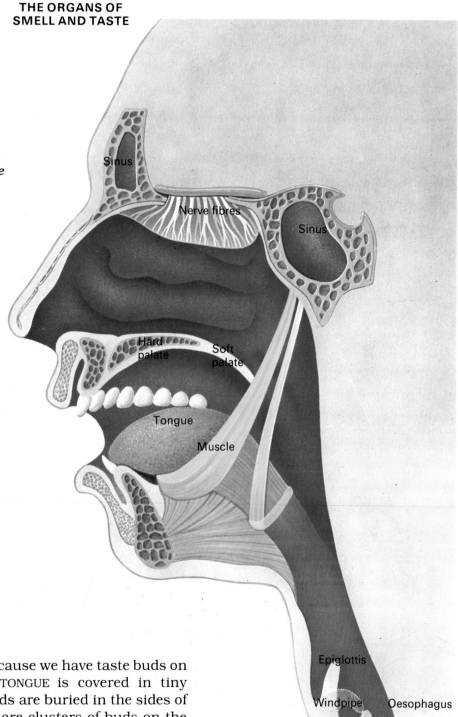

Taste

We can taste food because we have taste buds on
our tongues. Your TONGUE is covered in tiny
bumps. The taste buds are buried in the sides of
these bumps. There are clusters of buds on the
back, tip and sides of the tongue. NERVES running
from the buds to the brain tell you whether the
food you are eating is sweet, sour, bitter or salty.

Flavour is a mixture of the taste and the SMELL
of food. If you have a bad cold and your nose is
blocked, food hardly tastes of anything. The most
comfortable way to take bad-tasting medicine is
to hold your nose while you swallow.

*A cutaway drawing showing where
smells and tastes are picked up.
Nerve fibres high in the nose pick up
outside smells. Smell from food in the
mouth can enter the nose past the soft
palate. Taste buds cluster in groups
on the tongue.*

Tea

Tea is a refreshing drink that is made by pouring boiling water over the dried, chopped leaves of the tea plant.

Tea was first grown in China. It was brought to Europe by the Dutch in the 1660s. Today most tea is grown in northern India, China and Sri Lanka.

Teeth

Teeth are made to cut, tear or crush food so that it can be swallowed. Cutting teeth are called incisors; tearing teeth are called canines; and crushing teeth are called molars. Meat-eating animals have large canines for tearing flesh. Plant-eaters have sharp incisors and large molars for snapping off and grinding stringy stalks. Humans have all three kinds of teeth because we eat all kinds of food.

There are two parts to a tooth. The root, which has one, two or three prongs, is fixed in the jawbone. The crown is the part you can see. Tooth decay happens when bacteria mix with sugar. This dissolves tooth enamel, making holes that let infection get inside the tooth.

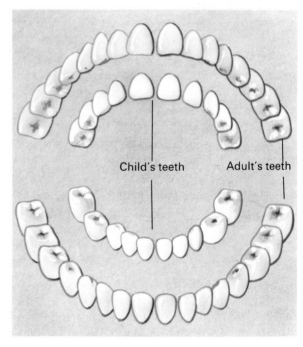

Above: Your first set of teeth are called milk teeth. There are ten on the top, and ten on the bottom. Each row has four incisors at the front, with one canine either side, followed by two molars. As you grow, these teeth fall out and are replaced by an adult set. These are the same as milk teeth but there are 16 molars altogether.

Below: The dentist drills away the decay in a tooth before filling the hole.

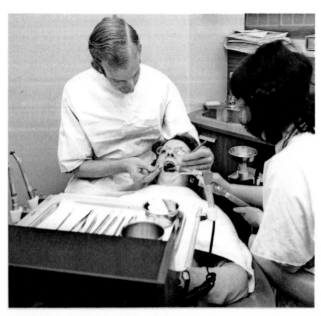

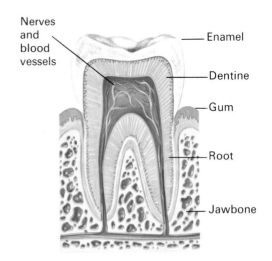

Above: There are three layers to a tooth. Inside is a cavity full of nerves and blood vessels. It is surrounded by a bony wall of dentine. This is covered by hard, shiny enamel.

Telephone

Telephones let you speak to someone far away. When you pick up a telephone receiver (shown in the picture on the right), a weak electric current is switched on. When you speak into the mouthpiece, you speak into a microphone.

Waves of SOUND from your voice hit a metal disc inside the microphone and make it vibrate. These vibrations travel along the telephone wires as electrical waves. When they reach the other end, they hit another metal disc in the earpiece. This changes the vibrations back into sound waves, which the person you are calling hears as your voice.

The first electric telephone, made by Alexander BELL in 1876, produced only a very weak sound over long distances. Today telephone networks use a worldwide system of cables and communications satellites.

The eyepiece of a reflecting telescope is at one side of the telescope, near the top. Light from the object passes down the tube and is reflected back by the concave mirror at the bottom. A small flat mirror directs these rays into the eyepiece.

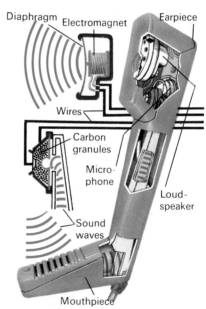

The mouthpiece of a telephone contains a small microphone. The sound waves from your voice make a diaphragm vibrate and this compresses carbon granules in the microphone. An electric current flows through the granules and this varies in strength as you speak. This varying current then flows along wires to the other telephone. There it enters a small loudspeaker in the earpiece. This contains an electromagnet which causes a diaphragm to vibrate as the incoming current varies. This produces the sound of your voice.

Telescope

Telescopes make things that are far away look nearer. They work by gathering the LIGHT from an object and bending it to make a tiny picture called an image. The image is then made larger.

There are two kinds of telescope. The LENS or refractor telescope uses two lenses fixed in a tube to keep out unwanted light. A large lens at one end of the tube collects the light. A smaller lens called the eyepiece makes the image larger.

The image you see through this kind of telescope is upside down. If you want to turn the image the right way around, a third lens is needed.

The other kind of telescope is called a reflecting telescope. Instead of a lens it has a curved mirror to collect light.

The idea of the lens telescope was discovered by accident in 1608 by Hans Lippershey, a Dutch spectacle maker.

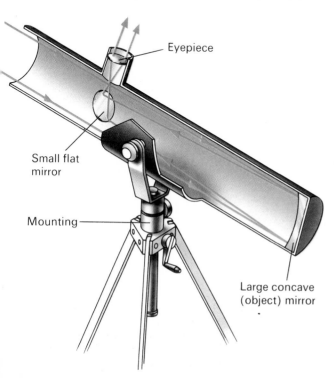

Television

Television is a way of sending sounds and pictures through the air by ELECTRICITY. Scientists have been interested in the idea of television since the 1880s. Although John Logie Baird was the first to show how television worked, his success was based on work by many other scientists from all

Below: The view behind a television screen. The main part of a television is the cathode ray tube. The large end of this tube forms the actual screen. The narrow end of the tube contains either one or three electron guns. These fire electrons through the shadow mask onto the chemical phosphor dots. The shadow mask is a thin plate behind the screen. It has vertical holes in it, and each hole is for one group of dots.

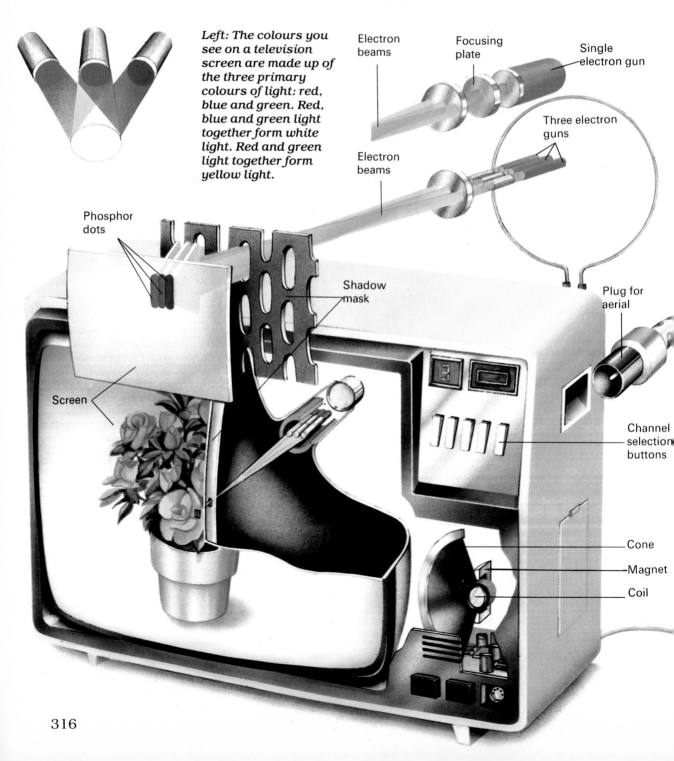

Left: The colours you see on a television screen are made up of the three primary colours of light: red, blue and green. Red, blue and green light together form white light. Red and green light together form yellow light.

Electron beams

Focusing plate

Single electron gun

Three electron guns

Electron beams

Phosphor dots

Shadow mask

Plug for aerial

Screen

Channel selection buttons

Cone

Magnet

Coil

over the world. Baird showed his set in 1926. The first television service opened in 1936 in Britain. Colour television began in the United States in 1956.

At first, all television was black and white. Few people owned television sets because they were very expensive. Now nearly every home has one.

Television works by changing LIGHT waves into electric signals. This happens inside the TV camera. A picture of what is happening in front of the camera forms on a special screen behind the LENS. Behind the screen is an electron gun. This *scans* the screen. It moves from left to right to cover each part of the picture. Each part is turned into an electric signal which is made stronger, then sent to the transmitter. All the signals are broadcast by the transmitter as RADIO waves. They are picked up by home TV aerials and changed back into electric signals. These pass into the TV set.

Inside the set is a large glass tube called the *cathode ray tube*. The screen that you look at is the front of this tube. The screen is covered with tiny chemical dots. In a colour set, these are arranged in groups of three:

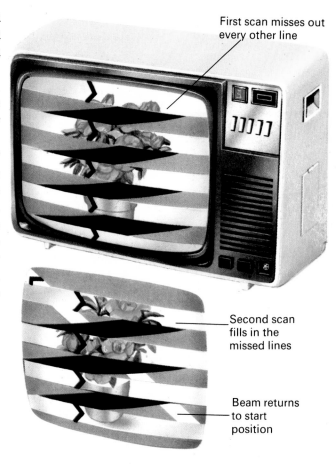

First scan misses out every other line

Second scan fills in the missed lines

Beam returns to start position

Above: The electron beams scan the television screen 50 times each second. The chemical dots glow red, blue, or green to produce the pattern that forms each picture. You can actually see the dots if you go very close to the screen.

Below: People who operate televison cameras wear headphones so that they can get their instructions from the programme director in the control room.

one red, one blue, one green. At the back of the tube is another electron gun. This fires a beam of electrons to scan the screen just as the camera gun does. As each electron hits the screen, it lights up a dot. These tiny flashes of colour build up the picture on your screen. You do not see lines of coloured flashing lights, because the electron gun moves too fast for the eye to follow. What you see is a picture of what is happening in the television studio.

Live television programmes show you what is happening as it happens. Most programmes are recorded on film or *videotape* and sent out later.

Temperature

Temperature is the measurement of heat. It is measured on a scale marked on a THERMOMETER. Most people in the world today use the Celsius or Centigrade scale. The Fahrenheit scale is most often used in the United States.

Some animals, such as mammals like man, are warm-blooded. Their temperature stays much the same. Humans can stand quite a wide range of body temperatures. A healthy man's normal body temperature is 37°C. When he is ill, his temperature might go up to 41°C or more, and he could still survive.

Other animals, such as snakes, lizards and frogs, are cold-blooded. Their body temperature goes up and down with the temperature of their surroundings. Many cold-blooded animals can survive until their body temperature drops almost to freezing point.

Below: Normal human temperature is 37°C (98.6°F). The human body can deal with different temperatures, but cannot adjust easily to extremes.

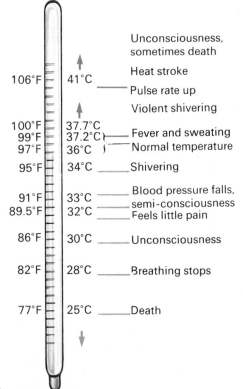

		Unconsciousness, sometimes death
		Heat stroke
106°F	41°C	Pulse rate up
		Violent shivering
100°F	37.7°C	
99°F	37.2°C	Fever and sweating
97°F	36°C	Normal temperature
95°F	34°C	Shivering
91°F	33°C	Blood pressure falls, semi-consciousness
89.5°F	32°C	Feels little pain
86°F	30°C	Unconsciousness
82°F	28°C	Breathing stops
77°F	25°C	Death

Tennis

Tennis is a game for two or four people played on a specially marked court, which is divided in half by a net 90cm high. If two people play it is called a singles match. If four people play it is called a doubles match.

Tennis balls must be about 50mm in diameter and weigh about 56.7 grams. A tennis racket can be any size.

A tennis match is divided into sets. Usually women play three sets and men play five. Each set has at least six games. To win a game, one player must score at least four points. Modern tennis is a simple version of an old French game called real tennis or royal tennis.

Chris Evert Lloyd, who won the Women's All-England Singles Championships at Wimbledon in 1981.

Teresa, Mother

Agnes Gonxha Bojaxhiu was born in 1910 in Skopje, which is now in Yugoslavia. She gave up her life in a Catholic convent in India to devote herself to helping the poor in the slums of Calcutta.

In 1948 she founded a new order of nuns called the Missionaries of Charity. The woman who had come to be known as Mother Teresa of Calcutta was awarded the Nobel Peace Prize in 1979.

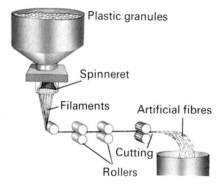

Plastic granules

Spinneret

Filaments

Artificial fibres

Cutting

Rollers

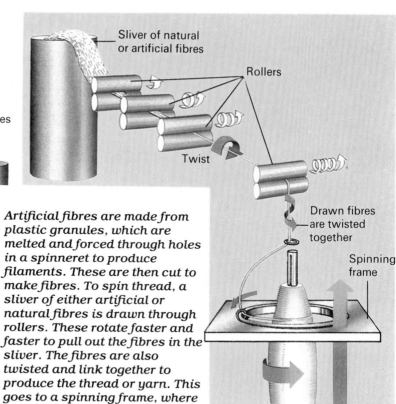

Sliver of natural or artificial fibres

Rollers

Twist

Drawn fibres are twisted together

Spinning frame

Bobbin

Artificial fibres are made from plastic granules, which are melted and forced through holes in a spinneret to produce filaments. These are then cut to make fibres. To spin thread, a sliver of either artificial or natural fibres is drawn through rollers. These rotate faster and faster to pull out the fibres in the sliver. The fibres are also twisted and link together to produce the thread or yarn. This goes to a spinning frame, where the thread is twisted again as it is wound on to a bobbin. The thread is then ready to be woven into cloth.

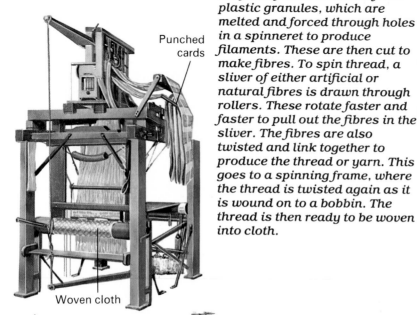

Punched cards

Woven cloth

The automatic loom was invented by Joseph Marie Jacquard. Cards punched with holes were fed into the loom to make it weave a particular pattern.

In 1779, Samuel Crompton invented the spinning mule, which could spin several kinds of yarn.

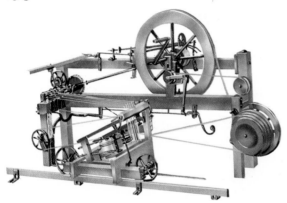

Textile

A textile is any cloth made by WEAVING. Before the INDUSTRIAL REVOLUTION, all cloth was made by hand from natural fibres of wool, silk, cotton or linen. Since then, scientists have developed many kinds of man-made fibre. Rayon is made from wood. Nylon comes from oil. There are even some fibres made from glass. Man-made fibres are cheaper and often easier to wash and take care of. Sometimes they are mixed with natural fibres to get the best of both materials.

Thailand

Thailand is a country in South-East ASIA. It sits in the middle of Burma, Laos and Kampuchea. The south coast opens onto

Above: Huge figures of demons guard a Buddhist temple in Bangkok.

the Gulf of Thailand, which is part of the South China Sea. Bangkok, the capital city, is on the coast.

Thailand is more than twice the size of the United Kingdom, and about 50 million people live there. Most of them live in the central part of the country. Many rivers flow through this area, making it very fertile. Most people are farmers. Rice is the main crop. They also grow cotton, tobacco, maize, coconuts and bananas. In the north there are large forests of teak, which is a major export. The peninsula in the south-west is very rich in minerals, especially tin.

Thailand was called Siam before 1939. Thai means 'free', so Thailand means the land of the free. There is a king, but the country is ruled by an elected government.

Theatre

A theatre is a place where plays are performed by actors and watched by an audience. The theatre may be just a patch of ground or a large, expensive building.

The earliest theatres we know about were in Greece. They were simply flattened patches of ground on a hillside. The audience sat in rows on the hill above so that they could all see the 'stage'. When the Greeks built theatres, they cut a half-moon shape in the hillside and lined it with rows

Left: The theatre at Delphi, built in the 4th century BC. The first stone theatres were circular, with seats completely surrounding the central earth floor. Later the seats were arranged in a semicircle. Behind the orchestra was a building from which the actors came to the stage. Later still movable scenery was used, while complicated machinery behind the building was used for special effects. For thunder, pebbles were rolled on copper sheets. Mirrors were flashed for lighting. The theatres were so skilfully built that even people sitting right at the back could hear every word spoken by an actor.

Above: One of the kinds of drama created by the Japanese is called kabuki. *This involves song and dance and was started in the 1600s. It is still popular today.*

of stone seats that looked down on a round, flat stage.

The Romans copied the Greek pattern, but they built most of their theatres on flat ground. The rows of seats were held up by a wall. The Romans built a theatre in nearly every large town in the Roman Empire.

In Britain, there were no theatre buildings before the 1500s. Troops of actors travelled around using their carts as stages. Later, they performed in rich people's houses and in the courtyards of inns. The first theatres to be built were made of wood and looked very much like inns. The stage jutted out into a large yard. Galleries of seats ran all around the sides. There were even seats on the stage, but only for rich people. These theatres had no roofs. When it rained, the *groundlings*, people who stood in the yard around the edge of the stage, got wet. SHAKESPEARE'S plays were performed in theatres like this.

Later on, theatres had proper roofs. The stage was moved back and the audience sat in rows in front of it.

Thermometer

A thermometer is an instrument that measures TEMPERATURE. It is usually a glass tube marked with a scale. Inside is another, thinner glass tube, which ends in a bulb containing liquid mercury or alcohol. When the temperature goes up, the mercury or the alcohol gets warm and expands (grows bigger). It rises up the tube. When it stops, you can read the temperature on the marked scale. When it gets cold, the mercury contracts (grows smaller) and sinks down the tube. If alcohol is used in a thermometer it is usually coloured red. Most thermometers measure temperatures between the boiling and freezing points of water. This is between 0° and 100° on the Celsius scale or 32° and 212° on the Fahrenheit scale. Most countries use the Celsius scale.

Medical thermometers, which are small enough to go in your mouth, measure your blood heat. Household thermometers tell you how warm or cold the air is inside or outside your house.

Use a household thermometer to keep a record of weather conditions.

Thermostat

A thermostat is an instrument that keeps a TEMPERATURE steady. It is usually part of a central heating system. It switches the boiler on or off when the temperature gets too low or high. Thermostats are also fitted in cars, spacecraft and other machinery.

Until recently, thermostats were made with metal strips inside. When the strips got hot, they expanded (grew bigger). They had to bend to fit into their space. When they bent, they broke electrical contacts. This switched the boiler or heater off. Modern thermostats are electronic. They can work in temperatures that would melt most metals.

Below: A metal strip thermostat. When the strip gets hot it bends. This stops the flow of electricity.

To heater   To heater

The Third World Fali tribe in the Cameroon live in grass huts with thatched roofs. Several huts are built together forming small villages.

Third World

The Third World is a polite way of describing the poorer nations in our world. The first two 'worlds' are the rich and powerful nations of the East, led by the communist countries of the SOVIET UNION and CHINA; and the western countries, of which the most powerful is the UNITED STATES.

The Third World countries are in ASIA, AFRICA and SOUTH AMERICA. Many of them supply the rest of the world with cheap food, minerals, timber and fibres, as well as cheap labour. This pattern of wealth in one part of the world and poverty in another is very difficult to change. The rest of the countries in the world do not want to give up the wealth and power they have been used to for so long. This means that many countries in the Third World go on getting poorer while the rich countries go on getting richer.

Thunderstorm

Thunderstorms are caused by ELECTRICITY in the air. Different electrical charges build up inside big rain clouds. When the charges are strong enough, a spark leaps from one charged part of the cloud to another. Sometimes the spark jumps from the cloud to the ground. We see the spark as LIGHTNING. Lightning heats up the air. The air expands (gets bigger) so quickly that it explodes, making the crashing noise we call thunder.

Since sound travels much slower than LIGHT, you always hear thunder after you see lightning in a thunderstorm. It takes thunder about three seconds to travel one kilometre. To find out how many kilometres away the storm is, you count the number of seconds between seeing the lightning and hearing the thunder, and divide the number by three.

Tide

Tides are regular movements of the OCEANS. They are mainly caused by the MOON. The moon is like a giant magnet. It tugs the oceans toward it as it loops around the earth. The earth is spinning at the same time, so most places get two high tides and two low tides about every 24 hours.

High tide happens when the water flows as far inland as it can. Low tide happens when it flows out as far as it can.

Right: When the sun and moon are pulling in the same direction at the oceans, there is a very high, or spring, tide. When the sun and moon are pulling against each other at right angles, there is a very low, or neap, tide. Spring tides occur when there is a full, or new, moon. The red arrows show the pull of gravity.

A storm cloud is like a giant electricity generator. The positive charge is at the top of the cloud and the negative charge at the base. Lightning is the spark between the two: first within a cloud, then from cloud to cloud, and then from cloud to Earth. The diagram shows a typical storm cloud. For a hailstorm, the top of the cloud must be above freezing level and there must be rapidly rising convection currents swirling up through the cloud. These carry up droplets which freeze near the top of the cloud and begin to fall.

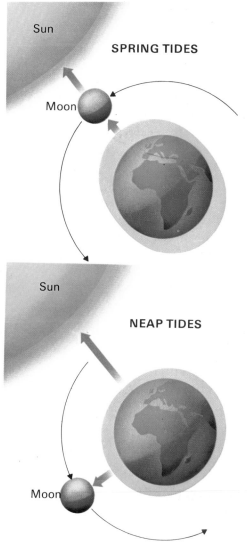

Sun

SPRING TIDES

Moon

Sun

NEAP TIDES

Moon

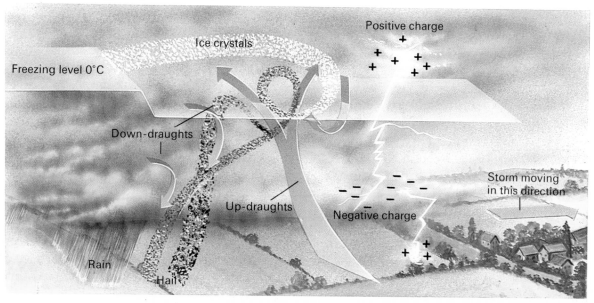

Ice crystals

Positive charge

Freezing level 0°C

Down-draughts

Up-draughts

Negative charge

Storm moving in this direction

Rain

Hail

Tigers are rarely seen on open ground. They prefer the cool shade of forests. If it gets too hot they like to go swimming.

Tin is found in the rich mud of river beds in Malaysia.

Tiger

Tigers are the biggest members of the cat family. They live in the forests of Asia and Indonesia, and hunt deer or large cattle. Tigers usually lie still during the day, and hunt alone by night. They are very strong. One tiger can pull a dead buffalo that is so heavy a group of men would find it difficult to move.

Until the 1800s, thousands of tigers roamed through the forests of Asia. Then men began to shoot them, and as a result they are now very rare.

Tin

Tin is one of the oldest metals known to man. People were mining tin before IRON was discovered. Tin was mixed with copper to make bronze.

Tin was mined in Cornwall long before the birth of Christ. An ancient people called the Phoenicians sailed from the Mediterranean to trade cloth and precious stones for it.

Tin cans are made from sheets of steel that have been coated with tin. Tin does not rust.

Tin is not a common metal. The main tin mines are in Bolivia, south-eastern Asia, and western Africa.

Toad

Toads are AMPHIBIANS. They look very much like FROGS. Toads have no teeth, a rough and warty skin and are usually fatter and clumsier than frogs. They spend less time in the water than frogs, but most of them mate and lay their eggs in water, and spend the first part of their lives as tadpoles.

Toads eat slugs, snails, caterpillars, insects and other small animals. They flick out their long sticky tongues to catch food.

Toads tend to live in drier places than frogs and they have better-developed lungs. All capture living prey, such as worms, slugs and insects; most catch it with a long, sticky tongue which is fired out at great speed.

Toads' tongues move so fast that you cannot see them. They can catch insects as they fly. If attacked, toads can produce poison from the two bumps behind their eyes. This poison covers their skin, and makes the toads harmful to most of their enemies.

Tobacco

Tobacco is made from the dried leaves of the plant *Nicotiana*, which belongs to the same family as potatoes. It was first found in America, but is now grown all over the world. The Spanish traveller Francisco Hernández brought it to Europe in 1599.

Tobacco leaves can be rolled together to make cigars, or shredded up to be smoked in pipes or cigarettes. Smoking is very bad for your health. It is particularly harmful to the lungs and heart.

Tongue

The tongue is a muscular, flexible flap inside the mouth. Only VERTEBRATES have tongues. Our tongues help us to TASTE and eat food, and to talk. The letters T and D for instance, cannot be said without using the tongue in a special way.

In toads, the tongue is at the front of the mouth. Snakes have forked or split tongues which can 'smell' the air. Cats' tongues are covered with tiny hooks of flesh. Cats can use their tongues like combs to clean their fur.

Tornadoes can cause a lot of damage. In 1925, a tornado in the United States lasted three hours, killing 684 people.

Tornado

Tornadoes are violent, whirling windstorms. Most of them happen in America, but they can occur anywhere in the world.

Hurricanes are strong winds that build up over the sea. Tornadoes build up over land, when large masses of CLOUDS meet. The clouds begin to whirl around each other. Gradually, they join together to make a gigantic, twisting funnel. When this touches the ground, it sucks up anything in its path—trees, houses, animals, trains or people.

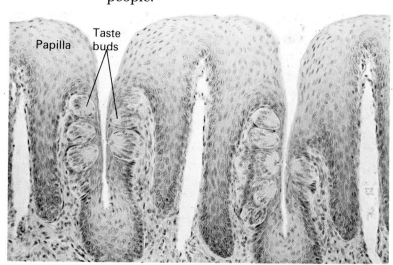

Papilla
Taste buds

Humans and other mammals have tongues covered with tiny bumps called papillae. *You can just about see them if you look in a mirror. Inside a papilla are taste buds and nerve endings. These make the tongue sensitive to taste, heat, pain and pressure. The tip of the tongue is the most sensitive spot in the body.*

Torpedo

A torpedo is a cigar-shaped weapon used to sink ships. It is propelled by an electric motor or engine. Its nose contains devices that guide it to its target. The *warhead*, behind the nose, has a device that makes the torpedo explode. Some torpedoes explode near a ship's hull. Others explode when they hit the ship. Surface vessels such as motor torpedo boats (below) and destroyers use torpedoes. So do submarines and aircraft. ROCKETS can carry them to distant targets.

Tortoise

Giant tortoises live in the Galapagos Islands and islands in the Indian Ocean. They can weigh up to 225kg and be 1.8 metres long. Some large tortoises live for over 150 years.

Tortoises are slow-moving REPTILES. They can walk only about 4.5 metres in a minute. When frightened, they pull their heads and legs inside their domed shells. The 40 or so kinds of tortoise live on land in warm parts of the world. They are similar to TURTLES and terrapins, but these reptiles live in water.

Touch

There are different nerve cells in your skin called receptors that respond to five main kinds of touch. These are light touch, heavy touch (pressure), pain, heat and cold. Receptors pass sensations along NERVES to the brain.

Pain receptors are the most numerous; cold receptors the least numerous. Some parts of the body, such as the tongue and fingertips, have more receptors than others.

We also have receptors inside the body. Usually we do not realize that these are working, except when they produce sensations such as hunger or tiredness.

Below: Different kinds of receptors in the skin:
1. *Pressure-sensitive endings*
2. *Heat receptor*
3. *Nerve fibres wrapped around hair bases*
4. *Free nerve endings, sensitive to pain*
5. *Touch receptor*
6. *Cold receptor*

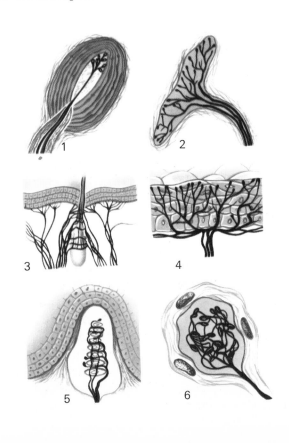

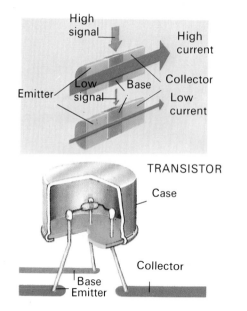

TRANSISTOR

A transistor has three layers. The inner layer, or base, *the* emitter *and the* collector. *An electric current flowing from emitter to collector is stopped by the base. If an electric signal being fed to the base increases, the base lets more current through. If it decreases, less current passes. Because the current is greater than the base signal, the transistor is acting as an amplifier.*

Transistor

Transistors are small ELECTRONIC devices. They are usually made to amplify (strengthen) electric currents in electronic equipment such as radios, televisions, computers and satellites. They can also switch electric currents on and off. Transistors have largely replaced other devices, called valves, which were once used for the same purpose.

Today complicated circuits containing thousands of transistors can be put into SILICON CHIPS that are only a fraction of an inch square. The first practical transistors were developed in the 1940s by the American scientists Walter Brattain, John Bardeen and William Shockley. The invention of transistors completely revolutionized electronics and millions of these devices are now made every year.

Tree

Trees are the largest of all PLANTS. They are woody plants with a thick central stem, or trunk. Most trees grow to more than 7 metres high. The biggest tree is a type of sequoia. These giants can grow to over 100 metres high, and can measure 25 metres around the trunk. Trees can also live a long time. One bristle-cone pine in California in the United States is nearly 5000 years old.

Above the ground is the *crown* of the tree. This is made up of the trunk, branches, twigs and leaves. The *roots* are below the ground. They are the fastest growing part of the tree. They support the crown like a giant anchor. The roots take in water, which has minerals dissolved in it, from the soil. The water is drawn up through the trunk to the leaves. A fully grown apple tree takes in about 360 litres of water a day.

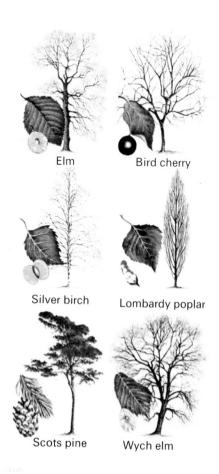

Elm

Bird cherry

Silver birch

Lombardy poplar

Scots pine

Wych elm

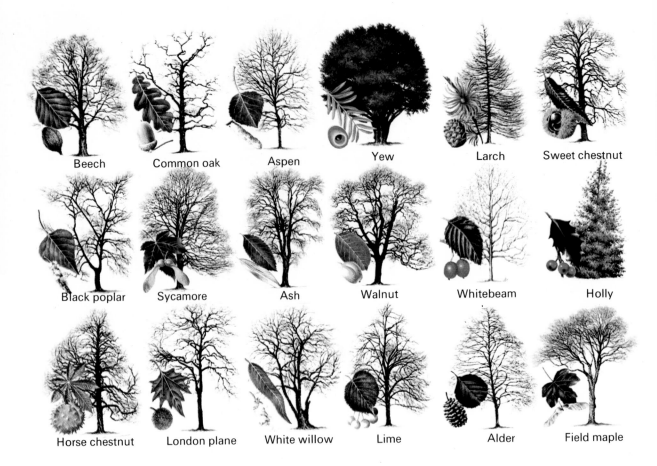

Beech   Common oak   Aspen   Yew   Larch   Sweet chestnut

Black poplar   Sycamore   Ash   Walnut   Whitebeam   Holly

Horse chestnut   London plane   White willow   Lime   Alder   Field maple

There are two main kinds of trees. CONIFERS are trees with needlelike leaves, such as pines and spruces. In place of flowers, they produce their seeds in cones. Most conifers are evergreens. This means that they do not lose their leaves in the autumn. Conifers grow in cold or dry regions.

The other kind of tree is the flowering, or broad-leaved, tree. Many of them, such as elms and oaks, are *deciduous*; that is, they lose their leaves in the autumn. But some broad-leaved trees, such as holly and many tropical forest trees, are evergreen. Broad-leaved trees have flowers which develop into FRUITS that completely surround the seeds. These trees are often called hardwoods, because of their tough, hard wood. It is harder than that of the softwood conifers.

The traditional tree of England is the oak. In Norman times the country was covered with great oak forests, in which wild boars roamed.

Above and on the previous page: These drawings of 24 common trees will help you to identify them. Points to look for are overall shape, the shapes of the leaves, and the appearance of the seeds.

Below: When a tree trunk is cut, you can see the annual rings. Each ring shows the new wood grown in the trunk in one year. The number of rings tells you the age of the tree.

Triangle

A triangle is a shape with three straight sides. Triangles are important in GEOMETRY. If we know some ANGLES and sides in a triangle, we can work out the others by using MATHEMATICS.

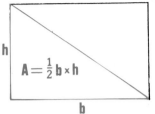 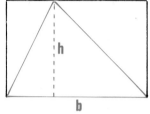

$$A = \frac{1}{2} b \times h$$

The area of a rectangle is found by multiplying its length by its width (or base × height). A triangle is half a rectangle. So the area of a triangle is a half of the base multiplied by the height.

The brightly striped Surgeon fish.

Trojan War

The Trojan war was fought in about 1200 BC between the Trojans of Troy and the Greeks. It lasted for 10 years. The poet Homer, in his poem the *Iliad*, tells the story of only a few days of the war. We know the story of the rest of the war from other writings.

Paris was a prince of Troy. He fell in love with Helen, the wife of King Menelaus of Sparta in Greece. Paris took Helen to Troy, and Menelaus with other Greek kings and soldiers went to get her back. They besieged Troy for years. In the end they won by tricking the Trojans with a huge wooden horse filled with Greek soldiers, which they left standing outside the city. The Trojans, thinking that the horse was a gift, took it inside the city walls. The hidden soldiers then opened the gates and Troy was destroyed. No one knows if the story was true.

Right: This Greek vase shows scenes from the Trojan War. A warrior is about to kill the Trojan king, who is on the ground. The goddess Aphrodite bars the way of Menelaus, who wants to kill Helen, his former wife.

Tropical Fish

Tropical fish are among the prettiest fish in the world. They live in the warm seas of tropical regions, often along the edges of CORAL reefs.

Many small, brightly coloured, freshwater tropical fish are popular aquarium pets. Marine fish can also be kept, but they are

more expensive and difficult to look after. They have to have salt water containing just the right amount of salt to live in.

Tropical fish live in warm water. Most tanks have a heater to keep the water at around 24°C. A cover on the tank holds the heat in and stops the water from evaporating (drying up). Electric light bulbs in the cover light the tank and also heat the water. Most aquariums have air pumps that add OXYGEN to the water and filter it to keep it clear. Water plants also provide oxygen. Food for tropical fish can be bought at pet shops.

The most common tropical freshwater fish is the guppy. Other common tropical fish are angelfish, barbs and neon tetras.

Tudors

The House of Tudor was an English royal family which ruled England from 1485 to 1603. The first Tudor King was HENRY VII. He was a grandson of a Welsh squire, Owen Tudor, who had married Henry V's widow. Henry VII came to the throne after defeating Richard III at the Battle of Bosworth. This ended the Wars of the Roses (1455–1485) between the houses of Lancaster and York. To join the houses, Henry VII, who belonged to a branch of Lancaster, married Elizabeth of York.

Henry VII was succeeded by his son, HENRY VIII. During the reign of Henry VIII the arts flourished in England. The King used Parliament to pass laws that broke all ties between England and the ROMAN CATHOLIC CHURCH.

Henry VIII was succeeded first by his son, EDWARD VI, then by his daughters, Mary I and ELIZABETH I. When Elizabeth died in 1603, the crown went to King James VI of Scotland, the first of the STUART kings.

The Tudors were strong rulers. During their time, England became richer and more powerful, especially at sea. The voyages of England's daring seamen led to more trade and new colonies. SHAKESPEARE wrote his plays during the reign of Elizabeth I.

Angelfish

The original angelfish *is shown above. The small variety below is from the Pacific. The Imperial can be 40cm long.*

Black and gold angelfish

Imperial angelfish

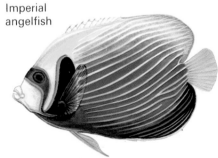

Below: The lyretail wrasse *swimming over a tropical reef.*

Tuna

The tuna, also called tunny, is a large, firm fish, rich in PROTEINS and VITAMINS. Most tuna live in warm seas, but they may swim into northern waters in summer. Different kinds of tuna include the bluefin, which may be 3 metres long, and the albacore. Tuna are the only fish whose body temperature is higher than that of the water around them.

The tuna's body is streamlined and it can reach speeds of 48km/hr. Tuna live in big shoals and feed on other fish.

Tunnel

Tunnelling is important in mining, transportation and water supply. The Romans built tunnels to carry water. And today, a tunnel that brings water to New York City is the world's longest. It is 169km long.

Different methods are used to build tunnels. In hard rock, the tunnel is blasted out with explosives. Cutting machines, like those used to drill oil wells, are used in softer rock. In the softest rocks, *tunnel shields* are used. These are giant steel tubes, the same size as the intended tunnel. The front edge of the shield is sharp and is pushed into the earth. The earth is dug out, and the tunnel behind the shield is lined to stop it from caving in.

Some tunnels under rivers are built by lowering sections of tunnel into the river. Divers join them together. When the tunnel is complete, the water is pumped out. Underground railway tunnels can be built in deep trenches. When they are finished, the tunnel is covered over.

The Channel tunnel joining Britain to France is one of the biggest tunnelling tasks ever undertaken.

Right: The tunnel diggers commonly used today are automatic machines called moles. Rotating cutters at the front of the mole dig out the soil or rock, which is then taken away by a conveyor belt. As the mole moves forward, engineers line the tunnel with panels to form its walls. The mole is powered by electric motors and hydraulic jacks. These receive hydraulic fluid along lines from the surface. Bad conditions such as waterlogged soil can slow down the tunnelling. But when conditions are good, the mole can dig out a trainsize tunnel at a rate of 5 metres an hour.

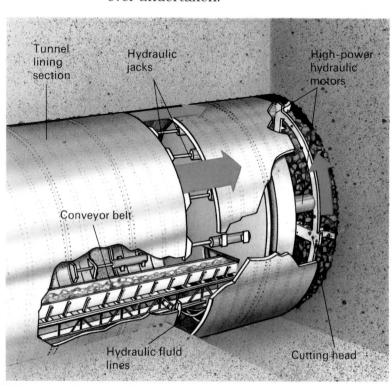

Tunnel lining section

Hydraulic jacks

High-power hydraulic motors

Conveyor belt

Hydraulic fluid lines

Cutting head

Turbine

A turbine is a machine, in which a wheel, drum or screw is turned around by fast-flowing water, or by steam or gas. Water wheels and WINDMILLS are simple turbines.

Water turbines are used in hydroelectric power stations. The force of water carried through a pipe from a dam turns the turbine. The turbine does not produce electricity. But as the turbine spins it drives a generator, which produces the electricity. Some turbines are wheels or drums, with blades or cup-shaped buckets round their edges. Other are shaped like screws or propellers.

Steam turbines are operated by jets of steam. They have many uses. They are used to produce electricity, to propel ships and to operate pumps. Gas turbines are turned by fast-moving jets of gas. The gases are produced by burning fuels such as oil. Gas turbines turn the propellers of aircraft.

Right: In a steam turbine, high-pressure steam is directed through fixed blades to strike the blades of a series of turbine wheels. The steam expands as it passes through each set of blades, driving the wheels round. The fixed blades direct the steam onto the turbine blades at the correct angle.

Turkish harvest. Wheat, sugar beet and barley are Turkey's chief crops.

Turkey

Turkey is a country which is partly in EUROPE and partly in ASIA. The small European part covers three percent of the land. It lies west of the waterway that links the Black Sea to the Mediterranean Sea. This part includes the largest city, Istanbul, which was once called Constantinople. The Asian part, sometimes called Anatolia or Asia Minor, includes the capital, Ankara.

Most of Turkey's 49 million people follow the religion of ISLAM. Much of the land is mountainous and large areas are covered

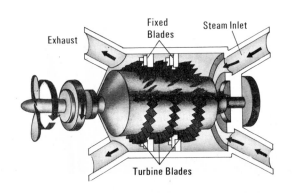

Exhaust — Fixed Blades — Steam Inlet — Turbine Blades

by dry plateaus (tablelands). But the coastal plains are fertile and farming is the main industry.

Turkey was once part of the Byzantine empire, which was the eastern part of the ROMAN EMPIRE. But after Constantinople fell in 1453, the Muslim Ottoman conquerors built up a huge empire. At its height, it stretched from southern Russia to Morocco, and from the Danube River to the Persian Gulf. But it declined after 1600 and collapsed in World War I. After that war Turkey's president, Kemal Atatürk, modernized the nation.

Turtle

A turtle is a REPTILE with a shell. Some turtles live in the sea, some in fresh water, and some on land. The shells of turtles are made of bony plates covered by horny scales. Turtles that live on land are often called TORTOISES. Most sea turtles have flatter shells than tortoises, and are more streamlined. Sometimes turtles are called terrapins, especially the kinds of turtles that people eat.

Marine, or sea, turtles spend most of their lives in warm seas. They swim great distances to find food, and eat water plants and small sea animals. Sea turtles go ashore to lay eggs. They usually bury their eggs in the sand, or hide them among weeds to keep them warm and safe.

Baby sea turtles hatch out on their own, dig themselves out of their nest, and head for the sea. This journey is dangerous because their shells are still soft. Crabs, snakes and birds are waiting to snap them up before they reach the water.

Typewriter

Typewriters are hand-operated writing machines. They produce letters and figures, which look like lines of type in a book. When you strike a key on the keyboard, it moves a metal bar. A raised letter on the end of this bar is pressed against an inked ribbon. This marks an inked image of the letter onto a sheet of paper which is held in a roller.

The first practical typewriter was invented in 1867 by an American, Christopher Latham Sholes (1819–1890).

Today's typewriters contain electronics. They can type semi-automatically and some can store the work that has been typed. They also have an error-correction key for erasing mistakes.

Left: Green turtles *hatching. This marine turtle is becoming rare because its eggs are eaten in Asian countries and it is used to make turtle soup. The* hawksbill *turtle nearly became extinct because its shell was used for 'tortoise shell' ornaments and jewellery. The largest marine turtle is the* leatherback. *It can weigh more than 725 kg and measure up to 1.8 metres long. The leatherback has smooth, leathery skin instead of scales.*

This Greek vase shows Ulysses and one of his men driving a stake into the eye of the one-eyed giant.

Uganda

Uganda is a small republic in the middle of East AFRICA. It was ruled by Britain until 1962, when it became independent. General Idi Amin seized power in 1971. Many people were murdered under his dictatorship. But in 1979, Ugandans and Tanzanian soldiers took over Uganda and Amin fled.

Part of Africa's largest lake, Lake Victoria, lies in Uganda. Most of the 14 million people are farmers. The main crops are coffee, tea and cotton. Uganda's capital is Kampala.

Ulysses

Ulysses is the Roman name for a Greek hero called Odysseus. His adventures during a ten-year journey home after the TROJAN WAR are told in HOMER'S poem, the *Odyssey*.

On his journey he was captured by a cyclops—a one-eyed, man-eating giant. A witch called Circe changed Ulysses' men into pigs. And sirens (sea maidens) lured his men to their deaths. When he finally reached home, his wife, Penelope, was surrounded by suitors. She had agreed to marry any man who could shoot an arrow from Ulysses' bow through 12 rings. Ulysses, in disguise, was the only man to do this. He then killed all the suitors.

United Kingdom

The United Kingdom of Great Britain and Northern IRELAND is the eleventh largest nation in Europe. ENGLAND, Wales and Scotland make up the island of Great Britain, which takes up most of the BRITISH ISLES. Northern Ireland, Scotland and

Below: Queen Elizabeth II opening Parliament. Members of Parliament are chosen by the people and form the government that makes Great Britain's laws.

Above: A Norwegian soldier on duty in Lebanon. He is there as part of a United Nations peacekeeping force.

Wales are mountainous. The highest mountain is Ben Nevis in Scotland. Plains and valleys cover much of England. The longest river is the Thames, which flows through southern England. The British climate is mild.

About 56 million people live in the United Kingdom. Few other countries are so crowded. Four out of five people live in cities such as Belfast, Glasgow and LONDON. London is the capital. Great Britain grows half of the food she needs. Her industries help to pay for the food that is bought from abroad. The United Kingdom manufactures a wide range of goods. Service industries, such as tourism, which provide services rather than producing goods, are increasing. Traditional industries, such as coal mining, are declining.

United Nations

Most of the world's countries belong to the United Nations. This is an association that works to keep peace and help people everywhere.

Each member country sends delegates to regular meetings of the United Nations' General Assembly in New York City. The General Assembly suggests how countries should behave. It cannot make them take its advice. But the United Nations' Security Council can ask member countries for troops to help stop nations from fighting.

The United Nations works largely through 14 groups. The Food and Agriculture Organization helps countries to grow more food. The World Health Organization fights disease. The International Monetary Fund lends countries money.

The United Nations has managed to prevent some wars and has helped millions of people.

United States of America

The United States of America is the world's fourth largest nation. Russia, Canada and China are bigger in area, and more people live in China, India and Russia. There are 50 states in the United States. Forty-eight are in the same part of NORTH AMERICA. The other two are Alaska in the north and the Pacific islands of Hawaii in the south.

The mainland of the United States stretches from the Pacific to the Atlantic. Long mountain ranges run down the Pacific coast. Inland are flat-topped mountains and basins. In this region is Death Valley, the lowest place in the Americas. Here too is the Grand Canyon, a huge gorge cut by the Colorado River. Farther east lie the tall peaks of the Rocky Mountains that run from Canada to Mexico. Beyond these stretch the central Plains where the mighty Mississippi River flows. Another mountain range, the Appalachians, runs down the eastern side of the United States.

The United States is a young country. In 1976 it was just 200 years old. The original 13 colonies declared their independence from Britain in 1776, when the REVOLUTIONARY WAR broke out. A peace treaty was signed in 1783, and two years later the

Above: Combine harvesters gather wheat. Today vast wheat fields cover the plains where prairie grasses used to grow and great herds of buffalo roamed.

Right: the Capitol building in Washington DC where the US government sits.

These clocks below show that the sun rises in the east of the United States three hours before it rises in the west. Because America is so wide, it is divided into four time zones.

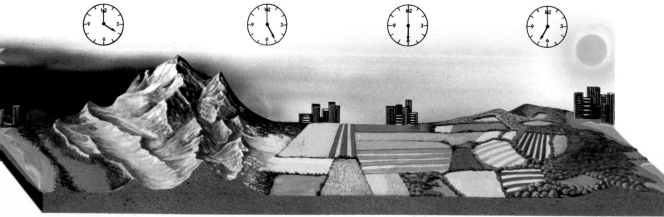

Constitution was drawn up. This is still the basis of US government today. George Washington was elected first president in 1789. By the mid 1800s the United States looked much as it does today. Explorers had added new land to the original colonies, and the country stretched as far west as the Pacific. From 1861 to 1865 the CIVIL WAR was fought between the South, which believed in SLAVERY, and the North, which wanted every person to be free. The northern states won and slavery was abolished. Between 1870 and 1900 thousands of Europeans came and settled in the United States. They were seeking land and a new life. By 1900 the country's population had doubled.

German submarine attacks on American ships brought the United States into WORLD WAR I in 1917. After the war, the Senate rejected President Woodrow Wilson's wish to join the newly formed League of Nations.

During the 1920s America was very prosperous. The ban on alcoholic drinks—the Prohibition—encouraged gangsters and 'bootleggers'. In 1929 the prosperous years came to an end when the stock market collapsed. This was called the Wall Street Crash, and the period of the Great Depression started. President Franklin D. Roosevelt was in office at this time. His New Deal policy was aimed at cutting unemployment and ending the depression.

In 1939 WORLD WAR II broke out. The United States entered the war in 1941, when the Japanese attacked Pearl Harbor in Hawaii. Toward the end of the war, Roosevelt died and Vice-President Harry S. Truman became president.

During the 1950s and 1960s the United States fought two wars in Asia. The first was defending South KOREA from takeover by North Koreans. The second war was against communist forces in VIETNAM.

The 234 million citizens of the United States include Eskimos, Indians and people whose ancestors came from Europe or Africa. Seventy in every 100 Americans live in cities. Washington DC is the capital but

Above: Disneyland in Anaheim, California, is a playground for both young and old. It was built by the film producer Walt Disney and opened in 1955.

New York is the largest city. Los Angeles and Chicago each have over two million inhabitants.

The United States is the world's richest country. Its farms produce huge wheat crops, and more oranges, meat, eggs and cheese than any other country. American miners mine more coal, copper, lead and uranium. The United States is the world's largest manufacturer of motor cars and chemicals.

Until recently the United States produced enough coal, oil and gas of its own to run its farms, factories and homes. But now it has to buy oil from abroad.

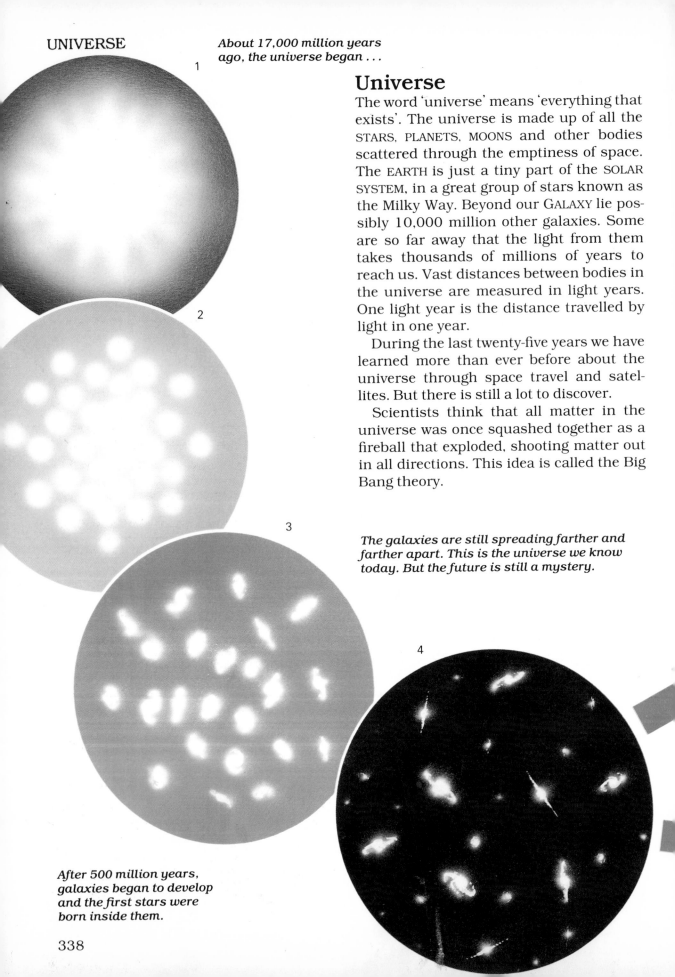

About 17,000 million years ago, the universe began . . .

Universe

The word 'universe' means 'everything that exists'. The universe is made up of all the STARS, PLANETS, MOONS and other bodies scattered through the emptiness of space. The EARTH is just a tiny part of the SOLAR SYSTEM, in a great group of stars known as the Milky Way. Beyond our GALAXY lie possibly 10,000 million other galaxies. Some are so far away that the light from them takes thousands of millions of years to reach us. Vast distances between bodies in the universe are measured in light years. One light year is the distance travelled by light in one year.

During the last twenty-five years we have learned more than ever before about the universe through space travel and satellites. But there is still a lot to discover.

Scientists think that all matter in the universe was once squashed together as a fireball that exploded, shooting matter out in all directions. This idea is called the Big Bang theory.

The galaxies are still spreading farther and farther apart. This is the universe we know today. But the future is still a mystery.

After 500 million years, galaxies began to develop and the first stars were born inside them.

Uranium

This metal is one of the heaviest of all known ELEMENTS. It was named after the planet Uranus. Uranium gives off RADIO-ACTIVITY. As it loses atomic particles it decays, and ends up, after millions of years, as LEAD. People working with uranium often need protective clothing to shield their bodies from radiation damage.

Uranium is the fuel used to make ATOMIC ENERGY in atomic bombs and nuclear power stations. If a uranium atom is split up, the pieces can bump into other uranium atoms and split them up. This goes on and on in a *chain reaction* that gives out a lot of energy. Uranium is mined in many countries. Most of the western world's uranium comes from the United States and Canada.

Uranus

The PLANET Uranus is 19 times farther away from the sun than the earth is. We cannot see Uranus just with our eyes. It was the first planet discovered with the help of a TELESCOPE. It looks like a greenish-yellow

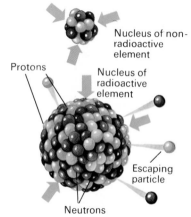

At the centre of every atom is a nucleus made up of tiny particles called protons and neutrons. If the material is like uranium and has many protons and neutrons, it may be radioactive and shoot out particles.

disc, with markings that may be clouds.

Uranus is unlike our earth in many ways. For one thing, it is much larger. You could fit 52 planets the size of the earth inside Uranus. The distance through the middle of

The diagram below shows two ways in which the universe might continue. 1. In the 'Never-ending' universe the galaxies will continue to fly apart until space is almost all black emptiness. 2. Alternatively, the galaxies may stop moving apart. Their gravity will then pull them inwards again, closer and closer, until they collide and explode in a 'Big Crunch'.

1. Never-ending universe

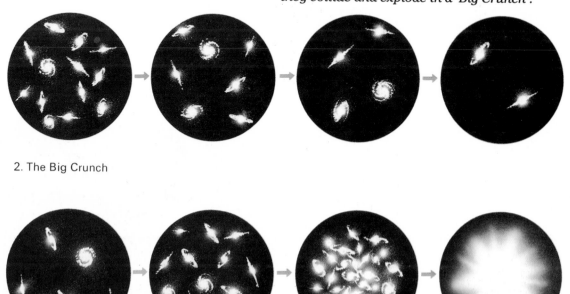

2. The Big Crunch

Uranus is nearly four times the distance through the middle of the earth.

Unlike our planet, Uranus is mainly made up of gases. Its whole surface is far colder than the coldest place on earth.

Uranus spins at a speed that makes one of its days about the same length as an earth day. But Uranus takes so long to ORBIT the sun that one of its years lasts 84 of ours.

In 1986, *Voyager 2* flew close to Uranus and took pictures that told scientists a great deal about the planet. It has at least 15 moons, one of which—Miranda—has mountains 26 km high.

When Voyager 2 *passed Uranus in 1986, it sent back to earth the most distant messages ever received from a space probe. One unusual feature of Uranus is that the tilt of its axis (shown by the red lines) is very extreme.*

Uruguay

Uruguay is one of the smallest countries in SOUTH AMERICA. It lies in the south-east, between the Atlantic Ocean and its two big neighbours, Argentina and Brazil. Uruguay was formerly a province of Brazil. It became independent in 1825.

Low, grassy hills and lowlands cover most of Uruguay. Many rivers flow into the big Uruguay River or into the river mouth called the River Plate.

Most of Uruguay's three million inhabitants are descended from Spanish or Italian settlers. Uruguayans speak Spanish. More than one in three of them live in the capital, Montevideo. Its factories make clothing, furniture and other goods. But most Uruguayans work in meat-packing plants, wool warehouses or on country ranches.

Vacuum

A vacuum is a space with nothing in it. It gets its name from *vacuus*, the Latin word for empty. In fact there are no complete vacuums. When you try to empty a container by pumping out the air, some air always stays behind. This partly empty space is called a partial vacuum. New air always rushes in to fill the space. This is how your LUNGS work. When you breathe in, your diaphragm contracts, making your chest larger. The lungs expand, making a partial vacuum. Air rushes in to fill the space.

You can see partial vacuums at work in many ways. The space does not always fill up with air. When you suck air from a straw dipped in lemonade, it is the lemonade that rushes to fill the vacuum and so into your mouth.

Vatican City

Vatican City is the Pope's home and head-quarters of the ROMAN CATHOLIC CHURCH. It stands on Vatican Hill in north-west Rome, and is the world's smallest independent country. It is only the size of a small farm and about 1000 people live in it. Yet it has its own flag, radio station and railway. It also issues its own stamps.

Vatican City is surrounded by walls and contains many famous buildings. These include the Vatican Palace, which has more than 1000 rooms; the Sistine Chapel, decorated by MICHELANGELO; and St Peter's Basilica.

Below: St Peter's Basilica, in Vatican City. The church stands over a tomb, which is believed to hold the body of St Peter, the first Pope. Michelangelo helped to design the church. It was begun in 1506 and took about 150 years to complete.

Vegetable

Vegetables are plants with parts that we can eat. They taste less sweet than the plant foods we call FRUIT. Vegetables such as lettuce and spinach are eaten for their leaves. Other vegetables are eaten for their roots or stems. Carrots and parsnips are roots. Celery and asparagus are stems. Peas, beans and sweet corn are seeds. Tomatoes and marrows are fruits.

Peas and beans supply body-building PROTEINS. Leafy and root vegetables provide

VITAMINS, minerals and fibres to help keep our DIGESTION working properly. Potatoes contain *starches*, which the body can burn up to make energy.

Veins

Veins are narrow tubes that carry used BLOOD from all parts of your body back to the HEART. Blood flowing through the arteries is pushed along by the pumping of the heart. Blood in the veins has nothing to push it along. So many veins have flaps inside them which close the tube if the blood begins to flow backwards.

Venezuela

Venezuela is a large country on the north coast of SOUTH AMERICA. Most of southern Venezuela is covered by flat-topped mountains. Here stands Angel Falls, the highest waterfall in the world. A grassy plain stretches across the middle of the country on either side of the Orinoco River.

Venezuelans speak Spanish. The country became independent from Spain in 1821.

Venezuela grows bananas, sugar cane, coffee, cotton and cocoa. But its minerals, especially oil, make it the richest country in the continent. A lot of its oil comes from wells in Lake Maracaibo, in the north-east of the country. Venezuela's capital is Caracas.

Alonso de Ojeda discovered Lake Maracaibo in 1499. He called the land Venezuela, or Little Venice, because the natives lived in houses on stilts.

There are 18 million people in Venezuela.

Venice

Venice is a beautiful city in ITALY, on the Adriatic Sea. It is built on a cluster of low, mud islands. There are more than 100 of them. The houses are built on wooden posts driven into the mud. Instead of roads, Venice has CANALS. Sometimes, the sea floods the city, which is slowly sinking into the mud at about 2 mm a year.

For hundreds of years, Venice was the

Above: A 'forest' of drilling rigs in Lake Maracaibo. Much of Venezuela's oil comes from this large shallow lake.

most important centre for trade between Europe and the empires of the east. The city became very rich and is full of palaces and fine houses built by merchants.

Below: A painting of Venice in the 18th century.

Venus (goddess)

Venus was the Roman goddess of love, grace and beauty. The Greeks had a similar goddess called Aphrodite. Many of the stories about Venus began as tales about Aphrodite.

Most stories say that Venus was born in the sea foam near the Greek island of Cythera. Although she was the most beautiful goddess, she married the ugliest god. He was Vulcan, the god of fire. But Venus also fell in love with other gods and with men. Venus and the war god, Mars, had a son called Cupid, the god of love. She also loved a Greek king called Anchises, and they had a son called Aeneas. The Romans believed that Aeneas helped to start the city of Rome.

Venus liked to help lovers. She started the TROJAN WAR, by making Helen of Troy fall in love with Paris.

Venus (planet)

The PLANET Venus is named after the Roman goddess of beauty and love. Venus is the brightest planet in the SOLAR SYSTEM. We see it as the morning star or the evening star.

Venus takes only 225 days to go around the sun. So more than three years pass on Venus for every two on earth. But Venus itself spins so slowly that one day on Venus

Above: Venus, the goddess of love, appears in the middle of this scene. It comes from a painting called Primavera *(Spring). It was painted 500 years ago by the Italian artist Sandro Botticelli.*

Below: The thick cloud over the surface of Venus holds in the heat. The midday temperature is 480°C.

lasts for 243 days on earth. It is the only planet to spin in the opposite way to the direction of its ORBIT.

Venus is about the same size as earth, but weighs a little less. It is also much hotter, because it is much closer to the sun. The surface of Venus is hidden under a dazzling white cloak of cloud. This may be made up of tiny drops of sulphuric acid. The atmosphere on Venus consists mainly of the gas *carbon dioxide*. This acts rather like a greenhouse roof, trapping the sun's heat. The rocks on Venus are hotter than boiling water. Above the hot rocks are fierce winds of more than 320 km/hr.

Verb

Verbs are 'doing' or 'being' words, such as *go, hit, choose, have, be*. Verbs tell you what people or things are doing, or what is happening to them.

We know who or what a verb describes by its place in a sentence. When you say 'the dog *bit* the man', you know that the dog is doing the biting, and not the man.

The way a verb is spelled is also a clue to what or who is being described. When we are describing ourselves, we say 'I *go*', but when we are talking about someone else we say 'he *goes*'.

We also add different endings to verbs to show at what time something is happening. Sometimes the verb is changed completely. For instance, we say 'I *go*' (meaning now), 'I *shall go*' (meaning in the future), and 'I *went*' (meaning in the past). We use the word *tense* to describe what time the verb refers to. For example, the past tense of 'I *run*' is 'I *ran*'.

Versailles

Versailles is a famous palace in France. It stands in a city, also called Versailles, just outside Paris.

Versailles palace was begun by LOUIS XIV in 1661, as a kind of 'holiday home' for the king and his court. It was built on the site of a hunting lodge. The most famous architects, sculptors and gardeners of the time worked on the palace and its magnificent park.

Louis XIV spent enormous sums of money on the palace. The great expense and luxury of the Versailles palace was one of the causes of the French Revolution.

Below: Louis XIV's magnificent palace at Versailles.

Vertebrates

Vertebrates are animals with a backbone or spine. The backbone is made up of short bones called *vertebrae*. This name comes from a Latin word that means 'to turn'. Most vertebrates can bend and straighten their backbones by turning their vertebrae slightly.

Many things make vertebrates different from other animals. Most have a bony case to protect their BRAIN, ribs to protect their HEART, LUNGS and other delicate parts, and one or two pairs of limbs. And most vertebrates have a SKELETON made of bone.

There are seven main kinds of vertebrate groups. The simplest kind are the lamprey group. Lampreys are eel-like fish with no jaw. They have a spine but no skeleton. Next come sharks and skates, which have a skeleton of cartilage. All other vertebrates have bones. They are the bony FISH, AMPHIBIANS, REPTILES, BIRDS and MAMMALS.

Vesuvius

Vesuvius is one of the world's most famous VOLCANOES. The mountain rises over the Bay of Naples in southern Italy. It is about 1200 metres high, but gets shorter every time it erupts.

The first eruption we know about hap-pened in AD 79. Nobody realized that it was an active volcano and so they had built towns and farmed the slopes of the volcano. For three days Vesuvius threw out ash and lava that buried the Roman cities of POMPEII and Herculaneum. Part of the wall of the old crater is still there. There have been nine bad eruptions in the last 200 years. The worst eruption in recent years happened in 1944 during World War II. The village of San Sebastiano was destroyed and Allied troops helped people to escape from the flowing lava.

Victoria, Queen

Queen Victoria (1819–1901) ruled Great Britain for 64 years, longer than any other British monarch. During her reign, the nation grew richer and its empire larger than ever before. She was the queen of many countries, including Australia, New Zealand, Canada and South Africa, and she was the empress of India.

Victoria was the daughter of Edward, Duke of Kent. GEORGE III was her grand-father. She was just 18 when she inherited the throne from her uncle, William IV. Two years later she married her German cousin, Prince Albert. They had four sons and five daughters. Prince Albert died of typhoid fever in 1861. His death left the Queen deeply unhappy. For many years she wore only black clothes to show her grief. She also stopped going to public ceremonies.

Below: Plaster casts made by bodies buried when Vesuvius erupted.

Below: Queen Victoria's reign began in 1837. This is an early portrait.

Left: The Viking ship found buried at Gokstad, Norway. We have learned a lot from it about how Vikings built their ships. Ships were very important to the Vikings. They sometimes buried their kings and chiefs in large ships. These 'tombs' were then burned or buried.

Vietnam

Vietnam is a country in South-East ASIA. It is only 55 km wide in some parts.

Vietnam used to be divided into two countries, North Vietnam and South Vietnam. From the 1950s until 1975, the two countries were at war. South Vietnam was supported by the United States. North Vietnam was communist. Now the whole country is communist.

Below: Refugees being rescued by helicopter during the Vietnam War.

Viking

The Vikings were a fierce people who lived in Norway, Sweden and Denmark. Between 800 and 1100, a great number of Vikings left their homes to raid villages and build settlements in northern Europe.

The Vikings sailed in long ships, which were faster than any other at that time. They were the first European people to discover North America. They sailed there from Greenland, but they did not settle there.

Vinegar

Vinegar is an ACID liquid. It is made when alcohol is left uncovered. The alcohol mixes with oxygen in the air and goes sour. Vinegar can be made from wine, cider or malt.

Vinegar is used to season and flavour food. People use it to make sauces and salad dressings. Food can be preserved (to stop it going bad) by keeping it in vinegar. This is called pickling. Onions and beetroot are often pickled in vinegar.

Virus

Viruses are very small living things that cause diseases in plants and animals. They are smaller than BACTERIA and can be seen only with a very powerful MICROSCOPE.

You can be infected with viruses by swallowing them or breathing them in. Some insects carry viruses, which they pass on when they bite you. Once inside the body, a virus travels around in the bloodstream. It gets inside a living CELL where it produces more viruses. Sometimes the cell is entirely destroyed by the viruses.

Diseases caused by viruses include measles, chicken pox, mumps, influenza and colds. Viruses are very hard to kill. INOCULATION helps to prevent these diseases.

When a virus enters the body, the blood produces substances called *antibodies*. After a while there are enough antibodies to kill all the viruses and the patient recovers.

Vitamins

Vitamins are chemicals that our bodies need to stay healthy. They are found in different kinds of food. There are six kinds of vitamins. Scientists call them A, B, C, D, E and K. Vitamin B is really a group of vitamins.

The first people to realize that certain kinds of food were important to health were sailors. On long voyages they got a disease called *scurvy* if they could not eat fresh fruit and vegetables. These contain vitamin C. From the 1700s, English sailors were given limes to eat to prevent scurvy. This is why they were nicknamed 'limeys' by the Americans.

No one food has all the vitamins we need. That is why it is important to eat a mixture of things. Some people take their vitamins in pills. No one really needs pills if they eat well. Very old people, young babies and women expecting babies all need more vitamins than usual. But too much of some kinds of vitamins, such as vitamin A, can be bad for you.

Volcano

A volcano is an opening in the surface of the earth. Burning gas, boiling rocks and ash escape from this opening. Sometimes they trickle out, sometimes they explode. If they explode, it is called an *eruption*.

In ancient Greek stories, volcanoes were the chimneys of the underground forge of the fire god. The Roman name for this god was Vulcan. Volcanoes are named after him.

Below: An Iranian boy being vaccinated. Edward Jenner, an English doctor, began the use of vaccine injections to protect people against virus diseases.

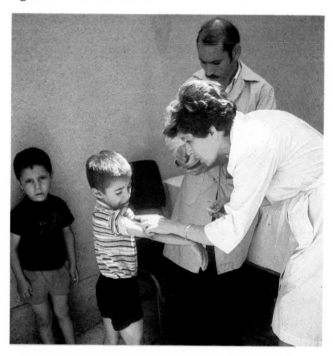

VOLCANO

Some volcanoes are gently sloping mountains with cracks, or *fissures*, in them. Hot liquid rock called *lava* flows out through the fissures. Other volcanoes are steep-sided mountains with a large hole at the top. These are called cone volcanoes. They are the kind that explode.

Erupting volcanoes can do a lot of damage. The city of POMPEII was destroyed by Vesuvius in AD 79. In 1883 Krakatoa, a volcano in Indonesia, erupted, causing a tidal wave that killed 36,000 people. Volcanoes can also make new land. An island called Surtsey, south of Iceland, was made by a volcano erupting under the sea in 1963.

If you look at where volcanoes are found around the world, they make a pattern of long chains. These chains mark the edges of the huge 'plates' that form the earth's surface. They are the weakest part of the earth's crust. One chain, called 'the ring of fire', goes right around the Pacific Ocean. Earthquakes, geysers and hot springs are all found in the same area as volcanoes.

Below: A cutaway picture of a volcano. The mountain (1) is made of layers of cold ash and lava sandwiched together. Hot lava (2) spouts up through a central crack (3).

Vole

Voles are small, tubby animals about 10cm long. They have short tails and very small ears. They belong to the RODENT family and are closely related to LEMMINGS. Voles live in all the cooler countries of the world. The bank vole and meadow vole are very common in Britain.

The vole lives in shallow burrows. Sometimes it shares tunnels made by moles. Bank voles dig out store rooms and bedrooms from the burrows and line them with chewed grass. They can run, climb, swim and jump.

The meadow vole lives in rough fields and on moors. Many meadow voles now live on the grassy slopes at the sides of motorways. They sit up and eat with their 'hands', like SQUIRRELS.

Water voles are often called 'water rats'. They are nearly twice the size of meadow voles. They live in river banks, where they dig deep burrows.

Volume

The volume of an object is the amount of space it takes up. You can find out the volume of something by measuring its height, width and depth and multiplying the figures together. So a brick with equal sides, each 10cm long, has a volume of 1000 cubic cm, that is $10cm \times 10cm \times 10cm$.

It is easy to find out the volume of boxes or bricks or anything with straight edges. Measuring the volume of something with irregular sides is more difficult. A very simple method was discovered by ARCHIMEDES, the Greek scientist. A story told about him says that he was getting into his bath, which was full to the brim, and water spilled over the side. He suddenly realized that the volume of water that spilled over was exactly the same as the volume of his body. This means that any irregularly shaped object—such as a piece of coal or a brass weight—can be measured by plunging it into water and measuring the rise of the water level.

The meadow vole has a blunt nose and tiny, rounded ears.

Vowels

Vowels are the letters A, E, I, O and U. Sometimes the letters Y and W are used as vowels. Vowels are pronounced with the mouth open. What they sound like depends on the position of your TONGUE in your mouth. The shape your lips make is also important. If they are pushed forward, as if you are whistling, you make an *oo* sound. If they are pulled right back, you make an *ee* sound.

Because the tongue and the lips can shape themselves in hundreds of different ways, there are hundreds of different vowel sounds. Sometimes two or three vowel sounds are run together to make a new sound. The vowel sounds in one LANGUAGE are often very difficult for speakers of another language to learn.

Wages

Wages are the money people earn for their work. Wages used to be paid according to the amount of work done—the weight of coal dug, or the number of shirts made. Today, most wages are paid for the length of time people spend working. Overtime, or time worked in addition to normal hours, is paid at a much higher rate. Trade unions were formed to see that their members were paid fair wages and given reasonable working conditions.

Wales

Wales is part of the United Kingdom of Great Britain and Northern Ireland. It lies to the west of England and is a country of low mountains and green valleys. The highest mountain is Snowdon, and Cardiff is the capital city.

The Welsh are descended from the Celts. English is their main language today, but about a quarter of the people still speak Welsh. Many Welsh people are fighting passionately to keep their language alive.

South Wales is one of Britain's biggest coalfields. Most of the people live in the coal-mining areas, or in industrial towns like Swansea and Cardiff. Steel is another important industry. In the mountains of north and mid-Wales many people are sheep-farmers.

Walrus

The walrus belongs to the SEAL family. Its enormous canine teeth look like two tusks. These tusks can be up to a metre long. The walrus uses them to scrape up the clams and shellfish it eats. It also uses its tusks to fight, and even polar bears keep away from fully grown walruses.

The Atlantic and the Pacific walrus both live in the cold ARCTIC. They are big animals. The male Atlantic walrus measures up to 4 metres and weighs as much as 1800 kg.

In the 1930s walruses almost disappeared through being hunted for their tusks and skins. Now there are laws against hunting them and their numbers are slowly increasing.

Right: Walruses live in large families on beaches and ice floes. Because so many of them live together they are very easy to catch and kill.

Below: Fishguard is on the coast of South Wales. Most Welsh people live in cities in the south because the north is mountainous.

Wasp

There are many different kinds, or *species*, of this insect. Some wasps are called social insects because they live together in large groups. These wasps have different jobs to do for the group. A few of them are queens, and lay eggs. Others are workers. They build the nests and collect the food. But most wasps are solitary insects. They live alone, build their own nests, lay their own eggs and collect their own food.

Wasps build nests in different places, depending on their needs. Some build in hollow trees, or in the roofs of houses. Others use holes in the ground, or hang nests from the branches of trees.

Wasps have a very powerful sting, which they use to stun their prey, or to defend themselves from their enemies—such as people!

Water

Water is the most common substance on earth. Seven-tenths of the world's surface is covered by water. Water is also the most important substance on earth. Without it life would be impossible. Life first started in water, and the bodies of all living things are mostly water.

There is no such thing as 'pure' water. Water contains MINERALS, which it has picked up from the surrounding earth and rocks.

Water exists in three forms. At 0°C it freezes into solid ice. At 100°C it boils into

Below: Water is made from two gases, hydrogen and oxygen. When two parts of hydrogen are combined with one part of oxygen, liquid water is formed.

Common wasp

Hornet

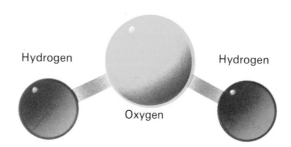

Hydrogen

Hydrogen

Oxygen

351

steam. Normal air takes up water easily, and CLOUDS are huge collections of water *vapour*. At any time, clouds contain millions of tonnes of water, which falls back to earth as RAIN. Some of this water stays in the soil or underground for years, but most of it returns to the oceans.

Weather

The weather—sunshine, FOG, RAIN, CLOUDS, WIND, heat, cold—is always changing in most parts of the world. These changes are caused by what happens in the atmosphere, the layer of air above the earth.

The atmosphere is always moving, driven by the sun's heat. Near the EQUATOR the sun's strong rays heat the air. At the North

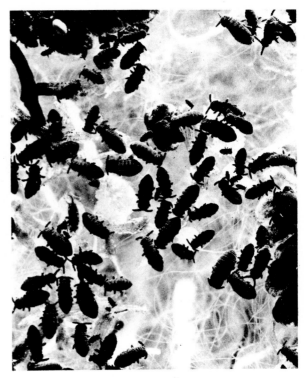

Right: Water often contains many tiny living things that are too small for us to see. This drop of water has been photographed under a powerful microscope.

Below: Still water has a kind of 'skin' on it. This is called surface tension. If you are very careful not to break it, you can even place a needle on this surface.

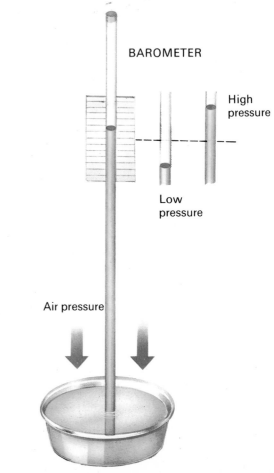

BAROMETER

High pressure

Low pressure

Air pressure

Right: The barometer shows differences in air pressure. A tube stands in a bowl of water. The tube has water sucked partway up it and is then sealed. As air pressure rises and falls, the water in the tube goes up and down. This can be a guide to the kind of weather we can expect.

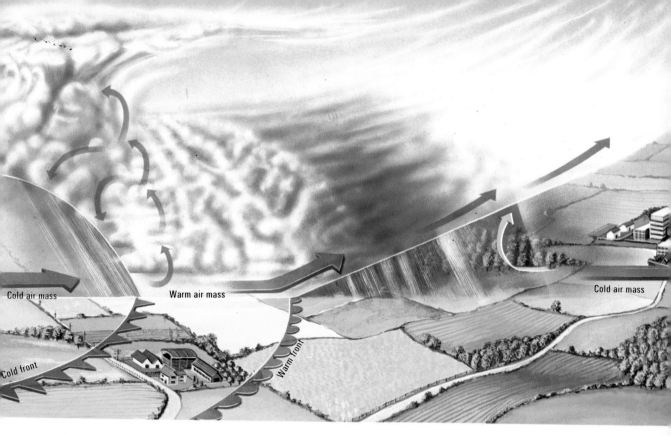

Cold air mass

Warm air mass

Cold air mass

Cold front

Warm Front

Depressions usually bring rainy and windy weather. In the depression above, warm air is being squeezed between two masses of cold air. The lighter warm air rises over the cold air. As it rises it forms clouds and rain. The edge of the advancing cold air is called a cold front. The edge of the advancing warm air is called a warm front.

Below: Three homemade weather instruments. The anemometer *shows wind speed. Its paper cups are fixed to a cork disc that spins on a nail. The* weathervane *shows wind direction. It swings around a nail set in a board marked with compass points. The* rain gauge, *made from a funnel, glass jar, and tin can, measures rainfall.*

and South Poles the sun's rays are weaker and the air is colder. This uneven heating means the atmosphere is never still. Huge masses of warm and cold air flow round and round between the tropics and the polar regions. As these wandering air masses meet, rise and fall, heat and cool, they cause weather.

When cold and warm masses meet, the air whirls inward in a giant spiral called a *depression*. Depressions bring clouds, wind, rain and summer thunderstorms. They can also cause violent TORNADOES and hurricanes.

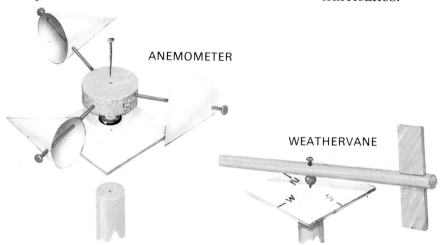

ANEMOMETER

WEATHERVANE

RAIN GAUGE

353

The meeting line between two air masses is called a *front*. When cold air pushes up behind warm air, it forms a *cold front*; when a warm air mass catches up with a cold mass, it creates a *warm front*. Fronts usually bring changes in the weather.

Weaving

Curtains and sheets, shirts and carpets, towels and trousers are just some of the many useful articles made by weaving. In weaving, threads are joined together in a crisscross pattern to make cloth (see the illustration below).

People have been weaving cloth to make clothes since the New STONE AGE. The oldest fabric we know of was woven nearly 8000 years ago in what is now Turkey. These first weavers learned to make linen from *flax*. By 2000 BC the Chinese were weaving cloth from SILK. In India, people learned to use fibres from the COTTON plant.

Meanwhile *nomads* (travellers) from the deserts and mountains of Asia discovered how to weave WOOL.

For thousands of years, making cloth was slow work. First, the fibres were drawn out and twisted into a long thread. This process is known as spinning. Then, rows of threads were stretched lengthwise, side by side, on a frame called a *loom*. These threads made up the *warp*. A crosswise thread, the *weft*, was then passed through from one side of the loom to the other, going over and under the warp threads. A *shuttle*, like a large needle, was used to feed the weft through the warp.

Spinning wheels and looms were worked by hand until the 1700s. Then, machines were invented for spinning and weaving. These machines worked far faster than hand looms, and cloth became cheap and plentiful. Today most woven fabrics are made by machine.

The modern weaving industry began in England when Edmund Cartwright, a clergyman, invented the first steam-powered loom. In 1787 he was using his new steam loom in his own factory. From then on other weavers improved on Cartwright's ideas until today looms turn out miles of cloth at high speed in highly complex patterns.

Below: How a loom works. The warp is a set of threads running the length of the cloth. The weft is another thread that goes across the cloth. A shuttle laces the weft over and under the warp threads from one side of the loom to the other. To help the shuttle pass through more easily, special frames raise some warp threads and lower others. The reed is pulled up to the cloth to tighten the weave.

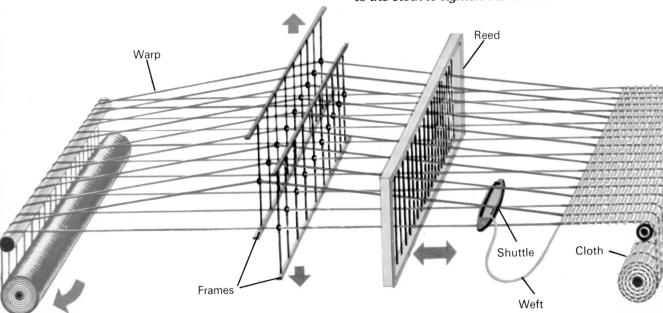

Warp

Reed

Frames

Shuttle

Cloth

Weft

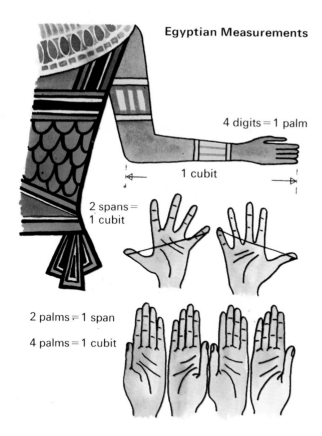

Egyptian Measurements

4 digits = 1 palm

1 cubit

2 spans = 1 cubit

2 palms = 1 span

4 palms = 1 cubit

Above: In ancient Egypt a span (across the hand) and a cubit (from fingertip to elbow) were used to measure length.

Above: Juice from sugar cane harvested in Jamaica will be made into sugar.

Weights and Measures

Weights and measures are used to work out the size of things. The two main kinds of measurement are weight and length. They answer the questions 'How heavy?' and 'How long?' Length is also used to find area and volume. There are several systems of weights and measures. The most common in the world is the METRIC SYSTEM.

West Indies

This chain of tropical islands stretches from Florida in the United States to Venezuela in South America. On one side lies the Caribbean Sea; on the other stretches the Atlantic Ocean. The islands are really the tops of a drowned range of mountains. Palm trees and tropical grasses grow here, where it is almost always warm. But fierce autumn hurricanes often destroy trees and houses.

The thousands of islands are divided into more than 20 countries. CUBA, JAMAICA, Haiti and the Dominican Republic are among the largest. Many West Indians are at least partly descended from Africans. Other West Indians have ancestors who lived in India or Europe. Most West Indians speak English, Spanish or French.

People grow bananas, cotton, sugar cane and other tropical crops. Some work in hotels. Tourists from many countries come here to swim and sunbathe.

The West Indies were discovered in 1492 by Christopher COLUMBUS.

Whale

Whales are big sea MAMMALS well built for living in the water. A thick layer of fat called blubber keeps out the cold. A whale's body is shaped for easy swimming. Its front limbs are shaped like flippers. It also has a broad tail flattened from top to bottom, not from side to side like a fish tail.

Unlike fish, whales must swim to the surface to breathe. They take in air through a *blowhole* (two slits), on top of the head. Baby whales are born in water. As soon as they are born they surface for a breath.

There are two groups of whales. Toothed whales like the DOLPHIN mostly catch fish. But killer whales are toothed whales that attack seals, penguins and other whales.

Baleen whales are the other main group

Above: The killer whales will attack and kill the biggest whales.
Below: Beluga (white) whales are born grey, but turn white as they grow older.

Above: The sperm whale is the largest toothed whale. It can measure 20 metres and weigh over 39 tonnes.

of whales. Baleen whales include the blue whale, the largest mammal that has ever lived. Each baleen whale catches tiny shrimplike creatures with a special sieve. This is made of a horny substance called baleen or whalebone. When the whale opens its mouth, long baleen plates hang from its upper jaw like the teeth of a giant comb. Hunting by man has made the biggest whales very scarce.

Wheat

Wheat is a valuable food crop. Grains of wheat are produced by a certain kind of grass. The plants are about a metre tall. Their thin stalks have 'ears' of grain at the top. Each ear consists of *kernels* of grain, and each kernel has a protective covering called the *chaff*. Kernels are taken off the stalk by *threshing*. This is usually done by machine. Threshing also removes the chaff. Mills grind the kernels into flour for making bread, breakfast cereals, cakes, pies, noodles and spaghetti. White flour is made from only part of the kernel. Whole wheat flour is made from the whole kernel. Each grain of wheat is mostly made of energy-giving *starches*. It also contains plenty of body-building PROTEIN, as well as FATS, MINERALS and bran.

Wheat grows best in dry, mild climates. Farmers sow the seed in winter or spring. They harvest it when the grain is dry and hard. Most wheat comes from the USSR, the United States, China and India. The world grows more wheat than any other kind of grain.

Wheel

Wheels are one of our most useful inventions. This is because a wheel turning on an axle is a very good way to move loads. It is easier to move a heavy load with wheels than it is to lift the load or drag it along the ground.

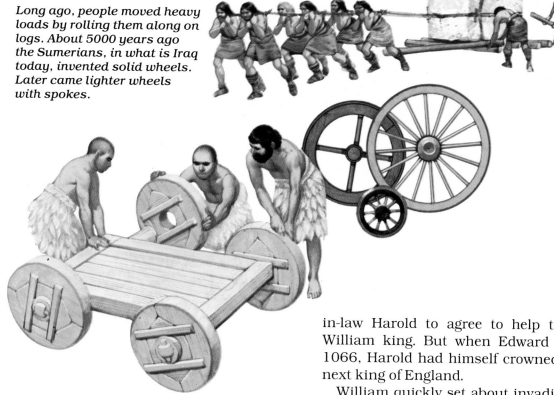

Long ago, people moved heavy loads by rolling them along on logs. About 5000 years ago the Sumerians, in what is Iraq today, invented solid wheels. Later came lighter wheels with spokes.

STONE AGE people may have learned to roll loads along on logs. No one is certain exactly when the wheel was invented. But Bronze Age people were probably the first to use the wheel about 5000 years ago. The oldest known wheels looked like slices cut across large tree trunks. But each solid disc was made of three parts. Wheels like this were used on carts. Some people think that the very first wheel was used to make pottery by Bronze Age people in Mesopotamia (part of what is Iraq today).

William the Conqueror

William the Conqueror (1027–1087) was William I of England, and England's first Norman king. Before that he was Duke of Normandy in northern France. (Normandy was named after the Normans or Northmen, also called VIKINGS).

When William visited England in 1050, his relative EDWARD the Confessor may have promised him the throne of England. In 1064 William forced Edward's brother-in-law Harold to agree to help to make William king. But when Edward died in 1066, Harold had himself crowned as the next king of England.

William quickly set about invading England to seize it for himself. His Norman army sailed across the English Channel in open boats. There were about 7000 troops, including knights who brought their war horses. William defeated Harold's ANGLO-SAXON army at the Battle of HASTINGS, fought in Sussex near where the town of Battle stands today.

William spent three years winning all England. To do this he built many castles, from which his knights rode out to crush their Anglo-Saxon enemies.

By 1069 the Normans had conquered one-third of England, and William had become the most powerful king in western Europe. He claimed all the land as his, but he lent some to his Norman nobles. In return, the nobles supplied soldiers for William's army. William's descendants ruled England for many years.

William of Orange

William of Orange (1650–1702) was a PROTESTANT ruler of the Netherlands, who became King William III of England, Scotland and Ireland.

In 1677 he married his Protestant cousin Mary. In 1688 the English invited William and Mary to rule them in place of Mary's unpopular father, the Catholic James II. James fled when William landed with his army. No one died in this so-called 'Glorious Revolution', and William defeated James in Ireland in 1690.

Wind

Wind is moving air. Slow winds are gentle breezes. Fast winds are gales. You can see the speed of the wind by its effect on trees and buildings.

Wind blows because some air masses become warmer than others. In warm air, the tiny particles of air spread out. This means that a mass of warm air is lighter than a mass of cold air that fills the same amount of space. Because warm air is light it rises. As warm air rises, cool air flows in to take its place. This causes the steady trade winds that blow over tropical oceans. CLIMATE and WEATHER largely depend on the wind.

A scale of wind speeds was worked out in 1805 by Admiral Sir Francis Beaufort. It is called the Beaufort Scale. In it the force of the wind is shown by numbers from 0 to 12. The number 0 shows that there is a calm in which smoke rises straight up. At 1 on the scale, smoke drifts slowly. By the time we get to 4 we have a breeze in which small branches are moving and flags flap. At force 7 whole trees are moving and it is difficult to walk against the wind. Force 12 is something that, fortunately, few of us will ever see. It is a full hurricane, with terrible damage to ships at sea and houses on land.

Windmill

Windmills are machines that make the wind's energy perform useful work. They were used in Asia as early as the 600s AD and came to Europe in the 1100s.

In early windmills a wheel with long sails was fixed to a tower. The whole tower could often turn to face the wind. As the wind turned the sails, the turning wheel moved machinery inside the mill. This machinery was used to do useful work such as turning heavy stone wheels to grind corn.

Nowadays, people are trying to make better windmills as a way of generating electricity. These windmills are usually on a tower made of steel girders. Some have sails like aircraft propellers which turn at a high speed when the wind blows. The propellers turn a generator which makes electricity.

Westerlies   Trades   Polar easterlies

MAJOR WIND BELTS

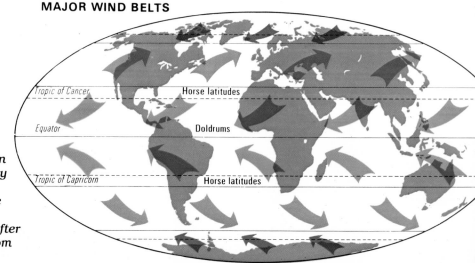

A map of the earth's main winds. They are set off by the sun's heat, which warms some parts of the earth more than others. Most winds are named after the place or direction from which they blow.

Tropic of Cancer   Horse latitudes

Equator   Doldrums

Tropic of Capricorn   Horse latitudes

Vines are grown throughout the warm Mediterranean countries, and in parts of central Europe, particularly in France and Germany. Europe is world famous for its fine wines. Italy makes more wine than any other country.

Wine

Wine is a drink made from plant juice, containing alcohol produced by fermentation.

Most wine is made from grapes. But you can make wine from other fruits as well. First the fruit is crushed. Then the juice is fermented in containers called vats. The wine is stored in casks until it is ready to drink. A well-stored wine tastes better the older it is. Sweet wines are rich in sugar. In dry wines most sugar has become alcohol.

Below: The grey wolf is also called the timber wolf.

Wolf

These CARNIVORES include the red wolf of South America and the grey wolf of the world's northern forests. A pack of wolves can kill a sick or injured deer much larger than themselves. When grey wolves are hunting, they howl to signal to each other where they are. Each spring a she-wolf has four to six pups.

Wood

Wood is one of the most valuable materials that people use. It can be sawed, carved and worked into almost any shape.

Thick timber is used for buildings and ships, while planks are made into furniture, barrels and boxes. Seasoned (specially treated) pieces can be shaped into musical instruments and delicate ornaments. Most house frames are wooden, and doors, floors, stairs and wallpaper are generally made from wood too.

The wood we use is the fibrous inner material of trees and shrubs. It is very

This book is made of paper that came from logs like these.

strong, and can support many times its own weight.

Softwood, which comes from pines and firs, is used mostly as pulp to make paper. Hardwood, which comes from broadleaf trees, is used to make furniture and for building.

Woodpecker

There are about 200 kinds of woodpecker. They are found in many parts of the world, but most live in America and Asia.

Woodpeckers have sharp, powerful bills with which they drill holes through the bark of trees. They reach in with their long tongues to fish out the insects that live there.

Most woodpeckers have bright colours and markings, especially on their heads.

Above: The great spotted woodpecker is the most common European woodpecker. It is well known for its habit of drumming very rapidly on dead branches.

Woodwind

Woodwinds are a family of MUSICAL INSTRUMENTS, played by blowing through a mouthpiece and into a hollow tube. Different notes are made by opening and closing holes in the instrument. Recorders, flutes, oboes, clarinets, horns and bassoons are all woodwind instruments.

Wool

Wool comes from the fleece of SHEEP. It is a very long and thick kind of hair and can easily be turned into yarn. The yarn may be woven into blankets, carpets and clothing, or it can be knitted. Woollen cloth is heavy and warm.

Wool has been spun and woven since STONE AGE times. Modern wool, however, comes from specially bred sheep that have good fine wool. The best wool comes from merino sheep. These are white sheep that originally came from Spain. Most wool is produced in Australia, New Zealand, Argentina and the Soviet Union.

Above: Sheep farming in Australia. The sheep are sheared and marked.

Below: The recorder is one of the easiest woodwind instruments to play.

World War I

Between 1914 and 1918 Europe, America and much of the Middle East were locked in the first struggle that could be called a world war. On one side were Germany, Austria-Hungary and Turkey. On the other were France, the British Empire, the United States and Russia.

The battle soon became a stalemate in the west. The two armies spent four years in trenches in northern France, fighting over the same patch of ground. But in the east, Germany had better luck. The Germans attacked Russia so strongly that by 1917 Russia withdrew from the war.

After the United States joined the war in 1917, the Allied armies slowly pushed the Germans back. In November, 1918 peace was declared.

Above: A scene of bitter fighting at Ypres in 1915.
Below: Some of the weapons first used in World War I.

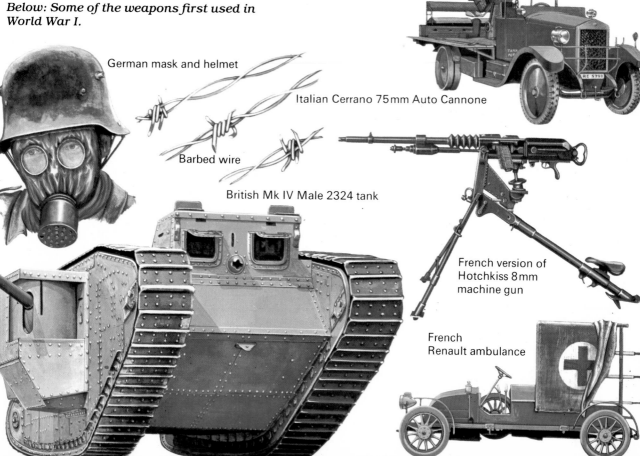

German mask and helmet

Italian Cerrano 75mm Auto Cannone

Barbed wire

British Mk IV Male 2324 tank

French version of Hotchkiss 8mm machine gun

French Renault ambulance

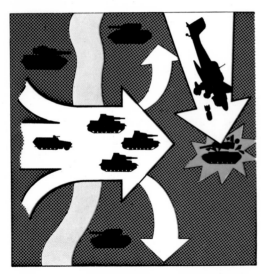

Above: Germany used blitzkrieg *tactics to smash through enemy lines with heavy weapons. Troops then poured through the hole. Right: After D-Day on June 6, 1944, the Allies sent many thousands of men into France.*

World War II

With the invasion of Poland in the autumn of 1939, Germany, Italy and then Japan entered into a six-year war with most of the major nations of Europe, Asia, Africa and America. The battles raged from the Pacific Ocean, China, and South-East Asia to Africa, Europe and the North Atlantic.

Germany's early attacks were hugely successful. Her armies swept through Europe and on into Russia and north Africa. However, the tide turned after 1941 with the entry of the United States into the war. By June 1944, Allied forces had landed in France and by May the next year Germany surrendered.

In the east, Japan's armies rolled through China, Malaya and Indonesia and captured many Pacific islands. In the end, Japan fell too, but not until two atomic bombs had been dropped on its cities by the United States.

Worms

There are hundreds of different animals with soft flat bodies that are commonly called worms. Some are very simple creatures, such as roundworms or flatworms. Others, such as earthworms, leeches and the larva of some INSECTS, are more complicated animals. Their bodies are divided into several segments.

Most of the simple worms are small. They usually live as parasites inside the bodies of animals or plants. Liver flukes and tapeworms are two such creatures.

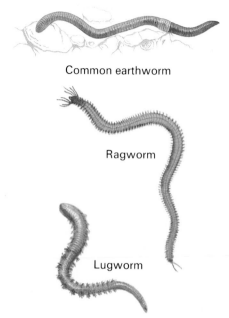

Common earthworm

Ragworm

Lugworm

Above: Three kinds of worm. The earthworm feeds by swallowing soil as it tunnels. The ragworm can swim weakly. The lugworm lives in burrows on sandy shores.

Below: Orville Wright was the first person to fly an aircraft on a controlled flight.

Wright Brothers

Wilbur and Orville Wright were two American bicycle engineers who built and flew the first aircraft. Their successful machine was made after years of studying small models.

The first actual flight took place at Kitty Hawk, North Carolina, in December 1903. Their simple petrol-engined craft flew for 59 seconds. Five years later they flew an improved model for 75 minutes.

The original Wright *Flyer* is in the National Air and Space Museum in Washington DC.

Writing

The earliest forms of writing were simple picture messages, or notches on sticks that were used for counting. Gradually, pictures that were used again and again became simplified. These symbols meant certain objects, like 'man' or 'house'. Egyptian HIEROGLYPHICS were used in this way.

In time, the symbols came to stand for sounds and could be combined to form words. Later still, alphabets of these sounds came into being. Vowels appeared with the ancient Greeks and Romans. Their alphabets were similar to the one we use today.

Below: Picture writing on a 5000-year-old clay tablet from the Middle East.

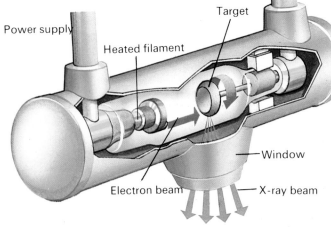

Power supply

Heated filament

Target

Window

Electron beam

X-ray beam

Above: An X-ray machine. When a filament inside the machine is heated, it produces a stream of electrons. A strong current passing through the machine forces a beam of electrons onto a metal target. As the target stops the electrons, they produce X-rays. Below: An X-ray photograph of a human hand. Bones block more of the X-rays than flesh does, so the photographic plate is less clouded where bones are.

Xerography

This is a way of copying writing or printing by using a machine called a *photocopier*.

The page to be copied is laid face down on a glass panel on the machine. Whatever is on the page is focused through a moving LENS onto an electrically charged metal plate coated with black powder. When a clean sheet of paper, also electrically charged, passes over the plate, the powder clings to it, making an exact copy of the original. When the paper is heated, the powder 'sets' so that the copy is permanent.

X-rays

X-rays are waves of energy like RADIO or LIGHT waves. They can pass through or into most living things. They can also leave an image on a photographic plate, making a picture of whatever they have passed through. Doctors can use them to take 'photographs' of the insides of people. This helps the doctor to find out if anything is wrong with the patient.

Wilhelm Röntgen, a German scientist, discovered X-rays by accident in 1895 while he was passing electricity through a gas.

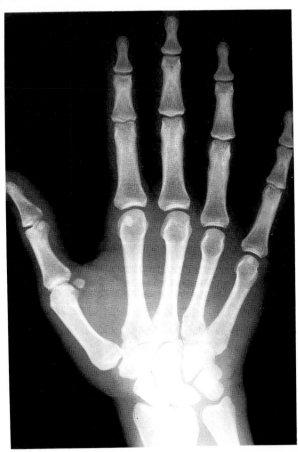

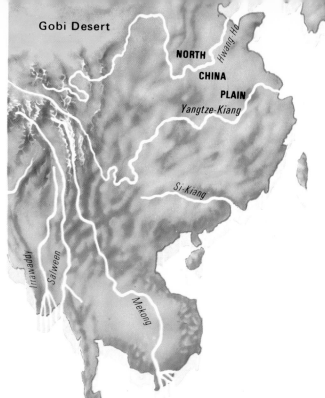

Above: The Yangtze and the Hwang-Ho are the two great rivers that cross China.

Yangtze, River

The Yangtze is the longest, most important river in CHINA. From its beginnings, high in the mountains of Tibet, it flows 5470km across the centre of China, pouring into the Yellow Sea near Shanghai.

The river takes its name from the ancient kingdom of Yang, which grew up along its banks 3000 years ago. Today, the Yangtze is still one of the main trade routes in China. Big ships can sail up it as far as Hankow, nearly 1125km inland. Smaller boats can reach as far as I-Ch'ang, which is 1600km from the sea.

Millions of people live and work on the Yangtze. Some live on the river itself in wooden sailing boats called *junks*.

Year

A year is the amount of time it takes for the earth to travel once around the SUN. It takes $365\frac{1}{4}$ days. A calendar year is only 365 days long. Every four years, the extra quarter days are lumped together to make a year of 366 days. These longer years are called leap years.

Yeast

Yeast is a plant, and it is also a kind of FUNGUS. The whole plant consists of just one CELL. It is so tiny that you cannot see it without a microscope. It is very useful because it turns sugar into alcohol and carbon dioxide gas. This process is called *fermentation*. Yeast plants do this because they do not produce their own food. They live on sugar instead. Today yeast is grown in huge vats. It is then pressed into cakes or small pellets, ready to be sold.

There are over 150 different kinds of yeast. The most important are the brewer's yeast and the baker's yeast, which are used to make beer and bread.

In wine- and beer-making, yeast turns the sugar in grapes or malted barley into alcohol, while most of the gas produced bubbles away. In bread-making, the carbon dioxide gas forms bubbles, which makes the bread dough rise.

Yoghurt

Yoghurt is a thick, sour-tasting, custardy kind of milk food. Yoghurt is a Turkish word for fermented milk. It is made by adding special BACTERIA to fresh cow's or goat's milk. The bacteria sours the milk and makes it thicken.

Yoghurt first came from the Balkans. People in Iran, Bulgaria, Greece and Turkey have eaten yoghurt for hundreds of years. Now it is a popular food all over the world. You can eat it with fruit, jam or honey, as a salad dressing, or in hot, spicy stews. Yoghurt is rich in VITAMIN B. People often eat it when they are trying to lose weight.

Yugoslavia is one of the most beautiful countries in Europe. Thousands of tourists go there every year. This town is called Sveti Stefan.

Yugoslavia

Yugoslavia is a country in south-east EUROPE. Most of it lies in the Balkans. It is a rugged, mountainous country. In the west, the mountains sweep down to the Adriatic Sea. Inland, the country is mostly scrubby and poor. Around the river Danube in the north, the land is fertile. Most of the country's farming goes on around here. Farmers grow wheat, barley, plums, olives and grapes, and keep a lot of cattle.

Yugoslavia's 23 million people come from different nations and speak many different languages. Most of them are Serbs, but there are also Croats, Slovenes and Macedonians. They also follow different religions. Some are Roman Catholics, some are Muslim and some belong to the Greek Orthodox Church. The capital city is Belgrade.

Zaire

Zaire is a huge hot and rainy country that sprawls across the heart of AFRICA. It includes most of the vast Zaire River, once called the Congo.

Much of Zaire is covered with thick jungle. There are lakes and highlands in the east and south. Copper, cobalt and diamonds are mined here. But most of Zaire's 31 million inhabitants are farmers. They grow tea, coffee, cocoa and cotton. The capital is Kinshasa.

Zambia

Zambia is a country in southern AFRICA. It is entirely surrounded by land. Zaire, Tanzania, Malawi, Mozambique, Botswana, Zimbabwe and Angola all share borders with Zambia. The capital is Lusaka.

The name Zambia comes from the Zambezi River. This runs across the western part of the country along the border with Zimbabwe. Zambia was the British protectorate of Northern Rhodesia until it became an independent republic in 1964.

Much of the country is rolling, highland plains. The majority of Zambians are farmers. But most of the country's wealth comes from its copper mines. Almost a quarter of the world's copper is mined here.

Below left: The flag of Zaire. Zaire once belonged to Belgium. It became an independent republic in 1971.
Centre: This flag, with a flying eagle representing freedom, was adopted on Zambia's independence.
Right: The 'Zimbabwe Bird' on Zimbabwe's flag comes from carvings found in the ruined city shown at the bottom of the page.

Zaire   Zambia   Zimbabwe

Most Zambians live in small villages like this one. They earn their living farming on small plots of land.

Left: Great Zimbabwe, an ancient ruined city in a valley in south-eastern Zimbabwe. 'Zimbabwe' comes from an African word meaning 'home of a chief'. It is thought that people lived here, on and off, from about 1700 years ago until the early 1800s.

Zebras share a waterhole with a herd of eland in the dry grasslands of Africa.

Above: Lake Kariba is on the border of Zimbabwe and Zambia. The Kariba dam provides water for the dry season.

Zebra

Zebras belong to the horse family. They live in the open grasslands of Africa to the south of the Sahara Desert. Zebras have creamy white coats covered with black or dark brown stripes. Each animal has its own special pattern of stripes.

Zebras live in herds. They feed on grass and are often found roaming the grasslands with herds of antelope. Although zebras can run very fast, they are often hunted by lions, leopards and hyenas. People also used to hunt them for their attractive skins and tasty meat.

Zeus

According to the myths and legends of the ancient Greeks, Zeus was the ruler of all the gods. He lived on Mt Olympus and was married to Hera. He was the father of the gods Apollo, Dionysus and Athena.

Zeus was the son of the ancient god Kronos. The stories say that Zeus and his brothers, Poseidon and Hades, killed Kronos and took over his throne and powers. Poseidon took the seas, Hades took the underworld and Zeus took the world and the sky. Zeus ruled over the sun, the moon, all the other stars and planets, and the weather.

Zimbabwe

Zimbabwe is a small country in southern AFRICA. It lies inland, about 240 km from the Indian Ocean. Only eight million people live in the country. About 97 out of every 100 are black Africans; the others are mostly whites. The capital is Harare.

Zimbabwe is bordered by the Zambezi River in the north. The Zambezi is famous for the Victoria Falls and the Kariba Dam.

Until 1965, Zimbabwe was the British colony of Southern Rhodesia. In that year, it declared itself the independent country of Rhodesia. Britain, however, did not recognize the new nation's existence. During the next 15 years, growing unrest and guerrilla warfare caused many problems in Zimbabwe. In 1980 the country became independent and was named Zimbabwe.

Zinc

Zinc is a hard, blue-white metal ELEMENT. It has been mined since ancient times and has been used in making BRASS for over 2000 years. Brass is an alloy of zinc and copper.

A large share of the world's zinc comes from Canada, Australia and the Soviet Union. Zinc mines usually contain other metals such as copper, gold, lead and silver.

Most zinc is used to *galvanize* steel. Galvanizing is putting a thin coat of zinc on steel to protect it. Zinc is also used to make cells in electric BATTERIES. As well as brass, zinc forms part of many other alloys including nickel and bronze.

Zodiac

The zodiac is the name given to the part of the sky in which the sun, moon and planets move. The first people to study the zodiac, over 4000 years ago, were the astronomers of ancient Babylon. They divided it into 12 sections, with a group of stars in each section.

Each of these 12 sections gets a name, called its *sign*, from the shape of the star group. The 12 signs of the zodiac are Aries (Ram), Taurus (Bull), Gemini (Twins), Cancer (Crab), Leo (Lion), Virgo (Virgin), Libra (Scales), Scorpio (Scorpion), Sagittarius (Archer), Capricorn (Goat), Aquarius (Water-carrier) and Pisces (Fish).

Each zodiac sign is linked to a part of the year. Pisces for example, covers the period

Feeding time at the zoo, always a popular sight.

February 19 to March 20. If your birthday falls during this period, Pisces is your birth sign. Astrologers use the positions of a sign's stars and planets to find out about people's personalities and to foretell their futures.

Zoo

Zoos are places where wild animals are displayed, cared for, bred, studied and sometimes saved from dying out. The first zoos were in ancient Egypt. In the Middle Ages in Europe, kings gave each other presents of apes, peacocks and lions. Private collections of animals were called *menageries*. Travelling menageries toured through Europe in the 1800s.

By the 1800s, scientists had sorted animals into groups and given them Latin names so that the same animal would have the same name throughout the world. This led to the building of the first public zoos, at first called zoological gardens. The very first one was London Zoo, opened in 1829. Early zoos seem cruel today. Modern zoos have more natural and spacious settings for their animals.

Below: The astrologers' 'clock' showing all the signs of the zodiac.

INDEX

Page numbers in *italics* refer to pictures.

ACKNOWLEDGEMENTS

THE NEW CONCISE CHILDREN'S ENCYCLOPEDIA

Cover: main picture Anglo-American Telescope Board; ZEFA tm, tr, br, bl.
Aldus Books 142 tr; J Allen Cash 70 bl, 90 t, 244; All-Sport 41 br, 310 tr; Australian News & Information Bureau 32 bl, tr, 185 tr, 314 bl, 360 tr; Barnaby's 3 bl, 39 tr; Belgian Tourist Office 46 tl; A G Bell 46 br; Bettman Archive 152 b; Bildarchiv Preussischer Kulturbesitz 35 br; Biofotos 43 br, 60 br, 138 b, 139 tl+r, 196 b, 330 br; Paul Brierley 296 b; BBC 269 t; British Museum 141 t, 160 t, 171 tl, 176 bl, 200 br, 277 t; British Sugar Corporation 306 t; British Telecom 85 m; British Tourist Board 66b, 211 br; BMW 217 b; California Institute of Technology 3 m, 30 r, 140 b, 299 b; C.G.T.O. 359 br; Michael Chinery 148 t, 352 bl, 369 t; Peter Clayton 284 t, 363 br; Bruce Coleman 194 b, 298 t, 333; Dave Collins 58 bl, 161; Commodore Computers 85 br; Cooper Bridgeman Library 34 bl; D A Courtney 70 tr; Department of Environment 3 br, 303 t; Zoe Dominic 37 t; Dutch Tourist Office 224 t; Mary Evans Picture Library 10 b, 127 b; Finnish Tourist Board 188 t; Ford Motor Company 217 tl; French Railways/Lafontant 196 t; French Tourist Office 265 b; Stanley Gibbons Ltd 252 t, 299 t; Giraudon 197 tl; Sonia Halliday 13 t, 56 br, 68 tr, 147 b, 248 t, 311 b, 320 b, 332 t; Robert Harding 84 tr; reproduced by gracious permission of Her Majesty the Queen 71 b, 202; Michael Holford 7 t, 27 bl, 99 r, 116 t, 159 t, 211 tr, 334 t, 341, 344; Alan Hutchison 346 b; Imitor 250 tl; Institute of Geological Sciences 94 r, 209 tr; Internationale Stiftung Mozarteum/Salzburg 219 tr; Italian National Tourist Office 271 tr, 273 mr; Jaguar Rover Triumph Ltd 217 b; Jamaican Tourist Office 355 tr; Japan Information Centre 269 bl, 321 t; Jodrell Bank Observatory 260; Robin Kerrod 11 t, 321 b; Zophia Kielan-Jaworowska 250 b; Kobal 77; Kobberstiksamling, Copenhagen 107 t; Lockheed Solar Laboratory 307; William MacQuitty 27 tr, 178; Mansell Collection 35 bl, 47 tl, 61 r, 84 tl, 95 r, 116 b, 179 bl, 180 tr, 194 tl, 200 bl, 252 b; by kind permission of the Marquess of Tavistock and the Trustees of the Bedford Estates 119; Mauritshuis, The Hague 26 tr, 203; Middle East Archives 154 t; Middlesex Hospital 364 br; Ernst Miller/Roebild 166; P Morris 3 tr, 25 t, 105 br, 106 tl, 129 tr, 234 br, 236 r, 324 tl, 329 tr, 356 ml; Tony Morrison 73 br, 238 b; James Muirden 30 l; Museo Pio Clementino Vaticano 277 b; NASA 16 b, 212 bl, 293 tr, 305 t; NHPA 17 b, 89 l, 146 t, 199 mr, 274 m, 278 t; National Coal Board 171 br; National Gallery, London 192 bl, 265 t; National Portrait Gallery 106 tr, 158 t, 222 tl, 345 br; Natural Science Photos 42 br; Peter Newark 78 t; Maurice Nimmo 236 l; Novosti Press Agency 186 br, 215 tr, 292 tl+r; Ordnance Survey 308 t; Ossterreichische National-Bibliotek 44 m; Photosource 184 br; Picture-point 245 bl; Pitti Gallery 26 br; Max-Planck-Institute für Aeronomie, Lindau, FRG 293 b; Popperfoto 183 br, 241 t, 254 tr; Press Association 334 b; Mark Redknap 20 r; J & M Ribière 136 t; Royal Astronomical Society 182; Rowntrees 145 tl; RTHPL 225 br; SACU 74 bl, 248 br, 283 t; SATOUR 26 l, 90 b, 285 b, 288 b; SCALA 206 tr, 235; Seaphot 104 br, 129 t+bl; SFP/Jean-Claude Pierdet 317 bl; Ronald Sheridan 71 tl; Siemens 165; John Massey Stewart 291 tr; Swiss National Tourist Office 310 br; Tate Gallery, London 27 tl; Jane Taylor 180 br; Enrico Tricarica 345 bl; United Nations 335; U S Capitol Historical Society 15 b; U S Environmental Protection Agency 286; U S Naval Laboratory 83 br; Universitets Oldsaksamling 346 t; Jean Vetut 301 l+r, 302 t; Vickers 282 b; Victoria & Albert Museum, London 27 br; Wadsworth Atheneum, Hartford, Connecticut, The Ella Gallup Sumner and Mary Catlin Sumner Collection 107b; Walt Disney Productions 104 l; C R Warn 368 bl; WHO 347; Diana Wylie 325 t; ZEFA 3 tl, 8 t, 9 t, 28 t+b, 29, 34 tr, 50 mr, 55 tl+tr, 56 tr, 63 m+b, 74 tr, 89 m, 94 l, 100, 108 t, 117 m+br, 121 br, 124, 128 br, 136 b, 144 t+b, 149, 160 b, 163, 170, 171 tr, 174, 176 tl, 177 tr, 177 br, 179 tr, 186 bl, 187 bl+r, 204 bl, 206 bl, 225 bl, 226, 227 bl, 237 bl, 262 b, 268 tr, 287, 289, 291 br, 295 br, 308 b, 310 tl, 311 t, 320 t, 322 tl, 336 tr, 336 m, 337, 350, 352 tr, 366, 368 tr.

Maxine Mentone